PODCASTING HACKS™

Other resources from O'Reilly

Related titles

iPod and iTunes: The Missing Manual
iPod Fan Book
iPod and iTunes Hacks
iPod Shuffle Fan Book
iPod Playlists

Digital Audio Essentials
Digital Video Hacks
GarageBand 2: The Missing Manual
Developing Feeds with RSS and Atom

Hacks Series Home

hacks.oreilly.com is a community site for developers and power users of all stripes. Readers learn from each other as they share their favorite tips and tools for Mac OS X, Linux, Google, Windows XP, and more.

oreilly.com

oreilly.com is more than a complete catalog of O'Reilly books. You'll also find links to news, events, articles, weblogs, sample chapters, and code examples.

oreillynet.com is the essential portal for developers interested in open and emerging technologies, including new platforms, programming languages, and operating systems.

Conferences

O'Reilly brings diverse innovators together to nurture the ideas that spark revolutionary industries. We specialize in documenting the latest tools and systems, translating the innovator's knowledge into useful skills for those in the trenches. Visit *conferences.oreilly.com* for our upcoming events.

Safari Bookshelf (*safari.oreilly.com*) is the premier online reference library for programmers and IT professionals. Search across thousands of electronic books simultaneously and zero in on the information you need in seconds. Read the books on your Bookshelf from cover to cover or simply flip to the page you need. You can even cut and paste code and download chapters for offline viewing. Try it today with a free trial.

PODCASTING
HACKS™

Jack D. Herrington

O'REILLY®

Beijing · Cambridge · Farnham · Köln · Paris · Sebastopol · Taipei · Tokyo

Podcasting Hacks™

by Jack D. Herrington

Copyright © 2005 O'Reilly Media, Inc. All rights reserved.
Printed in the United States of America.

Published by O'Reilly Media, Inc., 1005 Gravenstein Highway North,
Sebastopol, CA 95472.

O'Reilly books may be purchased for educational, business, or sales promotional use. Online
editions are also available for most titles (*safari.oreilly.com*). For more information, contact our
corporate/institutional sales department: (800) 998-9938 or *corporate@oreilly.com*.

Editor:	Brian Jepson	**Production Editor:**	Adam Witwer
Series Editor:	Rael Dornfest	**Cover Designer:**	Ellie Volckhausen
Executive Editor:	Dale Dougherty	**Interior Designer:**	David Futato

Printing History:

August 2005:	First Edition.

 This book uses RepKover™, a durable and flexible lay-flat binding.

ISBN: 0-596-10066-3
[C]

This book is dedicated to:
My mother Sharon and sister Jennifer, my wife Lauren,
and my daughter Megan—

They are my past, my present, and my future,
And those from whom comes all of my strength.

May take a week or it may take longer,
You've got the guns but we've got the numbers,
Gonna win, yeah, we're taking over. Come on!

—Jim Morrison of The Doors, from the song "5 to 1"

Contents

Foreword xi

Credits xiii

Preface xix

Chapter 1. Tuning into Podcasts 1

   1. Listen to Podcasts on the Web   1

   2. Rebroadcast Your Favorite Feeds   14

   3. Build Your Own Podcatcher   17

   4. Import Podcasts into iTunes   22

   5. Tune into Videoblogs   26

   6. Convert Text-Based Blogs into Podcasts   27

   7. Install Perl Modules   31

   8. Listen to Podcasts on Your PDA   37

   9. Podcatching with Your PlayStation Portable   46

Chapter 2. Starting Out 48

   10. Make Your First Podcast   48

   11. Professional-Quality Podcasting   52

Chapter 3. Quality Sound 61

   12. Set Up a Basic Home Studio   61

   13. Pick the Right Microphone   75

   14. Mix Your Podcast in Hardware   87

   15. Reduce Noise   94

16. Podcast in Surround Sound 100

17. Control Your Recorder with Your Mobile Phone 102

18. Construct Your MP3s 107

19. Train Your Voice 114

Chapter 4. Formats 121

20. Adopt a Format for Your Podcast 121

21. Build a Great News Podcast 127

22. Build a Great Story Show 133

23. Build a Great Personal Show 135

24. Build a Great Political Show 142

25. Make a Mystery Science Theater Podcast 148

26. Build a Great Music Podcast 153

27. Build a Great Review Podcast 162

28. Build a Great Sports Podcast 167

29. Build a Great Technology Podcast 172

30. Build a Beercast 177

31. Build an MP3zine 181

32. Produce Great Audio Theatre 185

Chapter 5. Interviewing 193

33. Record Great Interviews 193

34. Record Telephone Interviews 202

35. Record Interviews on Skype 209

36. Edit Your Interviews 214

Chapter 6. Blogging 222

37. Podcast Without a Blog 222

38. Blog Your Podcast 227

39. Manage Bandwidth 236

40. Tag Your MP3 Files 243

41. Feed Your MP3s to Movable Type 246

42. Podcast by Email 249

43. Syndicate Your Podcasts to the Radio 252

Chapter 7. Publicity 255

    44. Get Listed   255

    45. Launch a New Category   259

    46. Market Your Podcast   262

    47. Make Money with Podcasts   264

    48. Connect with the Community   267

    49. Join or Build a Podcast Network   268

Chapter 8. Basic Editing 272

    50. Choose the Right Audio Tools   273

    51. Juice Your Sound   286

    52. Automate Audio Hijack Pro   289

    53. Timestamp Your Show Notes   292

    54. Build a Simple Sound Cart for Macintosh   294

    55. Build a Simple Sound Cart for Windows   299

    56. Maintain the Gain   300

    57. Build a Sweet Sound   305

    58. Add Special Effects   310

    59. Fix Common Audio Problems   313

    60. Mix Multiple Tracks   316

Chapter 9. Advanced Audio 320

    61. Set Up a Home Studio   320

    62. Integrate Audio and Email Feedback   330

    63. Add Top, Bottom, and Bumper Music   332

    64. Record and Add Background Ambience   336

    65. Speech Synthesize Your Podcast Introduction   338

    66. Make a Mash-Up   345

    67. Grab Audio Legally   351

    68. Use Copyrighted Music Legally   355

Chapter 10. On the Go 363

    69. Assemble a Small Recording Rig   363

    70. Podcast from Your Car   369

    71. Podcast at an Event   372

    72. Create a Soundseeing Tour   374

Chapter 11. Videoblogging 379

    73. Start a Videocast   379

    74. Make a Quick-and-Dirty Prompter   383

    75. Build a Teleprompter   387

Glossary 391

Index 401

Foreword

Podcasting rules.

Well, no. It actually doesn't rule. In the world of online media, hyperbole often seems to be the principal coin of our realm.

But podcasting is one of the most important developments to hit the scene in a long, long time. It is the marriage of several genres, including weblogs, audio, radio, and TiVo-ish devices. It is made possible by the ever-powerful forces of technological progress, competitive instincts, and—this is key— our perfectly human wish to express ourselves.

Podcasting, simply put, is the idea of downloading an MP3 audio file to a digital device and listening to the program—a song, a lecture, a rant, whatever—at a time and in a place of your own choosing. Although the favorite audio device of our times is Apple's iPod, the word "podcasting" is actually miscast because we don't need an iPod to listen. For example, I listen to podcasts on my mobile phone, the device on which I now also listen to music.

Like almost everyone else reading these words, I've been a radio listener since my early days. In my car, the radio is one of the most indispensable devices. But the radio has always been a purely linear medium: to hear an entire show or song or segment, you listened to its beginning, its middle, and its end.

Audio remains a mostly linear form in any medium, whether broadcast or on the Net or, now, on podcasts. But digital audio is freeing us from the tyranny of live—the days when we had to listen to the programming as it was being broadcast if we wanted to hear it.

Podcasting's other great feature is its availability to more average folks in a way that is transforming all media these days. It's open to everyone who wants to be a creator, not just a consumer, in the new sphere that some call the *read-write Web*, a place where we can write content (almost) as easily as we can read it. Weblogs have captured most of the attention in this new world. As we move beyond text and pictures, we get things like podcasting. We can do it because the cost of the gear that we need to make high-quality content is dropping fast, while the power and ease of use grows.

I have a small caution to offer, however. Just because it has become easy to make an audio file doesn't mean everyone should do so. I've been assuming that it's an order of magnitude more difficult to create an audio program that large numbers of people might want to hear than to write a comparably high-quality weblog posting. Lately, I'm not so sure; as this book shows, audio production is getting much easier, and a new generation of multimedia-savvy people is coming along fast.

We definitely don't want to leave the podcasting to the experts. And even if your podcast is not very professional sounding, the important thing is this: if you're only doing a podcast for your family and close friends, they are going to find higher value in it than the listeners of popular podcasts will find in those programs—because they care so much about you and your life.

Let's remember, most of all, the basis for all this. Media are becoming a conversation, not a lecture.

Weblogs were the first major example of a *read-write Web* that podcasting is joining. Grassroots media now takes many forms, including journalism, with a host of sites being formed for the purposes of filling in the gaps the major media are leaving. But nonprofessionals have lots to offer in this sphere and others. When we have better tools to make sense of the conversations, we will be vastly better informed.

In a world of citizens' media, your voice matters as much as anyone else's. Media are plural, all of us.

So read this book. Learn some techniques. Absorb some tips. Then let's join this expanding global conversation together.

Dan Gillmor

Credits

About the Author

Jack D. Herrington is a software engineer with more than 20 years of experience in application development. He is the author of *Code Generation in Action* (Manning, 2003) and is the editor of the Code Generation Network (CGN) (*http://www.codegeneration.net/*). As part of his CGN work, he reviews technical books. That started the Bound Cast book review podcast (*http://www.boundcast.com/*), which was the genesis of the book you have in your hands.

His most recent professional work was at Macromedia, where he helped design and build several releases of Dreamweaver. Before that, Jack worked at Certive, a Redwood City, California-based Business Intelligence start-up. He has also worked at Axon Instruments in both California and Melbourne, Australia. Currently he is working at Leverage Software (*http://www. leveragesoftware.com/*). He is a frequent contributor to the O'Reilly Network (*http://www.oreillynet.com/*), DevX (*http://devx.com/*), and IBM's developerWorks (*http://ibm.com/developerworks/*).

Jack lives with his wife Lori, daughter Megan, and canine kids Sadie and Oso, in Union City, California. When he is not writing, he is a hiker, avid book reader, cook, and baker. You can catch up with Jack on his personal blog at Driving Sideways (*http://www.muttmansion.com/ds*).

Contributors

This book covers a diverse range of hacks, a feat that was possible only with a diverse group of contributors. The following people contributed their hacks and knowledge to this book:

- Jay Allison is an independent broadcast journalist and regular contributor to public radio's national programs. He has received five Peabody

Awards. His recent co-productions include "This I Believe," "Hidden Kitchens," and "Lost & Found Sound." Allison founded Atlantic Public Media (*http://www.atlantic.org*) to create new public radio stations on Cape Cod, where he lives. APM is also responsible for the Peabody Award–winning web site, Transom.org, which brings new voices to public radio, and the Public Radio Exchange (*http://www.prx.org*), which enables grass roots distribution of programming. Allison has also produced documentaries for ABC's *Nightline* and published essays in the *New York Times Magazine*.

- Originally a Fine Arts graduate with an interest in computers and interactive installations, Tim Baker has been a multimedia consultant and professional interactive and web designer since graduating in 1995. Tim has also been involved with the UK and international mash-up/bootleg scene since 2002, and he runs the MutantPop forum at *http://www.mutantpop.net/*, as well as more recently the Radio Clash mash-up podcast at *http://www.mutantpop.net/radioclash/*. He lives in London.

- Stacy Bond currently produces KQED's The California Report, a statewide public radio program heard by 650,000 listeners daily. Her shiny new production company, AudioLuxe (*http://www.audioluxe.org/*), is developing dynamic, innovative radio for a new generation of listeners. She writes and lives in San Francisco, with her husband and kitty.

- Originally from Los Angeles, Sam Curtis Coutin produced his first podcasts in October 2004: The Sports Pod (*http://thesportspod.com/*) and Podcat's Best Of (*http://podcat.com/*). Soon after, Sam launched My Sports Radio (*http://mysportsradio.com/*), the premier sports podcast network and directory. With an MBA from MIT and an entrepreneurial fire, Sam also runs Podcast Productions, a podcast consulting practice in San Francisco.

- Emily Donahoe works both as a freelance consultant and as a senior media trainer at Media Training Worldwide. She has trained CEOs, executives, authors, government officials, physicians, and public relations directors to be better communicators. Ms. Donahoe's recent client list includes Microsoft, Procter & Gamble, Environmental Protection Agency, Diners Club, AGI—Lexington Insurance Company, P.F. Chang's, Cendant Corporation (Hotel Group), American Kennel Club, Illumina, E-gain, National Multi Housing Council, American Spine Association, Jefferson Pilot Financial, Sovereign Bank, Minnesota State University, and the District Department of Transportation. Her clients have most recently appeared on *The Today Show*, *Sharon Osbourne*, the WB network, and New York One, and in print and Internet media including the *New York Times*, MSNBC.com, CNN.com, *The*

Atlanta-Journal Constitution, *The Boston Herald*, *The Daily News*, and *Newsday*. She taught public speaking at the University of California, San Diego for two years. Her CD with TJ Walker, "Fear No More: Exorcising Your Public Speaking Demons," is available through Amazon.

- Glenn Fleishman is a freelance journalist who lives in Seattle with his wife, son, and a dozen computers scattered around the vicinity. He writes about wireless technology regularly at Wi-Fi Networking News (*http://wifinetnews.com/*) and about Macs at TidBITS (*http://tidbits.com/*).

- Michael W. Geoghegan (*http://reelreviewsradio.com/*) is a well-known figure among podcasters and has been involved in podcasting since its earliest days. His show, Reel Reviews, was the Internet's first movie review, commentary, and discussion podcast. Michael has gone on to leverage his podcasting experience by producing a number of other popular shows aimed at the lifestyle and technology markets. He also offers his services as a consultant to businesses developing podcasting and portable media strategies.

- Brendan Greeley is the web editor and a producer for PRI's Open Source, which can be found at *http://radioopensource.org*. He has presented on podcasting at a number of national conferences, including at Harvard's Shorenstein Center, and he served for a year as the site editor of the Public Radio Exchange. His print work has appeared in the *New York Times*, the *New York Times Magazine*, and *The Wall Street Journal Europe*. He is the audio editor of the Little Gray Book lecture series in Brooklyn, and his audio work has been featured on Transom.org, Radio Netherlands, Wonkette, and Andrew Sullivan's Daily Feed as well as on public radio stations around the country.

- Brian Ibbott is from Arvada, Colorado, where he podcasts his show, Coverville, three times a week. Aside from a yearlong stint as a wedding DJ, Brian's professional career has always been in the technical services and web development industry. Brian has a wife, Tina, and a son, Tristan.

- Tony Kahn is a 35-year veteran of public radio and television. He has produced, written, hosted, and narrated more than 60 programs, including *Enterprise, Odyssey, Zoom, Nova,* and *Frontline*. He was the original host of PRI's The World, co-host of MPR's Savvy Traveler, a frequent contributor to Morning Edition and Marketplace, and a regular panelist on NPR's weekly quiz show, Says You. His work has been awarded 12 New England Emmys, the Edward R. Murrow Award, and numerous Gold Medals from the New York International Radio and Television Festival. His national docudrama, *Blacklisted*, starring Ron Leibman, Carroll O'Connor, Eli Wallach, and Stockard Channing, received numerous accolades as well, including the Best of Show of the New York Festival. He is currently the director and producer of WGBH's Morning Stories, public radio's first podcast and one of the most frequently downloaded podcasts now online.

- Viki Merrick is an editor for Transom.org (*http://Transom.org/*) and producer at Atlantic Public Media, where she produces local and national commentaries, essays, and slices of life from the new NPR stations for Cape Cod and the islands—WCAI and WNAN—and the weekly four-hour Arts and Ideas with Jay Allison. Currently she is a producer for the new NPR series This I Believe. Viki lives in Woods Hole, Massachusetts, with her two kids, Ben and Allegra.

- Gregory Narain is the founder and instigator of the social podcasting movement. Turning the focus away from the computer screen to capture public interaction, Greg has single-handedly turned podcasting into a new, engaging form of social entertainment for the masses. His SparkCasting.com venture provides both the technology and the platform to empower the revolution.

- Tony Palermo is a radio dramatist, sound effects artist, and educator who has written, directed, and produced hundreds of dramas and workshops for public radio, the Museum of Television & Radio, the United Nations, audio publishers, colleges, and schools. He performs and teaches across the U.S. and around the world. His most recent work has been with such stellar radio writer/directors as Norman Corwin, Jim Metzner, Yuri Rasovsky, Peggy Webber, Roger Gregg, Lindsay Ellison, and Tom Lopez. He has appeared with many performers from old-time radio as well as contemporary troupes. He predicted podcasting several years ago and feels it will revolutionize the radio industry.

  Tony hosts a Radio Drama Resources web site, where he helps others create and produce shows and offers instruction on script formats, scoring, engineering, directing, and how to make sound effects devices. Learn more at *http://www.RuyaSonic.com/*.

- Craig Patchett is the founder of The GodCast Network (*http://www. godcast.org/*), the first podcast network, and a former magazine publisher and book author. He currently produces four podcasts and hosts three, including Behind the Scenes, which provides podcasters with an inside look at how to create a podcast and make it work. Craig lives and works in San Diego.

- James Polanco lives in Oakland, California, and has been an established dance DJ for the past seven years. James is an avid technologist and is one of the founding members of Fake Science. James is currently working with fellow contributing writer Chris Walcott on developing new bands in their studio, Cedub Studio.

- Greg Smith is the developer of FeederReader, a program for the Pocket PC used to download all things RSS. Greg's extensive background in software development, electrical engineering, project management, business and financial systems, with occasional bouts of training, consulting, and amateur musicianship qualifies him to muck around in a lot of different areas.

  He is currently attempting to change the world using a Pocket PC, Visual Studio, and C#, and has been previously known to throw gobs of Perl, HTML, and C into vats of Solaris, Linux, and Windows. Greg lives with his beautiful wife and two kitties in Clinton, Mississippi.

- Phillip Torrone is associate editor of *MAKE* magazine and contributing editor to *Popular Science*. He has authored and contributed to numerous books on mobile devices and design. Phillip is also an Internet strategy analyst for the creative firm Fallon Worldwide, best known for its award-winning work on BMWfilms (*http://BMWfilms.com/*).

- Jeff Towne has been producing radio programs for more than 25 years, first with a Marantz cassette recorder and a four-track reel-to-reel tape recorder, and now on digital recorders and computer editing systems. In his more than 15 years with the nationally syndicated program Echoes, he has done extensive remote recording of interviews and musical performances, produced documentary-style features, and prepared shows for both satellite and web distribution. Jeff is also the "Tools Editor" for Transom.org, a Peabody Award–winning web site dedicated to channeling new work and voices to public radio. Transom.org's Tools Section provides technical training in sound acquisition, editing, and mixing.

- Adam Varga created the Dailysonic MP3zine after spending six months getting dirty and smelly on the Appalachian Trail. He is a New York City native with strong revolutionary tendencies. In his free time, he climbs mountains and makes music.

- Chris Walcott lives in Oakland, California, and has been a performing musician in the Bay Area for more than 20 years. In addition to playing in many rock/pop bands, Chris has also had the opportunity to play with the Oakland Opera Theater. Chris is most recently focusing on recording and song writing in his studio with fellow contributing writer James Polanco.

Acknowledgments

I would particularly like to thank my editor, Brian Jepson, for his work on this book. He always provided me with insight and advice. He was a true collaborator and I genuinely appreciate his efforts.

In addition, I would like to thank my wife Lori and daughter Megan for their sacrifices and support in this work. My mother Sharon Luria, and her husband Carlos, were both helpful and understanding. My good friend Mel Pleasant was also a great help in providing advice and perspective.

Tom Krymkowski, Danny Bringer, and Gregg McVicar were critical in the audio portions of this book. I would also like to thank Jon and Molly Coogan-Tyson, Todd Maffin, Tim Olson, Tim Dressen, Moira Gunn, Ryan King, Russell Holliman, Mikel Ellcessor, Martin Andrews, Jim Kloss, Jon Udell, Hugo Schotman, Chris Winn, and Baratunde, all of whom added their special mark to the book and without whom the book would have been much harder or impossible to produce.

The research and writing of this book was one of the most intense and exciting things I have ever done. I've learned more in the few months of writing this book than I have in any single short period in my entire life. I've made new friends, and explored a new world that I previously never had access to. To everyone who helped out, I am eternally grateful.

Preface

This book explores two main podcasting themes: how to listen to a podcast, and how to produce one on your own. While the majority of the book falls into the latter category, the first chapter discusses how to find great podcasts and subscribe to them without filling your hard disk.

The podcasting production chapters that follow we cover not only how to get the best sound with the lowest noise, but also how to produce a podcast that people will want to listen to because of what you say and do. These chapters also cover how to market your podcasts, how to interact with the community, and even how to get your podcasts on the radio.

Why Podcasting Hacks?

The term *hacking* has a bad reputation in the press. They use it to refer to someone who breaks into systems or wreaks havoc with computers as their weapon. Among people who write code, though, the term *hack* refers to a "quick-and-dirty" solution to a problem, or a clever way to get something done. And the term *hacker* is taken very much as a compliment, referring to someone as being *creative*, having the technical chops to get things done. The Hacks series is an attempt to reclaim the word, document the good ways people are hacking, and pass the hacker ethic of creative participation on to the uninitiated. Seeing how others approach systems and problems is often the quickest way to learn about a new technology.

How This Book Is Organized

The book is divided into several chapters, organized by subject:

Chapter 1, *Tuning into Podcasts*
> The hacks in this chapter teach you how to listen to podcasts through your browser and on a variety of different devices. You'll also learn how

to find good podcasts and share them with your friends, as well as how to tune into videoblogs.

Chapter 2, *Starting Out*

This chapter takes you through the basic hardware and software setup required to make high-quality podcasts. It also shows you how professional shows are produced, and how that knowledge can help you build a better podcast for yourself.

Chapter 3, *Quality Sound*

The hacks in this chapter cover in depth how to pick the right audio hardware for your podcast, as well as how to reduce noise to get that elusive clean sound.

Chapter 4, *Formats*

Having quality sound is one thing, but what do you say? Chapter 4 covers the formats of various shows, and provides examples of formats as well as case studies of many popular podcasts.

Chapter 5, *Interviewing*

Interviewing people is a great way to get compelling content for your podcast. Find out how to interview people, and how to edit the interviews, in this chapter.

Chapter 6, *Blogging*

This chapter concentrates on the mechanics of posting your podcasts to the Internet. Many options are available, and this chapter will help you sort them out while at the same time avoid being stuck with huge bandwidth bills.

Chapter 7, *Publicity*

The best podcast in the world won't go anywhere unless people listen to it. In this chapter, you will find out how to market your podcast, make some money off it, and work with the podcasting community.

Chapter 8, *Basic Editing*

There is a lot more to audio than just hitting the Record button and starting to talk. In this chapter, you'll learn the basics of audio editing, what applications are available, and how to understand and use audio effects and filters.

Chapter 9, *Advanced Audio*

The hacks in this chapter take things a step further and show you how to build your own home studio, integrate audio feedback, add sound effects, and more.

Chapter 10, *On the Go*

You can do only so much from the studio. Find out how to take your show on the road with the hacks in this chapter.

Chapter 11, *Videoblogging*

Add a new dimension to your podcast by creating videos in addition to your sound. This chapter covers the basics of videoblogging and shows you how to create a teleprompter to give your videoblogs a professional feel.

Conventions

The following is a list of the typographical conventions used in this book:

Italics

Used to indicate URLs, filenames, filename extensions, and directory/ folder names. For example, a path in the filesystem will appear as */Developer/Applications*.

`Constant width`

Used to show code examples, the contents of files, and console output, as well as the names of variables, commands, and other code excerpts.

`Constant width bold`

Used to highlight portions of code, typically new additions to old code.

`Constant width italics`

Used in code examples and tables to show sample text to be replaced with your own values.

Color

The second color is used to indicate a cross-reference within the text.

You should pay special attention to notes set apart from the text with the following icons:

This is a tip, suggestion, or general note. It contains useful supplementary information about the topic at hand.

This is a warning or note of caution, often indicating that your money or your privacy might be at risk.

The thermometer icons, found next to each hack, indicate the relative complexity of the hack:

 beginner   moderate   expert

Using Code Examples

This book is here to help you get your job done. In general, you can use the code in this book in your programs and documentation. You do not need to contact us for permission unless you're reproducing a significant portion of the code. For example, writing a program that uses several chunks of code from this book does not require permission. Selling or distributing a CD-ROM of examples from O'Reilly books *does* require permission. Answering a question by citing this book and quoting example code does not require permission. Incorporating a significant amount of example code from this book into your product's documentation *does* require permission.

We appreciate, but do not require, attribution. An attribution usually includes the title, author, publisher, and ISBN. For example: "*Podcasting Hacks* by Jack D. Herrington. Copyright 2005 O'Reilly Media, Inc., 0-596-10066-3."

If you feel your use of code examples falls outside fair use or the permission given here, feel free to contact us at *permissions@oreilly.com*.

Safari Enabled

 When you see a Safari® Enabled icon on the cover of your favorite technology book that means the book is available online through the O'Reilly Network Safari Bookshelf.

Safari offers a solution that's better than e-books. It's a virtual library that let's you easily search thousands of top tech books, cut and paste code samples, download chapters, and find quick answers when you need the most accurate, current information. Try it for free at *http://safari.oreilly.com*.

How to Contact Us

We have tested and verified the information in this book to the best of our ability, but you might find that features have changed (or even that we have made mistakes!). As a reader of this book, you can help us to improve future editions by sending us your feedback. Please let us know about any errors, inaccuracies, bugs, misleading or confusing statements, and typos that you find anywhere in this book.

Please also let us know what we can do to make this book more useful to you. We take your comments seriously and will try to incorporate reasonable suggestions into future editions. You can write to us at:

O'Reilly Media, Inc.
1005 Gravenstein Hwy N.
Sebastopol, CA 95472
(800) 998-9938 (in the U.S. or Canada)
(707) 829-0515 (international/local)
(707) 829-0104 (fax)

To ask technical questions or to comment on the book, send email to:

bookquestions@oreilly.com

The web site for *Podcasting Hacks* lists examples, errata, and plans for future editions. You can find this page at:

http://www.oreilly.com/catalog/podcastinghks

For more information about this book and others, see the O'Reilly web site:

http://www.oreilly.com

Got a Hack?

To explore Hacks books online or to contribute a hack for future titles, visit:

http://hacks.oreilly.com

Tuning into Podcasts

Hacks 1–9

I'll come home, eat, and surf the TV a bit, but usually there's nothing good on. Then around 11 p.m., I'll turn on [the] Dawn and Drew [podcast]. And it's like I'm hanging out with old friends.

—Scott Saunders

Congratulations, you just found 3,000 new friends to listen and talk to! These 3,000 podcasting friends talk about their lives, their work, their passions, and their interests in segments of audio and video every day from around the world. It's all free, and it finds you because you can subscribe to what you like.

This chapter is all about how to find and listen to podcasts, how to pass podcasts on to your friends, and how to listen to podcasts on iPods and other music players, as well as on devices that are more exotic.

HACK #1 Listen to Podcasts on the Web

Use your browser to find podcasts. Click a link, and in seconds, you'll be listening to the podcast in your favorite MP3 application.

You can listen to a podcast right now with the software you already have. Moreover, with thousands of podcasts to choose from covering every conceivable topic, you are sure to find something you like. This hack shows you how to listen to and subscribe to podcasts, how you can find the right podcast using directories, and how to manage your podcast download inventory.

Your first experience with podcasting starts with you pointing your browser to a podcast web site and clicking one of the show links. Here are some links to the perennial best of the podcast world:

The Daily Source Code (http://www.curry.com/)
>   This is Adam Curry's (ex-MTV veejay) 40-minute show, mixing podcast plugs, technology news, music, and more.

The Dawn and Drew Show (http://www.dawnanddrew.com/)
>   A popular comedy show featuring a young Midwestern couple with insights on relationships and technology.

Scripting News (http://www.morningcoffeenotes.com/)
>   The original podcast from Dave Winer. This is a combination audio/video blog that covers technology, politics, blogging, and a whole host of other topics.

The Rock and Roll Geek Show (http://www.americanheartbreak.com/movabletype/)
>   A popular and well-produced music show featuring new artists.

Coverville (http://www.coverville.com/)
>   A very well-produced music show featuring cover songs from a wide variety of artists. Clocking in at around 30 to 40 minutes per episode, this is a great way to enhance a workout or commute with familiar music played in a different style.

Reel Reviews (http://mwgblog.com/)
>   Michael Geoghegan's deep and insightful reviews into the classic movies of the past shed new light on our favorites.

When you surf to one of these sites, you will see what amounts to a blog with links on one or more of the entries to an audio file, usually an MP3.

Figure 1-1 shows that the Reel Review of *Repo Man* is located next to the Direct Download link. In addition, there is the standard podcast icon, which helps you identify podcasts.

Here is a list of the common browsers, and how they support the ability to listen to MP3 links:

Safari on Mac OS X
>   For sheer simplicity of previewing podcasts, Safari can't be beat. Clicking an MP3 link takes you to an almost-blank page where a reasonably sized QuickTime control plays the show and allows you to move around the audio randomly. When tabs are enabled, command-clicking opens the MP3 in a new tab. Right-clicking, or option-clicking, brings up a *context menu* that lets you open the MP3 in a new tab or a new window, or save it to disk.

Figure 1-1. The Reel Reviews home page

Firefox

> By default, Firefox plays MP3s right in the browser using your default
> audio player, such as the QuickTime player. If you don't want to play
> the file in the browser, you can copy the MP3's URL by selecting Copy
> Link Location from the context menu that appears when you right-click
> (or Ctrl-click on Macs with a single-button mouse) the MP3 link. Then
> paste the link into streaming audio applications such as QuickTime
> Player or Windows Media Player.

Internet Explorer

> On recent versions of Internet Explorer, clicking MP3 links will bring up
> the download dialog. Use this dialog to save the MP3 file to a conve-
> nient location on your hard drive. When the download is finished, click
> the Open button to open your default MP3 player. Older versions of
> Internet Explorer will bring up the media panel when you click an MP3
> link and start the embedded media player.

QuickTime, Windows Media Player, Real Audio, Sonique, and WinAmp
You can listen to podcasts in your favorite MP3 player application by using the MP3 file's URL. First, right-click the link in the browser, and use the context menu that pops up to copy the URL. Then use the URL playback feature of your favorite media application. In most players, this option is located in the File menu with a title such as Open URL. The media player will play from a streaming in-memory copy of the MP3.

I strongly recommend that you use headphones when you listen to podcasts in a public space, especially at the office or on a train. Podcasts aren't regulated by the FCC, or anyone else, for that matter, and they often contain profanity and discuss topics intended for mature audiences. This is part of the allure for some listeners. Podcasting opens up a whole new vista of creative expression that is currently unrestricted and looks to remain so.

Searching the Podcastosphere

You can search the world of podcasts using the Pod Razor web site (*http://www.podrazor.com/*). The engine catalogs the text portions of the podcasts' Really Simple Syndication (RSS) feeds. Then you can search this catalog using a search box similar to Google. If you are a Firefox web browser user, the Pod Razor site has a search tool that adds another engine to Firefox's search box. Just click the Firefox Search Tool link that appears on every page.

A new service called Podscope (*http://www.podscope.com/*) "listens" to podcasts and indexes them based on what it hears. Simply enter the phrase you are looking for into the search box and it will search the index to find any podcasts that match. From my experience, the service works reasonably well and is certainly worth a look.

Podcatching with iTunes

Once you have found the shows that you like, you will want to listen to each new episode as it comes out. Some are presented daily, while others follow a more random schedule. Thankfully, the ability to subscribe is baked right into the podcast architecture itself. Each podcast has an RSS file [Hack #37] attached to it. This file lists the recent shows, their date of publication, a title, some part of the text of the blog entry, and the URL of the podcast MP3.

iTunes offers the easiest way to subscribe to podcasts and to have them downloaded into your iPod. iTunes v4.9 was the first version to offer podcast support. If you don't have iTunes or you have an older version, you should go to the Apple iTunes site (*http://www.apple.com/itunes*) to download the latest version.

Once you have iTunes installed, click on the podcast icon to see your podcast subscription list. In Figure 1-2 you can see that I've subscribed to three podcasts and have a subscription pending with the Cinecast podcast.

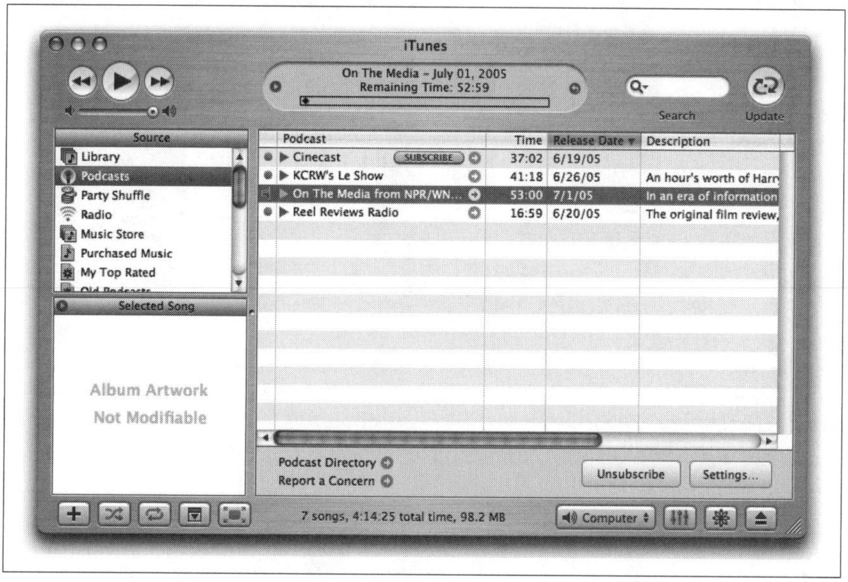

Figure 1-2. The iTunes podcasts subscription list

To find out what podcasts are available, click on the Podcast Directory link at the bottom on the window. This will take you to a special section of the iTunes Music Store, as you can see in Figure 1-3.

Click around to see what's available and then click the Subscribe button on any of the podcasts that appeal to you. These podcasts will be added to your podcast subscription list and will update automatically as often as you like.

You can alter how often iTunes checks for new episodes and how many episodes are saved by clicking on the Settings button when you have a podcast subscription selected. The settings dialog is shown in Figure 1-4.

Podcasts can be fairly large in size, often ranging between 10 and 40 megabytes, so you should set the podcasting subscription to save only as many as you think you will have the time to listen to. With a dozen or so subscriptions, you can easily consume several gigabytes of your disk and iPod space if you keep all of the downloaded episodes.

Figure 1-3. The podcast section of the iTunes Music Store

Figure 1-4. The podcast subscription settings

If you have your own podcast, then you should use the Publish a Podcast
link in the iTunes Music Store podcast directory to add your podcast to the
Apple directory.

Figure 1-5 shows the publishing page in the iTunes Music Store podcasting section. Paste the URL of your RSS feed, or one you would like to subscribe to, into the Podcast Feed URL field, and click the Continue button to start the publishing process. Then you will be asked to categorize the feed and specify the language and whether or not the content is explicit in nature. You will then be published on the Apple directory, which offers your podcast to listeners worldwide.

Figure 1-5. The iTunes podcast directory publishing page

Get the Right Podcatcher

If you don't have iTunes or don't want to use it, there are several Podcatcher applications for Windows, Mac OS X, and Linux. These Podcatchers have media players built right into them to make it easy to listen to the shows without ever leaving the program.

iPodder (http://ipodder.sourceforge.net/)

iPodder is an open source podcatcher written in Python that runs on Windows, Macintosh, and Linux. The podcatcher maintains a subscription list and automatically downloads new podcasts as they become available. The latest version supports BitTorrent (*http://www.bittorrent. com/*) for downloads. Using BitTorrent for downloads is increasing in popularity as the large size of MP3 files becomes a bandwidth issue.

iPodder was the first on the block and has a lot of grassroots support.

iPodderX (http://ipodderx.com/)

iPodderX is a popular Macintosh podcatcher that has the iPodderX directory viewer built in. You can find the shows you want in the directory and add them to your subscriptions list. iPodderX also integrates with iTunes to add new podcasts to your iTunes library as each is downloaded. iPodderX Lite is a freeware version of iPodderX, with a restricted feature set. The newest version of iPodderX is an RSS reader that will read text feeds as well as podcast feeds.

Doppler Radio (http://www.dopplerradio.net/)

Doppler is a podcatcher for Windows. Its feature set is roughly the same as that of iPodder, though it has some more advanced features such as history maintenance to remove old podcasts, and it has a smooth integration with iTunes. Multithreaded downloading and resuming interrupted downloads are upcoming features not present in the most recent version as of this writing.

PoddumFeeder (http://www.ifthensoft.com/poddumfeeder.html)

PoddumFeeder is a commercial Macintosh podcatcher. It supports subscriptions, directory browsing, and integration with iTunes and the iPod. This is one of the most polished of the Macintosh podcatchers. PoddumFeeder does not have an embedded media player. Instead, it loads all the downloaded podcasts into iTunes directly. It also features a headache-saving option for deleting podcasts from iTunes that you have already listened to.

The list of podcatchers is growing quickly, though most at the time of this writing were just in their first versions. The preceding list comprises production-ready podcatchers. Podcast Alley (*http://podcastalley.com/podcast_software.php*) maintains a complete and current list of podcatchers.

Podcatching

To demonstrate using a podcatcher I will use iPodderX for Macintosh. iPodderX starts with the list of available podcasts from the iPodderX directory.

The top-right pane of the window in Figure 1-6 is filled with the list of available podcasts. You can refine the list using the drop-down menu to select the category of podcasts that interests you. Clicking the plus (+) button will add the podcast to your subscriptions list, which is located on the lefthand side of the window.

Figure 1-7 shows the Coverville podcast feed list. By clicking an individual feed, you can see the list of available shows. And by clicking an entry in the list, you can start listening to the podcast through the embedded QuickTime

Figure 1-6. The iPodderX directory of podcasts

player. The little arrow next to each show in the subscriptions list launches your web browser and opens up the home page for that podcast.

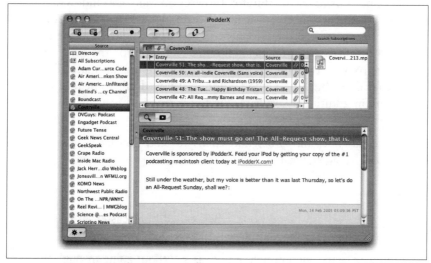

Figure 1-7. The list of Coverville podcasts

Using the Preferences dialog, you can specify how often the application should check for updates to the feeds, where the downloaded files should go, and whether the audio files should be added automatically to iTunes. If you are impatient and you want the program to check for new podcasts immediately, you can click the Check Now button on the main window.

If you bump into a podcast as you surf the Web, you can subscribe to it in your podcatcher. First copy the RSS link, which usually appears as an orange XML button or a button labeled RSS. Then use the Add a Podcast (or similar) menu item in your podcatcher and paste the URL into the Podcast Feed URL field.

Use Your Current RSS Reader

Another approach is to use the RSS reader you already have, assuming it supports *enclosures*. Enclosures are how RSS feeds specify binary files (usually multimedia files) along with each blog entry. This is a natural fit for podcasting, and as podcasting has been gaining in popularity, more of the established RSS readers have been adding support for enclosures.

NetNewsWire 2.0 Beta for the Macintosh automatically downloads enclosures. This is an all-in-one solution for the Macintosh if you are already using it to read the day's news via RSS. The downside is that NetNewsWire focuses on the RSS and not on podcasts, so there is no built-in media player or integration with iTunes. What you do with the MP3s as they come in is entirely up to you.

Another option is to use the Firefox browser on Mac or Windows. Use the Bookmark Manager to create a new live bookmark using the Add Live Bookmark command in the File menu. Then paste the URL to the RSS 2.0 feed into the Feed location field. Firefox will monitor the feed continuously. Firefox won't download the enclosures for you automatically, like a podcatcher does, but it is a good solution if you don't want to download and maintain additional software. Firefox is free and is available from its official site (*http://getfirefox.com/*).

If you use Bloglines (*http://bloglines.com/*) to read RSS feeds, you can use that service to read enclosures as well.

Blugg.com

Blugg provides a flash-based podcatcher, called bluggcaster, at *http://blugg.com/caster/*. The site is shown in Figure 1-8.

It's a fun way to try out a bunch of podcasts without going through the hassle of downloading them to a podcatcher. For example, Philip Torrone of Engadget uses bluggcaster on a tablet PC to have a little podcast radio station (*http://make.oreilly.com/*).

Figure 1-8. The bluggcaster on blugg.com

Using Podcast Directories

Several directories of podcasts are available for finding podcasts that interest you:

iPodder (http://iPodder.org/)
> This is the original podcast directory. It has a very comprehensive list of all the directories. It's also accessible in OPML form if you want to turn it into something else with XSLT and/or your favorite programming language.

iPodderX (http://iPodderX.com/)
> iPodderX maintains a very up-to-date directory of podcasts.

Podcast Alley (http://podcastalley.com/)
> Podcast Alley maintains a comprehensive list of podcasts, and it is the site where listeners go to vote for their favorite podcasts. On the home page are the top 10 ranked podcasts. A list of the top 50 is also available.

You can surf these directories to find the podcast you are looking for on the Web. When you find a podcast you like, copy the RSS 2.0 URL and paste it into your podcatcher's Subscribe dialog. Then the podcatcher will continuously monitor the feed, looking for new podcasts as they come along and downloading them for you.

RSS 2.0 is one of several different RSS standards. But it's the only one that allows for the specification of enclosure tags that makes podcasting possible.

Clean Up Podcasts from iTunes

Listening to podcasts can fill up your hard disk quickly. You can set some of the newer podcatchers, such as Doppler (*http://dopplerradio.net/*), to maintain your iTunes library for you.

In Figure 1-9, I have set Doppler to remove the podcasts for the feeds if they are still around after five days. You can also restrict the size to a specified amount of disk space, or have Doppler remove podcasts with a specific iTunes rating.

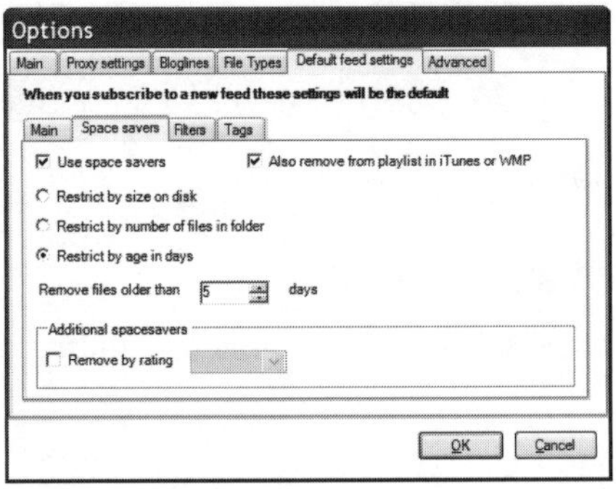

Figure 1-9. Doppler's space-saver options

iPodder (*http://ipodder.sf.net/*) has a tab for cleaning up the iTunes directory after downloading.

With iPodder, shown in Figure 1-10, you need to use the feed selection drop-down menu to select the feed you want to trim. Then use the list of downloaded items to select the ones you want to remove. Click the Delete button to delete the sound files from iTunes.

If you want more control over what items to remove, I recommend using iTunes' Smart Playlist feature. The Smart Playlist editor dialog is shown in Figure 1-11.

Using the New Smart Playlist command under the File menu, I built a new Smart Playlist. I added a filter that selects only the songs that were added within the last 10-day period. I also added an additional filter to select only those songs with a genre of Other (which is often used for podcasts).

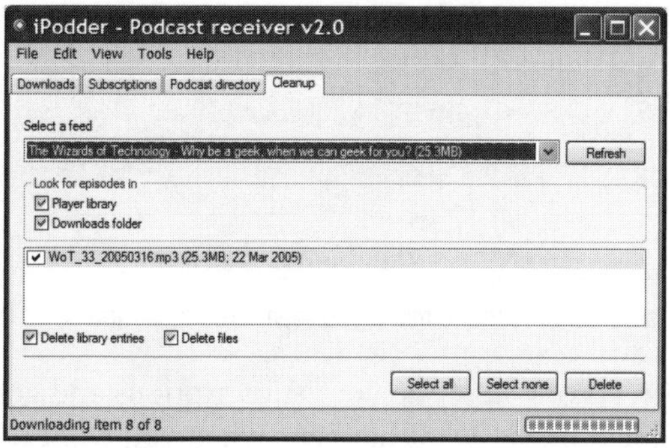

Figure 1-10. iPodder's cleanup tab

Figure 1-11. iTunes' Smart Playlist editor dialog

 Both iPodderX and Doppler Radio allow you to force the genre of the incoming podcast to a particular value. I strongly recommend doing that so that you can use easy Smart Playlist filtering.

When you click OK, you will see the new Smart Playlists in the playlists section. Double-click the Smart Playlist name to edit its name and set it to whatever you like. You can make these smart lists as elaborate as you want. For example, you can add an additional filter to allow podcasts below a certain rating. This will allow you to keep the podcasts you like and discard the rest.

It would be great if you could use the Delete key to delete all the items in the list at this point, but you can't delete items directly from a Smart Playlist. Mac users can use Doug Adams' Deleted Selected Files AppleScript (*http://www.dougscripts.com/*).

See Also

- "Tune into Videoblogs" [Hack #5]
- "Listen to Podcasts on Your PDA" [Hack #8]
- "Podcatching with Your PlayStation Portable" [Hack #9]

HACK
#2

Rebroadcast Your Favorite Feeds

Combine a bunch of feeds to make your own broadcast network.

Podcasting is like TiVo: you set up your subscriptions and get the shows you want as they come out. But what happens when you want to take your subscriptions on the road, or share them with your friends? This script allows you to create a single feed that pulls the most recent podcast from each feed you specify.

The Code

Save the following code as *network.pl*:

```perl
#!/usr/bin/perl -w
use LWP::Simple;
use strict;

# The list of feeds to retrieve

my @feeds = qw(
 http://www.curry.com/xml/rss.xml
 http://www.boundcast.com/index.xml
);

# The title of the network feed

my $networkName = "My Network";

# The URL of the home page

my $url = "http://www.mysite.com";

# A description of your network

my $description = "My very own network";

# Format the current date and time

my @days = qw( Sun Mon Tue Wed Thu Fri Sat );
my @months = qw( Jan Feb Mar Apr May Jun Jul Aug Sep Oct Nov Dec );

my @t = gmtime( time );
my $date = sprintf( "%s, %d %s %d %02d:%02d:%02d GMT",
```

```
    $days[ $t[6] ], $t[3], $months[ $t[4] ],
    $t[5] + 1900, $t[2], $t[1], $t[0] );

# Print the header portion of the RSS 2.0

print <<END;
Content-type: text/xml

<?xml version="1.0"?>
<rss version="2.0">
<channel>
<title>$networkName</title>
<link>$url</link>
<description>$description</description>
<language>en-us</language>
<pubDate>$date</pubDate>
<lastBuildDate>$date</lastBuildDate>
<generator>Network 1.0</generator>
END

# Iterate through each feed and find the first
# item with an enclosure then print it out

foreach my $feed ( @feeds )
{
 my $data = get $feed;
 while( $data =~ /(<item>.*?<\/item>)/sg )
 {
  my $item = $1;
  if ( $item =~ /<enclosure/ )
  {
   print $item;
   last;
  }
 }
}

# Print the footer

print <<END;
</channel>
</rss>
END
```

This script will read the RSS from the feeds you specify in the @feeds array.
Then it will combine all the feeds into a new, single RSS 2.0 feed with the
name, description, and URL that you specify. Modify the variables at the top
of the script before you upload it to your web server.

Running the Hack

To put the feed on the network so that it's visible from anywhere, you will need to upload the script to your ISP. The ISP needs to support Perl scripts and have the `LWP::Simple` library. You can use the script locally on Mac OS X by placing this script in your */Library/WebServer/CGI-Executable* directory. On Windows, you will need to install ActiveState Perl first. Then copy the *network.pl* script into your server's document directory [Hack #7].

Build a "Best of" Feed

Turning people on to podcasting can be difficult. The show that was great last week could be only so-so this week and could turn them off from the start. To make sure people have a great first experience with podcasting you can create your own "best of" feed with the free GigaDial service (*http://www.gigadial.net/*).

Start by creating an account with the service. Then create your own custom feed. From there you can add your favorite episodes to the custom feed. With a link to your feed and a copy of iPodder, your friends should have a great introduction to podcasting.

GigaDial, shown in Figure 1-12, doesn't stop there, though. You and your friends can collaborate on building the perfect feed because they can help maintain the list simply by logging onto the service and adding entries to your feed.

Here are some suggestions on other ways to use GigaDial:

Genre feeds
   Create several feeds that relate to a genre or theme and allow others to add recent podcasts into the theme.

Best-of-your-show feed
   Create a "best of" feed for your own show.

Short list for PDAs
   Create a single custom feed that limits what is sent to your PDA's podcatcher [Hack #8].

If you want to share your feed list with your friends, have a look at Bloglines (*http://www.bloglines.com/*). At this site, you can not only read blogs and listen to podcasts, but also publish your feeds so that you can easily share them with others.

See Also

- "Join or Build a Podcast Network" [Hack #49]

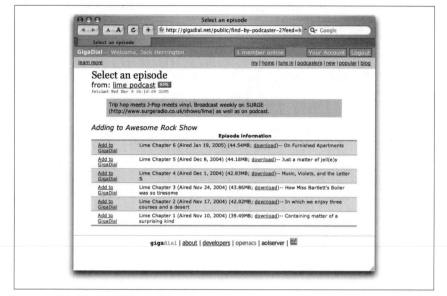

Figure 1-12. GigaDial's feed editing page

Build Your Own Podcatcher

H·A·C·K
#3

Using Perl, you can quickly build a command-line podcatcher for yourself.

Rolling your own command-line podcatcher, like the one shown here, gives you ultimate flexibility in what podcasts you download and when you fetch them. You can also hook up this script to a *cron* job or to a Windows batch file and download new podcasts overnight.

The Code

Save this code as *spc.pl*:

```perl
#!/usr/bin/perl -w
use Storable qw ( store retrieve );
use FileHandle;
use LWP::Simple qw( get );
use strict;

# The path to the history file that remembers
# what we have downloaded.

use constant HISTORY_FILE => ".history";

# The file that includes the URLs of all of the feeds

use constant FEEDS_FILE => "feeds.txt";
```

```perl
# The directory to use for output of the enclosure files

use constant OUTPUT_DIR => "enclosures";

# Loads all of the feeds from the feeds file and returns
# an array.

sub feeds_load( )
{
  my $feeds = [];
  my $fh = new FileHandle( FEEDS_FILE );
  while( <$fh> ) { chomp; push @$feeds, $_; }
  $fh->close( );
  return $feeds;
}


# Returns the filename from a URL

sub parse_filename($)
{
  my ( $fname ) = @_;

  # Remove the arguments portion of the URL
  $fname =~ s/\?.*$//;
  # Trim anything up to the final slash
  $fname =~ s/.*\///;

  return $fname;
}

# Parses a feed and finds the title of the feed and the
# URLs for all of the enclosures

sub parse_feed($)
{
  my ( $rss ) = @_;

  my $info = {};
  my $urls = [];

  while( $rss =~ /(\<item\>.*?\<\/item\>)/sg )
  {
    my $item = $1;
    if ( $item =~ /(\<enclosure.*?\>)/ )
    {
      my $enc = $1;
      if ( $enc =~ /url=[\"|\'](.*?)[\"|\']/i )
      {
        push @$urls, {
        url => $1,
        filename => parse_filename( $1 )
        };
      }
```

```perl
    }
  }
  $info->{enclosures} = $urls;

  $rss =~ s/\<item\>.*?\<\/item\>//sg;

  my $title = "";
  if ( $rss =~ /\<title\>(.*?)\<\/title\>/sg )
  {
    $title = $1;
    # Strip leading and trailing whitespace
    $title =~ s/^\s+//g;
    $title =~ s/\s+$//g;
    # Strip out the returns and line feeds
    $title =~ s/\n|\r//g;
    # Strip out any HTML entities
    $title =~ s/\&.*?;//g;
    # Strip out any slashes
    $title =~ s/\///g;
  }
  $info->{title} = $title;

  return $info;
}

# Grabs and parses a feed. Then adds the enclosures
# referenced in the feed to the queue.

sub feed_read($$)
{
  my ( $queue, $rss_url ) = @_;

  print "Reading feed $rss_url\n";

  my $rss = get $rss_url;
  my $info = parse_feed( $rss );

  foreach my $item ( @{$info->{enclosures}} )
  {
    push @$queue, {
      url => $item->{url},
      filename => $item->{filename},
      feed => $info->{title}
    };
  }

  print "\tFound ".scalar(@{$info->{enclosures}})." enclosures\n";
}

# Reads all of the feeds in the feed lists and creates
# a queue of enclosures to retrieve.

sub feeds_read($)
```

```perl
{
  my ( $feeds ) = @_;
  my $queue = [];
  foreach my $feed ( @$feeds )
  {
    feed_read( $queue, $feed );
  }
  return $queue;
}

# Loads the history file and returns its contents as a hash
# table. If a URL is in the hash table then we have already
# downloaded it.

sub history_load( )
{
  my $history = {};
  $history = retrieve( HISTORY_FILE ) if ( -e HISTORY_FILE );
  $history = {} unless ( $history );
  return $history;
}

# Saves the history out to the history file.

sub history_save($)
{
  my ( $history ) = @_;
  store( $history, HISTORY_FILE );
}

# Checks if a URL is in the history, and thus has already been
# downloaded.

sub history_check($$)
{
  my ( $history, $url ) = @_;
  return ( exists $history->{ $url } );
}

# Adds a URL to the history

sub history_add($$)
{
  my ( $history, $url ) = @_;
  $history->{$url} = 1;
}

# Downloads an enclosure and saves it out to a file in a subdirectory
# of the output directory. There is one subdirectory for each
# feed.

sub download_enclosure($$$)
```

```
{
  my ( $url, $filename, $feed ) = @_;

  my $dirname = OUTPUT_DIR."/".$feed;
  my $fullpath = $dirname."/".$filename;

  mkdir( $dirname );

  print "Getting $url...\n";

  my $data = get $url;

  my $fh = new FileHandle( $fullpath, "w" );
  binmode($fh);
  print $fh $data;
  $fh->close( );

  print "\tdone\n";

  return 1;
}

# Downloads all of the items in the queue that are not in the history
# already.

sub download_queue($$)
{
  my ( $history, $queue ) = @_;
  foreach my $item ( @$queue )
  {
    next if ( history_check( $history, $item->{url} ) );
    if ( download_enclosure( $item->{url},
         $item->{filename},
         $item->{feed} ) )
    {
      history_add($history,$item->{url});
      history_save( $history );
    }
  }
}

# Create the output directory

mkdir( OUTPUT_DIR );

# Read the feeds, build the queue, get the history and download
# enclosures that haven't already been downloaded.

my $feeds = feeds_load( );
my $queue = feeds_read( $feeds );
my $history = history_load( );
download_queue( $history, $queue );
```

The script starts at the bottom (after all the subroutines have been set up). The first thing it does is load in the feed list from the *feeds.txt* file. Here is an example *feeds.txt* file:

```
http://www.curry.com/xml/rss.xml
http://www.boundcast.com/index.xml
```

After that, the feeds_read subroutine downloads the RSS and parses it up, looking for enclosures.

The fun part of feed_read comes with the parse_feed subroutine that looks for the <item> and <enclosure> tags and then builds an array of hash tables to store what it found. All the enclosures from all the feeds are put into one big array called the *queue*. The queue is a to-do list of podcasts the script plans to download.

The script keeps a history of the files it has downloaded in a *.history* file that is loaded into a hash table. Both the queue and the history are passed to the download_queue function. This function will only download items that are not in the history. I could use the existence of the file on disk to decide whether to download the file. However, that means that I will have to keep the enclosure files in the output directory to make sure I do not download them twice. That limits my options in terms of what to do with the files after I download them. Therefore, I keep a separate history.

Running the Hack

On Windows machines, use ActivePerl (*http://activestate.com/*) or Cygwin's Perl (*http://www.cygwin.com/*) to run this Perl script. Perl is included on Macintoshes, though you might need to download the LWP::Simple module from CPAN [Hack #7] if you haven't installed it already.

I recommend using this script in conjunction with [Hack #4] to take the downloaded files and import them into iTunes. That script can also update your iPod automatically after all the files have been imported.

See Also

- "Import Podcasts into iTunes" [Hack #4]

Import Podcasts into iTunes

H A C K
#4

Use Perl scripts and iTunes' COM interface to automate MP3 importing on Windows; on the Mac, it's even easier.

iTunes for Windows supports a powerful scripting layer using Windows COM interfaces. ActiveState Perl (*http://activestate.com/*) complements this by making it easy to automate COM objects. I merged these two together to build a Perl script that complements the command-line podcatcher [Hack #3].

The podcatcher downloaded all the enclosure files into an *enclosures* directory that was organized by show. This means that the script in this hack needs to crawl the directory structure to find the MP3s to import them, and then update your iPod. This is not a problem, though, since the File::Find module [Hack #7] makes searching through a tree of directories a snap.

With the problem of finding the files out of the way, the script uses the Win32::OLE module to tell iTunes to import the files.

The Code

Save this code to a file named *addtoitunes.pl*:

```perl
#!perl -w
use Win32::OLE;
use File::Find;
use strict;

# iTunes refers to importing as 'converting' in its COM interface.
# So we convert each path.

sub convert($$)
{
  my ( $itunes, $path ) = @_;

  # Make sure it's an MP3 file

  return unless ( $path =~ /[.]mp3$/ );

  print "Converting $path\n";

  # Start the conversion

  my $progress = $itunes->ConvertFile2( $path );

  # Monitor the SLOW progress

  my $done = 0;
  my $lp = -100;
  while( !$done )
  {
    my $p = int( $progress->ProgressValue() );
    my $m = int( $progress->MaxProgressValue() );

    if ( $m > 0 )
    {
      my $percent = int( ( $p / $m ) * 100.0 );
      $percent = 0 if ( $percent < 0 );
```

```perl
      my $delta = $percent - $lp;
      if ( $delta >= 5 )
      {
        print "\t$percent%\n";
        $lp = $percent;
      }
      sleep( 2 );
    }
    $done = 1 if ( $p >= $m );
  }
  print "\n";
}

# Make sure we get a real path

my $searchpath = $ARGV[0];
die "Must specify search path\n" unless ( $searchpath );

# Start up iTunes

my $itunes = new Win32::OLE( "iTunes.application" );
die "Could not open iTunes\n" unless ( $itunes );

# Convert all of the files

find( sub { convert( $itunes, $File::Find::name ); }, $searchpath );

# Update your iPod. Comment this out if you don't have an
# iPod, or don't want it automagically updated.

$itunes->UpdateIPod( );

# Quit iTunes

$itunes->Quit( );
```

The script itself is very simple. It walks the directory that was specified as an argument on the command line to find MP3 files. For each MP3 file, it calls the ConvertFile2 method on the itunes object. This method returns a progress object that is polled to see how far the conversion has gone. On long files, this conversion process takes a while—a long while—so the script puts up a percentage indicator that tells us how much of the file it has imported.

As a bonus, the script tells iTunes to update the iPod after importing the files, which pushes the podcasts onto the player. You can comment out that line if you don't have an iPod or don't want to do automatic updating.

Running the Hack

I recommend running this script after the command-line podcatcher [Hack #3]. You can automate that by building a batch file that runs the podcatcher first, and then runs this import script. On Windows XP, you can specify that you want the script run at a specific hour of the day or week using Schedule Tasks, which is located in the System Tools section of the Start → Programs → Accessories menu.

On a Macintosh

On a Macintosh, you can use AppleScript or Perl to do the importing. Save this Perl script as *import.pl*:

```
#!/usr/bin/perl -w
use Mac::Glue;
use Mac::Path::Util;
use Cwd 'abs_path';
use strict;

# Convert the path to an absolute Mac path

my $macpath = Mac::Path::Util->new( abs_path( $ARGV[0] ) );

# Open iTunes and convert the contents of the path

my $itunes = Mac::Glue->new( 'iTunes' );
$itunes->convert( $macpath->mac_path() );
```

This script requires that the Mac::Glue and Mac::Path::Util modules are installed [Hack #7] on your system. Both of these modules are available through CPAN (*http://cpan.org/*). Mac::Glue is very cool; you can use it to drive any Macintosh application that supports AppleScript directly through Perl syntax.

Use the Terminal to run the script this way:

```
% perl import.pl /Users/jherr/mymp3s
```

This will import the directory you specify into iTunes.

See Also

- "Build Your Own Podcatcher" [Hack #3]

Tune into Videoblogs

#5 Subscribe to free amateur movies with ANT.

Videoblogs are the video version of podcasts. With RSS 2.0, you can now tune into these videoblogs the same way that you can with podcasts. ANT is a stable and high-quality client for videoblogs on the Macintosh.

On the righthand panel of the main window shown in Figure 1-13 is the list of subscriptions, and on the bottom panel is the list of downloaded videos that are available for playback. Once you have viewed a movie you can delete it from the playlist by selecting the entry and pressing the Delete key.

Figure 1-13. The ANT videocatcher

ANT comes with its own list of videoblogs that you can choose from. You can add your own as you find them. A great place to find videoblogs is the Videoblogging Yahoo! Group (*http://groups.yahoo.com/group/videobloggers/*).

See Also

- "Listen to Podcasts on the Web" [Hack #1]
- "Listen to Podcasts on Your PDA" [Hack #8]
- "Podcatching with Your PlayStation Portable" [Hack #9]

Convert Text-Based Blogs into Podcasts

Use the speech synthesizer on the Macintosh to turn text RSS feeds into podcasts and import them into iTunes.

If you get addicted to podcasts, you will find yourself wishing that your regular feeds were podcasts. However, those feeds are in text. Short of getting someone to read them, how do you get them into audio? You can use a speech synthesizer that turns the text into speech.

It might not be the most pleasant way to listen to text, but if you are at the gym and you want to get the latest technology headlines, you can use a speech synthesizer to read the headlines into MP3 files for iTunes [Hack #4].

The Code

Save this code as *asmac.pl*:

```perl
#!/usr/bin/perl -w
use LWP::Simple;
use FileHandle;
use Cwd;
use strict;

# The URL of the RSS feed

use constant URL => "http://www.mysite.com/myrss.xml";

# The artist name for the MP3s

use constant ARTIST => "Artist Name";

# The album name of the MP3s

use constant ALBUM => "Album Name";

# The output directory to put the MP3s into

use constant OUTPUT_DIR => "mp3s";

# Gets the feed and returns a hash of the RSS items, their titles
# and the temporary filenames

sub get_feed($)
{
  my $out = {};

  my $text = get URL;

  while( $text =~ /\<item(.*?)\<\/item\>/gs )
```

```perl
  {
    my $item = $1;
    my ( $title ) = $item =~ /\<title\>(.*?)\<\/title\>/gs;
    my ( $desc ) = $item =~ /\<description\>(.*?)\<\/description\>/gs;

    $title =~ /[\n|\r]/g;

    $desc =~ s/[\n|\r]/ /g;
    $desc =~ s/$\<\!\[CDATA\[//;
    $desc =~ s/\]\]\>//;
    $desc =~ s/\<.*?\>//g;
    $desc =~ s/\<\/.*?\>//g;
    $desc =~ s/\"//g;
    $desc =~ s/\'//g;
    $desc =~ s/,//g;
    $desc = $title . ". " . $desc;

    my $filename = lc $title;
    $filename =~ s/ /_/g;
    $filename =~ s/[.]//g;
    $filename =~ s/-/_/g;
    $filename =~ s/\\//g;
    $filename =~ s/\///g;
    $filename =~ s/^\s+//;
    $filename =~ s/\s+$//;

    $out->{ $filename } = {
      description => $desc,
      title => substr($title,0,30)
    };
  }

  return $out;
}

# Turns a story into speech as an AIFF file

sub speakstory($$)
{
  my ( $text, $filename ) = @_;

  open FH, "|osascript";
  print FH "set ofile to POSIX file \"$filename\"\n";
  print FH "say \"$text\" saving to ofile\n";
  close FH;
}

# Convert an AIFF file to MP3 with the right tags

sub convert($$$)
{
  my ( $aiffFile, $mp3File, $desc ) = @_;
```

```
    print "Creating $mp3File\n";

    my $cmd = "lame $aiffFile $mp3File --silent --tt \"$desc\"";
    $cmd .= " --ta \"".ARTIST."\" --tl \"".ALBUM."\" -h";

    system( $cmd );
}

# Get the feed URL and build MP3s for each of the entries

my $items = get_feed( URL );
foreach my $filename ( keys %$items )
{
    speakstory( $items->{ $filename }->{description}, "temp.aiff" );
    convert( "temp.aiff", OUTPUT_DIR."/".$filename.".mp3",
        $items->{ $filename }->{ title } );
    unlink( "temp.aiff" );
}

# Import the files into iTunes

print "Importing the MP3s into iTunes\n";

open FH, "|osascript";
print FH "set ofile to POSIX file \"".getcwd."/".OUTPUT_DIR."\"\n";
print FH "tell application \"iTunes\" to convert ofile\n";
close FH;
```

Running the Hack

To customize this script, change the URL of the feed in the Perl script, as well as the artist and album name. The output directory is just a temporary directory where the MP3 files go on their way to iTunes.

To run this hack you will need to install the LAME MP3 encoder [Hack #50] for command-line access. Download the most recent LAME *.tgz* file from *http://lame.sf.net/* and extract it. Then, cd to the top-level directory and run ./configure to configure the LAME distribution. Next, run make to build the LAME encoder. Finally, run sudo make install to install the LAME executable in the system.

Hacking the Hack

Some blogs offer two versions of their RSS feeds: one with a truncated version of the blog entries, and another with the complete text of each entry. You will want to point this script at the full-text version so that it will read the entire contents of each blog entry from the text in the RSS feed.

If a full-text feed is not available, you will want to hack the script to get the contents of each URL pointed into the feed. Then the script will need to extract the text of the entire blog entry from the target page to get the complete text. At this point, you can pass this full text back as the `description` field and let the script do the job of speaking the text into MP3 files.

iSpeak It

The iSpeak It application on the Macintosh (*http://zapptek.com/ispeak-it/*) is the commercial version of the RSS-to-speech application.

Figure 1-14 shows the iSpeak It main window that shows the text that will be converted into speech and then added to your iTunes library. You can specify a list of RSS feeds to read, or just use the ones that it has as defaults.

Figure 1-14. News headlines pulled from RSS, ready for text-to-speech conversion

Once the spoken news entries are encoded as sound files in your iTunes library, you can sync your iPod to iTunes and listen to the headlines on your way to work.

Admittedly, the computer speech generated by the system-standard Macintalk drivers is a little hard to take. Check Cepstral Voices (*http://cepstral. com/*) for some more-pleasing alternatives on Mac and Windows in the $30 range.

AutoCast

The equivalent program on Windows is called AutoCast (*http://autocastsoftware.com/*). The program requires the Microsoft Speech SDK Version 5.1. Full source code is available on the site.

See Also

- "Speech Synthesize Your Podcast Introduction" [Hack #65]

HACK #7 Install Perl Modules

A number of hacks in this book use Perl scripts. This hack covers installing Perl, Perl modules, and Perl support in your web server.

Perl is a widely used scripting language that I use in this book to perform a variety of podcast-related tasks. Perl comes preinstalled on Mac OS X and Linux, and it's easy to install on Windows.

If you have the time, it's worth learning Perl. The language syntax can be a little confusing at first but becomes familiar quickly. A lot of the value of Perl comes from the CPAN library of modules (*http://cpan.org/*), which covers every conceivable need.

Perl Modules for Podcasting

Here are some helpful Perl modules that should interest podcasters:

MP3::Info
> With MP3::Info your script can read and write the ID3 tags in MP3 files.

MP4::Info
> This retrieves information from MP4 (AAC) format files.

Ogg::Vorbis::Header
> This reads and writes information from an Ogg Vorbis file's header.

LWP::Simple
> This library allows you to fetch any URL with a single function call.

LWP::UserAgent
> This is the more functional version of LWP::Simple. With this module, you can simulate a web browser surfing to a site, logging in, getting cookies, making requests, and then leaving. You can automate any complex web task with LWP::UserAgent.

Net::SFTP

> The SFTP module gives you access to the full SFTP secure file-transfer standard. You can log into SSH hosts, navigate around, and upload and download files using simple function calls.

Net::FTP

> This is similar to the Net::SFTP module, but for the older FTP file-transfer standard.

XML::RSS

> This supports building RSS 2.0 feeds with enclosure tags using an object-oriented interface.

XML::Atom

> This is the corresponding interface to XML::RSS for the Atom syndication standard.

XML::DOM, XML::Parser, XML::Simple, *and* XML::XPath

> These modules, and many more in the XML family of modules, provide a wide variety of tools for reading, writing, and navigating XML documents.

XML::RSS::Parser

> This parses RSS feeds into objects to make it easier to navigate them.

Data::Dumper

> This is simply the easiest way to get a dump of the contents of any Perl variable. This is a very handy module when you are debugging Perl scripts.

Tk

> This is a free, platform-independent windowing toolkit that makes it easy to build graphical user interfaces (GUIs) that look reasonably good and respond well.

Mac::Glue

> This is a toolkit for using AppleScript automation to drive applications directly from Perl.

Installing Perl Modules on Linux and Mac OS X

One of the best Perl modules is the CPAN module, which automatically downloads Perl modules and installs them. Even better, if the module you want depends on other modules, it will download those modules first and install them before installing the module you requested.

To run the CPAN module, invoke this command:

```
% sudo cpan
```

sudo will run the script as root so that you can install modules in the main Perl library directory. The shell portion of the command line instructs the CPAN module to go into interactive mode. From here, you can type in install commands to download and install modules.

 If you have trouble running sudo, you need to use the visudo command to set yourself up as a "sudoer" with access to sudo. The visudo command must be run as root. If you don't have sudo installed, check the package repository for your Linux distribution.

The first time you run the CPAN module it will ask you a lot of questions about where it should look for modules. Make sure to specify a few sites so that if one or two go down you won't have any problems downloading and installing modules.

Once the setup is done the CPAN module will download the tarball of the module you requested and install it for you.

If you want to forego the interactive shell, you can request a specific module right from the command line, with this syntax:

```
% sudo cpan install XML::Simple
```

Installing web Perl scripts on Mac OS X. Apache comes preinstalled on Mac OS X. You will need to enable it by using the Personal Web Sharing option in the Sharing section of System Preferences.

Once Apache is active, you can copy your Perl script to the */Library/WebServer/CGI-Executables/* directory. Make sure the script is executable by changing its Unix permissions. The following shell commands copy a file called *network.pl* to the *CGI* directory and change its permissions to enable execution:

```
% cp network.pl /Library/WebServer/CGI-Executables/
% chmod 755 /Library/WebServer/CGI-Executables/network.pl
```

With this done, you should be able to use Safari to surf to the page on your local web server (*http://localhost/cgi-bin/network.pl*) and see the output of the script.

If you have trouble, you can try using this very simple script as a starting point:

```
#!/usr/bin/perl
print "Content-type: text/html\r\n\r\n";
print "<html><body>Hello!</body></html>";
```

The output is a web page that says "Hello."

Installing Perl scripts on your server. Installing Perl scripts on a Linux-, Unix-, or Mac OS X-powered web server is similar to installing them on Mac OS X. You copy the script into your *cgi-bin* directory, and change its permissions to 755 to make it executable. Unfortunately, the name and location of your *cgi-bin* directory changes with each ISP.

The good news is that installing Perl scripts is a common issue for ISPs, so they will have documentation on how to install them in their Frequently Asked Questions (FAQ) document, or in their knowledge base.

Installing ActiveState Perl on Windows

Windows doesn't come preinstalled with Perl. Can you believe it? Crazy. So, to run Perl scripts on Windows, you will need to install Perl first. The most direct way to do that is to install ActivePerl (*http://activestate.com/*). Use all the default options during the installation and you should have Perl installed in *c:\perl*.

Open a new command prompt so that you pick up the latest PATH setting, and run this command to test the Perl installation:

```
C:\> perl -v
```

If all is well, you will get a message that gives you the version of the Perl interpreter, some licensing information, and so on.

Another Perl installation option is to use Cygwin (*http://cygwin.com/*). Cygwin is a complete Unix environment for Windows that includes Perl among the available packages. You can use ActiveState or Cygwin Perl to run the scripts in this book, but ActivePerl integrates nicely with Internet Information Services (IIS). So, I recommend installing ActivePerl to use the scripts in this book. Thankfully the two Perls—ActivePerl and Cygwin Perl—do not conflict with one another if both are installed on the same machine.

Installing Perl modules on Windows. The ActiveState alternative to the CPAN module is a utility named ppm (Programmer's Package Manager). ppm can install any module in its repository. And there are a lot of modules in the repository! To see the complete list, go to the ppm site (*http://ppm.activestate.com/*).

To start an interactive session with ppm, type this at the command prompt:

```
C:\> ppm
```

From here, you can use install commands to install new modules:

```
ppm> install Mail-Box
```

This will install the `Mail::Box` Perl module. As with CPAN, the package manager will download any modules required to run the one you want to install, before installing yours.

One downside with `ppm` is that you can't specify the module name directly. Instead of `Mail::Box` you have to use the package filename, `Mail-Box`. Usually the translation is a simple conversion of the `::` to `-`. However, you might find that you need to search for the package name that corresponds to the module. To search, use this syntax:

```
ppm> search XML::RSS
```

You will get back a list of qualifying packages.

Installing Perl scripts in IIS. Windows XP and earlier editions allow the installation of a cut-down version of the IIS web server. To install it, use the Add or Remove Programs control panel, and then select Add/Remove Windows Components and the Internet Information Services.

Once IIS is installed, you can use the Internet Information Services manager in the Administrative Tools portion of the control panel to configure the IIS server. The first step is to create a new virtual directory that will host the Perl scripts. Navigate down into the Web Sites section and into the Default Web Site item. Now, right-click the righthand portion of the window and select Virtual Directory... from the New submenu.

The first step in the Virtual Directory Creation Wizard is to give the new directory a name. I called mine *scripts*. This is shown in Figure 1-15.

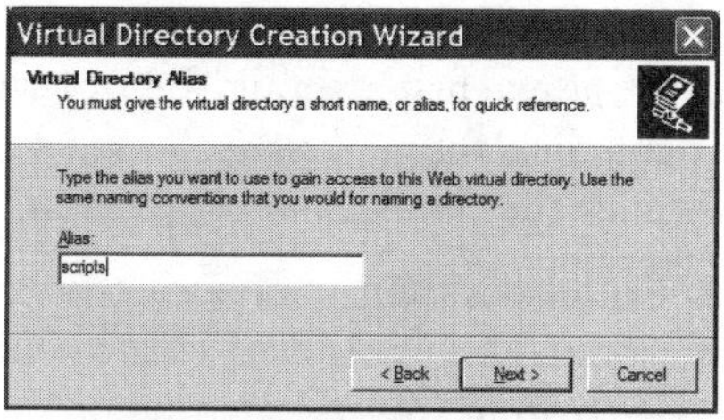

Figure 1-15. Naming an IIS virtual directory

Then you have to assign it to a real directory on your hard drive that will host the scripts. I used *c:\scripts*, as shown in Figure 1-16.

This means that any requests to *http://localhost/scripts/* will invoke the corresponding Perl script in the *c:\scripts* directory. So, *http://localhost/scripts/myscript.pl* becomes *c:\scripts\myscript.pl*.

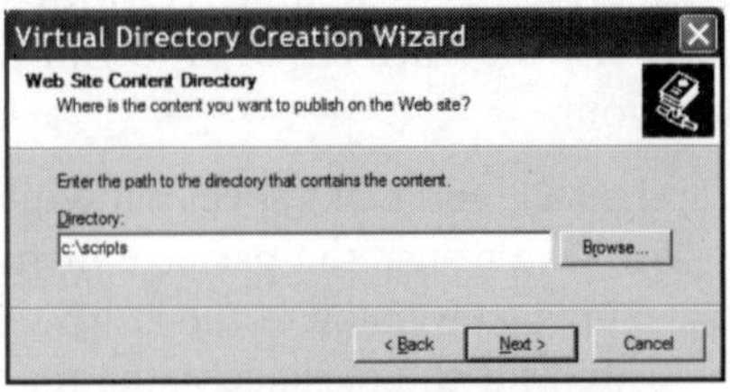

Figure 1-16. Assigning the virtual directory to a real directory

The last step is to set up the permissions on the virtual directory. I chose just to allow for execution of the scripts, by choosing the options shown in Figure 1-17.

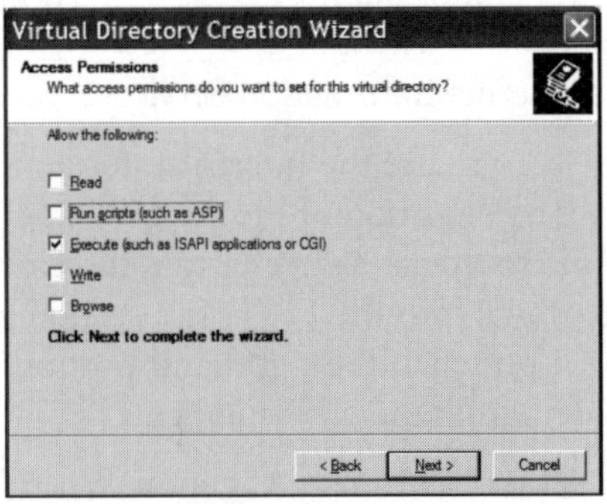

Figure 1-17. Setting the permissions on the directory

Once you have completed the wizard there is one last step. You need to tell IIS that scripts with the *.pl* extension should be run with ActiveState Perl. The first step is to right-click the new *scripts* virtual directory and select Properties. From here, click the Configuration... button.

This brings up the set of application mappings that specify which extensions go to which interpreter. Click Add to create a new mapping and to specify the mapping, as shown in Figure 1-18.

Click OK on the dialog in Figure 1-18, and then OK again on the dialogs that follow, until you are back at the IIS manager. Now you can add Perl scripts into the *c:\scripts* directory and access them through your browser.

Use this simple test script to make sure everything is working properly:

```
print "Content-type: text/html\n\n";
print "<html><body>Hello!</body></html>";
```

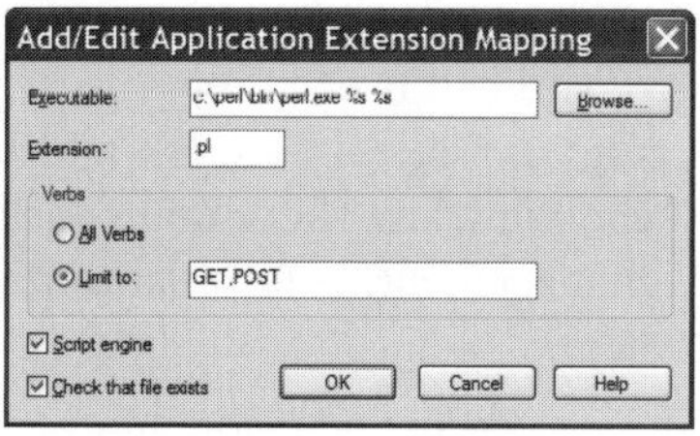

Figure 1-18. Assigning Perl to the .pl extension

Save this file as *c:\scripts\test.pl*. Then use your web browser (hopefully the new Firefox browser, downloadable at *http://firefox.com/*) to surf to *http:// localhost/scripts/test.pl*. If the web page shows the word *Hello*, you are cooking with gas.

Installing Perl scripts in Apache on Windows. Apache is an open source web server that provides an excellent alternative to IIS on Windows. Download the Windows installer for Apache (*http://apache.org/*). For the hacks in this book, I recommend using the 1.3 version of the server. Follow the installer and select that you want to run it as a service.

Next, create a script in the *c:\Program Files\Apache Group\Apache\cgi-bin* directory called *test.pl*, with the following contents:

```
#!c:\perl\bin\perl.exe
print "Content-type: text/html\n\n";
print "<html><body>Hello!</body></html>";
```

The trick here is to get the location of the Perl interpreter right. I used the default location for the ActiveState Perl interpreter. The location of your interpreter will vary if you installed it somewhere else.

After you have saved the test script in the *cgi-bin* directory, point your browser to *http://localhost/cgi-bin/test.pl* and you should see the word *Hello*.

How cool is that? Instant web serving with no muss or fuss.

HACK #8 Listen to Podcasts on Your PDA

Use a PDA to listen to podcasts on the go.

Why restrict yourself to MP3 players or your PC when you want to listen to podcasts? Your PDA makes for a very capable podcatcher. Web-enabled PDAs can grab podcasts for you without having to sync to a computer.

This hack covers podcatching clients for both Pocket PC and Palm-powered PDAs.

Podcatching with Your Pocket PC PDA

With a Pocket PC device, you can use an application such as FeederReader to download podcasts from a wireless network and listen to or view them wherever you are. You can view any show notes included in the RSS feed, and with integrated file management, you can automatically delete podcasts after you've listened to them.

The integrated feel of the Pocket PC, with the optional ability to view notes from the podcast, makes for a great experience.

Sneakernet or direct connect. You can treat a Pocket PC as a simple MP3 player to listen to podcasts: either downloading songs over ActiveSync or using a card reader. However, to really take advantage of podcasts, you'll want to consider installing an aggregator on the device.

To listen to podcasts you will need a decent amount of memory. I recommend at least 256 MB for a small number (5–10) of stored shows, with up to 2 GB to hold a large number of podcasts to listen to over a long weekend.

A walk-through using FeederReader. First, download and install Feeder-Reader (*http://FeederReader.com/*). You can install it into RAM or on a memory card. Installing it on a memory card will leave you more RAM for running programs. Using a program called CabInstl (search for "CabInstl" at *http://www.pocketgear.com/*) you can install the CAB file onto your memory card.

Figure 1-19 shows the process of installing FeederReader with CabInstl. After installing and running FeederReader, you can add a new feed by selecting that menu item and entering a URL, as seen in Figure 1-20.

Figure 1-19. Using CabInstl to install FeederReader

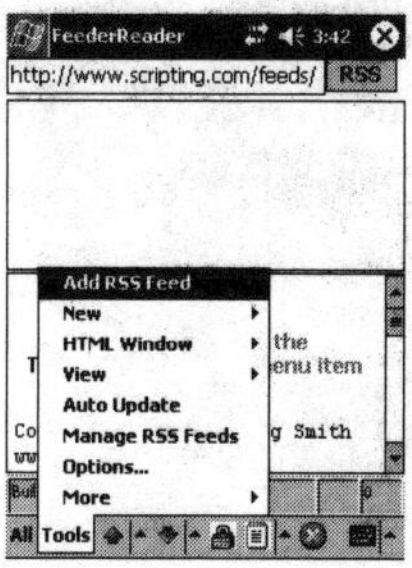

Figure 1-20. Adding an RSS feed

After adding all the feeds and arranging them into categories, select Update Enclosures (shown in Figure 1-21). This will download all enclosures in your podcast feeds. FeederReader downloads several podcasts at once. If any podcasts get stuck or time out, the remaining podcasts continue to download.

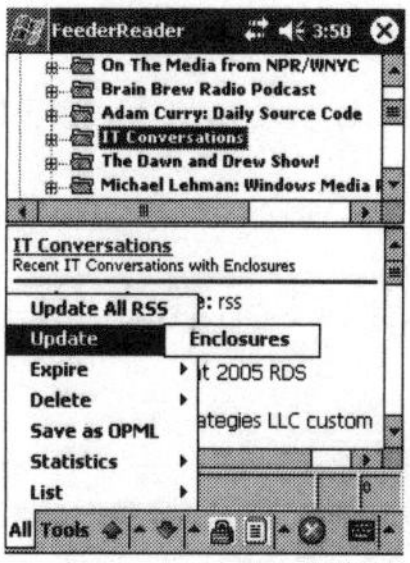

Figure 1-21. Checking the RSS feed for new podcasts

Then start the download by selecting the Enclosures option from the Update menu. You can see this in Figure 1-22.

At any time, you can bring up the Enclosure toolbar and tap the Play icon to play your downloaded podcasts. FeederReader will launch the appropriate player for the enclosure and let you continue reading other RSS feeds. You can listen to podcasts while you read news from RSS feeds. It works out great!

If the enclosure is a videocast instead, FeederReader will bring up the appropriate player for a videocast as well. It works with anything that the Pocket PC can display or play! To go to the next podcast or videocast, tap the Delete-Play Next icon (the right-facing triangle with the X superimposed on it) to automatically delete the previous podcast. This way, FeederReader is deleting the enclosure files right after you've finished with them.

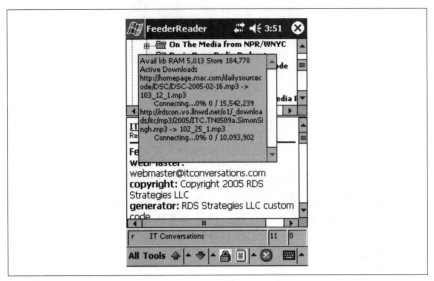

Figure 1-22. Downloading a podcast

Play is the Green arrow, and Delete-Play Next is the arrow with the X over it.

Figure 1-23 gives some more detail on the IT Conversations show that FeederReader downloaded.

Figure 1-23. Inspecting a downloaded podcast

The Pocket PC as an MP3 player. Some MP3 players can be mounted as hard drives without additional drivers on your desktop. With a Pocket PC, this is not directly possible. However, you can mount the Pocket PC as a drive on the desktop by using ActiveSync, the free program from Microsoft (it comes with every Windows Mobile Pocket PC and smartphone). When you do this, you can treat it as a mounted MP3 player and transfer files with the same techniques as you would an MP3 player, whether using Windows Explorer to copy and paste or drag and drop. You can also set it up to transfer automatically from other programs (such as iPodder).

Installing podcatcher software on a Pocket PC or smartphone allows you to download podcasts directly to your device without a desktop. As of early 2005, four programs for Windows Mobile devices directly download podcasts: Egress (*http://www.garishkernels.net/egress.html*), Pocket RSS (*http://pda.jasnapaka.com/*), FeederReader for the Pocket PC, and iPodderSP (*http://www.handango.com/*) for the smartphone. (Get it? The SP stands for Smart-Phone.) The developer of iPodderSP ported that program to the Pocket PC as well, and called it PiP, for "Pocket iPodder"; clever! While iPodderSP is a program dedicated to podcasts, the others are generic RSS aggregators in which you can also download nonpodcast RSS feeds.

In Figure 1-24 you can see iPodderSP zooming in on the Dawn and Drew show.

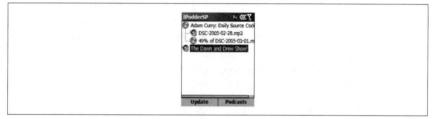

Figure 1-24. Zooming in on the Dawn and Drew show

It's all about the Net. To use these programs, your Windows Mobile device must have a connection to the Internet. Usually this is through WiFi, a cell phone (connecting with Bluetooth, IR, or a cable, and the cell phone data connection using, for example, EDGE), or ActiveSync with Internet Pass-through turned on (shown in Figure 1-25). Although a desktop is not required, it is sometimes helpful to connect with ActiveSync and take advantage of a broadband connection.

Many modern Pocket PCs come with integrated WiFi (usually 802.11b). WiFi combined with a broadband connection is one of the best ways to connect to the Internet for downloading podcasts. Remember that podcasts can be as short as 1 MB (one minute of audio of reasonable quality), but they can easily top 50 MB (one hour of stereo-music quality).

Unless you have a stable cell phone connection, and unlimited data for a fixed cost (more common in the U.S. than elsewhere), you'll likely prefer to download podcasts with a broadband connection and transfer them to your PDA through a WiFi connection or ActiveSync. GPRS data rates range from

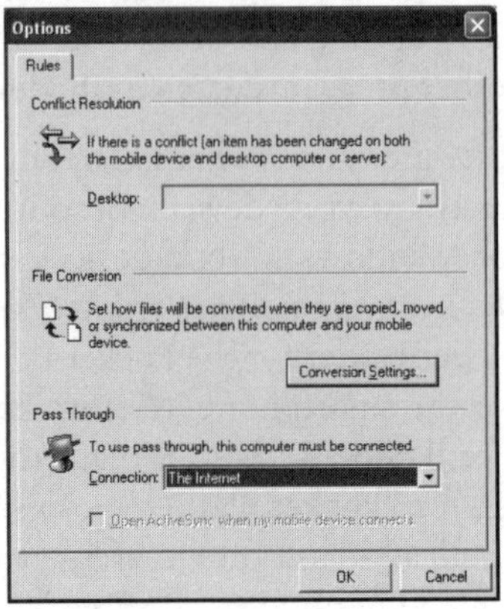

Figure 1-25. Setting up Windows XP for Internet pass-through

20 kilo*bits* per second to 50 kilobits per second (which averages 2–5 kilo-*bytes* per second). However, the newer EDGE data service offers between 6 and 15 kilobytes per second and 1xRTT hovers at around 7–12. (EV-DO is an improvement over 1xRTT that gets between *300 and 500* kilobytes per second in select U.S. cities.) A 20 MB file might take 1–2 hours over GPRS, 20–30 minutes over EDGE, but less than 5 minutes over ActiveSync and even less over WiFi and broadband.

One of the things that is crucial to a Pocket PC but less so for a connected desktop is a "resume" capability for enclosures. The Internet connection on a Pocket PC is much less reliable than an Ethernet-connected desktop PC. In addition, you might be in a position to download for only a few minutes as you whiz by a WiFi hotspot on the road. In these cases, you would not want to have to restart any enclosure downloads from the beginning. Most Pocket PC podcatchers support resuming a download. For resume to work, it also needs to be supported by the server. This is common, but not universal. This capability benefits the podcaster (or, rather, the one who hosts the file), so you might have luck in contacting them and letting them know about resume capability.

Let's play. So, you've got a flash memory card full of podcasts. Where do you start? You have three choices: browse the files within File Explorer, browse the podcasts with Windows Media Player (or another media player) and select one or more, or use integrated file management within your pod-catcher.

If your podcatching program saves enclosures in one directory, you can use File Explorer to browse and play those files. However, you might need to be careful about which downloads are complete and which are only partially downloaded.

Figure 1-26 shows the downloaded podcasts and videocasts. From here, you can sort them by date and delete them manually.

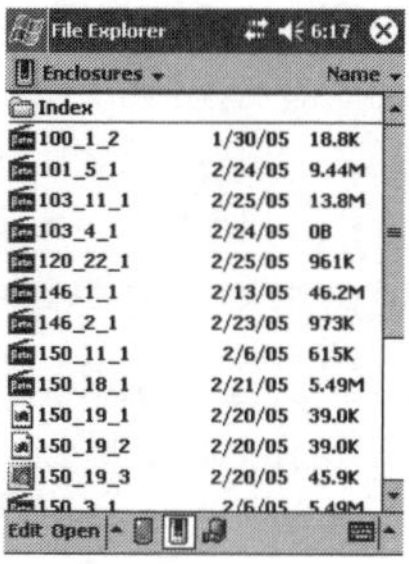

Figure 1-26. The directory of downloaded podcasts

The easiest way to play podcasts from a directory is to download all desired enclosures, listen to all of them, and then delete them before beginning to download the next group. If you delete the podcasts as part of your evening routine, you can download new podcasts overnight.

It can become difficult to determine when you can delete a podcast if you do not listen to all of them before beginning the next download. So, getting into a routine is highly beneficial. Better yet, use a podcatcher that has integrated file management.

Integrated file management. File management can be *integrated* into the podcatcher. It involves launching the player programs and deleting files when you are done with them. With an MP3 player or podcatcher without integrated file management, you can develop a routine with playing and deleting, but that requires some effort and consistency in your podcatching life. With file management, you play podcasts, and when the first podcast is done, you play the next one while deleting the first one. Prior to playing the next podcast, you can choose to keep it or wait to delete it later. Integrated file management is implemented in FeederReader, for example, with the Enclosure toolbar.

With integrated file management, the podcatcher can keep track of the type of enclosure to determine the best method of playing it. If you play an enclosure from outside the podcatcher, Windows Mobile uses the file extension to determine the program used. Depending on how the podcasting server is set up, you might not have the original extension of the file and the system might find it difficult to play the file automatically. As a last resort, if you know what type of file it is, you can open the appropriate program and load the file from within that program.

Podcatching with Your Palm-Powered PDA

Quick News from Stand Alone Inc. (*http://standalone.com/*) is a PalmOS RSS reader that supports podcast enclosures. To start the installation, make sure your PDA is ready to sync. Next, download the *QuickNews.rpc* file from the Stand Alone site. Use palmOne Quick Install to install the *QuickNews.rpc* file on your PDA. Then, press the HotSync button on your cradle or cable, or initiate a wireless hotsync to synchronize your PDA.

Once the Quick News application is installed, tap the Add Feed button to subscribe to a podcast. You will need to type in the URL of the podcast's RSS feed, as shown in Figure 1-27.

Figure 1-27. Setting up a Quick News podcast feed

If your PDA supports a network connection, click the application menu button and select Update All Locally to start the download. You can use the host computer to perform the download by selecting the Update All at HotSync command.

To download enclosures (as shown in Figure 1-28), which are the MP3 files of the podcast, you need to have memory installed in your PDA. Podcasts range in size from around 5 MB at the low end to around 25 MB at the high end. So, plan your memory card purchase accordingly.

You manage the list of feeds using the feed list screen that appears on application startup. This feed list is shown in Figure 1-29.

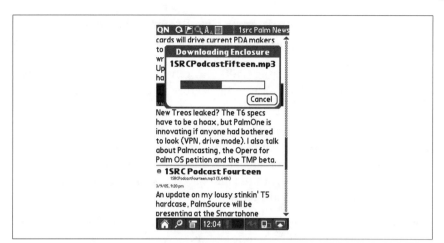

Figure 1-28. Downloading podcast MP3s directly with Quick News

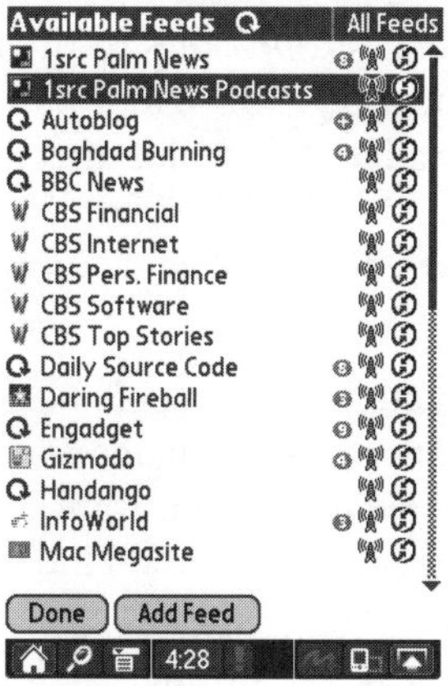

Figure 1-29. The Quick News feed list

Quick News is free for a 30-day trial period. You can purchase Quick News from the Stand Alone site for $14.95.

Some PalmOS PDAs come with MP3 player applications included in the pre-installed applications. Quick News does not play MP3 files directly, so if you don't have a player you will need to download and install one. I recommend Pocket Tunes (*http://www.pocket-tunes.com/*) and AeroPlayer (*http://www.aerodrome.us/*).

See Also

- "Podcatching with Your PlayStation Portable" [Hack #9]

—*Greg Smith*

Podcatching with Your PlayStation Portable

#9 Use your PlayStation Portable (PSP) to listen to podcasts.

Sony's new PlayStation Portable (PSP) unit can play MP3 audio files stored on its memory sticks. You can use this feature to listen to podcasts on the device.

Attach the PSP to your computer using the USB cable. Then select USB Connection from the Settings section of the Home menu. On both Macintosh and Windows the device will appear as a drive. Double-click the drive and navigate to the *PSP* directory. Cards that haven't been used in a PSP will not have a *PSP* directory yet, so just create one.

Once inside the *PSP* directory, create a subdirectory called *Music*, and another subdirectory within the *Music* directory, called *Podcasts*. The name of the *Podcasts* directory is really up to you, but the names of the other two directories must be *PSP* and *Music*.

Your can download the podcast *.mp3* files to the *PSP/Music/Podcasts* directory using the Finder (Mac OS X) or Windows Explorer. Or, you can set your podcatcher to download to that device directly by specifying that as the storage path for the enclosures. On Windows, the full path will be *<drive>:\ PSP\Music\Podcasts*, where *<drive>* depends on what the operating system allocates.

On Macintosh, the full directory will be */Volumes/<Card Name>/PSP/Music/ Podcasts*, where *<Card Name>* is the name you gave to the card in the Finder. This is *Untitled* by default. If you want to check the path for yourself, use the Go to Folder command in the Finder's Go menu and specify */ Volumes*.

Once the *.mp3* files are downloaded to the card, just stick the card in your PSP and use the system menu to navigate to the music icon. Once there you should be able to specify the card as the storage device and see the *Podcasts* directory. Click the *Podcasts* directory to see the podcast files. Click whichever you want to play.

If you see the "There are no tracks" message, you have put the files in the wrong location and you need to ensure that the directory structure is *PSP/ Music/Podcasts*, from the top level of the directory structure down. Check your owner's manual for more specifics if you are still having trouble.

Any audio you want to play on the device will have to be encoded as MP3 or Sony's ATRAC3plus format. You can download photos to the device as well by storing them in the */PSP/Photo* directory. Video can also be encoded for playback. PSP Video 9 (*http://pspvideo9.com/*) is a freeware Windows application that converts video from AVI or MPEG into Sony's MPEG4 format for playback on the device.

 When downloading photos from the Macintosh to a memory stick, the operating system will place thumbnails in the *PHOTO* directory that will confuse the PSP. Use the Terminal to find the *.jpg* files that start with a dot (.), and delete them.

See Also

- "Listen to Podcasts on Your PDA" [Hack #8]

## CHAPTER TWO

Starting Out
Hacks 10–11

*Podcasting gives you the power to compete
with Howard Stern, from your basement.*

—Joe Lipscomb

An hour from now you can be a podcaster. It's far easier than you think, and all you need are the microphone on your laptop and a connection to the Internet. Getting started early is very important. Podcasting is all about making mistakes and learning from them to create better podcasts. So, start right now and make your first podcast.

HACK #10 Make Your First Podcast

Use the hardware you have right now, and some free software on the Web, to make your first podcast.

If you don't have an internal microphone in your computer, you will need to get a microphone. Microphone solutions are available for all budgets. [Hack #12] covers the basics of sound input, and [Hack #13] will help you pick out the right microphone for your budget.

Once you have the sound input device covered, the next step is to download Audacity (*http://audacity.sf.net/*). This is a free application that runs on Macintosh, Windows, and Linux. It can record sound from any source, including the internal microphone on your PC or Macintosh laptop.

With Audacity installed, press the big red Record button and explain what you have in mind for your podcast. The meter bars attached to the window will show you when you are talking too loudly (by hitting the far side of the meter near the 0 mark) or too softly (by registering only slightly as you talk). Click the Stop button to finish the recording. When you are finished, you will have something that looks like Figure 2-1.

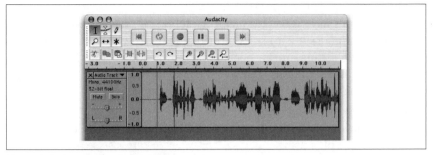

Figure 2-1. A recording in Audacity

As the recording is made, your voice is shown as a waveform on the display. Each word you say appears as a little blip in the signal that goes above and below the center line. The louder the word, the taller the blip.

Figure 2-1 shows a short period of silence at the beginning of the recording. I didn't start speaking until one second after I pressed the Record button. You can remove that period of silence by using the Selection tool, which is in the upper lefthand corner of the window. Next, select the period of silence and click either the Delete key or the icon with the scissors to cut the signal. You can do the same at the end of the signal to remove any trailing silence.

Digital audio is exactly like digital photography or video, in that you can do as many takes as you like or do as much editing as you please. It's all just RAM or disk space and you can delete what you don't use. So, relax and take as much time as you need to say what you want to say.

Being relaxed as you record your podcast is of primary importance in terms of getting a good sound. A number of handy tips for improving your vocal skills are outlined in [Hack #11].

With your audio file edited, you need to save that Audacity file to disk, and then export the file as MP3. For voice-only podcasts, I recommend using a 32-bit compression rate for MP3. You set that in the Preferences dialog in the File Formats tab.

You will be prompted for some information about your MP3 file. These are stored as ID3 tags that are embedded in your MP3. Getting the right content in those tags [Hack #40] is important for making it easy for your listeners to find and listen to your podcast.

With the MP3 in hand, now you have to put it up on the Web and link it to a Really Simple Syndication (RSS) 2.0 feed. Several solutions are available for this, depending on what you have today.

You have no blog, domain, or ISP

If you don't have a blog, domain name, or ISP, the easiest way to put together a podcast is to use Ourmedia. [Hack #38] walks you through the process of setting up an account and uploading your first podcast. Other similar options include Liberated Syndication, Odeo, and AudioBlog.

You have a domain, but no blog

If you have your own domain and ISP, you have several options. You can set up a blog using Movable Type or WordPress [Hack #38].

You have a domain, but don't want to run a blog

You can podcast without a blog using Podcastamatic or Dircaster [Hack #37].

You have a Radio UserLand, Movable Type, Word Press, or Blogger blog

See [Hack #38].

With most of these solutions (except for Liberated Syndication, Odeo, AudioBlog, and Ourmedia), you are going to have to find a place to host your MP3 file on the Web. MP3 files are a lot bigger than text files, so finding a place to put them can be difficult [Hack #39].

Once you have used one of these options to get your blog set up with an RSS 2.0 feed, and you've uploaded an MP3 file, you can create a new entry in the blog that points to your MP3 file. At that point, you are a podcaster! Point your podcatcher to your RSS 2.0 feed to make sure it downloads properly. Then go out into the podcastosphere and promote your podcast [Hack #46].

Where to Go from Here

The technical aspect of podcasting is only one part of the story. Once the microphone is switched on and the digital reels are virtually recording, what do you say? Content is king. Chapters 4 and 5 will give you some ideas about what to say and how to say it. [Hack #11] covers lessons you can learn from radio professionals to improve your podcast.

Still, the technical side of podcasting is a blast. You have a wide variety of amateur and professional microphones to choose from. Digitizing hardware is inexpensive and can greatly improve your sound. You can use cheap mixing boards and portable recorders to podcast anywhere, from your car to your local bar. The digital revolution has dropped the barrier to entry for communications, photography, and digital video. However, audio was not left behind. Chapter 3, Chapter 8, Chapter 9, and Chapter 10 cover your hardware and software options in detail.

Becoming a Critical Listener

Now that you are a podcaster, you will need to develop a new way of listening to podcasts. Instead of just laying back and enjoying, which you can still do, now you have to become a critical observer of podcasts. You are listening for several things:

Structure

> What is the show's format? What recurring elements, called *format elements*, does the show use to keep you listening to this podcast, and coming back for future podcasts? Is the interesting stuff in the beginning, at the end, or mixed throughout?

Style

> How are they presenting themselves? Are they professional or aloof? Are they just goofing around? Is their style related to what they are talking about?

Technical elements

> Are they using their blog in a unique or novel way? Have they put together something new with RSS? Do they offer a new way of contacting them with feedback? You should be on the lookout for all of these things when determining what to include in your show.

Content

> What's holding your attention? This is particularly important, since it's primarily what keeps people coming back to the show. When something moves you, listen to it over and over and figure out what is keeping you engaged.

You can learn from what does and doesn't work. When you hear something that works you will want to take that idea and see if it can work on your show. And when something falls over, you will want to make sure you aren't making the same mistakes.

This pertains not just to podcasts, but to anything on the radio, on television, or in what you read. The structures remain the same throughout. The narrative arc that moves you in a 30-second commercial can work in your podcast.

Think of yourself as that kid in his dad's workshop, taking apart a transistor radio to see how it works. You used to just listen to the radio, but now you want to see how it works, and see if you can make it better. Podcasts are just like little machines that you can dig into and see how they work, and then apply those lessons to your own podcast.

See Also

- "Set Up a Basic Home Studio" [Hack #12]
- "Pick the Right Microphone" [Hack #13]
- "Reduce Noise" [Hack #15]
- "Train Your Voice" [Hack #19]
- "Adopt a Format for Your Podcast" [Hack #20]

HACK #11 Professional-Quality Podcasting

Podcasting is new, but broadcasting isn't. Learn the established secrets of the broadcasting trade that will help you create professional podcasts with basic hardware.

Without even thinking about it, you are taking on the role of producer, writer, host, engineer, and editor of your own show. Understanding the different roles in a radio show can help you compartmentalize your work so that you can concentrate on each job. While you are in the host role, your mind should be fixed on the job of hosting, without thinking about the engineering or the production aspects of the show.

In this hack, I'll cover each role and give you some tips from the professionals that you can use in your own podcast.

The Producer

There are two levels of producer: the show producer, and the segment producer. The show producer is in charge of deciding how shows are organized, the theme of a show, and putting it all together. The segment producer handles an individual portion of a show, such as an interview or a comic bit.

A producer will tell you that a show needs a general theme and some structure. The theme is simply the subject of the podcast: some observation you had, a movie you want to review, or a story you want to tell. The structure of the show can be equally simple, with an introduction at the beginning, the show segment in the middle, and the credits and any plugs at the end.

The segment producer has two responsibilities: to research the topic and to author the *show prep* for his segment. This show prep is usually a set of notes that are given to the host before the segment starts. I'll cover what goes in the notes in the section titled "The Writer," later in this hack.

The podcast producer is concerned with finding guests for the show. The producer schedules a time to talk with the guest and does some research on the guest and what they are going to talk about.

Getting access to famous or important people can be difficult. As editor-in-chief of the Code Generation Network (*http://codegeneration.net/*) it's my job to secure interviews with interesting people. In general, I get access pretty quickly to people because it's a small field and people are interested in talking, but on two occasions, it took months of repeated calls and schedule choreography to get an interview [Hack #33]. But it was worth the wait.

Here are some tips I've followed to get some great interviews:

Have an elevator pitch
> This is a summary of why the person should come on your show and it should be very brief. The term *elevator pitch* implies that you should be able to explain the whole thing between floors in an elevator. In particular, you should know the size of audience you are giving the person access to, and why that audience is important to her. Also, find a way to appeal to the interviewee directly. Tell her why your interview will be different, and not just another whistle stop on the press tour.

Sound official
> In the process of getting an interview, you will talk with numerous people, all of whom have heard the same type of introductory lines over and over again. Have your salutation nailed when you start making the calls. "My name is Joe Schmoe. I'm from the *Daily Review*. I'm calling regarding an interview with Jane Doe about her new film, *For My Eyes Only*." Then be ready with the callback details, including a phone number and email address. The more blasé you sound, the better. Eagerness is a tip-off that you might be an amateur.

Keep notes
> As you talk with different publicists and people on the marketing machine food chain, keep a detailed journal of who, by full name, you talked to, and when and what they told you. It helps you to respond quickly and with authority when someone asks you who you talked to, why you talked with them, and what they told you.

Be persistent
> Publicists are busy, particularly when the person you are interested in is in demand. Keep calling, and keep a record of your calls. Always leave a message. If you're a small operation, you normally will not receive an answer. If they do contact you to tell you that you cannot have the interview, get them to tell you why, and try to rework your pitch to convince them to work with you.

Be positive and flexible

> If you aren't part of the big media machine, working with you is optional for publicists. Make it a pleasure for them to call you back. Be excited, positive, and entertaining, and make them feel good about what you are trying to do. Nobody is going to return your calls if you sound irritable or mean, if they have a choice. If you are a podcast show with 200 listeners, they are doing you a favor by setting up the interview. Be flexible in your schedule and work around their needs.

Be confident

> You have a good show. You understand your audience. You know the interview process and will do a good job at it. Have this in mind when you make these calls and talk with these people. Exuding confidence will reassure people that you are not a stalker looking for close contact with the stars.

Now, with the fundamentals in hand, I dub thee "press." Welcome to the club. We've got jackets. Now that you are one of the press, you can be on the press circuit for publicists. Publicists are your gateway to companies and individuals who want to flog their latest book, movie, product, or gizmo. A publicist's job is to get press that will generate sales, period. In general, companies don't have their own public relations group, or publicists. They contract that out when they have a product release.

The place to start is with the company web site and corporate phone number. Call them up and ask for the press relations department, and you will usually get a phone number or a voice mailbox. Leave your number and email (be pleasant, of course), and you are on your way. Have your elevator pitch ready for when the publicist calls back. You should also have a good answer to what your deadline is for the interview, and what times you have available. For the music business, you will want to start with the record label. Make a journal entry for when you called to remind yourself that you should call again if you haven't heard from them in a couple of days.

Timing is everything in terms of getting interviews. Understand that when a company isn't releasing software, or an artist isn't releasing a record, they are going to be in production on something new, or on vacation. It's when they release that they are most inclined to give interviews. If they aren't releasing at the moment, ask the publicist "what's in the pipe" and you will generally get a schedule of what is releasing (and when), and you should be able to get advance booking for the publicity train when the release does happen.

You should also have a clear idea of who you want to talk to. For example, if you want to interview someone at a software company, you will likely get the president, CEO, or a product manager for the software. You will likely not get access to the engineers that made the cool feature, unless you can convince the publicist that it will be a great interview that will sell the software. If you are trying to interview a band, you might want to start with the bass player or drummer and not the lead singer, as the former might not be in as much demand.

You can get local interviews with touring bands by checking out their concert schedule and getting in touch with their promoter. Local press is always good for ticket sales, so be sure to mention that you will be able to hype the tour with the local markets.

When you show up in person for an interview you should be dressed well and have all the kinks out of your sound setup before you get there. If you have a friend who can work the controls, bring her along as well so that you can concentrate on the interview. To add credibility, be sure to bring cards stating your show name and contact details. You should also bring the name, contact details, and any passes given to you by the promoter. Having microphones with flags (the little square boxes up at the top of the microphone that indicate your affiliation) also lends an air of credibility. Blank microphone flags are available in the $10 range from Microphone Flags (*http://www.microphoneflags.com/*).

After the interview. After you have completed the interview, the company might want to preview the recording to make sure they have been portrayed in the best light. You should work out these stipulations in advance. In addition, if you are thinking about doing an interview that is intended to portray the person in a negative light, you will want to make sure you are properly covered legally beforehand.

The last job of the producer for a given story is to complete the circle with the publicist once the interview is online. The publicist will want a link to the story to add to the company or artist web site. That creates a virtuous cycle where you publicize them and they, in turn, publicize you. You should also let the publicist know what the listener response was like. This will make it easier to get a follow-up interview later.

The Writer

The writer's job is to create the show prep or show notes that the host will use during the taping or the interview. The notes can be a Word document, or an OmniOutliner document. OmniOutliner (*http://www.omnigroup.com/*) has the advantage that the notes can be exported as OPML [Hack #44] and attached to the podcast blog posting later.

Organize your notes in the same way as the show, starting at the beginning with the show introduction, moving through each segment, and then into the closing credits.

As a podcaster, you are your own writer and host, so write the show notes the way you like to talk. In the beginning, you should write out almost everything you say verbatim. As you get more comfortable with the role of host, you can reduce the segment sections to just some notes. But you should keep the introductions, credits, and any plugs you want to make written out and in spoken form. People expect these sections to sound canned and formal anyway, so the stilted nature of reading copy verbatim is expected.

My recommendation is that you start out by having one sentence per line, a break of one line between paragraphs, and that you use a large font that's easy to read. Serif fonts are probably easier to read than sans-serif, so use something such as Courier. You should use underlines to indicate words you want to emphasize.

In general, it's easier to read from a printed copy. You can use a computer to read the copy if you don't want to print it. Just make sure you can use the arrow keys on your keyboard to navigate around your document. Computers also generate noise [Hack #15] from their fans, so be sure to put them out of the line of any active microphone.

If you are doing radio theatre [Hack #32] or you have a two-person show [Hack #20], you will want the show notes to have each host's name next to their corresponding lines. That way each person can follow along with the show. If you want to be super-slick, you can use a highlighter to emphasize your own lines on your copy.

For sections in the show where you just want to banter about a subject for a little bit, you should have notes specifying where the segment is to go, and some notes about the topic. You also should provide a good lead-in line so that the host can segue into the free-form segment.

The Engineer

The engineer's role is to get the show on the air and to make sure it sounds good. The sound levels should be consistent, and neither too soft nor too loud. Any audio segments that are going to be used should be right at hand. This book has a lot of material on how to get quality sound [Hack #50]. But what it all boils down to is that when you are the host, you should not be thinking about engineering issues. The setup should be reasonably foolproof.

The Host

As the host of the show, you are its face. All the preparation that has come through the producer, the writer, and the engineer has its payoff in your performance. But relax, it's not that big a deal. No, I'm serious, relax. It's the number one thing to remember when you are hosting. Stress tends to speed up your speech and make it sound tight and thin.

In his book *No Static* (Backbeat Books, 1999), Quincy McCoy lists three fundamentals for hosts. He calls them the 3 C's: Concentration, Composure, and Confidence. Concentration is critical to hosting a great show. Give yourself ample time and an ample number of takes to take the pressure off so that you can remain focused on the task at hand. When you are working alone, concentrate on your style and tone. When you are working with someone else, either a co-host or an interviewee, remain in the moment and focused on the conversation at hand. Having a computer with your show notes is handy, but it can be a distraction, so don't surf or read email when you are recording.

Composure is important in live interview settings. People will always move off of your interview script and into directions that you don't expect. You can't control everything and you shouldn't expect to. Keep your cool and get them back on track gently. It's also fine to get flustered or to delay. Just make sure you leave enough space to edit out those segments.

Keeping it cool also means working with your attitude. In particular, when you are interviewing a famous person, you need to keep in mind that you are the envoy of the listener. You are not there to be entertained by the person you're interviewing. Even though you might be jumping for joy inside, you need to stay on an even keel on the outside. Keep your autograph request until after the segment.

Confidence comes from two essential ingredients: experience and preparation. Experience is very important, which is why you should get into podcasting now so that you get over the mistakes everyone makes. Each time you do a show, review it to see what you could have done better, and make the changes in your next show. That will help improve your confidence in your ability to make mistakes and still get a great show at the end. Preparation is key as well. Having in-depth research and quotes will help you avoid any unexpected gotchas in an interview. Even if you think you know everything about a topic, you should still have notes that give names, titles, places, and times. Those are the easiest things to forget during the stress of an interview.

As I mentioned before, you need to relax, both mentally and physically. When you are taping your own segments, be sure to give yourself as much time as you need. And use as many takes as you like. Digital media is cheap and reusable. So, use a lot of it.

The physical component. On the physical side, it's important to stay hydrated. It's not natural to talk continuously for such long stretches of time. You will need to stay hydrated so that your voice remains smooth. Drink plenty of fluids, but nothing icy cold, and nothing with caffeine. Coffee and caffeinated teas will speed up your speech and increase your stress level. Decaffeinated herbal tea, particularly lemon tea, is the weapon of choice for most hosts in the battle against dry mouth and dehydration.

The microphone. You should always wear headphones that receive the monitor signal from the microphone [Hack #13]. This way you can adjust the position of the microphone and the strength of your voice to get the best possible sound. In fact, anyone who is in control of a microphone should be wearing headphones. Otherwise, people will tend to shift around and talk away from the microphone, which creates volume problems that have to be fixed in editing later.

Proper microphone technique is covered in [Hack #19]. But you should know at least the following fundamentals. Your mouth should be about a hand's-width away from the microphone, further for some microphones, closer for others. To avoid pops created by air rushing from your mouth, you should position the mic slightly above and to the right or left of the plane of your mouth. If a pop stopper [Hack #12] is available, you should use it.

You need to think of the microphone as a musical instrument. To get the best results you need to experiment with your position and the volume of your voice. You should always have a microphone stand. Holding the microphone will lead to annoying handling noise.

The closer you move to the microphone, the more the bass in your voice will come through in the signal. This is called *proximity effect*, and it's present in almost all microphones to some degree. This is the reason why you will see singers almost eat the microphone. You should experiment with just how close to or far away from the microphone you need to be to get the sound you want.

For a conversational show, you will want some proximity effect, but you will not want to have a tremendous amount of bass since this will ruin the illusion that you are standing right next to the person, having a conversation with him. Too much bass sounds unnatural and over-processed (or *wet*). A signal that is processed to the maximum degree is considered very wet, and a signal with no processing is *dry*.

Vocal styles. Using different styles as you talk in your podcast is like using different fonts in a document. For introductions and credits, you will want to use a more formal voice, with stronger and clearer enunciation. For conversational content, you should use a lighter tone, but you should still try to enunciate and talk a little more slowly than you normally do.

If part of your style is to shout or vary between loud and soft segments, be sure to include a compressor as part of your signal path. This compressor will ensure that you will not clip the signal when you yell or scream, and that your soft segments will be audible.

An alternative to compressors, which can make the sound unnatural if they are overused, is to *ride the gain*. Riding the gain [Hack #56] literally means having the engineer tweak the volume of the signal on the mixer as you talk, increasing the gain if you are soft and letting it off if you are getting boomy. Riding the gain is almost always done in music production, and is almost never done for radio work. On a one-person show, I strongly recommend using a compressor so that you can worry less about how loud or soft you are sounding and concentrate on making great content.

Practice. What all this boils down to is experience and practice. You need to learn how to write for voice so that you can read it into a microphone, and how to read so that you sound good. I recommend for your first few podcasts that you write the content in detail and then read it exactly, going through the entire thing several times. Do this each time with more improvisation both in content and style.

The next time you write for voice you will have a better idea of what makes for an easy, effective read. Over time, you will maintain the level of detail on the introduction and credit sections, but loosen up the script for the segments.

The Editor

Podcasts aren't live, so you will always have the opportunity to edit the show before you upload it to your server. Whether you choose to use that opportunity, and to what degree, is up to you and is largely a question of the type of show you are producing.

We will cover editing techniques in more detail in other hacks. But you should remember a few fundamentals. Leaving space around ums, ahs, and parts that you want to cut away is critical to being able to make clean cuts later, as is remaining fairly steady in your tone of voice. You must also remember to have at least 30 seconds of clear sound that you will use during editing at the beginning of the recording. You should remove leading and trailing blank segments [Hack #36] before encoding to MP3 [Hack #18] and uploading to the server.

Books

Several million words can and have been written on radio production. And in those words are valuable lessons for podcasters. One book in particular stands out: *Radio Production* (Focal Press, 1999), by Robert McLeish. This book is well worth your time and money if you are serious about broadcasting.

See Also

- "Train Your Voice" [Hack #19]
- "Adopt a Format for Your Podcast" [Hack #20]

Quality Sound

Hacks 12–19

There's no excuse for making poor recordings.
—Dave Isay

It is said that an engaging story can be played through a tin can and people will still listen. In reality, noise and a harsh sound will drive your listeners away before you even get to the good stuff.

This chapter will give you a solid start with the tools to make your podcast sound great, without having to spend a fortune.

HACK #12 Set Up a Basic Home Studio

Getting quality sound on the cheap is easy with today's digital tools, if you know what to look for.

For your first few podcasts, you should keep your setup simple. The internal microphone on your computer, or a very low-cost computer microphone plugged into the microphone port, is a good place to start.

You can use any reasonable set of headphones to monitor your sound. Monitoring your sound means sending the incoming microphone audio to your headphones as well as recording it to the output file. Monitoring yourself is critical because it gives you instant feedback. Is your voice too loud or too soft? Are you creating pops when you pronounce the *p*, *t*, or *b* consonants? Do you sound raspy or slushy? Monitors allow you to gauge this instantly and to make the appropriate changes. Without them, you will get to the end of the recording thinking you did great, only to find that you were a foot further away from the microphone than you should have been. The first rule of podcasting: any person controlling a microphone should be wearing monitor headphones.

Most any headphone will do, but you should disable any noise-canceling feature when you are recording. Otherwise, you will not get an accurate representation of your sound. Higher-quality headphones, such as the Sennheiser HD 570, are "open-air" headphones. These have great fidelity in playback and are a joy to wear. But these headphones make lousy monitors because they let in a substantial amount of room noise, including your voice, which can make you sound louder than the sound being recorded by the microphone.

When you have decided that podcasting is something you want to invest more time in, you will want to upgrade your recording setup. Your laptop's internal microphone or line-in port is great in a pinch, but neither was made with studio recording in mind. Additionally, their location inside the computer can introduce extra noise. Reasonable microphones [Hack #13] and recording equipment are moderately priced today and they can greatly expand the quality of the signal, and thus, your editing possibilities.

You can get sound into your computer in a variety of ways. The sections that follow will cover these options, and provide some hardware advice.

Headsets

Another simple option is a Universal Serial Bus (USB) headset, such as the DSP-400 from Plantronics (*http://www.plantronics.com/*; ~$85). With this headset, your voice is converted from an analog signal at the built-in microphone, to digital in the box attached to the headset. Then this signal is sent through USB to a driver in your computer. From there you can record the signal with any recording application.

Headsets such as the DSP-400 have unidirectional microphones that are targeted at your mouth, and thus will block out most outside noise. They also utilize noise reduction to take out background hiss and hum.

A headset is ideal for podcasting on the road. It can also come in handy when you are talking to your friends over Skype, or when you are boasting about your fragging skills in Halo.

Another headset alternative is the Bluetooth hands-free set you use for your cell phone. A fine example of this is the Jabra BT250 from Jabra (*http://www.jabra.com/*; ~$100). It works with your phone, but it can also work with your Macintosh. Just as with the USB headset, you can use it to record your podcast, as well as to talk over Skype [Hack #35] and to play video games.

USB Microphones

USB microphones for voice control have been around for a while. Now we are starting to see USB studio microphones such as the Samson C01U-USB (*http://www.samsontech.com/*), a large diaphragm condenser microphone that gets its power from USB and digitizes the signal in the microphone. The Samson lists for $234.99, but I was able to find it on the Web for well under $100.

PCI Cards

Desktop Windows, Macintosh, and Linux machines can host one or more PCI cards. A range of PCI sound cards work for both playing and recording sound. For reasonable sound, you will want a sound card that supports 24-bit recording at either 48 kHz or 96 kHz.

Table 3-1 shows a survey of recent sound cards.

Table 3-1. Various sound cards and their capabilities

Manufacturer	Model	Output	Bits	Rate	Price	Features
AudioTrak	Maya 7.1	7.1	18	48	$69.99	Mic, line-in
AudioTrak	Prodigy 192	7.1	24	96	$129.99	2 line-in
AudioTrak	Maya44 Mk II		24	96	$139.99	4 line-in, head-phone, MIDI, digital in/out
AudioTrak	Maya1010	7.1	24	96	$419	2 XLR, 8 line-in, headphone, MIDI
Creative Labs	Sound Blaster Live! 24-bit	5.1	16	96	$29.99	Mic, line-in, digital in/out
Creative Labs	Audigy 2 Value	5.1	24	96	$69.99	Mic, line-in, head-phone, digital out
Creative Labs	Audigy 2 ZS	5.1	24	96	$99.99	FireWire, mic, line-in, head-phone, MIDI, digital out
Creative Labs	Audigy 2 ZS Platinum	6.1	24	96	$199.99	FireWire, mic, RCA, line-in, headphone, MIDI, digital in/out
Creative Labs	Audigy 2 ZS Platinum Pro	7.1	24	96	$249.99	FireWire, mic, RCA, 2 line-in, headphone, MIDI, digital in/out

Table 3-1. Various sound cards and their capabilities (continued)

Manufacturer	Model	Output	Bits	Rate	Price	Features
Creative Labs	Audigy 4 Pro	7.1	24	96	$299.99	FireWire, RCA, 2 line-in, head-phone, MIDI, digi-tal in/out
Echo	Gina3G	—	24	96	$449	2 XLR, 6 line-in, headphone, MIDI, digital in/out
Echo	Layla3G	—	24	96	$499	2 XLR, 8 line-in, headphone, MIDI, digital in/out
E-MU	Emulator X 0404	—	24	96	$99.99	2 line-in, MIDI
E-MU	Emulator X 1212m	—	24	96	$199.99	FireWire, 2 line-in, MIDI, digital in/out
E-MU	Proteus X	Stereo	24	96	$199.99	2 line-in, head-phone, MIDI, digi-tal in/out
E-MU	Emulator X 1820	Stereo	24	96	$399.99	2 XLR, FireWire, 8 line-in, head-phone, MIDI, digi-tal in/out
E-MU	Emulator X 1820m	7.1	24	96	$499.99	2 XLR, FireWire, 8 line-in, head-phone, MIDI, digi-tal in/out
MOTU	2408mk3	—	24	96	$949	8 line-in, digital in/out
MOTU	24I/O Core Recording System	—	24	96	$1,420	24 line-in
MOTU	HD192	—	24	192	$1,799	12 line-in
M-Audio	Revolution 7.1 Surround Sound PCI	7.1	24	96	$119.95	Mic, line-in, headphone
M-Audio	Delta Audio-phile 2496	Stereo	24	96	$129.95	2 RCA, MIDI, digi-tal in/out
M-Audio	Delta 66	Stereo	24	96	$199.95	6 RCA, MIDI, digi-tal in/out
M-Audio	Delta 44	Stereo	24	96	$199.95	4 RCA, MIDI, digi-tal in/out
M-Audio	Delta 1010LT	AC-3	24	96	$299.95	2 XLR, 8 RCA, 2 line-in, MIDI, digi-tal in/out

Table 3-1. *Various sound cards and their capabilities (continued)*

Manufacturer	Model	Output	Bits	Rate	Price	Features
M-Audio	Delta 1010	Stereo	24	96	$599.95	10 RCA, 2 line-in, MIDI, digital in/out
Turtle Beach	Riviera	5.1	16	48	$29.95	Mic, line-in, head-phone, digital out
Turtle Beach	Catalina	7.1	24	96	$49.95	Mic, line-in, head-phone, digital in/out

Here is the key for the columns in Table 3-1:

Manufacturer and model

The name of the manufacturer and the model number of the card.

Output

This is the top end of the output from the card. Many of these cards are designed primarily to be the center of a home theatre system. Thus, they have 5.1 or 7.1 surround sound output. For podcast recording, all you really need is stereo. If you are going to use this as the basis of your home studio and you plan to do surround sound work, you will want to look into one of these surround sound cards.

Bits

The maximum bit-width for analog input recording. Many of these devices support one bit-width for recording the digital input and another for recording the analog input. I chose to put the analog input here because that is what you will be connecting your microphone to.

Rate

The maximum sampling frequency (in kilohertz) of the card. Again, many of these cards support higher rates (e.g., 192) for their digital inputs.

Price

The list price of the card in U.S. dollars. It's not unusual to get deep discounts off these numbers by checking a few Internet sources.

Features

Indicates which features the card supports:

XLR

Indicates one or more XLR inputs. XLR inputs are fairly uncommon on PCI sound cards. They mainly go with 1/8-inch or 1/4-inch inputs, or RCA inputs.

FireWire

Indicates card can also be used as a FireWire adapter.

Mic, RCA, and Line
> Indicates that the card supports one or more mic-in, line-in, or RCA pairs.

Headphone
> Indicates one or more headphone output jacks. Some of these cards use the front-left and front-right surround outputs to double for the headphone jacks.

MIDI
> Indicates that the card supports the Musical Instruments Digital Interface (MIDI) standard. This will allow you to use external MIDI devices such as keyboard and control surfaces as both inputs and outputs from your computer.

Digital In/Out
> Indicates whether the board supports digital input or output through an S/PDIF connector that is either RCA or optical. This is important if you want to use the card as the basis of a home studio with surround sound, or as part of a home theatre system. It's not so important for basic podcasting.

Each vendor listed in Table 3-1 provides a range of cards that go from just a few high-quality stereo inputs and outputs, to cards that can drive a home studio system. When a card has lots of ports, it won't be able to fit them all onto the backplane of the computer. One solution is to provide an additional unit that fits into a drive bay on the front of the computer. Another is to have an external breakout box that sits on your desk and has connectors and, in some cases, gain controls.

Better-quality microphones use the XLR cabling standard. That's a three-pronged connector that won't go directly into the mic-in or line-in of the card. In addition, with condenser microphones you will need to power the microphone with phantom power. You have several options:

Get a card with XLR inputs
> A few of these cards support XLR inputs directly. If you are working with a condenser microphone, make sure the card also provides 48-volt *phantom power*. This feature is often called a *microphone preamp*.

Use a microphone preamp or mixer
> Later in this hack, I'll cover some microphone preamps that provide gain control and phantom power, as well as convert your microphone's XLR output to ¼-inch unbalanced output that you can then run to your computer. A portable mixer unit can also provide phantom power and gain for your condenser microphone.

Use a microphone cable

For dynamic microphones, you can use a special cable that goes from XLR to ¼-inch unbalanced jacks, called a *microphone cable*. Depending on the card's input, you will also need to buy a small, ¼-inch to ⅛-inch mono or stereo adapter. These cost only a few dollars and are available from RadioShack.

As Table 3-1 shows, you have a wide range of options when it comes to PCI sound cards for your computer. It's good to understand the potential range of options. But all you really need for podcasting is a card that supports a high-quality, low-noise microphone or line input with 24 bits at 48 or 96 kHz. Cards that support that cost less than $100.

PC Card Adapters

Laptops don't have PCI card slots but they do have PC Card slots. A few vendors make high-end sound cards for the PC Card, as shown in Table 3-2. These range from basic surround sound and recording models to cards that can drive a whole studio.

Table 3-2. PC Card sound cards

Manufacturer	Model	Output	Bits	Rate	Price	Features
Creative Labs	Audigy 2 ZS Notebook	7.1	24	96	$129.99	Mic, line-in, head-phone, digital in
Digigram	VXpocket v2	Stereo	24	48	$729	XLR, mic, line-in, headphone
Digigram	VXpocket 440	Stereo	24	48	$849	XLR, mic, line-in, headphone, digital out
Echo	Indigo io 2-Channel	—	24	96	$229	2 line-in
RMS	Hammerfall HDSP	Stereo	24	96	$379	Headphone, MIDI, digital in/out

The Audigy 2 ZS from Creative Labs is sufficient for podcasting, but you will need either a microphone cable to convert your dynamic microphone to mic-in, or a microphone preamp or mixer to get the signal from a condenser microphone. The other adapters in the table illustrate what's available if you want to use your laptop as the basis of your home studio system.

USB Devices

Most laptops and desktop machines, and all Macintoshes, support the USB standard. This peripheral cabling standard has easy-to-use connectors and provides bus power so that devices can operate without external power adapters.

A number of USB sound recording devices are available, as shown in Table 3-3.

Table 3-3. USB sound adapters

Manufacturer	Model	Bits	Rate	Price	Features
Edirol	UA-20	24	44.1	$180	2 line-in, headphone, MIDI
Edirol	3-FX	24	48	$215	Mic, RCA, line-in, headphone, digital in/out
Edirol	UA-25	24	96	$299	2 XLR, 2 line-in, headphone, digital in/out
Edirol	UA-5	24	96	$355	2 XLR, RCA, 2 line-in, digital in/out
M-Audio	Transit	24	96	$99.99	Mic, line-in, headphone
M-Audio	MobilePre USB	16	48	$129.95	2 XLR, 2 mic, headphone
M-Audio	FastTrack USB	24	48	$129.95	XLR, RCA, line-in, headphone
M-Audio	Audiophile USB	24	96	$249.95	RCA, 2 line-in, headphone, digital in/out
Digidesign	Mbox	24	96	$595	2 XLR, 2 line-in, headphone, digital in/out
Tascam	US-122	24	48	$269	2 XLR, 2 line-in, headphone, MIDI

Each vendor in Table 3-3 provides a range of options that have a range of connectors for various input and output types. XLR inputs are the most important to podcasters because microphones have XLR outputs. And condenser microphones require phantom power, which these units can supply.

These units are fairly small—around the size of this book, but a little thicker. They take their power from the USB, so you have no messy secondary power cable or connectors to deal with, besides the USB cable that goes to the computer.

I looked at the following three devices for this book:

M-Audio MobilePre USB

This device, shown in Figure 3-1, has two XLR and instrument inputs assigned to the left and right channels, respectively. Optionally, the XLR input ports can supply phantom power. A monitoring headphones port as well as a stereo input for cheaper microphones also is available. In my tests, I often needed to crank the gain to get decent volume out of condenser microphones. The driver performed flawlessly, even when several applications were running on the host computer.

Figure 3-1. The M-Audio MobilePre USB

Edirol UA-25

The UA-25, shown in Figure 3-2, sports two hybrid XLR/instrument input ports, both of which can supply phantom power. Direct monitoring is supported through a ¼-inch stereo headphone jack that has its own independent gain. A built-in limiter suppresses signal peaks. The box also has MIDI and fiber in and out. The unit is capable of recording up to 96 kHz, the emerging recording standard.

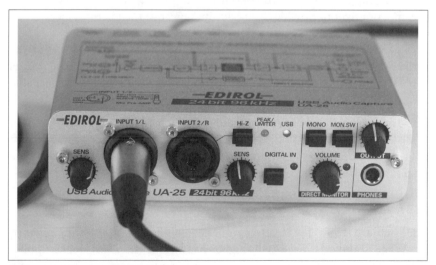

Figure 3-2. Edirol's UA-25 USB preamp

In my tests I found this to be a very hot box, requiring very little gain from the condenser microphones and injecting very little of its own noise. I did experience some hiccups with the driver on the Macintosh end. I recommend shutting down processor-intensive applications when recording.

Digidesign Mbox

On the face of it, ~$600 is a lot to pay for a two-XLR-channel USB recording box (shown in Figure 3-3). But in addition to a high-quality recording unit, you also get Digidesign's ProTools LE recording and editing software. This is professional-grade software that normally costs hundreds of dollars. When you account for that fact, the price looks really good.

The Mbox I tested had no issues with recording up to its maximum rate without injecting any artifacts. The driver that Digidesign installed had problems interacting with the launch of command-line applications on a Macintosh. To fix this, I simply moved */Library/Audio/Plugin-Ins/HAL/ Digidesign CoreAudio.plugin* to another location until I needed to use the Mbox again.

More details on ProTools are provided in [Hack #50].

One thing to watch out for is the level of phantom power that these USB boxes can provide to the microphone. USB provides enough power for peripherals such as mice, keyboards, and scanners. But these recording devices have a lot to do before powering the microphone. So, you might find you need an external XLR phantom power block, dedicated microphone preamp, or mixer to provide real phantom power to the microphone.

iMic. If your computer lacks a microphone or line-in port, as some of the earlier Macintosh portables do, your first option will be an iMic. The iMic is a USB adapter that has line-in, mic-in, and headphone ports. It's available from Griffin Technology (*http://www.griffintechnology.com/*) for $34.95.

You can get a microphone cable and a ¼-inch to ⅛-inch stereo adapter from RadioShack and plug your XLR dynamic microphones directly into your iMic. Condenser microphones will need built-in power, or an inline phantom power source.

FireWire

The step up from the USB peripheral standard is the IEEE-1394, or FireWire, standard. This is a higher-bandwidth standard that supplies slightly more external power than USB. Most Macintosh laptops and

Figure 3-3. Digidesign's Mbox with a Shure KSM27 (microphone not included)

desktops have FireWire installed. Cheap cards are available for Windows machines.

Just like USB boxes, these are external devices that record audio that sits on the FireWire device chain. These units generally provide more channels of audio than their USB cousins do.

Table 3-4 shows some FireWire audio boxes.

Table 3-4. FireWire audio adapters

Manufacturer	Model	Bits	Rate	Price	Features
Echo	AudioFire8	24	96	$749	2 XLR, 8 line-in, headphone, MIDI, digital in/out
Echo	AudioFire12	24	96	$999	12 line-in, MIDI
Edirol	FA-66	24	96	$495	2 XLR, 4 line-in, headphone, MIDI, digital in/out
Edirol	FA-101	24	96	$695	2 XLR, 8 line-in, headphone, MIDI, digital in/out
M-Audio	FireWire Solo	24	96	$249.95	XLR, 2 line-in, headphone
M-Audio	FireWire 410	24	96	$499.95	2 XLR, 10 line-in, headphone, MIDI, digital in/out
MOTU	Traveler	24	192	$895	4 XLR, 4 mic, 20 line-in, headphone, MIDI, digital in/out
PreSonus	Firebox	24	96	$499.95	2 XLR, 2 line-in, headphone, MIDI
PreSonus	Firepod	24	96	$799.95	8 XLR, 10 line-in, headphone, MIDI, digital in/out
Tascam	FW-1804	24	96	$749	4 XLR, 18 line-in, headphone, MIDI, digital in/out

These units are overkill for a podcast show, which needs just one or two microphones. Features such as digital I/O, MIDI, all the lines-in, and most of the XLRs will go unused. But if you are using podcasting as the starting point of your adventure in home studio work, these are ideal. They provide enough ports for a small band.

Mini-Disc or Flash Recorders

Another popular approach is to avoid recording to a computer altogether and record to a mini-disc or flash memory recorder instead. Both of these approaches provide the advantage of far less noise in the environment than if a computer were turned on. In particular, flash recorders such as the Marantz 660 have no moving parts and are thus completely silent. Recorded files are stored on the removable cards that you can read on your computer with a card reader.

Mini-disc recorders are becoming less popular because of two main factors. First, the recording time is limited. Second, the recorded files are on a mini-disc that is not easily accessible from a PC or Mac. So, the recorded sound needs to be played back into the computer and recorded in real time. This is a time-consuming pain.

Portable recorders are very handy for recording on the go [Hack #69].

Sample Setups

You have lots of options if you want to go from your microphone to your audio recording application. Here are some setups people have used successfully in podcasts:

Dynamic microphone to mic-in
> Perhaps the simplest setup is to use a dynamic microphone [Hack #13], a microphone cable, and a ¼-inch to ⅛-inch adapter to go from your microphone to the mic-in on your laptop or current sound card.

Condenser microphone to microphone preamp to line-in
> Use the microphone preamp to power a condenser microphone. Then take the output of the preamp's ¼-inch jack and use a cable and a ¼-inch to ⅛-inch converter to plug it into the line-in port.

Any microphone to USB preamp
> Attach either a dynamic or a condenser microphone to the XLR input of a USB preamp. Then attach the preamp to the computer with a USB cable. Driver software that comes with the device will allow you to record the sound from the microphone.

Any microphone to a FireWire preamp
> This is just like the USB preamp, except you use a FireWire device with a FireWire cable to the host.

Any microphone to a mixer to the line-in
> Use a mixer to take one or more microphones and mix them into a single-line output-level signal that goes to the computer's sound card. The mixer [Hack #14] provides phantom power for condenser microphones. Use the mixer's equalizer and gains to balance out the signal.

Any microphone to a solid-state recording device
> Solid-state recorders [Hack #69], such as the Marantz 660 and 670, have XLR inputs for microphones and can provide phantom power. Connect the microphone to the unit, and then record. When you are finished recording, use the USB connector to download the sound to your computer. Or eject the CF (compact flash) cartridge and put it in a CF reader connected to your computer to extract the MP3 or WAV files.

Any microphone, through a preamp to an MP3 recorder
> Small MP3 recorders [Hack #69], such as the iRiver, can record the line-in levels that come from a microphone preamp. Connect the microphone to the preamp using an XLR cable. Then use the ¼-inch jack on the output of the preamp to connect to the iRiver through a ⅛-inch to ¼-inch adapter.

These are just a few recipes to get you started with finding the right mix of audio hardware. One thing to keep in mind is that a longer signal path with more devices will invariably add unwanted noise [Hack #15]. It also adds complexity, which can lead to mistakes and hours spent tweaking device settings and rerecording lost sounds. Keep your signal path as simple and clean as possible.

Stopping Pops and Plosives

Plosives are the noises generated when the rush of air that comes when sounds such as the *p* and *b* sounds hit the microphone face on. You can prevent these popping sounds in several ways.

The most common way is to use a pop stopper, as shown in Figure 3-4. A pop stopper is a fabric mesh strung across a hoop that is then positioned in front of the microphone on a flexible arm. The mesh sits between you and your microphone and spreads out the rush of air. This will allow you to talk directly into the microphone's diaphragm without causing popping sounds. It will also reduce the amount of moisture that hits the diaphragm. This moisture can cause a condenser microphone to fail.

Figure 3-4. A Shure KSM27 with a stand and a pop stopper

Pop stoppers are relatively cheap. The one shown in Figure 3-4 costs around $25 and is available at music equipment chain stores. Instructions are available on the Web for making your own for a little less money. These involve nylon hose and an embroidery hoop.

Two additional techniques that can help you avoid popping sounds don't require the use of a pop stopper. The first technique is to train your voice to suck in hard consonants such as *p* and *b* instead of expelling them. It's an unnatural way to talk. To get there you will need to train with a vocal coach.

The second approach is far easier. You just change your position relative to the microphone. If you aren't talking directly into the microphone, the gusts of air you expel will rush harmlessly past the microphone. This is called being *off axis*. Well-trained singers [Hack #19] hold the microphone off to the side, at about 45 degrees from left to right. The microphone still picks up the sound, but it avoids plosive pops.

In addition to your position to the left or right of the microphone, you should also pay attention to your position above or below the microphone. Positioning the mic below mouth level can accentuate mouth and breath sounds. Positioning the mic at the same level as your mouth can create problems with plosives because of the rush of air going directly into the diaphragm. The ideal location is above your mouth. This will reduce mouth sounds while avoiding problems with plosives.

If you work without a pop stopper, I suggest that you position the microphone 45 degrees to the left or right and slightly above your mouth.

Pick the Right Microphone

HACK #13

Learn everything you need to know to pick the right microphone, or set of microphones, for your podcast.

No matter what kind of content your podcast will carry, odds are you'll need a microphone somewhere in the process. Many different microphone types are available, and some are specially tailored for a particular use. Matching the mic to your needs will give you better sonic results, and might even save you some money!

If all you want is to get your voice on a podcast, you can use the built-in mic on your computer or webcam, or get an inexpensive USB headset mic [Hack #12] or a basic computer mic with a mini-plug that can jack straight into your computer if it has a mic input. But if you want to get a richer, more professional, more radio-like sound, or if you are recording material out in the field, you'll want a better mic.

Dynamic or Condenser

Microphones come in two types: *dynamic* and *condenser*. In general, dynamic mics are more forgiving of rough treatment and do not require external phantom power. Condenser mics break more easily if dropped and require phantom power to operate, which must come from a recorder, a mixer, a preamp, an internal battery, or a separate power source. Condenser mics almost always provide louder output, reducing the amount of gain needed at the often-noisy preamplification stage. And condensers often give a brighter, more detailed sound.

Neither type is inherently better than the other is. Very commonly used in radio studios as announcer mics, dynamic mics such as the Electro-Voice RE20, Shure SM7B, and Sennheiser 421 produce very high-quality results. And the Shure SM57 and SM58 are reliable, inexpensive standards. In the field, the overall durability and lack of phantom-power issues make dynamic mics very attractive.

Large diaphragm condenser mics, such as the Neumann U 87 or AKG C 414, are standards for voice recording in studios. In recent years, inexpensive versions of this kind of mic have become easy to afford. These large, sensitive mics work best in a quiet, controlled space.

People often are confused between phantom power and preamplification. Although many microphone preamps provide phantom power, preamplification and phantom power are separate things. All microphones require a preamp stage to raise levels up to line level, but condenser mics, and some other types, also require a low-level current to charge the mic diaphragm, setting up the electrical differential between the mic's diaphragm and backplate. Most studio mics want to see 48-volt phantom power.

Some condenser mics, especially those designed to be used in the field [Hack #69], can accept a battery to provide the phantom power. This eliminates the need for an external box if your recorder or mixer will not provide power, but also adds another battery that can drain at the least opportune moment.

If you plan to plug directly into your computer or a small consumer recorder, it's easiest to use a dynamic mic, or a condenser mic that can get phantom power from a battery. If you are plugging into a mixer, a professional recorder, or some other device that provides phantom power, you can use either type of mic.

Pick-up Patterns

Mics can have various *pick-up patterns*, meaning the shape of the area around the mic where it is most sensitive. Some mics can be switched to change patterns, or you can screw *capsules* on and off to change the pattern, giving greater flexibility. Of course, these mics are usually more expensive than fixed-pattern mics, so if you're on a tight budget, you might want to choose a fixed-pattern mic that best suits your needs.

The most common directional pattern for announcer mics is called *cardioid* (see Figure 3-5), for its heart-shaped area of maximum sensitivity (mostly out in front of the mic but with a small lobe on either side of the capsule). Sounds to the sides and especially to the rear of the mic are largely rejected or at least reduced; sounds directly in front of the mic are picked up best.

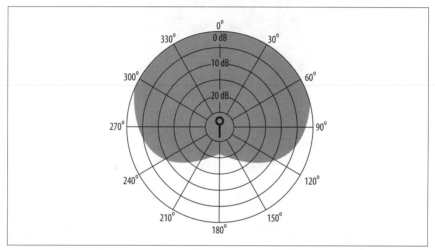

Figure 3-5. The cardioid microphone pattern

Hypercardioids have an even smaller, more focused pattern. The most directional mic is the *shotgun* mic, which is designed to highlight a narrow space, often from greater distances.

It's important to note that even the most directional mics do not completely reject sound outside of the pick-up pattern. Off-axis sounds are reduced in volume, but they also often acquire a phasey or muffled character, sometimes making extraneous sounds seem rather odd. Sometimes, what's most effective for one purpose, such as reducing feedback on a noisy rock concert stage, is not as pleasing for another, such as an intimate commentary in a quiet room.

The next most common pick-up pattern is called *omnidirectional* (see Figure 3-6), for its ability to pick up sounds in all directions equally. Because of the mic's design, it has less focus on a particular direction, but also, off-axis sounds are picked up more accurately and naturally, lending a more realistic ambience. Some people mistakenly believe that omni mics will pick up close and distant sounds equally, making the background too loud compared to the primary source. But these mics must still obey the laws of physics, and focus on the subject can be achieved simply by getting the mic in close. In most cases, to get good sound on tape, you must get the microphone close to the source because its sound pressure levels are dropping rapidly as you increase your distance.

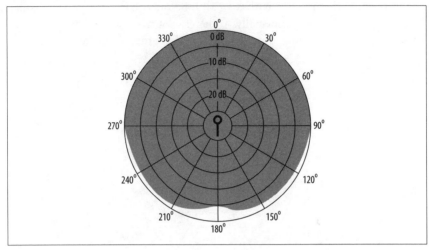

Figure 3-6. The omnidirectional microphone pattern

Omnidirectional mics have the added benefit of being less susceptible to handling noise and more tolerant of wind and plosives (popped *p* sounds and the like), and they create less "boominess" when close to the source. No mic is completely free from these problems, but omnis show less of this behavior than directional mics.

The more directional the mic, the more susceptible it is to handling noise, wind, and plosives, and the more of a boomy proximity effect the mic gets. But the more directional the mic, the less background noise it gets, which can make for a much more pleasing, immediate sound.

Microphone diaphragms. Among the varieties of microphones mentioned earlier is yet another distinction based on the size of the diaphragm. Dynamic or condenser, regardless of pattern, can each employ a large or small diaphragm.

Large-diaphragm mics are best suited for studio work in controlled environments, where they can be placed on a stand, preferably with a shock mount and a pop filter. The larger, more flexible diaphragm gives a richer, more detailed sound with a higher sensitivity, and so is generally preferable for primary announcing duties. But these large-diaphragm mics are very suscep-tible to extraneous noise and vibrations, and despite frequent claims by manufacturers of having integral pop filters, they always need additional foam or mesh pop-reduction devices. Many of these mics are meant to be addressed from the side, rather than the end of the mic, and cardioid mics will sound good from only one side. So, try a few positions for you and the mic until you find the perfect angle and distance.

Small-diaphragm mics can usually handle louder sources, and counterintu-itively, they actually can have a larger frequency range, due primarily to the smaller diaphragm having less mass. Some small-diaphragm mics can work very well as voice mics, but often they sound best when they're not directly in front of the subject, and instead are placed above or to the side so that the person is speaking past the mic, not directly into it. Handheld mics designed for singers can be good for recording the speaking voice as well, although the frequencies are sometimes "hyped" in the bass and treble to sound more vivid, which can be good or bad. Just don't use them like rock singers do, with the mic pressed right against your mouth! Back up about 6 inches and get off to the side, and those singers' mics, such as the Shure SM58, can sound great.

Choosing which pattern to use is largely a question of taste and production style. Some producers prefer the open sound of an omni, others the closer, tighter sound of a directional. Some even use short shotgun mics up close for interviews, giving a high degree of rejection of extraneous noise.

Lavaliers

Avoid the temptation to use lavalier microphones unless absolutely neces-sary. Clipped to a lapel or hanging around the neck, the lav mic is in a less-than-ideal position for good voice pick-up. Additionally, if the subject is moving around, clothes and cables will likely add unacceptable noise. Lava-lier mics are crucial in some circumstances, however: for instance, if the interview is being filmed, or if the subject is too self-conscious when having a mic pointed at him. But every time we do direct A-B tests, a lavalier sounds significantly worse than a well-placed handheld mic.

Choosing the Right Mic

No microphone is perfect for all users. When choosing a microphone, you have to decide what is right for you: omni or directional, dynamic or con-denser, handheld or lavalier, and mono or stereo.

You face a few additional challenges if you are using a small consumer recorder, or are recording directly into a computer's mic input, because the mic input is a high-impedance, 1/8-inch mini connector, and most pro micro-phones are low impedance with XLR connectors. You'll get better sound quality using a pro mic, even an inexpensive one, than you will by using a consumer mic with a mini connector on it, as long as you've got the right adapters. Get a high-quality converter cable, wired for this purpose, with a 1/8-inch mono connector on the recorder end if you are using a single mono microphone. You can find these on the Web from broadcast supply houses.

If you're using a relatively low-output mic, such as a dynamic omni mic, it can be worthwhile to get a cable that adapts from XLR to mini, adjusts the impedance, and shunts the plug-in power. The Shure A96F does all of these things. Louder mics are less likely to need this little boost.

For field recording, the most popular mics are omnis, such as the Electro-Voice RE-50 and the beyerdynamic M 58. A popular cardioid mic is the Shure SM58. Shotgun mics by Audio-Technica and Sennheiser are frequent choices. These mics are designed to be plugged into low-impedance XLR mic inputs, but they can work with a consumer recorder that has a mini input, and a good adapter cable.

Condenser mics require phantom power. That power can be provided by some recorders [Hack #69], a mixer [Hack #14], an external device, or sometimes an internal battery. Many of the small consumer mini-discs, video cameras, and some other recorders have something called *plug-in power*, which is similar to phantom power but cannot power professional mics, although it can provide power for electret mics designed to be used with these recorders.

In most cases, you will get better sound quality with a handheld micro-phone. Because you attach lavalier mics to lapels or wear them around your neck, they often pick up clothes rustle. In some circumstances, however, such as an intimate conversation during which an obvious mic would inter-fere with the feel of the interview, or a subject moving in such a way that keeping him "on-mic" would be impossible, a lav can save the day.

If you are going for the up-close, intimate feel that is so prized in audio pro-ductions, though, lavs can often disappoint, sounding distant or muddy.

If you are recording an intimate monologue or a typical radio-style announcement, your field-recording mics might leave you sounding a little weak or distant. That big, rich sound tends to come from a large-diaphragm mic, addressed from close by, in a quiet room. In a perfect world, you would use a big, expensive mic in a soundproof and acoustically treated booth, but that's not always practical. An inexpensive, large-diaphragm condenser mic, such as the Studio Projects B1 or the Audio-Technica 2020, can get you pretty close to that sound, if you can record in a room with some soft surfaces and not too much computer whirring or other extraneous sounds.

Mono or stereo? Stereo sound can add a lot to the vividness of your location recordings, but can be quite distracting during interviews. So, you might want a stereo mic for ambience and demos and a mono mic for interviews. The inexpensive stereo mics that are sold to go with consumer mini-disc recorders can get decent sound, and they can be more than sufficient to get some backgrounds for your piece, but they are not particularly durable, are often made of plastic, and have limited bandwidth, reducing high-frequency detail. The Sony ECM-MS957 and 907 are built to interface with mini-jack mic inputs with plug-in power, and they can sound good. If you want to step up a notch, some good choices are the relatively inexpensive Audio-Technica 822, the Rode NT4, and the Shure VP88.

Most conventional interview mics are mono, in that they produce only one channel of sound. Often you connect a cable from that mic to the recorder, which is wired to send that same signal to both the left and right channels of the tape or disc. This is often preferable to hearing the microphone in only one ear while monitoring the recording, but it doesn't make it stereo, since there's just an exact copy of the signal on both channels. It's easy enough to record just one channel and pan it to the center during your mix or to copy one signal to both left and right if that's easier. In fact, when transferring audio to the computer, it will save disk space to record only one channel onto your hard disk if the sound is not stereo.

Stereo is most commonly used to describe two tracks of audio, a left channel and a right channel, which are meant to represent a spatial orientation analogous to how our ears hear. You can make a stereo recording with two microphones, or with a stereo mic that has two mic elements in one housing. Depending on the recorder's input, the signals from the two mics or mic elements can be carried on two cables, or on a single cable.

Cabling can be very confusing, because the same types of wires and connectors can be used in very different ways. In the analog realm, you usually need one cable for each channel of audio, so connecting most gear will require a cable for the right channel and a cable for the left. RCA cables and ¼-inch *Tip Sleeve* cables that have a single ring on the jack carry only one channel of audio.

But for the sake of saving space, small, portable recorders, laptops, and a few other devices use stereo inputs or outputs on a single jack.

In that case, you can use one cable to transfer stereo audio, as long as it is a three-conductor cable with the correct *TRS* connectors on the ends. *TRS* stands for *Tip-Ring-Sleeve*, referring to the three conductors on the plugs. You'll see two black bands on the plugs—one near the tip, another ring about midway down—and the long sleeve of the shaft is a conductor as well. One-eighth-inch or "mini" TRS cables are commonly used for connecting the stereo headphone output of a small mini-disc recorder to the stereo mic input on a computer. Some stereo mics use a mini TRS (often just called a "stereo mini") plug to connect to the mic inputs of a mini-disc, a small portable DAT recorder, or a computer.

You might need adapter cables to interface a device that uses a stereo input or output with a mixer or audio interface. For instance, to connect a portable mini-disc to an audio interface such as the Digidesign Mbox, you need a cable with a mini TRS on one end and two 1/4-inch cables on the other. Plug the mini TRS into the headphone out of the mini-disc, and the 1/4-inch cables into separate left and right inputs of the interface.

Even professional mono mics can use an adapter cable that terminates in a mini TRS plug; in this case, because only one channel of audio is coming from the mic, the cable should be wired to send the audio to both the tip and the ring.

Field recording microphones. Table 3-5 lists a variety of field recording microphones. The microphones I've tested are shown in italics. Note that you can find all of these microphones on the Web for 30% to 70% off the prices listed in the table.

Table 3-5. Field recording microphones

Manuf.	Model	Type	Shape	Diaphragm	Price	Comments
Audio-Technica	ATR-30	Dynamic	Unidirectional	Small	$50	—
Sony	*ECM-MS907*	Condenser	Mid-side stereo	Small	$100	Good basic consumer stereo mic with a mini connector, designed to match with mini-disc recorders.

Table 3-5. Field recording microphones (continued)

Manuf.	Model	Type	Shape	Diaphragm	Price	Comments
Shure	SM57	Dynamic	Cardioid	Small	$148	The SM57 is very similar to the SM58, but without the pop protection from the ball-shaped windscreen. With careful placement a little off-axis, it sounds as good as an SM58.
Electro-Voice	635	Dynamic	Omni	Small	$178	An all-around workhorse reporter's mic.
Shure	SM58	Dynamic	Cardioid	Small	$188	The most popular, all-purpose vocal mic in the world. Very rugged; good sound.
Electro-Voice	RE-50	Dynamic	Omni	Small	$268	Has the same microphone element as the 635A, but with better pop filtering and isolation from handling noise.
Sony	ECM-MS957	Condenser	Mid-side stereo	Small	$300	A good-quality prosumer stereo mic with a mini connector, built to interface with small mini-disc recorders or DAT machines. Has a variable stereo "width" control. Is well suited to collecting ambience.

Table 3-5. Field recording microphones (continued)

Manuf.	Model	Type	Shape	Diaphragm	Price	Comments
Sennheiser	K6/ ME66	Condenser	Short shotgun	Small	$320	Modular; can fit a different capsule on a K6 power supply. Very tight pattern; good for recording from medium distance.
beyerdynamic	M-58	Dynamic	Omni	Small	$334	Has a better frequency response than preceding mics, as well as hotter output and a long handle.
AKG	C 1000 S	Condenser	Cardioid	Small	$338	Good frequency response. Uses standard 9-volt battery for phantom power.
Audio-Technica	897	Condenser	Short shotgun	Small	$370	—
Audio-Technica	822	Condenser	X/Y stereo	Small	$399	Nice-sounding prosumer stereo mic, with fixed-pattern X/Y stereo pick-up pattern. Cable terminates in a stereo mini connector or can split to two 1/8-inch outputs. Longer handle and metal construction make it a little hardier in the field than the smaller, plastic Sony mics.

Table 3-5. Field recording microphones (continued)

Manuf.	Model	Type	Shape	Diaphragm	Price	Comments
Rode	*NT4*	Con-denser	X/Y stereo	Small	$899	Affordable professional stereo mic with a fixed X/Y pattern. Comes with cables to connect to stereo mini mic inputs or to two XLRs. Excellent sound, but heavy and sensitive to wind and handling noise.
Neumann	*Series 180*	Con-denser	Variable	Small	$999	Very small.
Shure	*VP88*	Con-denser	X/Y stereo	Small	$1,266	Versatile professional stereo mic, with variable stereo width controls and available split mid-side output. Long, heavy handle.

Studio microphones. Table 3-6 shows a selection of studio microphones. The microphones I've tested are in italics. Note that you can find all of these microphones on the Web for 30% to 70% off the prices listed in the table.

Table 3-6. Studio microphones

Manuf.	Model	Type	Shape	Diaphragm	Price	Comments
Behringer	B-1	Condenser	Cardioid	Large	$120	—
Studio Projects	B1	Condenser	Cardioid	Large	$120	Good sound quality.
M-Audio	Nova	Condenser	Cardioid	Large	$130	—
Marshall	MXL 2006	Condenser	Cardioid	Large	$160	—
Audio-Technica	*AT2020*	Condenser	Cardioid	Large	$170	Good sound quality.
Rode	NT1	Condenser	Cardioid	Large	$349	Good sound quality.

Table 3-6. Studio microphones (continued)

Manuf.	Model	Type	Shape	Diaphragm	Price	Comments
Shure	KSM27	Condenser	Cardioid	Large	$575	Expensive, but great sound quality.
Sennheiser	421	Dynamic	Cardioid	Large	$650	Versatile mic that's effective on everything from voice to drums.
Electro-Voice	RE20	Dynamic	Cardioid	Large	$750	Perhaps the most common on-air announcer mic. Warm, flat sound. Good pop rejection.
AKG	C 414	Condenser	Variable	Large	$999	Classic, versatile, professional-level mic well suited for studio announcing.
Neumann	TLM 103	Condenser	Cardioid	Large	$1,300	More affordable announcer mic with Neumann sound.
Neumann	U87	Condenser	Variable	Large	$3,800	The big, warm announcer mic. Superb sound.

Purchasing Microphones

Any of the microphones in Tables 3-5 and 3-6 will serve a podcast very nicely. With this much variability in price, it's difficult to know how much to spend on a microphone. Compounding this problem is the fact that microphones are paired with preamps, and some combinations of the two will work better than others will. So, you might spend a lot of money on a mic and not couple it with the right preamp and get poor sound quality. Here are a few ideas:

- Talk with your friends in the real world and online about what combinations of microphone and amplifier are good for vocal work. Ideally, you should try out the equipment in person to see how it complements your voice and whether you can talk naturally and still get the sound quality you want. Audio conventions are another way to get access to different types of equipment.

- On the commercial side, check to see if your local music equipment store has microphones set up that you can try out. Another option is to rent an hour or two of studio time to record intros and outtros [Hack #63]. In addition to having clean intros and outtros for your podcast, you will also get experience with the different microphones and equipment in a studio [Hack #61]. At the time of this writing, studio time was widely available in major U.S. cities in the $40–$100 per hour range.

- Check the Web. You can read reviews of microphones on Sound on Sound (*http://www.soundonsound.com/*), though you have to subscribe to get to them. Harmony Central (*http://harmony-central.com/*) has user reviews of microphones. Electronic Musician (*http://emusician.com/*) has well-written and -researched reviews available for free.

See Also

- "Reduce Noise" [Hack #15]
- "Podcast in Surround Sound" [Hack #16]

—Jeff Towne

Mix Your Podcast in Hardware
#14
Mixers can look intimidating at first, but they are actually easy to use and very powerful.

Mixers are an inexpensive way to get your audio close to broadcast quality, with no digital editing. Figure 3-7 shows the Behringer UB1202 mixer.

Going from left to right on the setup you can see a number of horizontal strips. These are called *channels*. This mixer has an amazing 12 channels in it. The first four are mono channels capable of taking XLR [Hack #12] inputs. The XLR input of the first channel is highlighted in the upper lefthand corner.

Moving down the channel you can see a set of three knobs. This is a simple three-band equalizer [Hack #57] that can boost or reduce the low, middle, and

Figure 3-7. The Behringer UB1202 mixer

high frequencies on the channel. This is great for getting rid of high-pitched noises, adding some presence to a person's voice, or removing low hums.

Below the equalizer section, the next highlighted knob is the pan control. The pan positions the signal in the stereo space from left to right. By default, it's in the middle—dead center between the two channels. If you are recording two microphones and you want the output to be stereo mixed, you will want one to go slightly to the left and the other to go slightly to the right. This gives listeners a sense that they are at the table with the two people who are talking.

Right below the pan is the master gain for the channel. With this, you can boost or lower the amplitude of this channel relative to all the others. For a person with a soft voice you will want to boost it up, and for a louder person you should turn it down. The process of making small gain adjustments throughout the session is called riding the gain [Hack #56]. Another possibility is to use a compressor to manage the signal levels. More-expensive mixers have compression built right in as one of the effects.

All of the channels flow from top to bottom and from left to right. Inputs go in the top, flow through the channel to the channel gain at the bottom, and then go from left to right to the master gain on the far righthand side of the mixer.

The master gain is the slider with the rows of LEDs above it. The LEDs show your signal strength in real time. Moving the slider up will increase the gain of the entire mix. Moving the slider down will soften the entire mix. On a bigger unit, the channel gains are also manipulated with sliders.

The UB1202 also features several outputs. You can use two XLR output plugs at the back of the unit to connect to your USB preamp. You can also use the control room and tape outputs to go directly to the line-in of your computer or MP3 recording device.

If your microphones [Hack #13] are continuously soft, you will want to use the channel pregain knob, which is directly below the XLR channel input. This will boost the signal before it goes into the channel.

Some mixer models have built-in effects [Hack #58], though this one does not. These effects can provide reverb, chorus, flanging, compression, and a whole host of handy signal processing. For podcasting, you will likely want to use some compression to ensure that signals don't clip, and a slight reverb to add some vocal depth and sense of space.

If you plan to edit the recording digitally, you should keep the signal as clean as possible. I recommend using just the compression feature. The value of hardware compression is that you will keep the signal from clipping when it's converted from analog to digital either at the USB preamp or at the mic-in or line-in port. Software compression is good, but it can't fix a signal that's already been clipped by the analog-to-digital converter. It's best to have a hardware compressor to ensure that you never clip in the first place.

Even for a person who likes twiddling with knobs, a mixer can be intimidating. Here are three rules to live by:

- Don't tweak more than one thing at a time without checking what happened right after you tweaked it.
- If you find yourself in a completely messed-up state, just reset everything to its center or default position and try again.
- Tweak the knob to its full amount first. This will give you a sense of how far you can go and will allow you to dial it back in to find the right setting. If you are familiar with cameras this is similar to the technique of proper focusing; focus far out and then dial it back in to find the right detail point.

Here's one last tip from a father of a young child: keep your mixer away from the edge of the counter, and off the floor. Kids love to tweak those knobs and change subtle settings.

A mixer is an important component of your setup, as it drives your microphones and gives some initial processing to the signal to keep it loud, but not so loud that it clips. A mixer is essential if you plan to skip a USB preamp and go directly to the line-in or mic-in of your computer.

Mixers

When I think about a recording studio, I envision an engineer sitting in front of a gigantic mixer with hundreds of knobs and sliders. The mixers that are in studios can and do cost millions of dollars, but a mixer for home studio use can cost surprisingly little, in the $100 range, in fact.

Table 3-7 shows some of the portable mixers that are available on the market today.

Table 3-7. A selection of portable mixers

Manuf.	Model	Stereo in	XLR in	Effects	Phantom power	Computer interface	Price
Behringer	Eurorack UB802	4	2		X		$59.99
Behringer	Eurorack UB1202	6	4		X		$99.99
Soundcraft	COMPACT 4 Mixer	2	2		X		$109
Behringer	Eurorack MXB1002	1	5		X		$119
Nady	MXE-612	4	2		X		$119.95
Yamaha	MG10	2	4		X		$129
Alesis	MultiMix 6FX	2	2	X	X		$149
Nady	MXE-812	4	4		X		$149.95
Tapco	Blend 6	2	2		X		$149.99
Peavey	PV8	2	4		X		$155.99
Yamaha	MG8	3	4	X	X		$199
Alesis	MultiMix 8USB	2	4	X	X	USB	$199
Yamaha	MG12	4	4	X	X		$319
Alesis	MultiMix 12USB	4	4	X	X	USB	$399

Table 3-7. A selection of portable mixers (continued)

Manuf.	Model	Stereo in	XLR in	Effects	Phantom power	Computer interface	Price
Mackie	1202-VLZ Pro	2	4		X		$489
Mackie	1402-VLZ Pro	4	6		X		$659

The table is organized by price to illustrate how the number of channels and effects can vary as you go up the price scale.

Here is what the columns mean:

Manufacturer and model
> The name of the manufacturer and the model of the mixer.

Stereo in
> The number of stereo channels. Mixers have two different types of channels. The first is a mono channel that takes XLR inputs. The second is a stereo channel that takes 1/4-inch inputs for left and right, and can be used as either a stereo channel or two mono channels. For podcasting you will be using the mono XLR input channels for your microphone.

XLR in
> The number of mono channels with XLR inputs.

Effects
> There is an X here if the mixer has some built-in effects that you can apply to the signal. These effects usually include chorus, reverb, and flanging, among others. Many software packages can simulate the same effects on your computer, so this feature might not influence your purchase.

Phantom power
> All the mixers listed in Table 3-7 provide phantom power. I listed it in the table because it's so important to ensure that your mixer has this feature so that you can use condenser microphones. Small DJ mixers often don't include phantom power because they are meant to be used with cheap dynamic microphones. For high-quality podcasting, condenser microphones are necessary, so make sure your mixer provides the phantom power these microphones need.

Computer interface
> In a few cases, the mixer can record signals through a computer interface [Hack #12]. The standard of the interface is listed in this column. Though the ones in this list support the USB standard, some higher-end

mixers, such as those from Mackie, have plug-in FireWire cards for control and recording.

Price

The list price of the mixer in U.S. dollars. It's easy to find deep discounts on the Web if you shop around.

If you are going on the road you can take one of these mini-mixers with only two or four channels and have the output go into an iRiver MP3 recorder [Hack #69] or a Marantz portable recording unit. An example of this low-cost approach is the Beercast [Hack #30], which uses an iRiver, a mixer, and a few cheap microphones.

A mixer is handy in several situations. When you have more than two microphones you can use a mixer to fit them all into two channels, and you can set the gains and filtering parameters on a per-microphone basis. When you are recording phone conversations through a telephone hybrid, you will want a mixer to properly route and record the audio coming both to and from the phone.

Microphone Preamps

Condenser microphones [Hack #13] require phantom power to operate. You can get that power in several ways. Some condenser microphones (e.g., the Audio-Technica AT835B) have their own slot for a battery. This is the most direct way. Failing that, you will need to feed the microphone power through the XLR cable. Mixers, USB, FireWire preamps [Hack #12], and some sound cards provide this phantom power.

Another option is to use a dedicated microphone preamp. These devices serve two main functions: the first is to provide power to the microphone, and the second is to have gain control to amplify the signal. Some models provide equalization and other filters and effects to give a clean, warm sound.

Table 3-8 shows some of the microphone preamps on the market, sorted by price.

Table 3-8. A selection of microphone preamps

Manufacturer	Model	Channels	Phantom power	Effects	Price
ART	Tube MP	1	X		$57
Behringer	MIC100	1	X		$59.99
Behringer	MIC200	1	X	X	$69.99
ART	Tube MP OPL	1	X	X	$72
ART	Tube MP Studio	1	X	X	$86

Table 3-8. A selection of microphone preamps (continued)

Manufacturer	Model	Channels	Phantom power	Effects	Price
Rolls	MP13 Mini	1	X		$90
Alto	Alpha MicTube 2-channel	2	X		$114
M-Audio	Audio Buddy	2	X		$119.95
Behringer	MIC2200	2	X	X	$119.99
Presonus	TubePre	1	X		$129.95
Bellari	MP105	1	X		$150
Behringer	T1953	2	X		$169.99
Studio Projects	VTB1	1	X		$179.99
Presonus	BlueTube DP	2	X	X	$229

Preamps directly affect the warmth of someone's vocal sound, and can vary in price from $50 to $3,000. I chose to show the less expensive ones because I think these will work well for podcasts and they provide a nice, *phat* sound for your voice.

Here are the definitions of the table columns:

Manufacturer and model
> The name of the manufacturer and the model name or number.

Channels
> The number of input channels. On all of these devices, each input channel has both an XLR and a ¼-inch input jack, and an output XLR and a ¼-inch jack. This means you can use the device to convert from XLR to ¼-inch unbalanced to go to a computer's sound card.

Phantom power
> All of these devices supply 48-volt phantom power. It's called out here because it's one of the critical reasons for investing in a preamp.

Effects
> Some of these preamps come with built-in effects, besides the gain. These include equalization, output limiting, and more.

Price
> The list price in U.S. dollars. You can always find deep discounts on musical gear on the Web if you shop around.

If you plan to conduct interviews, you should invest in a two-channel model that can drive two microphones independently.

Most of the preamps in Table 3-8 are tube preamps that deliver a "smooth and fat" sound. Even if you don't need the phantom power or gain because some other device is providing this, you might want to consider a microphone preamp to thicken your voice and to add some warmth.

See Also

- "Set Up a Basic Home Studio" [Hack #12]
- "Set Up a Home Studio" [Hack #61]

HACK #15 Reduce Noise

Hum and hiss are annoying and distracting. Find out where the noise comes from and how you can reduce or remove it completely.

Hum and noise can ruin your recordings and turn off your listeners. What's even worse is that you are paying for noise [Hack #39], since a nice, clean signal will compress better. Better compression means a smaller MP3 file, which in turn means reduced bandwidth and disk space costs. Because software noise filtering distorts your sound, you will want to get rid of all the physical noise in your setup before turning to software noise reduction.

Find the Noise Floor

In a recording environment, the noise level is calculated in decibels. The studio's inherent noise is called the *noise floor*. The noise floor is the decibels of the noise in the room itself, which is called *environmental noise*. This also includes the noise of the sound recording system itself, which is called *signal path noise*. Since fewer noise decibels are better, you will want to lower your noise floor.

You should start by gauging your noise floor's current level. Then reduce your environmental noise, and then your signal path noise. Gauging your noise floor is fairly simple. You just record through your microphone [Hack #50] a sample of blank sound. Figure 3-8 shows a recording of the noise.

This is one of the few cases where you actually want a flat line.

The next step is to select the whole signal and use the View menu to plot the spectrum (see Figure 3-9).

The noise floor is the highest peak in the graph in Figure 3-9. In this case, it's near −40 dB, which is pretty bad. For a clean sound, you will want at least −60dB. Remember that less is better. A noise floor of −120dB means the studio and signal path are very clean.

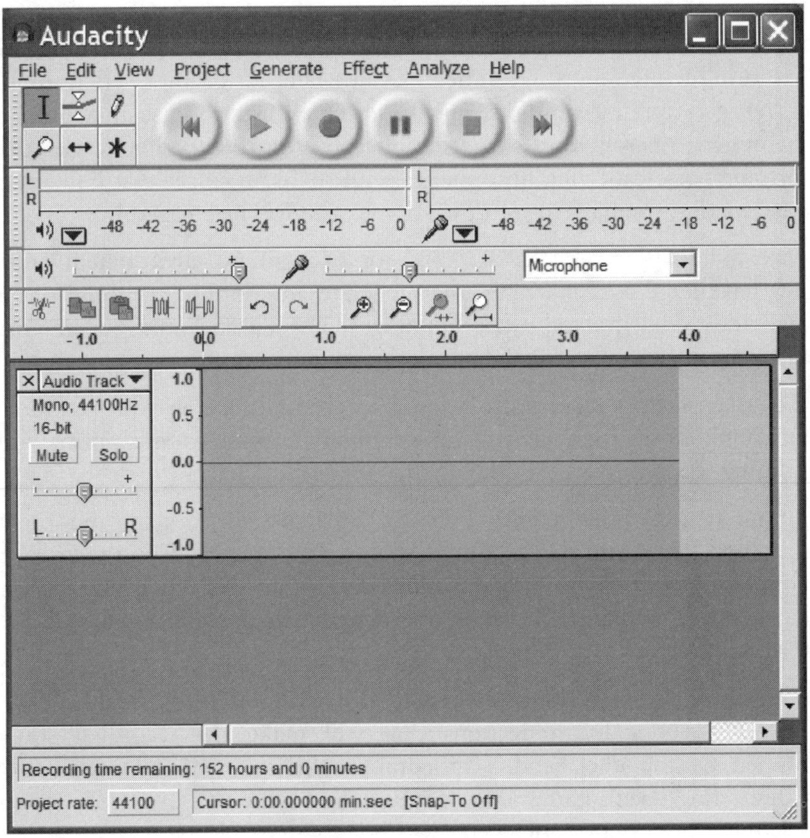

Figure 3-8. Audacity with a recorded noise sample

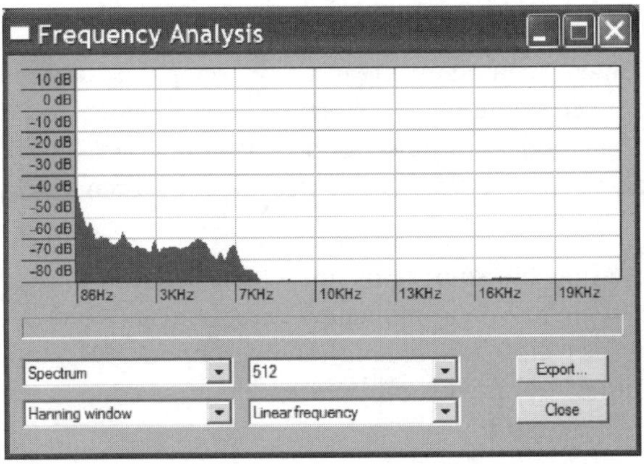

Figure 3-9. Spectral view of the noise floor

Eliminate Environmental Noise

Environmental noise is a little easier to track down than signal path noise. First, turn off anything you can hear. Ceiling fans, air conditioners, computers, refrigerators, air purifiers, and furnaces all create noise that humans tune out but microphones will detect. If you want to experiment with this, use some noise canceling headphones with no input to see just how much periodic noise you have in your own home. You will be amazed.

Office buildings are particularly bad for background environment noise. They have large A/C machines that generate an enormous amount of airflow. Additionally, some office buildings have started adding white-noise generators in areas with lots of cubicles to cut down on sound transmission.

All of these factors can lead to a low background noise in your recording. You should do as much as you can to eliminate these sounds during your recording session.

Another type of noise comes from the reflective surfaces in your room. Hardwood floors and desks bounce sound. The right angles in your room also reflect sound. Some simple ways to defeat these reflections are to close drapes, put carpeting on the floor, and hang or drape blankets on walls and horizontal surfaces.

Room size is also important. A standard-size bathroom is too small, and you will get quick sound reflections that will make the recording sound cramped. On the other hand, a cathedral will reflect sound and will give you an interesting reverb pattern that might not be what you expected. Try for something about the size of a small bedroom or den.

Basements are also ideal for recording, as they are below street level and thus have a protective barrier against outside noise. Recording late in the evening also cuts down on external noise.

Musical instruments can often sing just from the power of your voice. Cymbals and drums can bounce and distort sound even when you aren't playing them. So, if your podcast studio doubles as your home music studio, you should use blankets to cover up the instruments when you are recording podcasts.

Computers are horrible sources of noise. The internal fans are very noisy and their cases can leak high-frequency noise that can bleed into the audible spectrum. Laptops should be behind the microphone. Desktops should ideally be in another room, with cable extenders to get the keyboard, mouse, and video into the studio.

When you are recording out in the field be sure to use a *windscreen* for your microphone. A windscreen is the puffy black or red foam ball that goes on the live end of the microphone. This will cut down on wind noise.

Handling noise. *Handling noise*, a deep thumping sound that comes from moving your fingers around on the microphone, is the easiest form of noise to fix. If you are in a studio or at a fixed interview setting, use a microphone stand. Even better, use an isolation mount so that if the table is bumped you won't hear it in the recording.

When you have to hold the microphone in your hand, you can use the handlebar grip from a mountain bike to wrap around the microphone. This will reduce handling noise because your hand will not be in direct contact with the microphone.

Places to record at home. A home office is a good starting point when looking for a quiet place to record. You can use blankets to cover anything that could reflect sound. Another place to look is a walk-in closet filled with clothes. The clothes will dampen the sound. A garage could be OK, though you will need to look out for street noise, which can easily flow through walls that aren't insulated.

Places to record on the road. When you scout out a location, first make sure it's legal for you to be there. For example, ask permission from café owners, and make sure that you have the correct pass if you are in an area with restricted access. Then look for a room that's carpeted, has blinds to draw over the windows, and has linen-covered furnishings, such as beds or couches.

If you are recording yourself on the road in a hotel room, you can use the bed sheets and blankets to make a mini sound booth where you can record and isolate the outside noise.

If all else fails, try an outdoor location such as a park or a football field. It might actually be less noisy than your hotel room.

Eliminate Signal Path Noise

Everything between the microphone and your ears is called the *signal path*. Hum, hiss, crackle, and some types of pops are often created by problems with your signal path. One source of noise is particularly common: the 50 Hz or 60 Hz cycle noise that comes from power sources. This comes from the waveform used to transmit power via alternating current. In Europe, 50

Hz is used. In the U.S., 60 Hz is used. Either way, it comes out as a very low hum that's easily distinguishable.

These types of noises often have simple causes and easy solutions:

Don't mix audio cables with power cables
> Laying audio cables on top of A/C cables is a sure way to get a low, 50 Hz or 60 Hz hum. Keep your cables separated. If you have to cross two cables, you should cross them at 90-degree angles.

Use the shortest-length cable you can
> Don't run cables any longer than you need to. Cables are like antennas, and they will pick up noise. The longer the run the more noise they will pick up.

Buy good-quality cables
> Use shielded XLR cables for your microphones and all of your audio interconnects. Make sure the metal connectors on the ends of the cables are tight and that none of the connector's points makes a connection with the shielding. XLR cables are balanced, which means the signal is kept on separate lines from the shielding. This drastically reduces the amount of interference injected by the cabling.

Connect all A/C units to the same ground
> This avoids *ground loops*, which are another common source of 50Hz or 60Hz noise. If you can't connect everything to a single ground, you can add a transformer that should isolate the noise.

Use XLR microphones
> An XLR cable is less prone to interference than the two conductor cables of cheaper microphones. Quality microphones use XLR cables. Don't settle for anything less.

Another source of noise is the equipment itself. Microphones, preamps, and mixers all have inherent noise. With microphones, this is called *self-noise* and you can test this by leaving the mic on with no input and then bringing up the gain to its maximum point. In general, the better the quality of the microphone, the lower the self-noise. Of course, in this scenario it could also be your preamp. The only way to test that is to try your microphone on a different preamp to gauge the difference in noise levels.

In a complicated, multidevice signal path, additional noise can come from multiple gains. Each gain in the path will multiply the noise from the previous gain, and so on. A good rule of thumb is simply to remove any devices you aren't using from the signal path during a recording session.

If all of these quick tips failed and you still have some noise, try powering off each unit in the signal chain. Take it all the way back to the microphone and the preamp. Check for the noise there. If it's there, it's either a bad preamp or a noisy microphone. If it's not there, add your other signal processors and filters, one by one, until you find the one that's adding the noise.

Compressors, which are used to avoid the high peaks of vocal work, cause their own noise. For every dB of compression you use you get a corresponding dB of noise added to the noise floor. This is one reason to limit or remove compression from your signal path and to concentrate on controlling your vocal work.

Software Filtering Options

If all else fails, you can remove noise in post-processing by using software filters. High-quality software filters are available for removing hum, hiss, and A/C cycle noise, with little or no distortion to the signal. To help these filters you will need to record several seconds of empty sound at the beginning of your session. This section of empty sound will train the filter as to the ambient noise in the room.

Also, many software tools [Hack #57] will help you eliminate noise from your recordings.

Good Noise

Not all noise is bad noise. Some sounds, such as the clanking of coffee mugs in a café or the background music in a bar, can add ambience to your podcast [Hack #64]. This gives the listener a sense of place. Two tips will help you effectively use background ambient noise:

- Record some of it. That will help you both eliminate the noisy part of the signal later in post with a noise training filter [Hack #51], and give you some content to talk over as you fade into the segment.

- Random sounds are great, but sequential sounds aren't. For example, if you are at a ballgame, try not to record the score or other elements that will clue listeners in to when you made the recording. These audio cues are distracting and make it difficult to edit and rearrange the segment later.

See Also

- "Train Your Voice" [Hack #19]
- "Record and Add Background Ambience" [Hack #64]
- "Assemble a Small Recording Rig" [Hack #69]
- "Podcast at an Event" [Hack #71]

Podcast in Surround Sound

HACK #16 Use binaural microphones to give your podcast a three-dimensional sound field.

Podcasting brings listeners into your life. Podcasting with binaural micro-phones brings listeners into your head. The idea is simple: use two micro-phones to simulate your ears. The microphones [Hack #13] are usually small lavalier omnidirectionals that should sit as close to your ears as possible. Some people have even rewired headphones so that embedded lavaliers sit right on top of their ears. Others have gone as far as to build models of the human head with microphones that sit inside the ear canals.

Ideally, the two microphones will be matched exactly. Enthusiasts will go as far as to request two microphones with sequential serial numbers. Of course, this perfect matching costs money. A matched set starts at around $200 or $300. But cheaper unmatched sets that are suitable for experimenta-tion and podcasting are available in the $30 range.

Figure 3-10 shows the Low Cost Binaural Set ($75) from Core Sound (*http://core-sound.com/*), hooked up through its filter and into a Marantz 660 solid-state recorder [Hack #69]. The recorder has a left and right XLR input, both of which are tied into the microphones that connect to either side of the glasses right above your ears.

Figure 3-10. A set of binaural microphones on glasses, attached to a Marantz 660

The signal from the left lavalier goes into the left channel of a stereo recording, and the signal from the right goes into the right channel. The recording must be in stereo, with no mix between the two channels. When you edit these files, apply effects to both channels equally. When you make cuts, be sure to cut from both channels equally.

You can connect the headset to your computer and record that way, just as you would with a standard stereo microphone. This type of recording is best suited for fieldwork, where you can share your world in stereo just as you experience it. You can attach a binaural headset to the line-in of your portable recording unit. If it sounds underpowered, you will need to buy the battery kit that is sold along with the binaural headset.

Because the idea of binaural recordings is to simulate your ears, you need to both record at your ears and play back at your ears. So, use headphones when listening to binaural recordings to get the full stereo effect, with no balance or fade adjustments.

Here are some fun things to do with binaural podcasts:

Soundseeing tours
> Using binaural podcasts for a soundseeing tour [Hack #72] opens up a whole, new world. As people talk to the right or left or walk behind you, listeners will hear the sound exactly as you do.

Round tables
> Interview a group of folks and have some seated to your left and others to your right. Your listeners will be able to distinguish guests by their location.

Parties
> Go to a party and take in the small talk and conversation happening all around you.

Concerts and sporting events
> Experience the roar of the crowd [Hack #71] next to and behind you, and hear the game or the music in front of you. Motor sports are particularly good, as the cars zoom across the stereo field.

Binaural recording opens up a world of podcasting opportunities. For a small investment, you can get some binaural microphones, or make your own from instructions on the Web using microphones from RadioShack.

Binaural Tips

Here are a few binaural recording tips:

Use windscreens

As with any microphone, you should use windscreens on the binaurals if you plan on walking around outside. Even if there is no wind, your movement will create wind that comes through as a low-frequency whooshing sound [Hack #59].

Keep your head steady

It's natural for people to move their head during a conversation. If people on your left and right are involved in a conversation with you, you naturally move your head from side to side, as you would if you were watching a tennis match, so that you can concentrate on the person who is talking. This is very confusing if you are recording binaurally. Keep your head steady, and let the surround effect work for you. The same goes for walking around on tours. Try to walk from one steady position to another.

Explain the microphones

For whatever reason, binaurals don't seem to grab people's attention the way that other microphones do. Unfortunately, the way you act with these headphones to get optimal recording, such as not moving your head around much, will get you some attention. So, it's worth explaining to people where the microphones are and what they are doing.

As with everything, it takes practice to get the best sound. So, keep trying and learning from your experiences, even if the result doesn't come out the way you want the first few times.

HACK #17 Control Your Recorder with Your Mobile Phone

Use the awesome Salling Clicker system to control your whole computer, including your recording setup, right from your cell phone.

Computers, and in particular computer fans, make a lot of noise that can really screw up your recording [Hack #15]. But many podcasters use their computers to record their podcasts, so the computer has to be nearby so that they can turn the recorder on and off, play cuts, and read the show notes. Some podcasters invest in a home studio and have a great recording booth with clean sound, but their computer is on the other side of the glass wall. What can they do to control that computer remotely?

Sure, they could use a wireless mouse or keyboard, but the key and mouse clicks can be noisy. Plus, it's not as cool as this solution; using a cell phone.

With a program called Salling Clicker (*http://salling.com/*) for Mac OS X, you can use your Bluetooth-enabled phone to control every application on your computer. And you can arrange them on your keypad in any way you want.

Figure 3-11 shows the Salling Clicker Preferences panel. On the left is the menu for your phone, and on the right is all the stuff you can assign to buttons on the phone. Most of the items on the list come with Salling Clicker right out of the box. An excellent iTunes controller for navigating playlists and selecting songs is also available, as is a Keynote controller that lets you use a Keynote slideshow to prompt you when you have canned segments you need to record.

Figure 3-11. Scripts added to Salling Clicker

I added a few scripts to automate Audio Hijack Pro [Hack #50]. Audio Hijack Pro is a recording application that can take sound from all of the standard inputs, or from any application. An Audio Hijack Pro session is a combination of an input source, the recording specifications, and any effects processing for the signal.

This script starts the recording on a session named *bc*:

```
try
    tell application "Audio Hijack Pro"
        tell the session named "bc"
            stop hijacking
            stop recording
```

```
        end tell
    end tell
    tell application "SEC Helper"
        show screen message "Started" duration 1.5
    end tell
on error
    beep
end try
```

In this case, the script starts hijacking and recording a session named *bc*. To set this up on the phone I right-clicked in the lefthand panel of the Preferences pane and selected New Category. I named my new category Audio Hijack Pro. Then I right-clicked the Audio Hijack Pro category and selected New Script. I named this script *Start Recording*. Then I right-clicked that and selected Edit in the Script Editor. With the Script Editor, I typed in my script and saved it.

So far, so good. Now the script was in the library, but I couldn't get to it on the phone. So, I needed to create a new keypad layout that included the *Start Recording* script. I did this by clicking the gear below the phone menu on the lefthand side of the Preferences window, and selected the Insert Keypad option. I named my new keypad AHP, short for Audio Hijack Pro.

From here, I opened up the *Audio Hijack Pro* folder and dragged the *Start Recording* script onto the 1 button, as shown in Figure 3-12. I had already made the *Stop Recording* script, so I dragged that onto the 2 button. I could also have assigned some keynote or iTunes commands to other buttons. I'll leave those options to you.

The *Stop Recording* script looked like this:

```
try
    tell application "Audio Hijack Pro"
        tell the session named "bc"
            stop recording
            stop hijacking
        end tell
    end tell
    tell application "SEC Helper"
        show screen message "Stopped" duration 1.5
    end tell
on error
    beep
end try
```

It's pretty much the same as the original script for starting the recording, except in this case I stop it. The second section where I talk to the SEC Helper application is shown in boldface. SEC Helper puts up a beautifully beveled and semitransparent message box with the message you supply. In

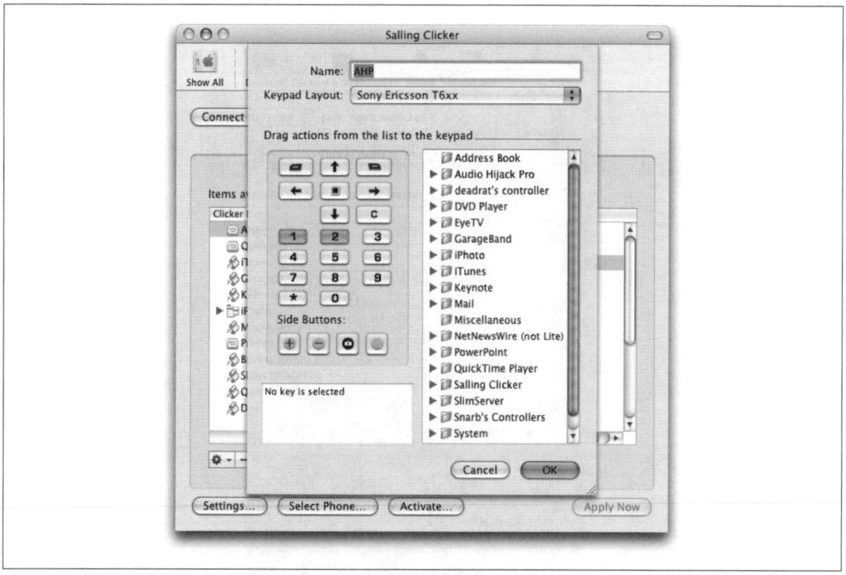

Figure 3-12. Attaching scripts to keys on the keypad

this case that message is "Stopped." You don't strictly need to do this, but it's super-sweet if you do.

SEC Helper can also write out messages to the phone. Salling Clicker is an insanely great piece of software. I was so blown away the first time I saw it that I changed cell phone providers and bought a cell phone that works with Salling Clicker that very day.

If you don't use Audio Hijack Pro for your recording, don't worry. You probably still can use Salling Clicker (any application that supports Apple-Script can work with Salling Clicker). And there are scripts out there for controlling Garage Band 2, Logic Express, Logic Pro, and Pro Tools.

Turning recording on and off is just scratching the surface of what Salling Clicker is capable of. You can script an entire dynamic interface with the phone that constantly updates itself from your machine. Figure 3-13 shows an example of the out-of-the-box iTunes controller as it's seen on my phone's screen. It's telling me the song, the album, and the playback time in real time. If I click the joystick to the right, it goes to the next song; if I click it to the left, it goes to the previous song.

ControlFreak

ControlFreak from mtvoid (*http://mtvoid.com/*) is the Windows alternative to Salling Clicker. You can use your phone to navigate around your desktop

Figure 3-13. A cell phone showing the Salling Clicker display

as well as to control it. ControlFreak is designed primarily as a media controller and doesn't connect to audio recording applications directly. But you can control audio recording applications through the desktop control functionality.

Other Remote Controls

Other options are available as well. The first is a Bluetooth keyboard and mouse. Logitech has two Bluetooth combinations, one at ~$180 and another at ~$250. Infrared keyboard and mouse combinations are cheaper, in the $50 range. But you need line-of-sight for those to work.

Another option is to use a small laptop that doesn't have a fan. Then use Virtual Network Computing (VNC) over WiFi to talk to the computer that's doing the recording. VNC allows one computer (the client) to see what's on another computer (the server) and to control it with the mouse and the keyboard. It's used in IT shops to control machines at a distance. What's even better is that clients are available for Windows, Macintosh, and Linux, and they are all interchangeable. So, you can control your PC from your Mac, or vice versa. Clients and servers are available at RealVNC (*http://realvnc.com/*). OSXvnc (*http://www.redstonesoftware.com/vnc.html*) is one of many VNC solutions for the Mac.

HACK #18 Construct Your MP3s

Use command-line tools to encode your MP3 files as well as to build customized MP3 files on the fly.

The MPEG-1 Audio Layer 3 format (MP3 for short) is a lossy compression format for audio. This means the sound going in will have elements removed to pack it into a smaller output size. The process of building an MP3 file from an input sound file is called *encoding*. The software that does this encoding is called an *encoder*.

MP3 first became popular around 1995. The first encoders did a poor job, so if you wanted an MP3 that was indistinguishable from a CD, you needed a *bit rate* of 256. (The bit rate relates to the amount of data stored per second in the file. The more bits, the better the sound.) Modern encoders, such as the latest version of the free LAME encoder (*http://lame.sf.net/*), produce CD-quality sound at a bit rate of 192.

Deciding what to remove from a recording to create the compressed file is fairly tricky. Modern encoders use a psychoacoustic model of our hearing to decide what to give the most bits to in the recording. Most of the time this will be the dominant frequencies in the segment being encoded. However, encoders are free to use whatever mechanism they think will produce the best sound for the given bit rate.

It follows that for less complex signals, such as a single human voice, we could spend fewer bits and still get a quality sound. This is why spoken-word podcasts encoded at 64 bits or even 32 bits still sound reasonably well. If you have a more complex sound, such as that of a music show, you should probably use 128-bit encoding.

Variable Bit Rate Encoding

Another option is to use variable bit rate encoding, or VBR. An MP3 file is organized into frames of data. Each frame has a header that indicates the number of channels, the sampling rate, and the bit rate. The bit rates can be altered from frame to frame. This is called variable bit rate, and it allows for a podcast to vary between complex musical segments and simpler spoken-word segments while achieving optimal compression overall.

The downside of variable bit rate encoding is that it's not guaranteed to be compatible on all players. I suggest you try VBR compression to see if it will make a big difference, and if it does, test it with a couple of modern clients to make sure it works.

ID3 Tags

Unlike records and CDs, the MP3 file format includes some information identifying the file's content. The first version of this identification standard was called ID3 v1.0 [Hack #40] and it contained enough room to put in a song title, an artist name, an album name, a year, a short comment, and a genre identifier.

Each field was given a set number of characters. Song name, artist, album, and comment were allowed a maximum of 30 characters. Year was given 4 characters, and the genre ID 1 byte. These are ASCII characters, so each is a single byte. Unicode support won't be available until Version 2.0. Version 1.1 of the standard cannibalized 2 bytes from the comment tag to provide space for a track number.

The specification hardcoded 126 different genres—from common ones such as Blues, Funk, Rock, and Reggae to more obscure Booty Bass, Primus, and Porn Groove. Podcasts tend to fit conveniently into genre #12, or Other.

The second version of the ID3 standard bears little resemblance to the first version. Instead of a single, small structure with a few fields, this version features a much more flexible tagged format. The format can store Unicode text for all the fields, which allows for internationalization. It can also store media such as pictures, large blocks of text such as original lyrics, and handy things for DJs such as beats per minute (BPM).

You can find more information on all of these standards at the ID3 site (*http://id3.org/*).

Encoding with LAME

LAME, free software that includes encoding functionality, is available on the LAME site (*http://lame.sf.net/*). It's an outstanding encoder that you can plug into your programs and use as a DLL or a library. You can also use it directly from the command line.

To encode a file from the command line you need to give it the name of the input file and the name of the MP3 file to create:

```
% lame mysound.wav mysound.mp3
LAME version 3.96.1 (http://lame.sourceforge.net/)
Using polyphase lowpass filter, transition band: 17249 Hz - 17782 Hz
```

```
Encoding hello.wav to hello.mp3
Encoding as 44.1 kHz 128 kbps j-stereo MPEG-1 Layer III (11x) qval=3
    Frame        | CPU time/estim | REAL time/estim | play/CPU |    ETA
    20/23    (87%)|    0:00/    0:00|    0:01/    0:01|   5.2245x|    0:00
average: 128.0 kbps                   MS: 23 (100.0%)

Writing LAME Tag...done
ReplayGain: -14.6dB
```

Here the *mysound.wav* file is being encoded as MP3 in the new *mysound.mp3* file. The encoder is using the 128 kbps bit rate (the default).

To change the bit rate of the encoding, add the –b option:

```
% lame -b 32 mysound.wav mysound.mp3
```

That command line encodes the same sound as before, but at the significantly poorer 32 kbps bit rate.

Bit rate is the main quality setting in MP3. The larger the bit rate setting, the better the quality. But LAME also provides another quality switch, -q, for setting the Q value:

```
% lame -q 0 mysound.wav mysound.mp3
```

Setting the Q value to 0 requests that the best-quality compression be done. The other side of the settings range is 9, which is the worst possible quality.

MP3 filters look for the dominant frequencies in the sound and concentrate on those. If your signal has noise, it might key on that noise and spend the bits where you don't want them. Another, more common case is that you present a lot of sonic energy in your voice above and below the audible spectrum. So, it's not really worth encoding it. Doug Kaye of IT Conversations recommends using low-pass and high-pass filters to optimize compression, with the low set to 10 kHz and the high to 80 Hz. This will allow the encoder to concentrate on the important sound.

Thankfully, LAME has low- and high-pass filters baked right in:

```
% lame --lowpass 10 --highpass 0.08 mysound.wav mysound.mp3
```

Both the low- and high-pass filters have settings in kilohertz. So, we set the low-pass filter to 10 kHz and the high-pass filter to 0.08 kHz (or 80 Hz).

Another handy feature of LAME is its ability to set ID3 tags:

```
% lame --tt "My Title" --ta "Me" --tl "My Album" mysound.wav mysound.mp3
```

In this case, we are setting the title to My Title, the name of the artist to Me, and the album name to My Album. LAME handles both versions of the ID3 tag format.

LAME has a lot more features than I covered here. For a complete list, use the --longhelp command-line argument:

```
% lame --longhelp
```

You can change the sampling frequency and the number of channels. You also can apply gain factors, do variable bit rate encoding, and a whole lot more.

Combine Without Re-Encoding

Two other command-line tools will aid you in your podcasting. *mpgtx* is a set of MP3 file tools that allows you to cut and join MP3 files without re-encoding, and SoX is a command-line tool that does signal processing on files.

mpgtx. Re-encoding MP3 files is a bad idea. MP3 is a lossy format, so each time you take an MP3 file, decode it, and then re-encode it, you lose quality. But encoding from an original file can take a while—a long while. So, what do you do when you want to be able to create several versions of a podcast, each with different ad placements [Hack #47]? Or suppose you provide a service, whereby you take several self-contained segments and string them together into one MP3 for the listener. Is there a way to do that on the fly with MP3?

Yes, you can split and join MP3 files in any combination of ways you like, without re-encoding. Several commercial software packages do it. But there is also the open source *mpgtx* (*http://mpgtx.sf.net/*) package. *mpgtx* is available for Windows, Mac OS X, and Linux.

To install *mpgtx* on Linux or Macintosh, first download the *mpgtx* gzipped tarball from the site. Then unpack it with the tar -xzvf command (or just let OS X do it for you). After that, run ./configure, followed by sudo make install to make and install the program.

On Windows, just download the binaries and install *mpgtx* wherever you keep your command-line utilities.

Once *mpgtx* is installed, you will have a host of new MP3 file commands at your fingertips. Three primary utilities are available: mpginfo, which gives you information about an individual MP3 file; mpgjoin, which joins multiple MP3 files into a single file; and tagmp3, which gives you control over the MP3 file's ID3 tags.

Here is the mpginfo commands report on the *mysound.mp3* file I made earlier in the hack with LAME:

```
% mpginfo mysound.mp3
mysound.mp3
   Audio : Mpeg 1 layer 3
   Estimated Duration: 00.63s
   128 kbps  44100 Hz
   Frame size: 417 bytes
   Joint Stereo: (Intensity stereo off, M/S stereo on)
   No emphasis,  original
   ID3 v1.1 tag
      ----------------
      title   : My Title
      artist  : Me
      album   : My Album
      track   : 0
      ----------------
```

I'll use three other MP3 files—*top.mp3*, *interview.mp3*, and *bottom.mp3*—to demonstrate how to build one MP3 from the sum of three MP3s. The *top.mp3* file is the introduction to the show, the *interview.mp3* file is the interview in the middle, and the *bottom.mp3* file is the credits and outtro [Hack #63]:

```
% mpgjoin bottom.mp3 interview.mp3 top.mp3 -o total.mp3
Now processing bottom.mp3 1/3 ...  100.00%
Now processing interview.mp3 2/3 ...  100.00%
Now processing top.mp3 3/3 ...  100.00%
```

This built a file called *total.mp3* from the sum of the three files. There are some limitations, but as long as the files are compatible in terms of sampling rate and bit rate, it will join them into the single, large file.

The third utility that is valuable to podcasters is the *tagmp3* program, which can set the ID3 tags in an MP3 file from the command line:

```
% tagmp3 set "%A:Me %a:My Album %t:My Song" total.mp3
Setting total.mp3 tag
% mpginfo total.mp3
total.mp3
   Audio : Mpeg 1 layer 3
   Estimated Duration: 02.98s
   64 kbps  44100 Hz
   Frame size: 208 bytes
   Mono,  No emphasis,  original
   ID3 v1.0 tag
      ----------------
      title   : My Song
      artist  : Me
      album   : My Album
      ----------------
```

With the first command, I set the artist, album name, and song name on the *total.mp3* file. Then I used the *mpginfo* application to make sure the ID3 tags were set properly.

The format items for the `tagmp3` set commands are shown in Table 3-9.

Table 3-9. The tagmp3 format syntax

Format item	ID3 tag field
%A	The artist name
%a	The album name
%t	The title of the song
%T	The number of the track
%y	The year
%g	The genre ID
%c	The comment

The *mpgtx* package contains three other utilities as well: `mpgcat`, which outputs the joined MP3 file to the standard output; `mpgsplit`, which extracts portions of the MP3 file into another MP3 file; and `mpgdemux`, which extracts a single MPEG file into multiple files with its component pieces.

SoX. SoX is an open source application that is available on Windows, Mac OS X, and Linux. It has two primary functions: it converts file formats, and it can apply a variety of effects to the sound it's converting.

To install SoX, start by downloading the source from the SoX site (*http://sox. sf.net/*). Then use `./configure` and `sudo make install` to build the SoX program and install it. On Windows just download the binary and install it wherever you like.

To convert a sound file, simply specify the input filename and output filename as command-line arguments:

```
% sox mysound.wav mysound.mp3
```

In this case, the *mysound.wav* file is converted to *mysound.mp3*. There are far too many input and output audio formats to list here, but this certainly covers all the standard file formats.

Next, you can apply a series of filters to augment the conversion:

```
% sox mysound.wav mysound.mp3 vol 0.5 pitch 300ms
```

This applies the "vol" filter, which tweaks the gain, in this case reducing the volume of the signal by 50%. Then it uses a pitch shift to up the signal to make it sound chirpy.

SoX supports a wide variety of effects: band pass filter, chorus, echo, fade, high pass, low pass, pan, phaser, pitch shifting, reverb, reverse, silence, stretch, and volume adjustments [Hack #58], as well as editing functions such as trimming away portions of unwanted signals.

I strongly recommend that if you are going to do a series of SoX operations, you use lossless formats such as *.aif* or *.wav* to do the operations. This will ensure that you don't lose data on each conversion.

Other Encoding Formats

Several alternative audio formats are worth knowing about. Here is a list of the lossless formats that will preserve audio, with no drop in sound quality:

WAV
> The Microsoft lossless sound storage format. There is no compression. The format is linked intimately to the structure of Intel processors.

PCM
> Short for pulse code modulated, this is the format that is used on CDs.

FLAC
> The Free Lossless Audio Codec is a file format that provides between 30% and 70% compression, without loss of sound quality.

AIFF
> This is the Audio Interchange File Format, which is commonly used on Macintoshes.

There are a few more lossy formats as well:

AAC
> The Advanced Audio Coding file format is the next-generation MP3 file format, with better compression as well as support for more channels, higher sampling rates, and better sound performance in the higher frequencies. Apple is a strong proponent of this standard. The songs from the iTunes music store are AAC files.

AC-3
> The Dolby compression standard used in Dolby Digital systems, this supports multiple channels to enable surround sound as well as variable bit rate encoding.

MP2
> This is the predecessor to MP3 and is a higher-quality lossy format commonly used by the broadcast industry.

Ogg Vorbis
> An open source lossy codec and file format that is gaining in popularity, this was developed in response to a licensing threat to MP3. Audacity supports Ogg Vorbis import and export without the addition of a codec.

WMA
> The Windows version of MP3 for its Windows Media Player and some portable devices, this is a direct competitor to AAC. Both of these formats support digital rights management (DRM).

Because of its immense popularity, MP3 is universally supported on all operating systems, often with multiple players. But it's worth knowing about these formats so that you can recognize different formats as you see them.

See Also

- "Choose the Right Audio Tools" [Hack #50]

HACK #19   Train Your Voice

Use professional techniques and training to improve your podcasting voice.

You should keep two things in mind when you sit down to record your podcast: speak well for broadcast (diction, enunciation, etc.) and speak into the microphone [Hack #13] correctly. Both of these issues are relatively easy to address with a few key tips.

Speaking Well for Podcasting

"Speaking well for broadcast" is something that calls to mind bad associations for many people. The idea of talking in "radio voice" (defined for most by the sound of early morning DJs or public radio smooth talkers) is the stuff of *Saturday Night Live* lampoons. Besides, there is of course no right or wrong way to speak for broadcast; it is, at its simplest, a pure and representative form of communication.

However, broadcasting (and by extension, podcasting) as a medium sometimes requires adjustments to have your voice, speech, and message be heard through the prism of an intermediary device (the microphone, for example) as you intended. It is common for people to be unhappy with the sound of their recorded voice. The idiosyncrasies of their speech or the lack of coherence and drive in their delivery can cause their broadcast to land on listeners' ears very differently than they imagined it would when they first conceived their message.

The speaking guidelines that follow are enormously helpful in terms of preserving the integrity of your message in auditory media. While working, be sure to record yourself every time—nothing will be more useful than hearing yourself. The following skill sets—techniques of the trade—are set forth as options to diversify and clean up your speaking for podcasts.

Diction and Enunciation

These are the issues that most American speakers have in their speech that come out in auditory media:

Hard r
>Most American accents (with the exception of some New England and Southern accents) have very strong *r*'s in their speech. (When British actors learn American dialects, one of their first points of focus is hitting their *r*'s!) It might help to try easing up on them a bit when they crop up in their diphthong (i.e., "See here! More of their poor art!") or triphthong (i.e., fire, power) state.

Popping ps *and other stop-plosives*
>The sounds of *p*, *b*, *t*, *d*, *k*, and *g* are known as *stop-plosives*. The most common problem with these sounds is that when they are overarticulated (or overworked), too much air is "exploded" from the lips, and this air unnecessarily frames or relishes the consonant sound. (This is a typical speaking problem that sound engineers have to correct in prerecorded radio and voiceovers, for example.) Be sure to give nice, closed endings to these sounds, and listen for the pops on playback.

Dropping off t, nt, d, nd, *and* ing *endings*
>Be sure to drive through and lightly hit the ends of your words. Don't drop off in the middle of a word. This is an important tip to honor for the sake of clarity.

Leaky s
>Think of this as the snakelike sound that happens when an *s* sound is pushed too hard. Move through *s* sounds quickly and avoid overworking them.

The sound in you *("liquid* u*")*
>This sound can blend in with the word before it, often sounding like *chew*. Be sure to make this its own sound.
>
>Try this: practice the phrase "can't you, won't you, don't you," giving a crisp end to the *nt* ending and a separate start to the *you*.

Pitch, Power, and Pace

You can develop three key aspects to the way you speak: pitch, power, and pace. These are covered in the sections that follow.

Pitch. You are always speaking on notes of the musical scale, known as *pitch*. Americans are known for speaking in a very small range of pitch—whenever they want to emphasize something while speaking, they tend to do it with volume instead of pointing it up with pitch. Try going up and down in pitch, even if just a touch, to pull out or point up key words or ideas for your listeners. This is a key tool for adding nuance and increasing "listenability."

> Try this: when reading a paragraph, try going *up a half step* in pitch every time you begin a new sentence, until you hit the middle of the paragraph, at which point start taking each sentence *down a half step*. This exercise is good for getting the idea of pitch variations in your ear, and helping you find what's useful.

Power. *Power* is the volume at which you speak. Speaking more loudly or softly at times is a main way of emphasizing a point. Although it is important to speak well and clearly—even into an all-hearing microphone—this is an aspect of speaking that you might want to use with caution when recording. Speaking too loudly will overpower the microphone; speaking too softly will make listeners work too hard to hear you.

Pace. *Pace* refers to the speed at which you speak. You can point up key ideas and phrases by varying the rate of your speaking. Rushing through sentences is a far more common problem than speaking too slowly. Be sure also to speak at an even pace when recording your podcast. If you're a habitual "fast-talker," it might feel at first as though you are speaking at an agonizingly slow rate. However, chances are good that you're speaking at just the right speed for the first time! Ask for a second set of ears to help you gauge until you get the hang of it. But generally, slower is far better than faster.

> Try this: time yourself reading a paragraph at your normal pace. Then read it again, aiming to *double* the time it took you to read it the first time.

Punctuation. The general rule of thumb is to go up a half step in pitch at commas, and down at periods. This is a simple but important rule for clarity. Also, punctuation is an internal indicator of how things are to sound, in terms of both pitch *and* pace. Use punctuation marks to guide your rate of speaking, too.

Try this: read a paragraph, and count a slow "1...2..." under your breath to time a pause every time you come to a comma or period. Then, read it again, *thinking* the "1...2...." This will set you on the right path to honoring your punctuation.

Speaking into the Microphone Correctly

Here are some things to concentrate on:

- Speak about six inches from the microphone.
- Enunciate clearly.
- Speak at a reasonable pace.
- Speak at a volume that you normally would if you were talking to someone in the room with you.
- If you're speaking at a louder than normal volume, pull back a bit from the microphone so that you don't overpower the mic. (You know the singers you see who hold the mic out when they're belting? That's why!)
- Don't move too close to the microphone (sometimes called "eating the mic"). The microphone will pick you up just fine.
- Don't move too far away when speaking at a normal volume. Remember, six inches is the optimum distance from the microphone when speaking in normal tones.
- Don't speak too quickly. Not only will you not be understood, but also the microphone can pick up all the sounds of your lips and breath, working double time to keep up with your speed. The result is that your speech will sound chewed. You probably don't want to embellish your podcast with all sorts of strange saliva-y sounds.

Other Resources

You can find additional coaching or help with the voice and speech aspects of your podcast in several places. Broadcasting coaches, classes, and schools are in most major metropolitan areas. Speech classes, offered for actors, can also be a resource; most of them work off Edith Skinner's famous book, *Speak with Distinction* (Applause Books). This book covers the world of diphthongs and triphthongs, of front, mid, and back vowel sounds, of stop-plosive and affricate consonants, and of nasal continuants. It teaches all of the sounds of standard American English, and how they should be used (an invaluable resource for anyone who speaks for a living).

Media trainers are experts in how to deal with all types of media. They offer both classes and individual training sessions that can be tailored to your needs, and most of them train for radio. Media trainers can also be a place to start for accent coaching, though there are speech experts who do this as well, and often do it better. Look for speech therapy credentials or graduate-level, Skinner-based speech work when shopping for an accent coach.

Accent coaching can make a huge difference, in a relatively short amount of time, for non-native English speakers or anyone with a regionalism that they feel interferes with the clarity or integrity of their message.

Talking Naturally

It's not easy to sound like you're talking; this will make sense the second you sit down in front of a microphone. After working with a slew of first-time producers and essayists at Atlantic Public Media, we learned that comfort with a microphone is sometimes a matter of finding the right trick. If you're fine with your own tracking, file these away for the next time you have a nervous guest in your studio.

Imagine someone else. Imagine that you're speaking to someone across the room. Move the mic away from you, turn down your levels, and find an imaginary person six feet away. Tell her your story. Let your voice reach out across the room. Some stories come with the quality of something confessed in a closet, so for those you want to bring the mic in, or better yet, use a closet and turn off the lights. Another common technique is to pretend you're on the telephone. A telephone is a microphone that everyone is used to.

Talk as though you're talking to a close friend. A good recorded script requires a certain kind of self-honesty. Don't be coy or clever with your voice because that will come through in the audio. Whether you're the reader or you're directing someone else, this is key, so don't let yourself or anyone else get away with it! If a performance gets stale or uncomfortable, tell the story of what's on the page instead of reading from it.

You have to start with headphones so that you can hear whether anything weird is going on in the background. But sometimes, it's best to take off the headphones. Some readers are shocked by the sound of their own voice so close in their head; it freaks them out. Worse, some people—you know who you are—are in love with the sound of their own voice. In this case, headphones will only encourage a person to hang on to every rumbly bass that is produced; you know, the Stentorian approach.

In defense of headphones, the biofeedback can also be very soothing. You suddenly can hear what you are doing wrong, without cringing. For the very timid, bring the headphones back out after the second read. It can be miraculous.

Warming up. Sing like an opera star, just for a second. This works particularly well if you're recording someone terrified by the mic. First, it breaks the tension because everyone sounds silly in a falsetto, and second, if you move your voice around it's easier to settle into your natural pitch. I think of it, when tracking someone else, as cracking their resistance.

Get yourself in order. Stand up. It will straighten out the air column. It makes you sound like you know what you're doing. Use a music stand or something similar to prop your copy on so that you never tuck your chin.

Remove everything from your person, especially noisy clothing (e.g., leather and nylon). Nervous people pick at things, move around, tap pens, and jiggle change. Microphones pick this up, particularly the tapping pen, and if listeners can't see what you're doing, they're going to wonder what the noise is.

Guests like being taken care of. Studios can be intimidating; explain to a reader exactly what is happening. Adjust the mic yourself to a comfortable height for them; give them some water, and make them feel comfortable with the equipment around them. Usually people want to start off sitting down, but are relieved once you make them stand up, since they can breathe better. Another way to get a reader to relax after a read or two is to let him know that you already have something usable, and encourage him to try a few more just to experiment. You will find that these later takes will be less stressed.

Reading technique. If you are reading from a script, read three times. You're likely to nail it in three takes. One of those times, watch the script while listening to make sure nothing is missed. You can also do it with your eyes closed, or looking somewhere else, and that is often a way to hear whether the energy is waning or if there's not a proper emphasis or feeling placed on a part of a phrase or a word.

Figure out where to breathe. People tend, strangely, to breathe unnaturally when they're trying to sound natural. You might need to look through a script to find and mark natural places to take a breath.

Try not to stress the obvious word. If the words are good enough, they'll come across.

Know that everything is magnified. Every time you push a phrase, or trail off, the impact on air is far greater than in a conversation. Audio gives you room for subtlety. Use it.

Edit yourself while you're recording. Often you can hear things you can't see on the page. If you're having trouble saying something or if it feels unnatural, change it. If you wouldn't normally say it that way out loud, don't say it into a microphone.

—Emily Donahoe and Viki Merrick

## CHAPTER FOUR

Formats
Hacks 20–32

The answer gets to the heart of what makes narrative work: whenever there's a sequence of events—this happened, then that happened, then this happened—we inevitably want to find out what happened next. Also, and this is key, this banal sequence has raised the question, namely, what's this guy saying? And you'll probably stick around to find out.

—Ira Glass

This chapter covers the role of format in podcasts, starting with an in-depth look at the why and how of formats. Then the hacks in this chapter dig into the individual format types, and present some case studies along the way.

HACK #20 Adopt a Format for Your Podcast

Apply the elements of a format to your podcast to give listeners a reason to subscribe to your show.

To format or not to format. That's a question many podcasters ask. Some believe formats smack of radio and are completely inappropriate to the ad hoc podcast, and others believe a format can help get content to listeners in the best way possible.

Deciding if a format is right for your show starts with understanding the term.

In its broadest sense, the term *format* refers to a show's style. There are sports formats, talk formats, news formats, and others.

But more specifically, the term *format* refers to how material within a show is *arranged*. In that sense, a format is an invisible framework on which your content rests. For example, you can format a sports show in several different ways: you can feature a series of three quick interviews separated by music clips, or you can feature one long interview bookended by music clips. Both are sports shows, but they are formatted differently. How you arrange those blocks of sound is how you "format" your show.

Formatting starts with choosing an overarching theme for the show's content. Will it be a political show, a review show, a music show?

Once you have a theme, envision your ideal listener. Start with yourself; how would you like to hear the theme approached? With one guest, or with many guests? With lots of music and not much talking, or the other way around? If you're doing a music show, for example, you could play a lot of music and occasionally interview a musician…or you could host a talk show about music and feature an occasional performance by a guest.

Ultimately, some details of your format will change with each podcast, and others will stay the same. All that's important in this initial planning stage is that you decide what your listeners will enjoy hearing.

Decide on a Duration

How long should you make your podcast?

First, think about your listeners. What do you want to tell them in an episode of your show? How long will that topic hold your listeners' attention? Ask a few friends interested in your subject matter how long they might invest in listening to a show such as the one you're developing. Also, your listeners are likely to be doing something else while the show plays in their ears, such as working out, biking, or commuting. You can always match the length of the show to the length of that supposed activity.

Having some boundaries for the duration of the show is important for listeners, because it lets them know what to expect. It's also important for you, because it helps you to know how much content to put together.

Podcasts generally range from 15 minutes at the short end to 40 minutes at the long end. There are no hard and fast rules about time in podcasts, and that's one of the great aspects of this medium. Typically, you want to start shorter and then go longer as you build your experience, or if the day's topic warrants it. One technical limit is 80 minutes; beyond 80 minutes, your listeners will no longer be able to burn a CD to listen to your show.

Another reason to decide on a duration for the show is to ensure you have enough time to produce it. An average podcast takes up to eight times the duration of the show to produce. A 15-minute podcast will take up to 2 hours to research, script, record, edit, and post. Shows that are mostly talk will take less time, and complex music or interview shows will take more time. You should know there are trade-offs when it comes to production time: for example, you can save some time by not writing a script, but the unscripted recording might take longer to edit.

 Here is a quick formula for determining duration: start with the number of free hours you are willing to commit to your show each week. Then divide that number by 6 and you will get a general duration for your show.

Block Out the Show

Radio shows map out their format, based on a clock. They literally have a clock on a piece of paper, similar to Figure 4-1, that shows how long each segment of the show will be and what it will contain.

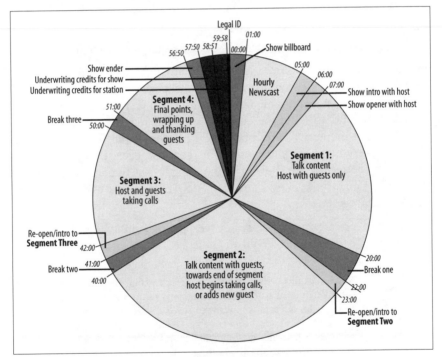

Figure 4-1. A simple radio clock for a one-hour show

A show is made up of blocks of sound known as *elements*. *Production elements* are standardized elements that are generally the same in each episode. These include such things as theme songs, introductions, and credits, and the way they're presented helps establish the show's identity. For example, using upbeat production elements creates the sound of a fun show.

Content elements, also known as *segments*, are the real substance of the program. These can be interviews, in-depth reports, or sets of music.

Between segments, radio relies on *transition elements*, which carry the listeners' ear from one piece to another. Usually these are bits of music, sound effects, or short bits of talk introducing the next radio segment.

But that's radio. Can these ideas apply in podcasting?

Elements offer predictability. They give a structure to the show that listeners can depend on, while allowing the host to be creative within that structure.

If you are already podcasting, you're probably using some basic elements. You likely have an introduction to start every show. And you probably have a farewell (a production element known as an *ender*) to wrap up your podcast.

But you can also use elements to set your podcast apart from others, by coming up with some regular segments that are unique to your show.

For example, David Letterman and other late-night television hosts have opening monologues. The audience tunes in, expecting the show to follow a certain format. But Letterman also has his "Top Ten List." When Dave moved from NBC to CBS, the contract specified that CBS would get the "Top Ten List property." That's because a portion of the viewing audience shows up every night looking for the Top Ten List, even if they don't stick around for the rest of the show. The monologue is a standard content element in late-night talk shows, and the Top Ten List is a content element unique to Dave's show.

Format elements are the not-so-secret weapon that broadcasters, and narrowcasters, use to engage and hold an audience.

> *Narrowcasting* is the opposite of broadcasting. *Broadcasting* is the term used to describe traditional radio and television content. Broadcasts are meant to serve a wide audience base and thus must appeal to a large spectrum of people, whereas podcasts can service a much smaller and narrower portion of the audience; thus, narrowcasting.

Create Great Content Segments

A great content segment does two things:

- It engages the listener by *sounding interesting*. This means if you're telling a story, you'll use an appropriate tone of voice (i.e., somber for a serious story), vary your pacing, and use dynamic language or good writing to keep listeners involved. If you're playing music, you'll put the songs in an appealing sequence, vary the rhythm or style a little or a lot, and create an evocative mood for the show. The way your content is presented *aurally* helps to engage your listeners.

- Great content informs, entertains, or inspires. What do you have to offer that's unique? Figure that out, and build your show around it. Perhaps your news show reveals behind-the-scenes details your listeners don't have access to. Your talk show might feature someone with an unusual personal story, prompting your listeners to think about an issue in a different way or inspiring them to take action. If you're presenting an opinion, try to offer a fresh and well-reasoned perspective.

To develop great content, ask yourself if you'd listen to this segment, and be honest. Would it keep you coming back? Test it on a few friends, or set up an email address and ask your listeners for feedback directly. Don't get stuck thinking you have to include things you don't care about. If you find yourself wanting to listen to a segment you've produced over and over, you know you've hit the mark.

Overall, great content *can* be listened to and enjoyed more than once. It's unique and universal at the same time. If it's engaging, your listeners will want to share it with others. And if you consistently create great content, your listeners will keep coming back, and their word of mouth will help build your audience.

Create Great Production Elements

At the very least, podcasts need an introduction and an ender. In the introduction, you introduce the hosts, and give the name of the show and a catchy phrase that describes what the show is about. Your ender should have whatever credits and sponsorship information you want to share with listeners. You should also thank the audience for listening, ask for feedback, and let them know they can find out more on your web site.

There are other production elements as well. A *billboard* or *rundown* is a short element that acts like an appealing contents listing for your show. Keep it conversational, and describe what you are going to talk about in the order it will appear in the show. In this way, you encourage listeners to stay with you for the entire podcast.

Another production element is a *teaser*. This offers just a little information to get listeners excited about a segment that will appear later in the show. That works well on radio, but not as well in a podcast, where the person can just fast-forward to the segment. What *does* work is teasing your next show at the end of the current show.

Another production element is a *promotional spot* or *promo*. This is an element that isn't *within* your show, but instead, takes the form of a short (30-second or so) commercial for your podcast. It contains a clip from the show, or a teaser that will get people excited. Ideally these should be scripted and tightly edited. Promos come in handy when you want to trade spots with another podcast to attract more listeners, or when you want to show up on Podcast Bunker (*http://podcastbunker.com/*).

A Few Lessons Learned

While researching this chapter, I had a chance to talk with a number of podcasters about what works and what doesn't. Here are some fundamental lessons they have learned:

Experiment

> Try out new format elements continuously. Request feedback from your listeners and use this feedback to dictate how you do your show. Everyone we talked to said that with every podcast, they were getting better and better. Strive to do the same.

Keep it light and have fun

> Listeners can tell if you are bored, angry, or uninterested. Listening to your podcast is optional. And normal people don't stick around for something unpleasant. Follow Ben and Jerry's motto: "If it's not fun, why do it?" Listeners look at podcasters as friends, and who wants friends that are angry or unpleasant?

Respect the audience

> If you think your time is valuable, you are not alone. Your listeners think their time is valuable, too. Listening to your podcast needs to be a rewarding experience for them. So, spend the time to design and write a podcast that provides a unique perspective and is worth the audience's time.

Strive for saucer eyes

> Keeping your audience engaged is critical to keeping them coming back. Broadcasters call the effect of total engagement *saucer eyes* because of the look that people give you when they can't wait to hear what's next. If you hear a story that holds your interest, break it down and ask yourself what you liked about the content, and what about the way it was told kept you enthralled.

Keep it simple

> Storytelling through audio works best when you have a linear narrative flow from the beginning to the end, and when you have only a few characters and key themes. Have a few larger points you want to get across

in your podcast story and keep returning to them and reinforcing them. A story should have a beginning, a middle, and an end.

Multiple hosts

Adam Curry makes the single-host format look drop-dead easy. The reality is quite different for the average human who doesn't have years of MTV experience. A multihost format is much easier to pull off because you can think about what to say next as your co-host is talking (of course, be sure to listen actively enough to your co-host so that you can respond appropriately). It's also easier on listeners to hear two people have a conversation than it is to listen to one person rant. So, grab a buddy and podcast together.

Remember, the most unique and important part of your show is *you*. Tell us what *you* care about, give us *your* thoughts in your own voice, and do the show *your* way. If you care about what you're saying, we will, too. Be yourself; that's what will keep it interesting for listeners.

—Stacy Bond

HACK #21   Build a Great News Podcast

Create your own podcast news show to shed light on stories that never would have been covered otherwise.

Podcasting is a new frontier in terms of more than just technology. While several national and international news outlets (e.g., National Public Radio, the BBC, etc.) are starting to make their content available as podcasts, a few independent "cyberjournalists" are among the first using the medium to offer standalone news coverage. This fits the independent spirit of journalism. You can become a member of the fourth estate by creating a news show that presents a unique point of view and explores topics that never would have been covered otherwise.

As a podcaster, you are your own editor, producer, and host. This means you'll have the flexibility to dig up information and uncover stories that interest you, but it also means you'll have to be extra vigilant when it comes to getting the facts right.

Types of News

Several different styles of news shows lend themselves to podcasting. The exception is breaking news, which is a real-time format where the news is reported as it's happening. Podcasting isn't suitable for breaking news because podcasting is a time-delayed medium. But you can still cover the same stories as conventional news; you just need to concentrate on providing exclusive information or unique analysis and perspective.

Here are several styles of news that are ideal for filling a podcast:

Specialty or trade journalism
> Use your area of expertise to cover stories that are unique to your industry or your personal interests. This is the essence of narrowcasting [Hack #20]. This approach almost guarantees you'll have listeners, because you'll be targeting a niche market.

Civic journalism
> Advance the public good by promoting an understanding of community issues. Civic journalism explores the rights of community members, and presents the voices of those who are participants in the issue at hand. Civic journalists must be extra vigilant to avoid advocating or promoting one side over another.

General-interest news
> Go a step further when it comes to the stories you'd find in a daily newspaper. These stories can be about anything of regional or national interest. Your challenge is to advance the story, or to provide a fresh or alternative perspective. Find a way to narrow your coverage by focusing on a geographic area, or on stories about a particular topic.

Investigative reporting
> To tackle this kind of reporting, you'll need to use your skills in research, winning people's trust, and putting puzzles together. This is in-depth reporting on topics not yet noticed by other media. Thorough investigative reporting is incredibly time consuming: you need to be sure your sources are reliable, double-check the information you uncover, take complete notes, and avoid missteps that can get you into legal trouble.

News analysis
> Explore topical issues and provide perspective on the "news of the day." Sunday morning television news programs are examples of news analysis shows. Instead of talking to the "news makers," a group of analysts, reporters, and columnists talk to each other *about* the news. As the host, you should provide facts, ask for analysis, and then play devil's advocate, challenging analysts to defend their opinions with facts and evidence.

If you experiment with different styles of journalism, don't do so within the same podcast. Listeners expect you to be consistent. You compromise your integrity as a reporter or producer when you blend styles, because each kind of journalism serves the public in a different way. Decide which style of journalism you're most interested in, and work within that style for a while to avoid confusing your audience.

Once you decide which style of journalism is right for your podcast, decide on a format. Any of these styles of journalism could easily fit into a news-talk format, and with a bit more work, they could fit into a magazine-style format.

Newsgathering

Newsgathering starts with observation. Look at the world around you, read a wide range of periodicals, and talk to people you encounter every day. Eventually you'll notice something out of the ordinary or you'll find a small piece of information to follow up on. How you follow up on that information is related directly to how accurate your news reporting will be.

Solid journalism is based on thorough research. As you look into a possible story, *keep an open mind.* Many times a reporter begins looking into one story, and finds a different story altogether. Don't get so focused on what you *think* the story is that you close your mind to other directions for the story.

Sources

To build a story, you need facts, and facts come from different types of sources. Each story you report should come from a variety of sources. Never rely on a single source for a story.

Official sources. Civic, municipal, or commercial institutions employ people for the specific purpose of talking to the media. These people will give you "the party line," or the institution's perspective. Always weigh information from official sources critically, because their goal is to protect the institution's reputation.

Institutions such as the military, or police and fire departments, have "public information officers," who are often listed in the front of the phone book. Most government entities, businesses, and other organizations list media contact information on their web sites. When in doubt, call the main phone number and ask to speak with the person who handles media requests.

Ask the organization's press contact to arrange for you to talk to someone within the organization who's close to the issue. This is standard procedure, so most of the time, they'll assume you want an interview with that inside person anyway. Be sure you know in advance the name or title of the person you want to interview, and have a firm grasp on the issue you want to find out about. Once you reach the source, be ready to do more listening than talking. Remember to keep an open mind, while also thinking critically about what you hear.

Don't be surprised if you have to try more than once to get an interview with a key person. Communications people are always busy, especially when their organization is in the news, and naturally, they will serve larger media outlets first. If you are patient, and you develop a relationship with the press contact, you will get an interview eventually.

You might be tempted to forego official sources, but this is not a good idea in most reporting. Government entities, large corporations that benefit from tax breaks, publicly traded companies, and service or utility companies are all accountable to the public. As a journalist, you are representing the public's interest by pursuing an official source.

Unofficial sources. Unofficial sources are integral to good reporting. The ideal unofficial source will have personal experience related to the issue, or a long history of following the issue at hand. Often, you have to think creatively to come up with a good unofficial source. Networking can help: sometimes you can ask a more obvious source if he knows of anyone else you should talk to.

Publicity sources. These sources come to *you* with information. But for that to happen, you'll need to get onto their press lists. Companies, grass-roots organizations, publishers, trade associations—they all send out press releases. You can turn a press release into a story by thinking critically and looking at all sides of the issue. Generally, there's a high noise-to-signal ratio when it comes to publicity material—you'll discard more information than you'll follow up on.

Analysts. An analyst's job is to stay informed and write or think about issues. Universities, think tanks, and other journalism outlets are a few places to find analysts. Be aware that while some analysts attempt to be unbiased, others, such as those with conservative or liberal think tanks, have a very specific perspective to promote.

Other sources. You can get information to help you understand an issue for reporting or discussion on your show in a variety of nonsource ways. Review past news articles, conduct interviews off the record (see the next section for what's involved with that!), research web-based information, and examine public records.

Journalists follow the *two-source rule*. This means you confirm information you get from one reliable source with another reliable source, or you find multiple, independent accounts of the information. Always be sure you can verify the facts you are reporting.

Touchy Situations

Reporting the news is a serious endeavor, and mistakes can have serious ramifications. The following subsections cover some of these common issues and provide advice and resources to keep you out of trouble.

The public's right to know. You can gain access to government documents under the Freedom of Information Act (FOIA), which weighs the public's right to know against an institution's desire for secrecy. The Society of Professional Journalists offers an FOIA toolkit (*http://spj.org/foia.asp*). The Freedom Forum (*http://www.freedomforum.org/*) keeps tabs on FOIA requests in progress.

Anonymity. Never promise anonymity to a source. Even if you are going to grant anonymity, always qualify that by saying you will "do your best." Journalist shield laws vary from state to state. You might be compelled to reveal a source at a later date.

You can allow a source to speak off the record, but you *can't* use that information in your story. *Off-the-record information* is used as background only, to help further your research. A source who won't give her name might not be trustworthy, or might have an axe to grind. You'll have to do your homework, and find someone else willing to go "on record" with the information.

Follow these steps to decide if you can leave a source's name out of a report:

- Is this person's information or perspective *essential* to the story? If the answer to this is yes, ask the following questions:
  — Am I placing the person in economic jeopardy by identifying him? (An example is a salesperson that could be fired from his job for blowing the whistle on price-fixing practices.)
  — Am I placing the person in physical jeopardy by identifying her? (An example is a victim of spousal abuse who's in hiding from her abuser.)

An unpopular view is *not* a reason to grant anonymity to a source. Never do this. If you do, your integrity will be compromised severely.

Slander. Slander [Hack #67] is something a podcaster needs to watch out for. Don't let these potential pitfalls scare you, or keep you from building a great news podcast. The most exciting aspect of journalism is navigating the various truths of all sides in an effort to tell the story accurately. That's why there is so much publicity when a journalist fakes a story or doesn't do the proper research. The challenge of always "getting it right" is part of what makes the calling an honorable one.

Resources

Here are a few resources for podnews journalists:

The American Press Institute (http://mediacenter.org/)
    Offers a cyberjournalist's site, as well as a journalist's toolbox.

The Pew Center for Civic Journalism (http://pewcenter.org/)
    Offers tools and techniques for journalists who seek to advance the public good.

The Poynter Institute (http://poynter.org/)
    Offers blogs, columns, and email lists related to journalism and journalistic ethics. The center also answers ethics questions for journalists on occasion.

Radio College (http://radiocollege.org/)
    Offers books and articles about journalism. The site is geared toward independent radio producers, but almost everything there applies to podcasting as well.

Fairness and Accuracy in Reporting (http://www.fair.org/)
    Keeps the media on its toes. You can learn a lot by reading what they have to say about mainstream and alternative media outlets.

With these resources, your commitment to thorough reporting, and your enthusiasm for your subject matter, you should be well on your way to building your own narrowcast news show.

See Also

- "Adopt a Format for Your Podcast" [Hack #20]
- "Grab Audio Legally" [Hack #67]
- "Use Copyrighted Music Legally" [Hack #68]
- "Assemble a Small Recording Rig" [Hack #69]
- "Podcast at an Event" [Hack #71]

—Stacy Bond

HACK
#22

Build a Great Story Show

Find out how to interview to get a great audible story for your podcast.

Since January 2004, WGBH-FM has broadcast a weekly series of short radio pieces called Morning Stories, which are narratives from ordinary people about some significant moment in their lives.

Our storytellers come from widely different backgrounds (they include a housecleaner from Brazil who is in the U.S. illegally, a postal worker, a tenured university professor, a retired high school teacher, a Cambodian immigrant, a blue-blooded Bostonian, a Jewish grandmother, victims of domestic violence, and seers of past lives). But their stories share a common goal: to give listeners a feeling for what it is like "to be the other guy."

In public radio, stories that make a strong personal connection with a listener are said to have *driveway potential*—i.e., they keep the listener glued to the radio, even after he has parked his car. At their best, these stories also make us want to retell them, in our own words, to someone else. Whatever their style or subject, stories this vivid and infectious tend to have some common elements:

- A dramatic story line that whets our appetite for what happens next
- Specific incidents, behaviors, and details that are easy to visualize (not, for example, "Full of self-reproach, I took it out on others," but "I came home and kicked the dog")
- A narrator with a genuine tone of voice, able to express or suggest the emotions the story inspires

Most of us are not professional raconteurs, able to tell a great personal anecdote to a stranger on demand; so, how do you get people with little or no radio experience to talk on the radio about something significant that happened to them in a way you just can't forget?

Basically, get them to feel that the experience they want to tell us is happening to them there and then. We are all born storytellers, I believe, hardwired to make sense of important experiences by shaping and passing them on in story form. The closer we get to the heat of the moment that our story is about, the more lively, compelling, and relevant the details of our account are likely to be.

At Morning Stories, we have learned that one of the most effective ways of getting vivid, first-person accounts is through an hour-long recorded "talk" with the producer. Starting with the topic or experience he wants to explore, the storyteller is encouraged to re-experience some of the moments and feelings that most moved him in the past and that move him now. In the course of the hour, we can usually get more than enough images and incidents from which a three- to six-minute story can be edited. On occasion, a fully formed story takes shape on its own.

Talk might be the wrong word to use, because in this process, the main job of the producer is to listen—actively—with all his senses and imagination, for what the teller says that strikes a genuine human response and for what the teller has not yet said that might make the story take full shape and come alive.

Experience helps, of course. But there are some skills you can learn that are specific to the art of interviewing for a story.

Listen for Specifics

Is the teller giving you images and details you can respond to, or can flesh out with memories and experiences of your own?

One of the great powers of audio as a medium is that it involves us in finishing the picture with sensory memories and images from our own experiences. This is part of the process that lets us turn someone else's story into our own.

The villain the storyteller brings to life in her own story becomes real to each of us in our own way—based on my own experiences, my villain might have a mustache, a dark felt hat, and a limp, and yours might not. But both are real.

Echo the Teller's Emotions

The teller's tone of voice is a crucial part of his story. It reflects the emotions, spoken and unspoken, that he feels. The more you can encourage him to experience the emotions his story brings up, the more real and richer his tone of voice will be.

Listen to what he is feeling as he speaks, reinforce the feeling if it seems vague, and when in doubt, make sure you've got him right. "You must have been scared…" or "What an embarrassing situation…" or "That makes me feel sad" are examples of responses that let the teller know you're listening to what he is feeling and that you want to know more.

"Listen" to Your Own Reactions

Regardless of whether you actually talk about it out loud, be aware of what in your own life the teller's story is bringing spontaneously to mind. Can you see, hear, smell, or feel what the person is describing in your own mind, out of pieces from your own memories and experiences? Are you interested, vitally, in what happens next because it has touched on something that matters deeply to you? Is what he is saying perhaps leading to someplace you have already been? Is he leaving a clue that might lead you both to where the story wants to go?

We have discovered that most of the stories we end up using on Morning Stories are not the stories the tellers start out thinking they are going to tell. Rather, they are the stories that come to life as part of the process of talking and being listened to.

In a sense, during the hour they spend together, the storyteller and producer are on a journey through only partially mapped territory, with the teller leading and the producer one step behind. The teller's job is to report what he sees and feels, and the producer's job is to follow behind, to keep the storyteller from wandering off track. Trusting the process will get you both where you need to go.

See Also

- "Adopt a Format for Your Podcast" **[Hack #20]**
- "Record Great Interviews" **[Hack #33]**
- "Edit Your Interviews" **[Hack #36]**

—Tony Kahn

HACK #23 Build a Great Personal Show

Create a show that opens a personal window on your life, without exposing yourself to privacy risk.

Blogging opens up a whole new view on people's lives with details that many thought would be too personal to share. Bloggers talk about their fears, their triumphs, their jobs, and their relationships at an intimate level of detail. Some have even been fired for doing so.

Podcasting, or audio blogging, raises the level of personal intimacy to a new high. Now instead of writing your fears, you are saying them to us as if we were sitting next to you. We can hear the emotion in your voice. But instead of whispering it to one person next to you, you are saying it loudly through the headphones of people across the world.

There is no one formula for how to create a great show about your personal life. However, there are some tips and techniques that can alleviate the potential risks and help build an audience through content that is compelling.

The Listener Is Right Next to You

When you are talking into your microphone, imagine that the microphone has disappeared and you are talking to someone right next to you. This is, in fact, what you are doing. You aren't addressing a group of people, you are addressing an individual with headphones on.

As you are talking, that individual is creating an image of what you are saying in her mind. When you talk about your dog, she pictures a dog she knew. This is what broadcasters call the *theatre of the mind* and it's what makes audio such an engaging medium. Unlike TV, audio requires listeners to construct images from what you are saying.

Understanding the theatre of the mind leads me to the first principle of effective storytelling: detail. Detail is critical in telling a story that engages listeners. Describe the colors of the leaves, the scent of the room, and the feel of your dog's fur. Detail helps build a better picture of the scene in your listeners' mind.

The second principle is to tell a story [Hack #22]. Stories have beginning, a middle, and an end. Listeners understand the structure of stories and enjoy having them told. Stories are a series of events that starts with the introduction of a scene and some characters: "I went to the supermarket this afternoon to do some shopping." Following that are some events that affect the characters: "On the way out I clumsily crashed into an old man and our groceries flew everywhere." More events are layered on: "We sorted through the groceries and then we got to talking." Now you've got the listeners hooked because even this inane story can grab attention. The listeners want to know what happens next.

Personal stories can end with either a traditional conclusion (e.g., "And they all lived happily ever after"), or better yet, a personal revelation. Either way, you should always tell listeners how this made you feel. They are tuning into your podcast because they want to know more about you. And how you feel and respond to events is much more revealing than the events themselves.

This simple story I used as an example is constructed with what's called a *linear narrative*. The story starts at the beginning and goes through to the end. This is the simplest type of *narrative arc*. But there are others as well. You can start in the middle with a scene that draws listeners in, and then jump back to the beginning to give a sense of context. Movies such as *Memento* and *Pulp Fiction* are examples of more complex narrative arcs that break the mold of simple linear storytelling.

Format Still Works

Even though your show is an informal chat about your life, you still have a
discernable format [Hack #20]. Even the simplest show has an introduction at
the beginning of the show and credits at the end as its format elements. Here
are some other format elements that you can use in your show to keep people coming back:

Specific observations
> A segment dedicated to a particular type of occurrence. An example is
> the "Stupid Driving Move of the Week" in which you talk about the cra-
> ziest thing you saw on the road this week.

Movie, book, podcast, or music reviews
> A short review segment [Hack #27] where you discuss what you liked about
> a recent movie, book, podcast, or music CD. Tell listeners how it made
> you feel and what gets you excited about it. For example, when I sat
> down to write a review for *Wired* magazine I was given this advice: write
> the review, and then write a cover letter telling us what really gets you
> going about it, and then throw away the review and send us the cover
> letter.

Best spam of the week
> Read the silliest spam message you got this week, and then riff on it.

Games
> Games that you play with your listeners, or games that they send you
> that you play yourself, are very engaging and will keep people coming
> back. As an example, Adam Curry started a game on his Daily Source
> Code (*http://www.curry.com/*), whereby listeners would send him a song
> mash-up that he would try to identify. It was an entertaining way of
> connecting with his audience.

My unique perspective
> Jobs often afford us a unique perspective on life. Tell us a story from
> your job that gives us a new view on the human condition. For exam-
> ple, a blogger who worked as an adult video store clerk got some atten-
> tion when she shared her observations about the store's customers and
> their habits.

This is just a list to get you started. Get creative with your format elements.
People will keep coming back for these daily or weekly segments, even if
they don't like the rest of your show.

Don't Get Fired

Telling personal stories that engage listeners is great, particularly if those stories are honest ones about your life. But is there such a thing as too much information? When it comes to your job, the answer is definitely yes. Here are some basic rules to keep you out of hot water at work:

Let them know you are podcasting
> Tell your boss that you are podcasting. Let her know what it is, where she can find it, and what you intend to cover in your podcasts. Get her feedback about what is in bounds and what is out of bounds. Make sure you know what you can say about the work you perform, the clients, and your co-workers.

Don't use real names
> Don't mention your co-workers, bosses, or subordinates by their real name.

Don't divulge confidential information
> Don't talk about the job that you perform, particularly if there are intellectual property concerns. If this is a corporate podcast you might be obliged to do so, but that's not a personal podcast.

Don't state company policy
> Company policy is for the company's web site, intranet, and internal documentation. It's probably not interesting either. So, why bother?

The best advice is to steer clear of work altogether. Even talking about how much work has affected you or your relationships can cause problems. Nothing demonstrates this more clearly than the story of Heather Armstrong, the woman behind Dooce (*http://www.dooce.com/*), who was fired for talking about her work on her weblog. In fact, the term *dooce* is now used to describe someone who has been fired for weblogging (*http://urbandictionary.com/define.php?term=dooce*).

Don't Expose Too Much

The question of how much to expose on a personal podcast or blog is something you'll have to weigh. It's a matter of personal taste, but in a world where identity theft is increasingly prevalent, you should follow some basic security precautions:

No full names
> Ideally you shouldn't use your full name. And you certainly shouldn't use the full name of your friends or relatives.

No addresses

People don't need to know exactly where you live. The region or the state should be sufficient for listeners to draw a mental picture about you and your surroundings.

No home or work phone numbers

Don't give listeners your home, cell, or work numbers. If you want to establish a comments line, which is a good idea, use a voice-mail-to-email solution [Hack #62].

No schedules

There is no legitimate reason why listeners need to know your exact personal schedule. Let them know you will be at a conference in a particular city if you expressly want to meet up. But knowing when you fly in and out and where you are staying can only help someone who wants to hurt you.

You should also cleanse your site of address information. Keep your resume on your computer and send it out as email to those who need it. Better yet, remove the physical address and phone numbers from the web version.

Great Personal Shows

As part of my research for this hack, I contacted a few personal podcasters. Here are some hints and tips they had to pass along.

BugCast. Joel Benge podcasts his NGR BugCast (*http://nogagreflex.com/*) from his car on the way to and from work. He uses his Treo 650 cell phone [Hack #69] to do the recording. Then he edits in some prerecorded tops, bottoms, bumpers [Hack #63], and any audio feedback [Hack #62] he has gotten from his listeners.

For content, he picks some issues of the day—usually what he hears over the water cooler or while talking to friends. Then he jots them down to take them with him on his ride. He then riffs on the topic for between 7 and 15 minutes.

He is careful to make sure he never talks about his clients or his workplace. And he takes a little care to protect his identity, but since he has been blogging for five years he has already been out there a while.

For feedback, he uses one of the free phone-message-to-email services and directs that to a Gmail account. He integrates that feedback in digital form in subsequent podcasts.

Obi Show. Louis Hill (a.k.a. Obi) does a stream-of-consciousness podcast called the Obi Show (*http://obiwanadobe.com/*). He talks about politics, tech stuff, games, and anything else that sparks his interest. But he keeps away from personal stuff—anything about his family is strictly off limits for privacy reasons.

It's a pretty loose format. There is an introduction, then usually 20 minutes of free-form riffing on the topics that come to mind, then the credits and the outtro. Sometimes he will bring in some Creative Commons music [Hack #68] to spice it up.

He never does any editing on the show. He believes the "less polished style" is part of the show's appeal. It takes him about two hours to go from concept to preparation, and then recording, encoding, and uploading, on a 20-minute show.

He's been doing this since November 2004. This makes him one of the older dogs on the podcasting block. He's gotten some listener feedback and has used it to drive the show now and again, but most of the time he sets his own course for each show based on what "catches his eye."

This and That with Jeff and Pat. Jeff and Pat use their 30-minute conversational to talk about the news of the day, what's going on in the world of technology, and any other topics that interest them. They prepare by writing a list of topics prior to recording. They keep the spontaneity by refusing to look at each other's lists.

There is some structure to the This and That show (*http://thisandthatpodcast.com/*). Jeff, the technician of the two, prerecords some segments [Hack #20]. And they have two format elements that are in every show. "Getting to Know You" is a segment in which they tell listeners new and interesting factoids about themselves. And the locally oriented "Dallas Minute" segment covers regional issues with a narrowcasting focus.

So far their private lives have been largely out of the show. But they understand that over time their audience will want them to get more personal. They have made some efforts to keep their last names a secret, but it's not a huge deal to them.

Jeff records the show, usually in one shot, on a hard-disk recorder that doubles as a music studio setup [Hack #61]. It takes two to three hours of post-production time to put the show together. And they edit out any flubs, dead air, and other problem spots. He uses some compression, a little reverb, and a few sound effects. Most of this comes from his music hobby, which explains the quality of the equipment and the resultant recordings.

They have a growing audience base, and a local magazine called *D* featured a story about them. Most of the traffic comes in from the U.S. and Canada. They are constantly working on the show's format and are integrating the feedback they get from their listeners.

Inside the Magic. Richard Brigante is not a casual Disney fan. He lives a mere 20 minutes from Walt Disney World, visits the parks frequently, and keeps up-to-date with all the Disney news and rumors. A couple of years back he and a friend ran the Real Disney web site (*http://realdisney.com/*) until maintaining it became too much to handle. Now, with podcasting, he has a new medium for bringing Disney news to the faithful with his Inside the Magic show (*http://distantcreations.com/insidethemagic/*).

Each week he summarizes the news and rumors from a number of sources, including Utilidors (*http://utilidors.com/*), WDW Magic (*http://wdwmagic. com/*), and Intercot (*http://intercot.com/*), among others. He summarizes all of these as show notes. Then he records on his Mac using GarageBand [Hack #50] and uses iTunes for the encoding. His experience with TV and movie production has helped a lot.

Part of his mission is to bring the Disney magic to people who aren't at the parks. Another is to provide a unique perspective to his listeners by sharing news and rumors that aren't always along the Disney party line. For example, he supports Roy Disney in his battles against Michael Eisner, and doesn't hesitate in voicing his opinion of The Walt Disney Company in his show and on the web site. The response he has received from the podcast has been roundly positive and it shows the opportunities presented for this type of narrowcasting.

Viking Youth Power Hour. The Viking Youth Power Hour (*http://www. thefeedlot.org/vikingyouth/*), according to Matt, is about getting together with his friends and doing what they do best: "cracking wise about the universe." At the start of each show, they have an invocation whereby they bring some person or thing into the show that sets the theme. Then Brian, Jason, Alex, and Matt (the show's hosts) riff on that theme.

The show is what the four hosts call a "communal experience," whereby they talk over, under, and around current events or whatever else. They are quick-witted enough that the result is hardly "cracking wise," and in fact has become one of the highest ranked news podcasts.

They have a fairly simple setup. They all have Marshall MXL-990 microphones [Hack #13], which are fed into a Behringer UB1202 mixer [Hack #14], which then goes into an M-Audio MobilePre USB interface [Hack #12] and into either a Mac or a Windows box running Audacity [Hack #50]. They all spend about three hours per week on show prep, and the resulting audio is edited and mixed in three to eight hours after recording.

They want their show to compel people to act. As Matt says, "Podcasting isn't about being a passive spectator; it's about designing the world—and the world of information—in the manner that is agreeable and desirable to you."

See Also

- "Adopt a Format for Your Podcast" [Hack #20]
- "Record Great Interviews" [Hack #33]
- "Record Interviews on Skype" [Hack #35]
- "Edit Your Interviews" [Hack #36]
- "Integrate Audio and Email Feedback" [Hack #62]
- "Add Top, Bottom, and Bumper Music" [Hack #63]

HACK #24   Build a Great Political Show

Blogging changed the way American politics work. Podcasting will extend that reach. Find out how to make a political show that is compelling and entertaining.

Congress repealed the Fairness Doctrine in 1986 and the talk-radio world has never been the same. Before this repeal, the FCC had mandated that shows had to give equal time to opposing sides on an issue. After this was lifted, pundits such as Rush Limbaugh fundamentally changed the nature of talk radio by giving it a hard push in one direction, with no representation of the alternative viewpoint. Throughout much of the U.S., this has resulted in a strong shift toward conservatism on the radio dial. And only recently have newcomers arrived to present alternatives.

Podcasting provides another outlet for this strongly charged political talk-show format, and already a number of podcasts have replicated this formula. The first essential element in a political show is timeliness. The show the listener receives today should be relevant to the news of the day. To do that you need to keep up with the news. Here are several resources for current news and political information in the U.S.:

The White House (http://www.whitehouse.gov/), the House of Representatives (http://house.gov), the Senate (http://senate.gov), and the Supreme Court (http://supremecourtus.gov/)

These sites provide access to the press releases and opinions of the three major branches of the federal government: executive, legislative, and judicial.

GPO Access (http://www.gpoaccess.gov/crecord/index.html)

This is the site for the Congressional Record, where you can find quotes from the floor of the House and Senate updated on a daily basis.

C-SPAN Archives (http://www.c-spanstore.org)

This is where you'll find the video archives of the C-SPAN network. Though C-SPAN is mandated by the government, it is actually a privately held company and the material on this site is copyrighted. You must ask permission before using the material in your podcast, unless you believe it falls within the realm of fair use. An email address for asking permission is provided in the Contacts section.

Google News (http://news.google.com/)

Google aggregates articles from all the major news sources into one easy-to-search interface. In addition, you can subscribe to the news service and get updates when articles are posted that match your search criteria. It's an excellent way to have the news come to you.

CNN (http://cnn.com/) and Fox News (http://foxnews.com/)

These news networks provide a news-alert service that will email you when major news events take place.

RSS

If you already have an RSS aggregator, use it to keep up with the news by subscribing to your favorite news sources!

In addition to these sources of timely news and information, you can use archives of historical material in your podcast. The C-SPAN Archives (*http://c-spanstore.org*) has video archives of all the C-SPAN footage you can use with permission (located under the Request Form link on the lefthand side of each page). The History Channel has a series of speeches of historical significance (*http://historychannel.com/speeches/*). This material is copyrighted and you need permission to use it. The Internet Archive (*http://www.archive.org/*) has a wealth of Creative Commons material, including famous speeches that you can use freely in your podcast.

Fair Use of the News

According to section 107 of the U.S. copyright code, you can use material freely if that use is for "comment" or "review." These are deemed "fair use" according to the law. Quoting from articles and news sources for the purpose of giving your own opinion is generally considered fair use. Ideally, you should cite the article, the source, and the author.

Format

Once you have the news of the day at hand, it's time to work on the format. In general, it's easier to get a two-host format [Hack #20] to work for listeners instead of a one-host format. Unless he has credibility, an individual host will sound like he's ranting. With two hosts, listeners get the impression of a dialog, even if both hosts are presenting the same viewpoint.

Political shows run on trust. Listeners trust you with their time because they believe you will present them with news that interests them, and that you will interpret it for them in a way that they can agree with. The two-host format allows each host to interrogate the other by asking the questions they believe the audience would be asking. Every format element you bring into your show should reinforce the message that you are a trustworthy source of valid opinions.

The content trick that works particularly well in political formats is the technique of *large-small-large*. You start with an idea in the large. Then you provide a small anecdote that demonstrates the larger point. You finish by extrapolating the smaller anecdote back to the larger theme for your listeners. Here is an example:

> The economy is really going downhill. I met this guy a couple of days ago who had been out of work for 2 years and he had 20 years of experience in his field. There are people like this all over. I'm telling you, the economy is in a tailspin.

Start with a sweeping statement, followed by a small illustrative example, and then come back to the bigger picture again.

Another way to build trust is to invite the listeners to test you. Tell them to check the stories linked from the blog for themselves. Even if only a few take your invitation to heart, the rest will be impressed by your confidence. This will only serve to increase their trust in you.

Segment ideas. Besides the usual news item with opinion segment and listener mail, you can use a lot of other format elements as periodic features in your political show:

Interviews

Interviews are ideal for political shows. They give politicians an opportunity to reach an audience with their message, and they provide a way for listeners to get the answers they want to questions on the issues of the day. Because podcasts are time shifted, you should use tools such as your blog to get questions from your listeners by posting ahead of time who your guests will be and asking for potential questions.

The objector

Have a weekly segment during which you talk with a person on the other side of the political spectrum. This type of segment can help your credibility greatly, as it shows how you can dispatch your political enemy quickly.

Specific news item

Cover a particular type of news item, or a news item from a particular source, each week. An example is a "Crazy Conservative Nonsense" or "Wacky Views from the Left" segment.

Reviews

This is a weekly segment during which you review [Hack #27] a new book or movie from the political angle.

Call-in games

Pick a listener with whom to play a game in which he can win a prize. You can really get creative with this one in terms of thinking up a game that's entertaining but not so difficult that no one can win it.

Format elements such as these can keep people coming back to your show, even if they don't like what you have to say most of the time.

Using the Blog

Making the best use of the text portion of the blog related to your podcast is critical for the political show format to work. Make sure it has links to the resources you talked about in the show, as well as more material that supports your reasoning.

Always keep the comments open with this type of podcast. Furious debates can increase your listener base and get you coverage in the wider press.

What Doesn't Translate

It's easy to think of podcasting as just another way to transmit the same audio that could go over the radio. But you can't just translate the formats that work so well on radio directly into your own podcast. The first difference between the two media is that podcast listeners aren't skipping through the dial, and generally they listen to the podcast from start to finish. You don't need to bring listeners who "just tuned in" up to speed, so there is no need to repeat yourself the way radio hosts need to. If you listen to a radio show, you'll notice that it covers surprisingly little in an hour—at most, one or two topics. If you want your podcast to run as long as these shows, you will be able to cover a lot more ground because you don't have to repeat yourself.

The second difference is the fact that radio shows, particularly talk-radio call-in shows, are live. The live nature of the show allows the host to cover events in real time. This is not something you will be able to do in your podcast. The call-in nature of the show is also different. A live show has is a continuous conversation in which listeners can hear what's said and then call in to respond. With a podcast, your call-ins will need to be scheduled in advance.

Aspiring Rush Limbaughs or Al Frankens need to understand the differences between radio and podcasting media. You can make podcasts succeed in the political spectrum, but the format of these shows will be dramatically different from their radio cousins.

Great Political and Opinion Podcasts

To get a better feel for what works and what doesn't work for political and opinion show formats, I asked some podcasters to share their insights with me.

Two Rights. Bill Rice and Keith Burwell like to think of their Two Rights podcast (*http://tworights.com/*) as a more thoughtful and balanced approach to conservative political commentary than what listeners can find in traditional media. Disenchanted with the drama and extremism of radio talk shows, they seek to engage listeners in a dialog.

Each show takes about three hours to produce. There is some preparation time up front during which each host writes his own notes and researches his own topics for the show. The two hosts don't combine their notes because they think the interplay will be more genuine and energetic if they approach the show separately. Recording takes about 30 to 45 minutes. Then come editing, encoding, and uploading.

Their hardware setup comprises a Windows PC, a couple of RadioShack microphones [Hack #13], and a Behringer Eurorack UB802 mixer [Hack #14]. They use Audacity [Hack #50] for recording, mix-down, and encoding.

They tried a couple of different formats, even some with music and advertisements, and they let their intuition and their feedback guide them to a three-segment format. In the first segment, they cover the hot news items of the day. In the second segment, they do reviews and commentary. And in the final segment, they focus on "higher-level" ideological or academic political issues.

They prefer two hosts to one because the interaction of the hosts is more appealing for the audience and results in less of a rant-type show. In the long run, they would like to see the show work its way into the legitimate media, and perhaps even use it as a vehicle for their own political aspirations.

The Randi Rhodes Show. On the professional side of the podcast spectrum is the Randi Rhodes Show (*http://therandirhodesshow.com/*). It's both a podcast and a broadcast radio show on the fledgling Air America Radio network (*http://airamericaradio.com/*). Air America started in 2004, but Randi was on the air in Florida well before that. Randi works the liberal side of the American political divide with her one-woman radio show that goes for four hours a day.

Four people are on the show staff: the host (Randi); a producer who writes the comedy bits, produces the web site, and performs administrative tasks; another producer who books guests, screens calls, and does research; and a technical director who runs the board and picks music.

Each member of the show puts about four hours of preparation time in before they go live. They edit bits, write scripts, update their web site, and do research. Their sources include the *New York Times*, the *Washington Post*, the *Los Angeles Times*, the *Guardian*, the BBC, Media Matters, BuzzFlash, and numerous blogs.

The show has mainly a call-in format [Hack #20], with listeners calling in live to talk about the day's events. But they do have some scripted comedic bits. The interaction with the audience is primarily over the phone, but the message board and blog play a big role in communicating with the audience and in building the trust that's so critical in a single-host format.

John Edwards' podcast. John Edwards, the Democratic candidate for vice president in 2004, started his own podcast in 2005. His personal podcast (*http://johnedwards.com/*) is a combination of policy statements, personal perspectives about his life, his family, and his children, and their responses to the email questions they get.

The technology of the podcast is as homespun as it sounds. They have a microphone on their kitchen table that John and Elizabeth use in combination with a Macintosh running GarageBand [Hack #50]. They use GarageBand to create license-free, podcast-safe sound loops [Hack #63] to run under segments of the podcast. And they use iTunes to do the encoding to MP3.

What excites John about podcasting is how he can talk directly with what he considers a grass-roots political community through the podcasting medium. "Podcasting is an important medium because it lets me have a personal conversation with the grass roots about a variety of issues," John says. "The truth is, we need to strengthen the grass roots' voice in every way possible. Podcasting helps us do that."

See Also

- "Adopt a Format for Your Podcast" [Hack #20]
- "Record Great Interviews" [Hack #33]
- "Edit Your Interviews" [Hack #36]
- "Podcast at an Event" [Hack #71]

HACK #25   Make a Mystery Science Theater Podcast
Create podcasts that act as an alternate soundtrack to some of today's worst movies.

> He did a good job cleaning up the place. / But his bosses didn't like him, so they shot him into space. / Now they send him cheesy movies. The worst they can find. / He has to sit and watch them all while they monitor his mind. / Now keep in mind Joel can't control where the movies begin or end. / Because he used those special parts to make his robot friends.
>
> —"Mystery Science Theater 3000" theme song

"Mystery Science Theater 3000," or MST3K to its fans, was a show running from the 1980s through the 1990s that started on public access television and then went national with Comedy Central and, later, the Sci-Fi Channel.

The idea was simple: talk extremely clever and funny trash about very bad movies for two hours. The central portion of each show had the three main characters—a human (Joel or Mike) and two robots (Tom Servo and Crow T. Robot)—silhouetted against a screen that showed the movie. You could hear the movie's audio track, with the characters' snide comments on top of it.

The show was a cult hit, and a feature film was produced. But today it's rarely shown in reruns, even though fans, known as *mysties* (subcategorized into Joel or Mike fans), are hardcore in their love of the show. Check out the show for yourself at its official site, *http://mst3k.com/*.

Podcasts present a new opportunity to create alternate commentary and soundtracks for movies. To test this idea I got together with two friends to provide extra commentary to George Lucas's *Star Wars Episode II: Attack of the Clones*. We learned several things in the process:

More is merrier
> Several hours of funny commentary is a lot for a single individual to fill. Having more people in the mix makes it easier to relax and find the right time to jump in with your commentary. It also opens up opportunities to riff on what the other co-hosts are saying.

Preparation is key
> Watch the movie at least twice. Use the first time to take some notes and to get some ideas. Use the second time for the actual taping. Use sources such as the Internet Movie Database (*http://imdb.com/*) to research the actors and their previous films. The database also has comments, quotes, and goofs from the movie. Films that were more popular will have better information.

Timing is critical
> For the audience to follow along with you they have to be in sync with the commentary. Get your recording setup ready, and then rewind the film to the beginning of Chapter 1 and hit Pause. The readout should read 00:00:00. When you start recording, say, "Press Play on my mark in 3, 2, 1, mark," or something like that. Then press Play on your mark and have at it.

Running gags
> While you are doing your homework on the movie, find some running gag for a couple of the characters. With the "Episode II" edition of the show, we used Queen Amidala's hair and outfits, which changed from scene to scene, often at inappropriate times. It's fun for the audience, and it's easy to extend over the film.

Pick the right movie
> Not all films are good comedic material. Make it easy for yourself. Pick something that's pretty bad to start with: old Schwarzenegger films, mid-80s teen films, B movie sci-fi flicks, or *Catwoman*. These films have enough bad acting, outrageous accents, and horrible effects to keep you occupied for the whole movie.

Gear up the audience

It's worth giving your listeners a few ideas about how they should listen to the show. I recommend using open-air headphones such as the Sennheiser HD570. Another option is to use just one side of the headphones because the commentary is mono, and leave the other side off so that you can hear the movie.

These should get you on your way to the right content. But what about the sound setup?

The Sound Setup

For the first show, we set up everything in my living room. We used two different studio microphones: a Neumann U 87 and a Shure KSM27 [Hack #13]. These went into the left and right channels of a Marantz 660 solid state recorder [Hack #69]. We monitored the recording levels by watching the indicators on the front of the unit.

We set the Neumann U 87 in omnidirectional mode so that we would sound uniformly close to the microphone. The Shure KSM27 is a cardioid microphone that has no setting. The output of both microphones was roughly similar, but we chose to go with the Neumann in the end.

We positioned the microphones above the coffee table in front of the couch. They were dead center between the three of us and about 4 feet away.

To hear the movie, we connected the RCA output of the DVD player into a headphone amplifier that fed three different headsets and allowed us to tweak the levels individually. You can just as easily use a cheap headphone splitter from RadioShack.

Ensuring that the movie sound doesn't bleed into the recording is critical, for two reasons. The first concerns legal issues (we discuss this in the next section). The second concerns the lack of perfect synchronization. Watching video where the sound is slightly out of sync is an extremely frustrating experience. If you have some or all of the audio track in your recording and the video is more than 100 milliseconds off, your audience won't be able to watch the movie and listen to your audio for very long. Let your listeners use open-air headphones to listen to your sound and the movie simultaneously.

Legal Issues

As we noted, you should be aware of some legal issues if you incorporate parts of a movie, such as the soundtrack, in your recording. You can avoid legal issues by making sure you have perfect isolation so that the audio from the copyrighted work doesn't bleed into the recording.

Even so, is this legal? Movies are copyrighted, and copyright law provides for what's known as fair use. There are a number of fair use scenarios, a few of which apply to this activity. The first two are commentary and criticism. If you are providing commentary on or critiquing a film, that's usually fair use according to section 107 of the U.S. copyright code. It helps that the film industry calls alternate soundtracks *commentaries*.

Two other fair use options might also apply. The first is parody, where you are mocking the film. The other is for teaching, if you are using your commentary as a teaching tool.

Keep in mind that since this is a new activity, it hasn't been tested in court. And a company with a registered trademark can sue you for damages if it feels your work has hurt the film's marketability and is infringing on its copyright. If you have reservations about the legality of this activity, but you still want to pursue it, get the advice of a copyright attorney and request permission from the copyright owner to use the film.

It certainly can't hurt that listening to your podcast legally requires that individuals either rent or buy the DVD, or record the film on their DVR or VHS unit.

More Ideas

Providing comedic commentary is just one possibility for this new medium:

Scene-by-scene critique
> Break down the classics such as *Casablanca*, *Gone With the Wind*, and *The Godfather* with a scene-by-scene critique.

A whole new audio track
> Create a whole new audio track for the film. I saw this done live in Australia with a comic troupe spoofing on a cheap Greek Hercules movie. I laughed so hard I was in pain. Because it was originally in Greek, the lack of synchronization with the characters' lips made it even funnier.

Little-known facts
> Use the material in the Internet Movie Database (*http://imdb.com/*) and other movie-specific fan sources to create an informational soundtrack that augments the viewing experience.

Try something other than movies
> Spoof your favorite shows, such as *Star Trek*, *Scooby-Doo*, or *Teletubbies*. All of these are available on home video. Or folks can tune their TiVos in to the show and find the episode for which you are providing a new audio track.

Who knows; maybe you can make the next MST3K. There are certainly a lot of recent bad movies worth spoofing. And since you aren't including the copyrighted material in your podcast, the gloves are off.

If you do create an MST3K soundtrack for a film, be sure to register it with MST3K (*http://mst3k.com/*). They have an archive of fan productions, both live and filmed.

How MST3K Was Produced

As part of my research for this hack, I had a chance to talk with Mary Jo Pehl, who played Pearl Forrester and was a writer for the show. Each show was produced in seven to nine days. The first three days were spent watching and rewatching the movie, brainstorming ideas and lines, and coming up with ideas for dialog for the host segments. The host segments were the portions in which Mike or Joel and the robots appeared in the ship and not in front of the screen.

On the fourth and fifth days, they edited the dialog they came up with for the characters, and assigned the lines. The lines were specified with a time code that indicated where they should come in.

Day six was a rehearsal day. On day seven, they shot the host scenes; on day eight, they shot the movie sequence. About 98% of the lines you heard were directly from the script. While the first shows on cable access were unscripted, later shows had between five and eight writers. Each writer was free to concentrate on portions of the film they thought would yield the best comic gold. The last day was for editing and cleanup.

Picking the right movie was a matter of finding one that had enough dialog to spoof and wasn't so poorly made that it didn't work as a film. In all, the movie would be viewed four to five times before it would end up as a produced show.

Mary Jo's advice to all of us potential Joels and Mikes: "Have fun with it; don't be afraid to use all your knowledge base, no matter how trivial or inconsequential it might seem. Look, a bunch of complete nerds made a good, fun living doing just that on MST3K."

> If you're wondering how he eats and breathes, and other science facts, / then repeat to yourself *"it's just a show"* as you breathe and just relax. / For Mystery Science Theater 3000.
>
> —"Mystery Science Theater 3000" theme song

See Also

- "Adopt a Format for Your Podcast" [Hack #20]
- "Produce Great Audio Theatre" [Hack #32]

—*James Polanco and Jack Herrington*

HACK #26 Build a Great Music Podcast

Create a music show that exposes your listeners' minds to new music.

So, you've decided that you want to create a music-based podcast. Excellent. Music is the common denominator that joins all of us, and it's a way of sharing memories or introducing us to new artists, songs, and even styles. In this hack, I'll take you through the process of developing a great music-based podcast, from determining the type of show you'll produce, to getting your music together, and finally, to producing your show.

Choose a Show Theme

The first step is to determine what kind of music show you want to produce. Chances are you already have an idea for this, but if you don't, take a moment to think about whom your audience will be. Adults? Kids? Everybody? Also, think about the theme of your show. My show, Coverville (*http://coverville. com/*), features the best in musical cover versions. Your show could showcase a specific style of music, such as Latin music or heavy metal. It could be a regional show that features artists from a specific geographic area. Or you could develop a show that focuses on a certain time period, such as the 60s or the 70s.

> The show Radio Clash (*http://www.mutantpop.net/radioclash/*), out of London, focuses on *mash-ups* [Hack #66], which is when DJs extract the vocals from one song and place them over another song that has had its vocals stripped.

Once you've determined your show's theme, you need to come up with an estimated length. One of the benefits of podcasting is that you're not limited to a specific time slot. Your show doesn't always have to be 30 minutes long, for example. But you want to give your listeners an idea of what to expect. The average pop song is 3 minutes and 20 seconds long. A show that includes six average songs, including talking and an intro, will take about 30 minutes. Keep in mind that more-successful podcasts are less than an hour in length. This is, in part, because of the trade-off between file size and show length. A longer show can take more time to download, which can become a deterrent for listeners.

Licensing: Not a Minor Detail

A major factor that you shouldn't overlook is licensing [Hack #68]. This is a huge topic among music-based podcasters right now. A copyrighted piece of music has two licenses: a *composition license* and a *mechanical license*. A composition license is the license that the musical piece's writer or composer holds. In the U.S., three agencies hold these licenses: ASCAP (*http://www.ascap.com/*), BMI (*http://bmi.com/*), and SESAC (*http://sesac.com/*). A copyrighted piece of music will be registered with one of these three agencies, which will distribute royalties to the writer of the piece of music whenever it is performed. A mechanical license is based on that performance of the song. The mechanical license for a song is owned by any combination of the artist, the recording company, and the Recording Industry Association of America (RIAA; *http://riaa.com/*). To play a piece of music in your podcast, you must meet the requirements for both the composition license and the mechanical license.

Usually you can acquire the composition license by paying royalties to ASCAP, BMI, or SESAC. Look in the liner notes of the CDs containing the music you'll be playing to see which of those three agencies the music is licensed to. If you won't be playing any music licensed to SESAC, for example, you won't need to pay them royalties. As of this writing, the annual royalty costs for each of these three agencies are roughly $288 for ASCAP, $275 for BMI, and $170 for SESAC. These figures are based on the assumption that you are making less that $12,000 per year on your podcast. For specifics, please consult the web sites of each agency.

Acquiring the mechanical license is a bit more difficult, as no license models are available through the RIAA or the Harry Fox Agency (*http://harryfox.com/*) that address the technical issues associated with podcasting. Both of these hold the mechanical licensing keys to a large number of popular artists. In these cases, your best bet is to get permission from either the artist that performed the song, or the recording company that the song is licensed to. Again, you can find this information in the CD liner notes, or on the artist's web site. With an eloquent letter of introduction, in many cases the artist or recording company will be happy to grant permission to play their music in your podcast.

Here is the letter I use:

My name is Brian Ibbott, and I host and produce an Internet radio program called Coverville that showcases the best in cover versions of songs. I have about 11,000 subscribers, and I've been featured recently in *BusinessWeek*, the *New York Times*, *USA Today*, and *Time* magazine. I invite you to listen to my archives at *www.coverville.com*.

I'm writing because I was hoping to be able to acquire permission to play your music on my show. Of course, I would also include links to your site as well as to locations where your music can be purchased.

I appreciate your time! I look forward to hearing from you.

Thanks,

Brian Ibbott

coverville@gmail.com

www.coverville.com

Celebrating the best in cover songs since…well…last year.

A simple way of avoiding the licensing problem altogether is to focus on independent artists. An immeasurable amount of excellent music is available in all styles, released by independent artists. Several good resources for independent music are available on the Web, including GarageBand (*http://www.garageband.com/*). Keep in mind that it's still essential to ask for permission to play independent artists' music in your podcast, and permission will likely be granted more freely.

> The Insomnia Radio podcast features independent artists only—and those who have given their permission to Jason, the host, for inclusion in his podcast. This subverts the licensing issues completely, with no concerns for the RIAA.

Assemble the Pieces

Once you've determined your show's style and content, you can begin the fun process of gathering your music. For the most part, it's a good idea to be consistent with the file format of the tracks you'll be playing. For compatibility across the board, I recommend that you keep your music in MP3 format, encoded at a bit rate that balances good quality with small file size: 128 kbps to 192 kbps. Gather your music in a folder or playlist in your music program where you can see track length and artist information. Group your songs into playlists based on individual shows, so you can see which songs sound good together, and so you can make sure the total time will be close to the show length you decided on earlier. Having a few shows' worth of music prepared ahead of time will allow you to ensure that you have plenty of content for future shows, and will shorten the amount of time it takes to cement your podcast's style or "feel."

For consistency, you might want to have a theme song at the beginning of your show. Many podcasters begin their shows with a piece of music [Hack #63], or music with spoken information about what their show is about. Whether you are planning on using a copyrighted piece of music or something you've composed yourself, you'll want to make a special version of the track that automatically fades out at the point at which you'll start talking in your show. On the Mac, I use Soundstudio [Hack #50] to open the track, go about 30 seconds in (when the first verse or chorus has ended), and fade the track out to about 10% of its original volume. This way, I don't have to quiet the track manually as I'm recording the show.

Speak Up!

And now we move on to your voice. Narrate your show. Here's your chance to release your inner DJ! A music podcast without any sort of dialog about the music or the artists you're playing is unfair to your listeners and to the performers whose music you're playing. Your listeners might want to know why you picked the track you're playing, or if it's not a well-known song, the artist's name and where they can find the song. If you've gone through the trouble to get permission from an artist to play her song in your podcast, the least you can do is give her credit, and let people know where they can find out more about that artist! Not to mention the fact that ASCAP and BMI require that you *don't* provide a list of the songs in your podcast on your web site. So, the only way for your listeners to know what they're hearing is for you to tell them.

You'll need some software to amplify your voice and provide other necessary (and unnecessary) effects. On the Macintosh I recommend Audio Hijack Pro [Hack #50] (*http://rogueamoeba.com/audiohijackpro/*), as it's a Swiss army knife of audio tools and plug-ins. Experiment with different effects to see how your voice sounds, but at a minimum, consider using a compressor filter to bring your highs down and your lows up. As you talk, you might get really excited and start talking louder, forcing your listeners to adjust their volume knobs on the fly. Or you might start talking quietly at points, again forcing your listeners to compensate. With a compressor [Hack #56], consistency in volume is mostly taken care of for you.

Plug a pair of headphones into your computer so that you can hear your voice as you speak. This is a great tool to use when you're experimenting with different filters and plug-ins, since you can hear the results immediately. You'll use the headphones when you're recording the show, so you can monitor the sounds that your listeners will hear.

Dan Klass demonstrates a very clear microphone and effect setup for his podcast, Old Wave Radio (*http://new80s.blogspot.com/*), which features new artists performing tracks that easily could have come from the New Wave sound of the 1980s.

Know What You're Playing

Ready to record your first podcast? Keep in mind that you won't be playing your music directly from your playlist organizer, for two good reasons. First, it is difficult to end the playing of one track before the playing of the following track begins. It can be downright impossible if you have built-in segueing turned on in your playlist organizer, as the second track might start playing as early as 10 seconds into the end of the previous track. The second, and more important reason, is to allow you to set the volume of each track individually. All CDs are not recorded at the same volume level, and you don't want to irritate your listeners by playing two consecutive tracks in your podcast that force them to reach for the volume knob on their MP3 player while they're listening! I can't stress this point enough: get your track volume levels as close as you can to each other.

In your playlist, locate the individual song file for each track. In Apple's iTunes, you can Ctrl-click the track and choose "Show song file" from the pull-down menu that is displayed. The song's file is shown in its location on your hard drive. Then, open the file in an individual track player. I recommend using QuickTime, which is available for both Macintosh and Windows. QuickTime allows you to set each track's volume, as well as identify sections of the track to play, if there is additional audio in the beginning or end of the track that you don't want to include. I organize all the Quick-Time windows along the right side of my screen (as seen in Figure 4-2), in the order that I'll play them. Make sure also to open a QuickTime window containing your theme song, as well as anything that you'll play at the end of your show.

Do your research! Get information about the tracks you'll be playing, from the artist and title of the song to additional information that your listeners might find useful: the album that the track is available on, where the band is from, maybe some trivia about a member of the band, and a more popular band that she came from. Anything you find interesting about the track, your listeners might find interesting as well. A good source for music and artist information is All Music (*http://www.allmusic.com/*). You'll find a very detailed background for many bands, with discography and Billboard charting information.

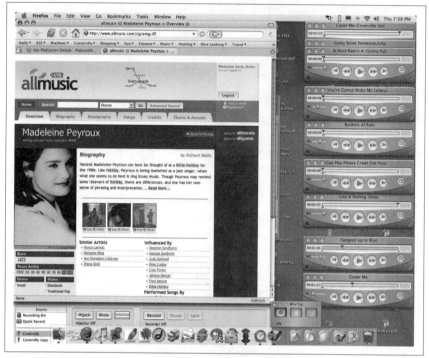

Figure 4-2. Brian Ibbot's desktop during the recording of Coverville

Also, listen to the beginning and end of each track. Roughly figure out how much time passes in the song before the singer starts singing, and whether the song has an abrupt ending—with or without singing—or a fade out. You'll use this information to keep from talking over the singing, or from starting a new track before the singing has stopped on the old one. As you do more and more of these, you'll get better at anticipating how much you can say before the singer starts. Also, if the song fades out with a repeating chorus, you can start your *back-announcing* (telling people about the song you just played), after the first fully repeated chorus or when the track fades out to about 50% of its normal volume.

This is a good opportunity to make sure the tracks you'll be playing sequentially sound good together. Playing two acoustic tracks, or two concert tracks together, eliminates the abrupt sound-quality changes that occur if you follow either with a studio track, for example. Try to match the styles and tempos of the songs you put together. For example, don't follow a trash-metal track with a sappy 70s love ballad. Also, and here's a trick that's not well known, try to pair "major chord" and "minor chord" songs together. For those of you who are not familiar with the *major* and *minor* terms, certain musical chords evoke a happy sound (major), and certain musical chords evoke a sad sound (minor). Try to keep the majors and minors together. This keeps the "mood" consistent between tracks.

Choosing the Recording Software

Several pieces of software are available for recording your show. I use and recommend WireTap [Hack #50] (*http://ambrosiasw.com/utilities/wiretap/*). Basically, WireTap has one job: to record all the sounds that come out of your computer. If you've set your "voice" program to *play through* (in other words, as you talk into your microphone, you can hear your voice through your headphones), WireTap will be able to record your voice as well as the music.

Another popular option is to combine the free Audacity program (*http:// audacity.sourceforge.net/*) with an audio direction tool called Soundflower (*http://www.cycling74.com/products/soundflower.html*). On its own, Audacity will record a single audio channel, whether it's your music or your voice—so on its own, it's not a great recommendation for podcasters. Soundflower is a tool that lets you direct audio from one application to another. So, you can use Soundflower to route the music from QuickTime and your voice from Audio Hijack Pro to Audacity. More tools are being introduced every day, so check podcasting forums such as Podcast Alley and the Yahoo! Podcasters Group to learn about new tools that might be even easier to use than the ones I describe here.

Recording Your First Podcast

Finally, you're ready to record your show. There are two steps:

1. Press Record.
2. Have fun.

Part of the charm of podcasting is its informality. Address your listeners as you would speak to your friends, and don't get too hung up in preventing "ums" and "ers." A lot of tools will allow you to edit your podcast after you've recorded it, so if it really worries you, or if you make a major mistake, you can go back and edit it later.

For my show, I start recording, and I give a little introduction about what the listener can expect on the show. I do this for two reasons. One is that I use this as a simple tag to get my listeners excited about what's coming up. I also do it to provide a favor to those listening on an iPod Shuffle or other flash-based MP3 player without a display. Without a display, listeners on these devices will not know if the track they're listening to is one they've heard until they reach the introduction.

After my introduction, I play the intro music track, and right before the song starts to fade, I start talking. I introduce myself, give a really quick description of the show (for new listeners), talk about my sponsor, and introduce the first song. As I'm introducing the song, I start playing the song as a music bed (if there is an intro), and I stop talking before the singer begins. Then, I turn off my mic and fade out the introduction music if it's still playing.

Promoting Your Podcast

Get a few shows under your belt before you do too much self-promotion. Many shows don't get their rhythm until the third or fourth show, and you might find that tweaking your show's theme appeals to you. Don't lose heart if your show doesn't sound like you expected. As you get your theme and your technical issues cemented, your show will sound more like the show you intended to produce. Once you've gotten the hang of doing your show, after the second or third podcast, start mentioning it on relevant forums [Hack #48] and submitting announcements to other podcasts that play recorded announcement files [Hack #46]. Word will spread about your show, and your audience will find you. Most importantly, make sure you're having fun producing your podcast. It absolutely comes through in the sound of your show if you enjoy doing what you're doing.

Great Music Podcasts

I had the opportunity to talk with a few music podcasters about what makes their podcasts great.

Caribbean Free Radio. Georgia Popplewell uses her skills as a video producer and music magazine editor to create her fantastic Caribbean Free Radio (*http://caribbeanfreeradio.com/*). If you haven't listened to it, give it a try. It can turn your cold winter train ride into work into a breezy walk on a sunny island beach in her home in the Antilles.

She structures the show as a set of three or four songs, sourced primarily from local artists she knows. The order of the songs is random, but the final track is usually down-tempo. In between the songs she adds some talking segments that are either interviews or her own commentary. The shows run around 20 minutes. Those 20 minutes take about two to three hours to produce, which includes scripting, recording, editing, a mix-down, and encoding.

She scripts her own talking segments first, but then ad-libs during recording. She's still not happy with her how her voice sounds and feels that sometimes she talks too quickly.

She produces the podcast using video tools. She records at home with a camcorder with XLR inputs and an Electro-Voice RE50 [Hack #13]. After that she uses a combination of Final Cut Pro, QuickTime Pro, and Soundtrack [Hack #50] on a Macintosh to record the show and put it together.

She's shocked at how the show has taken off. She originally intended it to be a small show for promoting the new music of the Antilles. But great music has built her a large following. Recently she has been trading links with other shows, as well as experimenting with new format ideas such as sound-seeing tours [Hack #72] and story segments [Hack #22] such as those in Tony Kahn's Morning Stories.

Lime. Lime (*http://lime-radio.com/*) is hard to describe. In its first season it was a set of eight podcasts that had a mix of music with a few vocal stingers between songs. Its second season was more scripted, with characters and plot arcs, but still with a lot of great music. Its third season, which is in production now, relies more on the spoken segments, while still having the music mix. Mike Jewell's ever-changing format seems to be working, as Lime is one of today's most popular music podcasts.

The production of a season starts by scripting out the plot arcs. Each show is written, then vocal actors are brought in to record the spoken segments. Those are mixed with a variety of different songs to create the finished episodes. Mike uses two Rode NT5 microphones [Hack #13] and an M-Audio FireWire 410 [Hack #12] connected to his Macintosh to do the recordings. The mix-down is in Logic Pro. He also uses Audio Hijack Pro [Hack #50] for sampling, and he uses speech synthesis software [Hack #65].

He organizes the music to fit the scene he wants to create. Most of the songs he picks are comparatively gentle because he expects the show to be "background music." He recommends leading into a slow track with something that ends with an echo or a slow-down. For something more assertive he recommends leading in with a song that comes to a sudden finish or sting. Most of all, he likes to keep listeners guessing and never gives them what he thinks they expect.

See Also

- "Adopt a Format for Your Podcast" [Hack #20]
- "Make a Mash-Up" [Hack #66]
- "Grab Audio Legally" [Hack #67]
- "Use Copyrighted Music Legally" [Hack #68]

—Brian Ibbot

Build a Great Review Podcast

Create a review show that tells your listeners about the best movies, music, and books, with insight they can find nowhere else.

Podcasting is perfectly suited for the review format, and such shows became popular quickly. Putting together a review show is straightforward, assuming you do some homework first. When podcasting first got started, I jumped in with the first movie review, commentary, and discussion show, called Reel Reviews—Films Worth Watching (*http://reelreviewsradio.com/*). While my goal was to talk about great films readily available on DVD, the lessons I learned in producing the show hold true for any review format show.

Using my experience, let's examine how to produce a great review show.

Talk About What You Know and Enjoy

Roger Ebert is such a mainstay among movie reviewers because you can tell he has a passion for film, and he enjoys talking about it, studying it, and critiquing it. As is often the case, subject matter for which the presenter has enthusiasm can often lead to compelling listening. When setting up a review show, make sure it is a topic about which you can speak with some authority and enthusiasm.

Creating a podcast involves a commitment to your listeners; they are counting on the fact that you will continue to produce shows. If your subject matter is not something that you get excited about, rethink whether you should proceed. In my case, I have been talking about film for years to anyone who was interested. As such, making the transition to a podcast just involved letting a few thousand more people in on the conversation.

Know Your Audience

It is imperative that you clearly define who your audience is. Think about whom you want to attract as listeners and how best to provide the content they will find useful. These decisions will have an impact on the length of your show, what (if any) accompanying material you put with your reviews, and ultimately how you will market the show. This is some of the most critical planning you will do when creating your show. I cannot stress its importance enough.

Have Clear Points to Convey

The secret of a great review show is in the preparation. Think through the major themes and points you want to identify and highlight for your listeners. Is there a theme you can use as a bridge to tie together the individual points? When talking about film, art, or music, this is often an effective method.

Unlike other types of podcasts, review shows have some unique requirements. A review show's goal is to convey facts and impressions about the review subject. This is where it can get challenging for the podcaster. To ensure that you get all the important points covered, you need to make some choices.

The most important choice you must make is how you will prepare. Let me share what has worked for me. When I first started podcasting, I would outline five or six bullet points I wanted to make sure I covered, and then simply started recording. This proved to be a very natural style for me; I was comfortable and reasonably satisfied with the results. As I continued to produce additional shows, I felt it was important to include more and more detail. I thought this would add to my movie commentary. This culminated in one particular recording that I must have started over 15 times, as I kept getting lost in my rather detailed outline.

That was the breaking point. I tore up the outline, jotted down the five or six bullet points, and ended up recording it with no further hassle. That day, I learned that I am much more comfortable just speaking. If I can create a podcast in which I "talk" to my listeners, I feel that I produce a much more compelling and interesting show. Invariably by using this technique, I always forget to mention something, but my listeners don't know that, and I have yet to get a complaint about something I didn't say. While as a podcaster you might be frustrated that you forgot something, the beauty of audio is that it is transitory, and people experience it in a linear fashion. It allows for much more leeway than the written word, where someone can search back and forth.

Of course, there is another option: the scripted show. Some people have been successful with this approach, so it is important to consider. If you are more comfortable being completely prepared, you can script out your entire show. This will ensure that you don't miss any points. It will also dramatically increase the amount of time required to prepare your show.

If you choose to script your show, it is all the more important to concentrate on your delivery. People are generally turned off if you sound like you are reading. Frankly, if you are reading, you should just post the text. This is why it is important to interject your personality into your presentation. Make sure you accentuate the high points and drive home your conclusions regarding the material you are reviewing.

Conclusion

Not everyone will agree with you, but nothing is worse than a reviewer with no conviction in her opinion. Frankly, some controversy regarding your opinion will foster debate and added attention to your podcast. Right or wrong, you will earn listeners' respect by being genuine and truthful in your opinion.

Podcasting is an extremely rewarding experience. When running a review show, it is an exciting experience to find out that people have made a decision based on your reviews and opinions. In my case, I get email everyday from people who have rented or purchased the films I discuss in my podcast. For me, that was the whole goal: to discuss and encourage people to see great films.

Great Review Podcasts

Here is how some other review podcasters have gone about making their podcasts stand out.

(Cool) Shite on the Tube.   Mix lots of beer, a few movies, and three Australians, shake well, and you get the (Cool) Shite on the Tube podcast (*http://coolshite.net/*). Bruce Moyle, Chris Rattray, RDon, and Q-Dog take their knowledge of movies and their ability to sit around and trash films to its logical conclusion as a review show. Their podcast is a vivid illustration of the value of the multihost format, particularly in review shows. The interplay between the hosts gives the podcast its infectious appeal while making it much easier to produce. The fun they have as a group talking about the movies comes through in the show.

The raw and uncut feel comes from the minimal editing and preparation. They watch the movie on Tuesday. Then Bruce cuts a few snippets of audio out of the movie. On Sunday they get together to have a few beers and record the show. They use GarageBand, Audio Hijack Pro [Hack #50], a cheap amplifier, and a Styrofoam cup to hold the microphone.

They've taken most of the feedback they received about the show to heart, and are working on making some improvements.

Overall, the difficulties in producing their show are minor: getting together on time can be tough, and remembering to turn on the microphone is critical. Their advice for review podcasters is to drink, and redo everything a couple of times the first time out.

Cinecast. Adam Kempenaar and Sam Hallgren of the Cinecast movie review podcast (*http://cinecastshow.com/*) take the buddy film approach to movie reviews. They use the two-person format to feed off of each other's insight into each film. They don't script their show too much. They prefer instead to use the conversational tone of the podcast medium to engage themselves and their listeners in a dialog about the film. Sometimes the reviews run in their ideal range of 15 to 20 minutes, but other times they get so caught up in the conversation that time flies and the podcast ends up being much longer.

Adam has been reviewing movies for five years for the *Daily Iowan*. He was self-conscious at first and would validate his reviews against what other critics were saying. But now he has the confidence to avoid any reviews before he has seen the movie and has settled on his own opinion.

Their advice for potential movie reviewers is to *take it seriously*. You can be funny, but you should keep it professional. Create a format and write some notes so that it feels like a well-produced show. But more importantly, use your unique perspective to provoke listeners to think about the film's meaning and to get at what the film was trying to say. Have confidence in your own critique and express it with conviction.

Various and Sundry DVD podcast. The Various and Sundry DVD podcast (*http://variousandsundry.com/*) grew out of Augie De Blieck Jr.'s text blog. Each week he would take the listings for the DVDs to be released on Tuesday, and copy and paste the ones that interested him it onto his blog with some of his own comments. It became a huge hit because it gave his listeners a shopping guide to take with them on their Tuesday DVD purchasing trips. It was an easy next logical step to turn his DVD blog into a DVD podcast.

The format is pretty straightforward. He uses TextEdit to fill his show notes with the DVD release list. Then he goes to the Internet Movie Database (*http://imdb.com/*) to do some research on the films that interest him or his listeners. He is thinking about adding some show format elements, but it's a commitment of time that he doesn't have.

On the recording side he keeps it simple. He uses Audacity [Hack #50] and a Sony ECM-MS907 [Hack #13] that hooks into his G5 Power Mac. He uses a stand to keep the microphone steady, and a windscreen to keep the plosives down. He records in one shot, and if he messes up, he just stops, goes back to the beginning of the sentence, and starts again. Then he edits it all down in post-production. He can take up to an hour to get a 5- to 10-minute show to sound right. Once he's finished editing, he uses the MP3 export in Audacity to build the podcast file, and edits the ID3 tags in iTunes. Then he uploads the file to the server with a hand-coded RSS 2.0 [Hack #37] file.

Through his podcast, he has created a bidirectional conversation with his audience. He has heard from his listeners that his recommendations have encouraged them to try out DVDs they wouldn't have otherwise. And his listeners have broadened his viewing taste as well.

For the comic-book fans out there, he also has a comics podcast called the Pipeline Comic Book Podcast (*http://comicbookresources.com/rss/*) that does for comics what his first podcast did for DVDs.

His advice to would-be DVD reviewers is to hold your ground on your opinions, even in the light of negative feedback. And keep your show on a schedule that people can follow predictably, to build your audience.

TheForce.Net. TheForce.Net (*http://theforce.net/*) covers everything in the Star Wars universe, including the movies, the games, the books, the action figures, and more. Erik Blythe, having done his own personal podcast, thought The Force Network readers would enjoy a news and commentary podcast dedicated to their favorite topic. He uses Sonic Foundry to record from his Plantronics computer microphone [Hack #12]. Then he mixes down with Sony's ACID [Hack #50]. The result is around 15 minutes of engaging Star Wars news and opinion.

He starts by laying out each show into three segments: news, commentary, and a featured item. The news is sourced from TheForce.Net site, or through other fan sites. News about the movies must come directly from Lucasfilm press releases. Rumors must have multiple sources. For his feature segments, he does interviews and round-table discussions from Star Wars conventions. He has a scripted intro and outtro [Hack #63]. His outtro segment encourages his listeners to contact him with feedback on the show, which so far has been roundly positive.

The listeners have responded best to the commentary segments. Erik believes this is because he knows what he would like to hear and he uses that to guide the show. He keeps mind of his pacing through the show and is careful not to lose listeners' attention with dull content. The key, according to Erik, is to keep the listeners' mind engaged with fresh news and commentary on the Star Wars universe, which provides them with new points of view.

See Also

- "Adopt a Format for Your Podcast" [Hack #20]
- "Mix Multiple Tracks" [Hack #60]
- "Grab Audio Legally" [Hack #67]

—Michael W. Geoghegan

 ## Build a Great Sports Podcast

#28 Create a show that brings a unique view on the passion of the sports world to your podcast listeners.

The NBA Finals, the World Series, and the Super Bowl are the three most widely covered sports events on American mass media. But what about the Snocross Worldwide Championship? For that you'll need Sledhead Radio, the podcast dedicated to snowmobiling.

When I launched the first sports podcast in October 2004, there were less than 50 podcasts to speak of worldwide. Now, in addition to The Sports Pod (*http://thesportspod.com/*), sports junkies worldwide have access to hundreds of sports podcasts on just about every sport known to man. When you consider that only a few years ago, listeners had access to only one or two local sports radio programs, it's no wonder why listeners describe podcasting with a sense of liberation. The geographical nature of sports provides the prime example for how podcasting thumps traditional radio. Great sports podcasts require consistency, quality, content, and distribution, and with the ammo that follows, you will be on your way to All-Star status.

Podcast Your Passion

Sports stirs up the emotions like nothing else, to the point that blatantly biased arguments are celebrated under the guise of "talking smack." Loyalty and passion are of the highest priority, and the experiences of our youth programmatically bind us to our favorite sporting events. Your job is to exploit that passion within yourself. Capture it, organize it, and publish it, for the world to experience along with you.

Gill Alexander is a Washington, D.C. native and radio veteran now living in San Francisco. As a kid, he dreamed of the day when Washington would have a hometown baseball team. When the Washington Nationals were born, Gill's excitement led him to launch The Nationals Play-By-Play podcast, where he podcasts the team's games, play by play, from his living room. "My friends and I always wished we could broadcast the games and tell it like it really is," he says. Podcast your passion, and you'll enjoy the process and increase your chances for success.

Segment Ideas

Here are some ideas for segments that you can use in your show:

Opinions
> This is the most common of segments. Be human, be yourself, and be opinionated.

News and Updates
> People mistakenly claim that sportscasting doesn't lend itself to podcasting. Nonsense. In this increasingly global society, transplants are a significant part of your prospective audience, especially if you are focused on events or a team from a specific geographic region. Obviously, the podcasts with news and updates segments are more time sensitive, and they work better in a daily format.

Interviews
> When a new book is released, it's promoted heavily. Watch the new releases in Amazon.com's sports section. Find a subject who would be a good fit for your audience, contact the publishing company, and get the interview. Jesse Knight from Basketball Babble says, "I heard that playground legend Demetrius 'Hook' Mitchell was promoting his new DVD. So, I Googled him, found the production company, and called them up, and two days later I was interviewing Hook on a Skype-Out call."

Countdowns
> Count down the best teams or athletes of all time, in your particular genre.

Contests/Trivia
> Ask a trivia question, and give away a small Amazon gift certificate for the winner. Ask listeners to post their answers in your Comments section to preserve integrity.

Watchin' You
> Some athletes are so fascinating that they deserve their own segments. Pick your athlete, and give an update on him during each show.

Debates
> Bring on a friend, a blogger, or another podcaster, and debate a hot issue in your genre.

Call-Ins
> Encourage audio feedback through one of the free voice mail services out there, and through email. For example, the Quick Takes podcast

consists of listeners calling in and responding to each other, through a K7 (*http://k7.net*) voice mail line.

Crystal Ball Player

Let's look into the future. Do you hate listening to TV sportscasters or just wish they would say what they were really thinking? Well, play-by-play podcasting could change the way we take in sporting events. While the podcaster watches games on TV, she podcasts her commentary.

Sports News Resources

Here is a list of key resources for integrating relevant content into your podcasts:

Google Alerts (http://google.com/alerts)

Google Alerts keeps you current on news and web items, as they happen. Just surf to the site, and enter the keywords relevant to your podcast. If you have a weekly podcast, it's best to set up a daily notice for this system so that you are up-to-date when you do your podcast.

For example: The Lakers Podcast with Jesse Knight and Steve Carbone.

Keywords: lakers, kobe nba, "kobe bryant", "phil jackson" lakers, jerry west lakers, "lake show", "magic johnson"…

The advanced search tool makes it simple to produce ideal search scenarios, so you aren't overloaded with stories.

ESPN (http://espn.com/)

If you're in the sports podcast game, chances are you already watch ESPN Sports Center regularly. Keep the TV on ESPN News, or listen to the live 24/7 feed on podcast production day. Most importantly, check *ESPN* for news stories relevant to your podcast.

Amazon.com New Releases in Sports (http://www.amazon.com/)

If you do interviews, check Amazon's list of new releases in the sports section and see who has released books and videos recently. Contact their publisher and publicist and request interviews.

Directories

You should register your sports podcasts with these directories:

ipodder.org Sports Directory (http://ipodder.org/directory/4/podcasts/categories/sports)

The iPodder directory of sports podcasts.

My Sports Radio Directory (http://mysportsradio.com/)

A directory that is specific to sports podcasts.

*Podcast Alley–Sports (http://podcastalley.com/podcast_genres.php?pod_genre_
id=2)*

> Podcast Alley's list of sports podcasts. It's always up-to-date because
> this is where people vote for their favorite podcast.

Great Sports Podcasts

I had the opportunity to talk with a few sports podcasters about what makes
their podcasts great.

Triathlete's Garage. Brett Blankner uses his Triathlete's Garage podcast
(*http://triathlon.blankner.com/*) to bring a personal perspective on training
for and competing in triathlons. And that view starts literally in his own
garage, where he uses Audacity, a Lansing boom microphone, and his HP
computer to bring you into his world.

Triathlons are grueling events. They comprise three stages: biking, swim-
ming, and running, any of which is enough sport for the average person. But
triathlons blend all three into a single event. The training for this sport is
equally intense. To keep his triathlete listeners going, Brett creates shows
that contain upbeat music, interviews, and segments of his perspectives,
based on his experiences. He even blends in soundseeing tours [Hack #72] from
the races he competes in using a MuVo MP3 player [Hack #69] with a voice
recorder.

He records the podcast on the one day a week he takes off from his intense
training. He uses his garage/studio to do the recording. Starting with some
experiences from the week, he adds any interesting sounds he has recorded
as well as any news or tips the audience would appreciate. When he's done,
he uses Audacity [Hack #50] for the final mix to MP3 before uploading to the
site, and then modifies his hand-written RSS 2.0 feed [Hack #37] to point to the
latest show.

His audience is a blend of athletes, people interested in the sport, and his
own family. The feedback he gets from the show is mostly positive. Sometimes he even gets some technical advice from his listeners that he uses to
improve the show's sound quality.

But it's not all about sound quality, he warns. He thinks the show works
because of his enthusiasm for the sport and the fun that he has creating the
show. The show completes an emotional circle with the audience: he trains,
competes, and then shares his personal victory with the podcast world.

Southern Sports Week. If you are more of a fan than a participant, you should check out Kit Baty's Southern Sports Week (*http://kitbaty.com/ssw*). Kit's 20- to 30-minute podcast covers the sports news from the Southern states as well as items he considers "off the radar" of the mainstream sports press.

Show notes are Kit's first step when building a show episode. These include the headlines he wants to talk about, stories he has researched, and any emails he wants to talk about. Then he uses Audacity [Hack #50] and his Plantronics headset [Hack #12] to record the show. It takes about 45 minutes to put together a show. It can take around an hour if it's an interview show.

He's pretty harsh on his voice, saying that he sounds like "an NPR host who hasn't yet hit puberty." But his production value and confidence increase with every podcast, as does his listener base. In the long run, he wants to have a listener base large enough to get him into coaches' press conferences and Southern sports events, with full press credentials. For now, he is satisfied with providing an alternative to what he sees as fresher and more free-form than what is on commercial sports radio today.

Fantasy Focus. In case you missed it, Fantasy Baseball has become a multi-million-dollar industry over the last decade. Bill Powers' Fantasy Focus (*http://podsumer.com/fantasyfocus/*) is the first podcast to cover Fantasy Baseball. Bill and his co-host, Chris, create one podcast a week. The show's format evolves as the season progresses. Before the season starts, they cover the fantasy drafts. And once the season starts, they cover the hot fantasy players and the match-ups that are coming up.

To produce the show, they use Cool Edit [Hack #50], which is now called Audition and is sold by Adobe. It takes between five and seven hours to produce a single show, from drawing up the show notes to recording and through to editing and uploading. They get highlights of recent games by purchasing them from the Major League Baseball site (*http://mlb.com/*).

Most of the feedback so far has been from men who share their passion for fantasy sports. Once the season gets started, they use the email they get to suggest team strategies and trade proposals with their audience.

See Also

- "Adopt a Format for Your Podcast" [Hack #20]
- "Grab Audio Legally" [Hack #67]
- "Assemble a Small Recording Rig" [Hack #69]
- "Podcast at an Event" [Hack #71]

—Sam Coutin

Build a Great Technology Podcast

#29   Bring technology advice and trends to your listeners, with a cutting-edge technology podcast.

Technology-themed shows can be a lot of fun and can be useful to listeners, but keep in mind that this particular audience will be demanding and smart, and you'll need to be extremely passionate and informed about your topics if you want to pull this off successfully.

While there is no secret formula, I've discovered some things in my podcasting career doing technology-oriented shows that have worked for some reason, at least most of the time.

Raw Is Better

Raw is an odd term, but it's the one word I think of when I think about the audio shows I do. Technology shows with nontechnical hosts on any medium (TV, radio, and now podcasting) are easy to spot. Usually these shows are hosted by someone who "almost sorta gets it," but they never sound quite right. Folks in the technology trenches aren't usually the most polished speakers, but there's a rawness to what they're saying that's genuine and can't be faked. And just about every subject contains so much minutia that if you're going to rattle off the benefits of, say, Linux, you better make sure you've either spent the last few years banging away at the console or you're interviewing a Linux expert. This isn't a top 40 station; it's a podcast, and it's meant for a sliver of the population, not for everyone. Your listeners will appreciate the familiar tech-hacker as opposed to the slickster DJ.

Interview Experts

You can't be an expert on everything, but it's usually pretty easy to spot who is the expert in a specific area of technology. When I want to hit a topic that I think might be interesting to my audience, but I'm not an expert in that topic, I usually try to find some of the experts in the field. This sounds hard, and besides, why would anyone want to talk to a lowly podcaster? Well, I've found that book authors promoting their books and bloggers looking to get the word out about subject matter in which they're experts are usually good candidates. I've interviewed [Hack #33] corporate types, but usually you have to get past a few layers of PR or marketing people before you can get to an engineer or developer. The best way to do this is to tell them up front that you'll be asking some pretty technical questions, and to send over a few sample questions to scare them. It also helps to attend tech conferences—

catching someone out in the hallway for a five-minute chat after they just did a killer demo on stage seems to make a good segment.

Review Technology by Using It

When I review technology (software, gadgets, or whatever), I generally review only those things I've bought or have tried in real-world settings. A good example of this is when I installed an XM Satellite radio in my wife's car—after installing it, using it for a few weeks, and recording some audio of some of its traffic and "extra" features, I felt I could speak to it in a way that folks could relate to. Why we bought it—the commute times, the technology that makes it work, geographic area, pricing—these are all considerations you usually don't get from the two-minute tech reviews you see on TV or hear on syndicated radio. After you get a few of these hands-on, real-world reviews of your own gear under your belt, it might be a good time to contact some of the companies that make the products you want to try. Having them listen to how you review a product will help them get an idea of what you have planned. It's also good to let them know your review might take a while longer than a more superficial review, since you're actually going to use the product or service in a real-world setting.

Try New Things

Because your audience likely will be more technical than you are, it's OK to try new recording setups and conferencing methods. If you're finding that Skype does a better job with five-way recording than recording a phone-based system, that information likely is useful to your audience. Did you get a new mic? Let the audience know—I've always felt it was my duty as a technology podcaster to run across the technology minefield for my audience, alerting them of what's good and what not to step on. While others might have other motives with their podcasts, one of my goals is to grow new tech podcasters—some of your listeners might take a page from your book and start their own podcasts. By opening up the kimono on how and what you do for your show, you'll be helping this process along.

Leave Politics Out

I'm saying this only because I've noticed that it's the biggest source of complaints. When people download a technology show, they really want the dirt on tech, not some weird Red States versus Blue States debate. Technology is one of the rare topics that many people can be part of and can enjoy. For some reason, "talk radio" and even "talk podcasting" encourage all sorts of heated topics, which is fine; just keep them out of a tech show. With that said, you should talk about the politics of legislation and the laws that affect technology; just leave out the ideology that the politicians often inject.

Show Notes

Tech podcasts are filled with tons of information about a wide variety of topics. Because of this, you'll need to provide all references in your show notes. I've generally found that breaking the show notes into time sections with a one-sentence descriptor, time code, and URL helps a lot. Show notes with a good description also help casual listeners to figure out if they want to listen to your show. In addition, they help the search engines index your content, since it's going to be a while before search engines are able to index audio. Here's an example:

01:30—Google offers new mapping service (and here's a hack for it…)

Many people have told me they listen to shows as they're commuting to work, and that once they arrive at their desk, they check the show notes for something they enjoyed or want to learn more about.

File Formats

The most common format for podcasts is the venerable MP3 [Hack #18], but depending on your audience, there might be demand for another format. If your show is Windows-centric—let's say it's about Windows Media devices—by all means, supply your podcast in Windows Media Audio (WMA) format. Is your show about open source? Go with the Ogg Vorbis format, but use it in addition to MP3. I try to supply an MP3, WMA, and Ogg file for direct download, as well as via torrent when it's possible. It's a little extra work, but there's nothing better than someone getting the format they really want, right from you.

Feedback

You can get feedback about your shows in many ways. I usually provide my email, instant messaging, and Skype addresses and encourage folks to send comments, but you also can get feedback in a few other ways. When I first began podcasting, I'd post my audio on my site and send a link to one of the many IRC rooms where my friends hang out. This quick sanity check usually saved me a ton of embarrassment if I goofed on a filename or audio compression, but it also gave me some initial reactions to my shows. I don't suggest doing this in IRC channels you're not familiar with or don't have friends in, since it's somewhat spammy.

Another way to get feedback and to get some extra content for your show is to use a free voice mail service [Hack #62]. If you use Skype, you're already set; just tell people to call and leave you a message. I really like k7.com's service. It's a free voice mail system that sends you an email with a WAV file attached. You can even request a "vanity number" so that people can dial words. Here's one of mine: 206-888-MAKE.

Sameness Kills

This is the most important consideration. I've stumbled along, creating technology podcasts for more than a year now, and each show, each email from a listener, makes every new podcast a little bit better. My final tip is to make shows *you* would want to hear, and talk about things that no one else is talking about. The worst thing in the world, the killer of all great things, is sameness.

Great Technology Podcasts

As part of writing this hack, I was able to talk in person and through email with a few technology podcasters. In the next several subsections, I pass along their experience and advice.

TechNation. Moira Gunn's TechNation radio show (*http://technation.com/*) is distributed nationwide through NPR. It also is podcast via Doug Kaye's IT Conversations (*http://itconversations.com/*). Moira's show comprises two or three interviews with people she believes have a keen insight into technology and its impact on society.

Today, she interviews Nobel Prize winners, famous scientists, and the CEOs of multinational corporations. But early on, producers were skeptical as to whether the technology format would work. And Moira, even with her background in engineering and science, initially was overwhelmed by the breadth of the topic. The more technology trendsetters she interviewed, the more she was able to frame their work in a larger context, and to pass that understanding on to her audience.

She prepares for the interviews with a set of around 8 to 20 written questions. For the first question she goes right to the heart of the topic. Follow-on questions provide the background material for her listeners. She likes to let her guest guide the conversation, and she uses her written questions in a random order.

On a good day, she can get everything she needs in 23 minutes or so, but the segment sometimes runs longer, depending on the guest. She admits that not every scientist or engineer makes for a great interview. She gets a couple every season who can't answer questions or who can't separate fact from opinion.

The show never lacks for guests. Most are booked several weeks in advance and are sourced from a network of around 140 publicists that Moira has developed over the years. Cutting the final show takes from 3 to 10 days. The finished show is sent as an MP2 file to Doug Kaye, who splits up the segments into individual podcasts for IT Conversations.

Moira wants the show to discuss technology's impact on our society. So, she stays away from product-pitch segments and late-breaking news. She likes to find questions for the show that the guest might not have heard on his press tour, and she likes to give an outlet to scientists, philosophers, and engineers who would not have the opportunity to reach a wider audience otherwise. From the wide appeal of her show, it's clear that Moira's approach is working.

Zdot. Tim Shadel found that no show written and produced for Java programmers was available for him to listen to during his commute. His Zdot podcast (*http://timshadel.com/blog/*) afforded him the ability to create content just for engineers. This is not a "for dummies" technical show. It's in-depth coverage of architectural and technical Java topics. And it's presented three days a week in 10- to 20-minute installments because that's just the amount of time that commuters have to listen to the show.

He starts with a Java topic that interests him and writes some notes with some major points highlighted. Then he records the show in a single shot using Audacity [Hack #50]. He edits out the "ahs" and "ums," and then he drops in the show's canned intro and outtro [Hack #63] using a multitrack Audacity session [Hack #60]. With a few effects such as gverb [Hack #51] and some noise removal, the show is ready for encoding and uploading to his Word-Press blog [Hack #38].

Even through some hardships, he has kept doing the podcast because it gives him a way to relate his ideas and experience to other programmers.

See Also

- "Adopt a Format for Your Podcast" [Hack #20]
- "Mix Multiple Tracks" [Hack #60]
- "Grab Audio Legally" [Hack #67]
- "Use Copyrighted Music Legally" [Hack #68]

—*Phillip Torrone*

HACK #30   Build a Beercast

Use cheap hardware, lots of beer, and good friends to create entertaining podcasts.

Beercasting is a talk show recorded on location in a bar or pub near you. Unlike your traditional talk show, a Beercast stars regular people as the hosts—such as your friends, co-workers, and loved ones.

Every night, thousands upon thousands of interesting, and brutally honest, conversations take place. The real shame is that often we can't even remember some of the more brilliant utterances the next morning. Beercasting's goal is to capture those conversations and to share them with anyone who's interested.

Beercasting has nothing to do with beer—well, not entirely. Beercasting is about the open and honest conversations held between folks. It just so happens that once a little liquor is stirred into your average chit-chat session, the floodgates are blown wide open. The *beer* in *Beercasting* refers to the most popular truth serum: beer.

How Does Beercasting Work?

Beercasting uses a simple, topic-based format that's similar to your average TV or radio talk show. Beercasters gather in small groups of from two to four people and discuss various topics, one at a time. The main difference between Beercasting and those other talk shows is that there's no real host; everyone's a star in their own Beercast.

The term *Beercast* is used to describe the final, published conversation. To ensure that listeners get the most out of the experience, and to prevent people from rambling on for too long, each Beercast focuses on one specific topic. Topics cover anything and everything, from relationships to politics and everything in between.

The topics can be selected from the existing Topic Archive available on the Beercasting.com site, or can be made up on the fly while recording.

How Do I Organize a Beercast?

The first thing you need to do is pick a date to hold your first Beercast. Though you might be anxious to get started as soon as possible, you'll want to leave yourself enough time to get people to clear their calendars.

It's always best to hold a Beercast on a night that you know works well for your group. If you plan to Beercast from home, you shouldn't need much more than a week's notice (this depends on your friends, of course). Don't forget to account for days off, birthdays, and other important dates.

For Beercasts that will be held in bars and pubs, you'll definitely want to leave yourself a couple of weeks, minimum. Bars often have events and other things going on that could rain on your parade. The best nights to plan for are Monday through Wednesday, which are their slowest nights.

Location, location, layout. Once you've picked the date, you're ready to decide where to hold your Beercast. As they say in real estate, it's all about location, location, location. You want to make sure the place you choose for your Beercast is centrally located and easy to commute to and from.

If you plan to Beercast from a bar or pub, drop into the places you're considering and make sure they're OK with you coming by and recording. Stay away from the über-corporate chains, as they'll often have policies against this sort of thing.

Aside from location, you have to consider the layout. Remember, background noise is the enemy. Not all spaces are created equally, and most are acoustically hostile when it comes to recording conversations.

Avoid noise like the plague. If you're going to Beercast from home, you want to stay away from the street, ductwork, computers, and anything else [Hack #15] that tends to be noisy. If you're destined for a bar or restaurant, you want to consider many other things:

- The jukebox or the volume of music from the overhead audio system
- Customer chatter
- Street noise

By choosing a slow night at a bar, you can bet that fewer people will be chattering in the background and the bar will be more willing to help you out.

Despite the noisier conditions when recording out in the wild, it's still recommended that you head out to the local watering hole for one simple reason: it's a great way to meet new people.

Party people. The last, but certainly not least, step in planning your Beercasting event is to gather the troops that you want to attend. Theoretically, you need only one person (yourself) to do a Beercast, but that's not nearly as much fun as you should expect to have.

The ideal size for a Beercast is four people, or multiples of that (assuming you've got additional equipment). Avoid the temptation to pile 20 people around a microphone, since it just doesn't work. When too many people get together, they start to chatter and side conversations form.

A great Beercast is powered by great conversation—choose your participants accordingly. Mix up the age, gender, and race of the people involved, and don't be shy to recruit "innocent bystanders" that are standing by, wondering what you're doing. Strangers invariably guarantee something new and unexpected. For your first Beercast, invite your most vocal and zany friends to participate. They'll be sure to draw a crowd…as they always do.

What Do I Need to Do a Beercast?

Beercasting can cost you as much or as little as you want. Naturally, the more you invest in your equipment, the better the end results will be. You do need to have a few critical components, however.

First and foremost is the recording device. This is the most critical piece because without it, there will be no record of the Beercast. All kinds of different recording devices are available to you, including cell phones, voice recorders, MP3 players, and mini-disc recorders [Hack #69]. Use whatever it takes to get started! In the long run, however, an MP3 player with a dedicated line-in is the recommended hardware. This will make it easy for you to get your show published, and it will get you the best results.

The only other thing you need to get your Beercast recorded successfully is a microphone [Hack #13]. Again, you can spend as much or as little on a microphone as you want, but note that spending lots of money does not mean you'll get better results. The one thing to avoid is using *any form* of built-in microphone. Generally speaking, internal microphones are not of the greatest quality and they yield poor results. A $10 RadioShack microphone goes a long way.

Topics. To have a good Beercast, you've got to have good topics. The most important thing to remember is that when you record a Beercast, you've got two audiences: the attendees and the listeners.

Choosing topics can be the most difficult part of preparing for a Beercast. The difficulty is that you have to ensure that everyone at the table can participate. In general, it's best to stay away from topics that are too controversial, as the discussion will get heated and fall apart quickly.

Catering to your listeners is a slightly different issue. The rule of thumb is to talk to your friends, not to the audience. It's easy to get into a "show" mode in which you talk for the sake of being entertaining. In reality, people are listening because they are interested in what's being said about the topic. They don't want to hear more of the same as what they can hear on the radio. The best-rated shows are the ones that are spontaneous, candid, and authentic.

If at any point you're feeling uninspired, check with the Beercasting.com Topic Archive to find a listing of every topic the Beercasting community has ever covered. The rating system we use makes it easy to find the things that audiences are interested in.

Publicize the Beercast

Once your Beercast is complete, you have one more task you have to complete: marketing. *Beercasting* stands for more than simply the name of the activity. It's also a service that helps you get your message out.

When your Beercast is complete, upload it to the web site (*http://beercasting.com/*). From there, the files will be processed and published to your squad's home page automatically. Instantly, thousands of new people will be able to download your Beercast.

Of course, this is only half of the battle. The other half of the promotion is something you must handle. You will receive an email from Beercasting.com once your show is published. Then you can use your promotion tools to notify everyone who attended the Beercast.

Once that's done, sit back and wait for the comments.

Vancouver Beercast Squad

Kris Krug met Gregory Narain and some other friends at the Northern Voice for a few beers and some Beercasting. It went so well that after Greg left, nobody wanted to stop. So, he created the Vancouver Beercast Squad and now he Beercasts regularly. At first he Beercast with just his local blog buddies. Instead of writing for their own separate blogs, they got together in one spot for some beer and straight talk. The first group comprised 15 people, and others were jockeying for seats at the table. Beercasts held more recently have comprised between 5 and 10 people.

His setup is simple: two cheap microphones, stands and cables, four headphones, some splitters, and his PC. He can set it all up and be ready to go in 15 minutes. He records with Audacity [Hack #50] and then uses Adobe's Audition to encode it into MP3s. He's really not that worried about the quality, since there is so much background noise from the bars. They have covered such topics as geek dating tips, why reality TV sucks, and the Iraq war, among others.

The bar owners he has worked with have been more than happy to give him permission to do the Beercast. In some cases, they have even given a free pitcher or two to get the party started. It's good business to hold activities that encourage people to come to the bar.

A lot of the feedback he gets is requests to join in the fun, or to borrow his hardware to set up more Beercasts. Everyone who is involved enjoys it and wants to learn how to build their own Beercasts.

See Also

- "Pick the Right Microphone" **[Hack #13]**
- "Mix Your Podcast in Hardware" **[Hack #14]**
- "Reduce Noise" **[Hack #15]**
- "Adopt a Format for Your Podcast" **[Hack #20]**
- "Assemble a Small Recording Rig" **[Hack #69]**

—*Greg Narain*

HACK #31   Build an MP3zine

Create a magazine-style podcast that your listeners can thumb through with their iPods.

MP3zines have all the benefits of print magazines, and all the conveniences associated with MP3 audio, RSS, and the World Wide Web. They have a table of contents, articles, advertisements, letters (or voice mail) to the editor, and editorials. But, they are distributed as podcasts. I am the editor, and one of the contributors, for the Dailysonic MP3zine (*http://dailysonic.com*). In this hack, I'll share the philosophies that guide us, and some of the lessons that we've learned in building Dailysonic.

Dailysonic's primary goal is to create unique and engaging content for our listeners. Five key elements work together to create the quality content in our show:

- Having multiple contributors who are willing to challenge themselves and try new things
- Constructing a show with interesting and engaging content, in a way that is easy to understand and navigate
- Using content that balances the elements of familiarity and surprise to keep current listeners and attract new ones
- Harnessing the potential of music/sound's abilities to transport listeners, connect with the human element, and elicit emotion
- Using the Web and the audio together, to create a complete interactive experience

Once the newness of podcasting's technology wears off, content will be the only thing that matters. We spend the majority of our time brainstorming, researching, and writing. It is important to have variety among our segments so that we have something of interest for everyone. We have segments for world news, underground and indie music, the human element, fringe and urban culture, travel, and technology.

Having multiple contributors makes the job of producing top-notch content a lot easier. Each contributor brings his unique perspective to the program. I recommend that you find people who want to contribute content and who can deliver it on time. Get your friends and colleagues involved, or collaborate with other podcasters.

The Internet makes it easy to collaborate with people who are far away. Our contributors record, edit, and produce their segments remotely, convert them to MP3, and email or FTP them to me. We also use Skype extensively for interviews [Hack #35].

Structure

Starting with a rundown makes it easy for listeners to navigate the show. Similar to a table of contents, a rundown briefly describes each segment in the episode, and lists the minute marker for each segment so that listeners can skip around easily and can take advantage of the medium's on-demand nature. The rundown also goes on the web page. This makes it even easier for listeners to navigate the episode, and allows potential listeners to decide if the episode is of interest before they download or subscribe.

Our segments are timed so that they start at whole-minute markers. It's much easier for a listener to remember "the 12-minute marker" than it is for him to remember "the 11-minute, 46-second marker." We use music, public service announcements, and advertisements to fill in time and round out minute markers.

When choosing segments for an episode, I think about familiarity and surprise. Familiar elements (such as a theme song, a steady host, or recurring segments) are important in making listeners feel at home and giving them something to expect. But too much familiarity can lead to a show that's boring or too exclusive (i.e., rehashing the same inside jokes, over and over). On the same note, too much surprise can turn listeners off or make them feel uneasy.

Recurring segments [Hack #20] give listeners something to look forward to and a reason to come back for more. Having regularly recurring segments gives you and your contributors a specific framework to work in, which is helpful when you're having trouble coming up with new ideas. It's much easier to write a segment on a specific topic (e.g., travel) than it is to write about anything under the sun.

Segments can recur daily, weekly, and even monthly. For example, every day at the two-minute marker, we discuss important world news. We have a daily one-minute radio drama that serves as Dailysonic's "cartoon." Every Tuesday, we have a three-minute segment called "Isaac Dolom's Science Hour." Also, each week, we have a music series about a different artist, genre, or theme.

Challenging Yourself

To create surprising content for your listeners, you have to surprise and challenge yourself. One feature that comes to mind is the one I did on the Idiotarod—a shopping-cart race through New York City, which is based on the Iditarod, the Alaskan sled dog race.

At the time, I had no experience doing sound work in the field and I didn't feel comfortable approaching people on the street for interviews. When I arrived at the start of the race, I was overwhelmed by the size of the crowd. When I saw "real" television cameras I even questioned my legitimacy as a reporter. But when the race started, I stepped up and captured the sound of hundreds of shopping carts rolling along the asphalt, and the crowds cheering wildly.

I made some mistakes. I accidentally recorded over the beginning of the race. But as the day rolled on (no pun intended), I became more comfortable approaching people with a microphone. I even ran alongside some of the racers to conduct interviews on the go. I learned some valuable lessons about working in the field, interviewing people, and properly using my portable mini-disc recorder [Hack #69]. At the end of the day, I felt much more confident in my abilities and I was glad that I challenged myself. The Idiotarod feature (*http://Dailysonic.com/excerpts/Idiotarod.mp3*) came out great, and it was a welcome surprise for Dailysonic's listeners, who until then mostly had been hearing pieces done in the studio.

The ambient sounds of the shopping-cart race transported listeners to that very time and place. The quiet of early morning, the tacky music and fluorescent hum in the supermarket, the sounds of a backroom poker game or of children at play; all of these sounds can transport listeners to another time and place. One of the best ways to get these sounds is to record them yourself with a mini-disc recorder and a stereo microphone.

Sound connects listeners with the human element. Another of Dailysonic's contributors, Anni, prefers to conduct interviews in cafés or other public spaces, as opposed to the quiet and sterile studio environment. The background chatter [Hack #64] of a café is enough to remind listeners that Anni and her interviewee are real people, just like they are. All too often, mainstream media flattens people's personalities, and it turns nonactors into actors. Our magazine is about people, and we want them to sound genuine.

Music

Music plays an important role in Dailysonic's production. It does all the same things that field-recorded sound can do: it transports the listener, connects with the human element, and elicits emotion. All the members of Dailysonic have extremely strong musical tastes. It's an unspoken duty of ours to expose listeners to the great music that mainstream radio all too often ignores. Aaron, another one of Dailysonic's contributors, has been known to spend hours sifting through crates of vinyl in antique stores, looking for that ultimate musical gem.

We weave music [Hack #63] into every aspect of our magazine. The music we play under the news tries to match the mood of the day's headlines (usually somber indie rock). Sometimes we choose songs for their message. For a story on the suicide rate among farmers in India we chose songs by Radiohead, a band that repeatedly has spoken out against globalization and supports fair wages for workers. On St. Patrick's Day, we use music by bands from Ireland. During our travel segments, we match the music to the region we visit.

Using the Web Site

A web site is the second face of your magazine podcast. We encourage our listeners to visit our web site, where we offer links to follow up on the topics we discuss and the music we play. We use the web site to post photographs from field pieces, outtakes, and extended versions of interviews. And we interact with our listeners through a message board where they discuss the shows and interact with each other.

In encouraging listeners to visit the web site both before listening to the show (to download the show and/or view the rundown) and after (to follow up on a segment or music), the listener both sees and hears ads. This allows advertisers to reinforce their brand through multiple media, and to gauge the ads' success by tracking click-throughs.

Be Unique

Don't try to imitate radio or print magazines. Use the unique qualities of the podcast medium to create something new. At Dailysonic, we are constantly learning, growing, and trying to refine our format and content, with both our listeners and the nature of this new medium in mind. There is no formula for a good podcast. Nevertheless, I hope that in sharing the importance of quality content, the power of sound and music, and the added value of a web presence, I got your gears turning. We are all learning as we go. The more that this learning is made into a collective process, the greater our collective output will be.

See Also

- "Adopt a Format for Your Podcast" [Hack #20]
- "Integrate Audio and Email Feedback" [Hack #62]
- "Record and Add Background Ambience" [Hack #64]
- "Assemble a Small Recording Rig" [Hack #69]
- "Podcast at an Event" [Hack #71]

—Adam Varga

HACK #32 Produce Great Audio Theatre

Write stories, build scripts, and produce audio theatre for segments of your podcast.

When we think of radio theatre, we imagine the classics such as "The Shadow" and "The Lone Ranger," shows from decades past when there was no television. Today's audio theatre is far more diverse than these shows were. We have audio books in which a single narrator plays several parts. We have shows such as This American Life (*http://thislife.org/*) that tell personal stories through clever use of narration and music. And we have plays set as audio theatre with full productions. These are popular in Britain, where the BBC presents full productions of drama, comedy, science fiction, and more.

Audio theatre provides you with a new outlet for your creativity and a new way of expressing complex topics through storytelling and parody. What's better is that you will be able to do it all with the audio setup you already have for your podcasts. All you need are some inspiration and enough writing skill to put together a script. From there, you use the three key elements of audio theatre—dialog, sound effects, and musical cues—to tell your story in a way that engages listeners.

This hack concentrates on small, five- to seven-minute productions that you can integrate into your podcasts. In radio, these are called *sketches*, and they are held as separate constructions from the unstructured portions of the show because they are scripted and are produced in advance. They involve up to four people, one or more microphones, some music, sound effects, and a script. The principles for the creation of sketches scale nicely to the size of a complete audio theatre production of a longer play.

The Story

A clear story is the foundation of any great audio theatre segment. Stories are available on the Web, but it's more interesting to do an original production. To give you some starters, here are some easy sources for stories:

Politics and current events
> Nothing makes an easier target for parody than the recent hijinks of your least favorite politicians. Listeners already know the characters, and with a little narration, it should be easy to bring them up to speed on current events.

Pop culture
> Just like politics, pop-culture icons from the worlds of music, movies, and commercials make excellent familiar targets for parody.

Life reenactment
> Use stories from your life and reenact them through a short skit, with you and a friend playing out your roles, or even inverting them.

Religious or classic works
> Use portions of classic fiction stories or events from religious works (which are filled with lots of short stories).

Jokes
> Use a joke as the basis for your sketch.

Urban legend
> Urban legends can be very funny and engaging.

These are some simple starting points, but you should let your own creativity be your guide. Movie productions spend a lot of money on props and effects to tell a story. With audio theatre, the story is primary, with some music and a few effects thrown in to help set the scene. With the financial portion of the equation removed, you can tell as elaborate and fanciful a story as you choose.

With the story in mind, you need to decide on the characters and the narrative arc of the story. An arc starts with a setup in which you introduce the characters, their relationships, and the setting. Then, the story creates a conflict among the characters, and finally, a resolution. This is the standard three-act linear formula: setup, conflict, and resolution.

A linear narrative works best in audio theatre. A timeline that jumps around, as exemplified in movies such as *Pulp Fiction*, works on film but is confusing to listeners in audio. Clarity is critical in audio theatre because listeners effectively are blind. They can see only what you tell them, and what they can hear in the music or effects. For example, unless you as the actor tell your listeners what you're holding in your hand, your listeners will never know you're holding a gun.

The Script

With a story that has characters and a narrative arc in hand, the next step is to write the script. Start by writing out the scenes as an outline of the whole story. Detail what is supposed to happen in each scene, and then which characters are in the scene. Try to avoid having several scenes where no action occurs. Otherwise, you will bore your listeners and they won't stick around for the end. In addition, I recommend having between one and four characters in any scene. Using more than that will make it difficult for listeners to keep track of who is saying what.

With this outline in hand, you can write the script. The script needs to be formatted so that the actors can read it quickly. I recommend using the Courier font, in bold, at 12 points with a wide margin to create a paragraph width of around 5 inches. At that rate, a page of script is about 45 seconds of audio. So, a five-minute sketch is roughly six or seven pages.

Each line is a cue. A cue is either a line of dialog, a sound effect, or a musical reference. The lines should be numbered on the page, restarting with the number 1 on each page. Following the number, you should include the character's name and the line of dialog, sound effect, or music reference. You should underline sound-effect lines, and start them with the word *Sound*, followed by details on the sound effect to be used. Here is an example script that I wrote for a section of Shakespeare's *Macbeth*:

```
1.  MACBETH:        That will never be. Who can impress the forest?
                    Yet my heart throbs to know one thing. Tell me,
                    if your art can tell so much, - shall Banquo's
                    issue ever reign in this kingdom?
2.  SOUND:          THUNDER.
3.  MUSIC:          WEIRD MUSIC-UP. DUCK FOR VOICES.
4.  ALL WITCHES:    Seek to know no more.
5.  MACBETH:        I will be satisfied. Deny me this, and an eternal
                    curse fall on you! Let me know!
6.  SOUND:          INTENSE BUBBLING-SLOWS-STOPS. THUNDER.
7.  MACBETH:        Why sinks that cauldron? And what noise is this?
```

```
 8.  FIRST WITCH:      Show!
 9.  SECOND WITCH:        Show!
10.  THIRD WITCH:            Show!
11.  SOUND:            THUNDER.
```

Keep in mind when you are writing your script that your listeners aren't in the room with you. They can't see you. So, anything you want them to see will have to come from the dialog or the sound effects.

The Studio Setup

Thankfully, the same requirements that make for a good podcasting studio also make for a reasonably good audio theatre setup. A large-diaphragm studio condenser microphone [Hack #13] will serve nicely for recording several voices. I recommend positioning the microphone at around collarbone level, with a pop filter placed such that you won't be able to get closer than eight inches to the microphone. The proximity effect is not helpful when recording dialog for audio theatre.

Whatever setup you choose, you should endeavor to create most of the sound for the show in the live performance. If you leave editing to post, you will find that you can mess with the sound for days or weeks to get it to feel right. It's far easier to create a live setup that will produce most of the sound you need, and reserve post-performance editing for adding music and doing any necessary trimming.

The Performance

Recording the sketch starts with picking the right actors. If you have the luxury of actually picking voice talent, you will want to choose individuals whose distinctive voices help flesh out the characters. In the likely event that you are doing the voice work yourself, you should try experimenting with different voices or accents.

Keep your studio quiet during the recording session. Extraneous noises confuse your listeners and distract them from the plot. Try not to laugh, sneeze, or cough. If you are walking around, take off your shoes unless the walking sound is important to you. If you are using multiple microphones, assume that they are all live. And try to keep the page-turning noise to a minimum. It can help to print the script single-sided to avoid the noise of flipping a page, and to allow you to move the pages from side to side. Plastic page protectors also help reduce noise, as does stapling the script in the lower left-hand corner so that the pages fall down as they are read.

Here are some simple hand signals you can use to communicate among actors:

Open hand
> Indicates that the person should stop, like a traffic cop stopping traffic.

Pointing finger
> Indicates when a music, effect, or dialog cue should start.

Drawing circles with your finger
> Tells the speaker to "speed it up." The motion is similar to the motion of circling your finger on the side of your head to indicate insanity.

Hooking two index fingers together
> Indicates that the cues need to be tightened up so that gaps are removed between the lines of dialog.

Pulling your ear
> Indicates to the speaker that he needs to increase his volume.

Putting your finger to your lips (shhh)
> Tells the recipient that she needs to be quieter.

Slitting your throat with your finger
> The sign for "cut" and indicates that the scene is over, or at least that this segment of the recording is over.

All the actors involved need to have copies of the script, and one of the people should act as the director. The director wears headphones, monitors the sound, and conducts the performance to indicate when actors should start and stop, to introduce sound effects, and to give nonverbal cues.

I recommend recording short productions several times to get the timing right. The first few times should be a recorded rehearsal with the production version coming from one of the later recordings. Especially when you are just starting out, it can be difficult to read prepared scripts with a style that feels unscripted. Professionals call this "lifting the script off the page," and it comes only after the actors have rehearsed several times so that they feel comfortable with the words.

Sound effects. Sound effects [Hack #58] are a very important part of audio theatre. They provide an element of realism to the story that dialog can't provide. The ideal sound effect complements the action taking place in the dialog.

You have two options for introducing sound effects into a production. The first is to inject a digital sound effect directly [Hack #58] into a recording. You can do this live by using a cart program [Hack #54] [Hack #55], used in combination with Audio Hijack Pro on the Macintosh or Total Recorder Pro on Windows PCs [Hack #50]. I recommend using a reverb effect on the sound effect before using it in your show so that it sounds natural in the context of the recording. If you want your listeners to feel that the actors are far away, the gunshot one actor fires at the other also should sound far away. Another method for making a prerecorded effect sound more natural is to record it to a CD or tape, and then play it back through a portable CD player and record it with the studio microphone that will be used in the show.

The second option for sound effects is to do them live, with devices or with what is at hand. Here are some basic effects that will get you started:

Thunder
Shake a 2×4-foot, high-impact polystyrene sheet/panel (.60 mil).

Walking through a jungle
Shake two little egg shakers and make vocal animal sounds.

Shoveling dirt
Shovel gravel in a gravel box.

Birds
Twist a little bird call and make vocal bird sounds.

A plane flying and sputtering
Apply a vibrating pen toy to a cardboard box, and move it.

On the radio
Hold a coffee mug off to the side and talk normally. This will create a boxy effect that is similar to talking through a phone or over the radio.

One particularly useful tool is a *crash box*, which is a metal tin (a large popcorn tin works nicely) that's filled with noisy junk and is duct-taped together. You can use this to simulate crash noises. You can also do a lot with just your mouth if you experiment a little. Just get creative with it.

Another important effect is the *walla*. A walla is a crowd noise sound, like the sound of a bar crowd or the roar of a stadium at a sporting event. It's easy enough to get with four or five friends mumbling in a random way. What's important is that there are no discrete words in the sound to distract listeners from the important primary dialog underneath which the walla is layered.

Always keep in mind that listeners will hardly notice if you miss a sound effect. But listeners will get confused by too much background sound or effects. Don't overuse the powerful tool of sound effects.

Music. Adding appropriate music to the start and end of a production or around each scene can provide listeners with a strong sense of place and time. As with any other podcast music, you will need to work through the licensing issues [Hack #68]. Which music you use depends entirely on your production's theme and in which portion of the show it's used. For the introduction, I recommend using something light, perhaps the beginning of a piece of music. For the conflict sections, use something with some more tension and drive. Then, at the conclusion of the production, use the end portion of a piece of music.

Using Apple's GarageBand or Sony's ACID is an easy way to create music that is license free and won't be so strong as to distract listeners from the story. In particular, stay away from sounds that are primarily in the treble clef. These can be distracting. Instead, keep with something fairly rhythmic in the bass clef.

Mix-Down and Encoding

The final phase after the recording is to use multiple tracks [Hack #60] in your sound editing application to layer any music or effects. Create another track, and then import and position the sound effects where necessary. If you chose a multiple-microphone recording setup, you will need to pan the recorded tracks to the right and left, and position them within the sound field. I recommend keeping the stereo spread between the 10 o'clock and 2 o'clock positions, if you think of the left and right sound field as the top of a clock between the hours of 9 and 3. Having the actors in discrete left or right positions is gimmicky and distracting.

I recommend keeping your first few productions as technically simple as possible. Unless stereo is required, go with mono, with just a few sound effects and music for the intro and the outtro [Hack #63] to set the scene.

One very helpful effect to use on productions is a reverb or room simulator [Hack #51]. These provide the illusion of different rooms and spaces, eliminating the need to build different sets that would provide genuine room reverberation.

More Resources

To learn more about audio theatre, check out my site, RuyaSonic (*http://www.ruyasonic.com*). From there you can get scripts, word templates, and articles on writing and production. You should also check out Crazy Dog Audio Theatre (*http://www.crazydogaudiotheatre.com/*). Crazy Dog has a terrific audio piece on how script writing for audio is fundamentally different from writing for film. Audio Theatre.com (*http://audiotheatre.com/*) and the Independent Radio Drama Productions site (*http://www.irdp.co.uk/*) also are excellent resources.

Legal Issues

If you plan to make money off of your audio theatre segments, you should have your actors sign releases. These should define the expected profit, how it will be calculated and distributed, and what percentage, if any, each player receives.

Wrapping Up

My final advice to you is to keep the production simple and the script creative. Don't confuse listeners by trying stories that are too complex, and have too many characters or effects. And don't bore listeners by doing something so conventional that it's predictable.

Audio theatre is a blast to create and it makes for great listening when it's done well. Experience is what it takes to do it right, and that experience comes from making a lot of mistakes. Still, it's fun trying your hand at some acting, and audio theatre makes it cheap and easy to do.

See Also

- "Pick the Right Microphone" [Hack #13]
- "Reduce Noise" [Hack #15]
- "Mix Multiple Tracks" [Hack #60]
- "Adopt a Format for Your Podcast" [Hack #20]

—Tony Palermo and Jack Herrington

Interviewing

Hacks 33–36

*I've learned that it's really, really hard to tell
people's stories in an honest way—and in a way
that's interesting to a passing listener. It's hard
to make the first phone call, it's hard to sit in
someone's living room and ask them about their
grief, and it's so hard to whittle that tape down
to a few moments. But it can be so incredible.*
—Karen Callahan

Interviews can be a powerful addition to your podcast format [Hack #20].
Through your interviews, your listeners will meet people they never would
have had the opportunity to meet in person. They might also hear stories of
people just like themselves that touch their hearts.

The hacks in this chapter teach you how to prepare for interviews, how to
record them, and then how to edit them to get the results you want. Along
the way, you will learn a few tricks of the trade from the pros.

HACK #33   Record Great Interviews

Finding the right people to talk to, and having the right form, can mean the
difference between a compelling story and a stifled mess. Learn the
techniques the pros use.

Getting the perfect interview is a combination of getting the right guest,
doing the preparation, and having the right techniques, both technically and
personally. This hack will walk you through everything you need to know.
And if this doesn't satisfy your needs be sure to check the Transom (*http://
www.transom.org*) site for even more on interviewing techniques.

Preparation

The best way to prepare for an interview is to do your homework. Hit the Web and find out all you can about the person you will be interviewing. Take lots of notes in a text editor or in an outliner application. Once you think you have exhausted what you can find out about the interviewee and the subject of the interview, you should organize your notes to make them easy to search through as you are developing your questions.

The next step is to find a perspective. In his book *Radio Production* (Focal Press, 1999), Robert McLeish gives four categories of interview that help you decide what you are looking for from the interview, and what questions to ask:

Informational interview
> You are interviewing for facts you will use in a story in which the interviewee plays a key role. Recording the interview is just a convenient way of taking notes, or you might use fragments of the interview in the story.

Interpretive interview
> You are presenting the interviewee with situations or scenarios and are asking him to provide his perspective and analysis. You as the interviewer need to present the facts and then ask the interviewee to provide an analysis of those events.

Emotional interview
> You and the interviewee walk through an emotional experience as she relates how it made her feel at the time it occurred. In these interviews, you need to remain in the moment with the interviewee and relive the experience with her. Then, work with the interviewee to express her state of mind for your listeners. Ira Glass of the weekly radio show "This American Life" is the master of the emotional interview.

Documentary interview
> You walk the interviewee through past events in a linear timeline. Your job is to draw out as much detail and perspective as you can. Your job also is to pick a starting point in the story, and then take notes as you go that help you ask follow-up questions to gather more detail where the interviewee was vague. Errol Morris's documentary interviews are legendary. He is famous for his grueling, 10-hour interview technique. Check out his work in the movies *The Fog of War* and *Fast, Cheap & Out of Control*.

With this in mind, you need to develop a set of questions that draw the required information or perspective from the interviewee. In all cases, your job as the interviewer is to represent your listeners. This means asking the questions you know your listeners would want asked, even if you already know the answers.

For podcasting interviews, you will likely be using a combination of information and interpretive questions in your interview: asking your subject the when, where, and how of an event, then asking him for his opinion or reaction to a related event.

What questions you ask will vary widely among interviews, but the fundamentals of compelling audio remain. You want to bring your listeners into your interviewee's world by extracting as much detail about the story and about his reaction to it as you can. Avoiding the brushoff and asking questions that probe for deeper detail is a hallmark of a great interviewing technique. Try to find questions that shed new light on the topic and help your listeners understand things in a new way.

How you order your questions can make or break an interview. If you are willing to spend a lot of time in editing, you can rearrange the question and answer blocks to create the story you are trying to tell. But it's easier just to spend some time figuring out the most important parts of the story and placing them near the end, as a crescendo. In addition, you might want to take an exciting question from the middle of the interview and put it at the beginning to get your listeners involved in the story right away. This early punch, followed by some background questions leading to the hard-hitting questions at the end, makes for a very engaging interviewing style.

Location and Hardware Setup

If you're recording more than one person at a time, get them to gather around you, and follow the conversation with your microphone. In general, it's risky to let the interviewee hold the microphone [Hack #13]. Sometimes lavalier mics can be helpful, but they attract noise and eliminate your control. Try to interview away from hard surfaces such as walls. For example, don't record across a desk because you can get phase cancellation from the reflected sound.

If you want a quiet interview, try to get it while seated on a couch in a room that has curtains and a rug. Set everything up the way you like it before you start. Be sure to check for interfering noise, such as air conditioners, fluorescent lights, refrigerators, traffic, radios, noisy crumpling of candy wrappers in front of the microphone, etc. Get away from noise [Hack #15] or have it turned off. A musical background is very difficult to edit. Loud hums are annoying because they add nothing and don't make sense.

Often, a noisy environment is exactly what you want. And be sure also to get the noise by itself, without any talking over it.

I often like to move around during interviews. Get your interviewee up and walking around, and ask him to show you what happened in addition to talking about it. This can relax people and take their minds off the recording. Have the person describe where you are and what you're doing. Refer to objects and sights around you. But try to keep the mic close to the interviewee. All this will reinforce a sense of place, action, and immediacy for your listeners. Moving around also gives you a variety of acoustical environments as structuring options in your final piece: possibilities for movement in time and space.

For "voice of the people"–type interviews (a.k.a. Vox Pop), go where people are waiting. If it seems appropriate, walk right up with your sentence about what you're doing and attach the first question to it. I've heard it suggested that the best recordings come from people wearing funny hats.

Preparing the Interviewee

Spend a few moments with the person before the recorder [Hack #69] starts rolling to let him know how the interview is going to play out. Let him know if you are going to edit the interview to clean up his voice, and let him know the kinds of things you will be editing out. If you are not going to be editing the interview, be sure to let him know that as well.

If you have some time before you get started, let him know the first question you're going to ask. This will allow him to prepare a response, but also will get him mentally prepared for the interview, and will avoid the freeze-up you get when you hit an interviewee with a tough question right out the box. Some interviewers go as far as to send all the questions to their interviewee in advance.

In addition, you should inform your interviewee about the mechanics of the interview: how long it will take, how many questions you will be asking, the type of information you are looking for, and how you will use it. Once the interview is complete, and the content is posted, you should complete the loop by contacting the interviewee to let him know the content is available.

Interviewing Technique

Remember eye contact. Don't let the mic be the focus—otherwise, it occupies the space between you and the person you're talking to so that you have to stare through it. I usually begin by holding the mic casually, as though it's unimportant. Sometimes I'll rest it against my cheek to show it has no evil powers. I might start off with an innocuous question ("Geez, is this as bad as the smog ever gets out here?"), and then slowly move the mic, from below, into position at the side of the person's mouth, but not blocking eye contact. You'll find your own way of being natural with the mic, but it is important.

Don't be afraid to ask the same thing in different ways until you get an answer you're satisfied with. Remember that you can edit together the beginning and ending of two answers, but be sure to get the ingredients. If a noise interferes with a good bit of recording, try to get it again. You can blame it on the machine, but it might be better just to wrap the conversation back to the same place so that you don't get the quality of someone repeating himself.

For repeat answers or more enthusiasm, try: "What?!" or "You're kidding!" or "Really??" Remember to ask why, especially after a yes or no response. Don't forget the preface: "Tell me about...." Let people talk. Allow silence. Don't always jump in with questions. Often, some truth will follow a silence. Let people know they can repeat things—that you're not on the air. It's OK to screw up. And remember to offer something of yourself (don't just take). Think of your listeners' innocence; ask the obvious, along with the subtle.

Save the hard, abstract, or conceptual questions until later in the interview. Lay some groundwork before getting into these all-encompassing questions so that your listeners understand where the questions are coming from. Asking "What is the purpose of your life?" as the first question out of the gate is just going to get you a blank stare.

If you interrupt or overlap your voice with your interviewee's voice, you won't be able to edit yourself out. This will eliminate that sense of the interviewee communicating directly with your listeners; instead, your listeners will be eavesdroppers on your conversation. It commits you to a production decision. If you want to leave your production options open, don't laugh aloud, or stick in "uh-huh" or other vocal affirmations. You must let your subjects know you're with them, but use head nods and eye contact and develop a silent knee-slap and guffaw.

Microphone Technique

If you do want your presence in the interview, think about perspective. Do you want your voice to be very on-mic? If so, you should move the mic up to your mouth for your questions. Do you want to defer the primary focus to the interviewee, but have your questions legible? Then, pull the mic back half way toward you, or speak up loudly.

For close-mic interviewing, keep the mic about 6 inches from the speaker's mouth and a bit off to one side to avoid P-pops (plosives). Go closer if he speaks very quietly, or further away if he is loud.

Use mic distance as a volume control—i.e., move in for whispering and out for loud laughter. Don't change the volume at the machine for this kind of quick change. You can use the built-in limiter or automatic gain control (AGC or ARL) in very changeable level situations. If your background is very noisy, and you want to tone down the noise level, mic your subject even closer (2–4 inches) and reset your record levels.

Equipment Issues

Become comfortable with your equipment. If you are comfortable, everyone else will be. Check, clean, and test all your equipment before you go out. Put in fresh batteries. Make test recordings. Be over-prepared. Be a Boy Scout. Have everything set up before you walk in. Sit in the car (or the subway station, or the bushes) to load and label your first tape, prepare your next tapes for fast changes, set your levels, etc.

Wind, handling, and cable noise are some of the most common recording problems. Use windscreens/pop filters [Hack #12] and try to get out of the wind. With the body of the microphone, as with so many things, learn to have a light touch. Don't let the mic cable bang around or rustle on your clothes. Check that all your cables have good, noise-free connections at both ends. Monitor with headphones to check for these problems.

For recording most sounds or voices, you want the meter peaking at a little above zero, never pegging at the limit. In general, shoot for a record level between 5 and 8 on the mic input knob. Recording levels are critical. You are trying to keep your levels as high as possible without distortion—by recording at a nice, hot level, you rise above hiss and electronic noise. Setting levels is a balancing act between distortion at the top and noise at the bottom. Don't use the Pause button, as it uses up the batteries. Occasionally during recording, check to make sure the recorder is actually working.

Omnidirectional, dynamic mics [Hack #13] are the best choice for all-purpose interviewing and basic sound gathering. Unidirectionals are good for noise rejection from the sides and rear and for stereo in pairs, but they are sensitive to wind and handling. Powered mics (electrets and condensers) have good response and high output, but they are sensitive to wind, handling, humidity, and dead batteries.

Try recording with headphones. They are almost essential for stereo recording. And they're always helpful for catching wind noise, handling noise, cable rustle, RF interference, P-pops (plosives), hums you didn't notice, nervous scratching, and other hazards such as forgetting to turn on the tape recorder. If for some reason you must conserve batteries, unplug the headphones.

Recording Ambience

Get all the sundry sounds [Hack #64], such as phones ringing, dogs barking, and clocks ticking—they can be useful for editing. Leave the machine running for stuff that seems irrelevant: it might not be. Yes, leave the recorder running. If you turn it off, your interviewee will say the best thing you ever heard. Don't pack up your stuff until you are gone. Allow people the chance to say things in conclusion. Ask them who else you should talk to. You might want to record them saying their names and what they do. Record sounds from various distances and perspectives. Experiment. For example, a toilet flush sounds very different when it's recorded from five feet away than when it's recorded with the mic resting on the plumbing.

You can't record too much. Collect and catalog sound effects and ambiences. Save everything, including your notes. Don't erase. Take plenty of extras: spares of everything, depending on how long you'll be on location, including assorted microphones, cables, tape recorder batteries, microphone batteries, tapes, AC cords/adapters, extension cords, windscreens, headphones, lots of plug/jack adapters, patch cords, mic stands, shock mounts, Rowi clamps, goosenecks, duct tape, electrical tape, cleaning and de-magnetizing gear, pens, paper, and labels. Label everything. Make safety copies of precious stuff on your computer.

Remember that you can always use your recorder as a dictating machine, either for on-location narration or for note taking. Don't forget to look as well as listen. Note specifics about what you see and feel. Immediately after an interview, make some notes about what you remember…what mattered.

Be a Good Interviewee

To create a compelling interview, the interviewer must ask thought-provoking questions, and the interviewee must be right there with insightful answers. Here are some tips to help you give great interviews:

Know the format
> Before you sign up for the interview, ask what the interview will be about and what the format is. Find out if the interview will be edited or live. If it will be live, you will want to know what the first question is so that you have time to prepare and so that you don't freeze up. A good interviewer will do this prep. But sometimes you will be the most

experienced person in the room. If you are presented with an option about live versus edited, always pick edited. With edited interviews, you can try multiple ways of answering a question and you will have time to think about your answers. If you are concerned with how you will be edited, make your own backup recording.

Know the audience

What audience will you be talking to, and what do they want to get from the interview? Interesting people have complex lives, only a portion of which might be interesting to the listening audience. You need to take that into account when you figure out your key themes and write your notes for the show.

Key themes

Unless it's an oral history or a storytelling session, you will be there to talk about something; a new podcast, a new book, whatever. You should have two or three key themes in mind on that subject. As the interview progresses, expound on these themes. You don't have to be exclusionary of other background information. But tie the background information back into your themes.

Let's say you are talking about your new Frisbee podcast. You have three key themes in mind: the idea of the podcast, when the podcast is updated and where to find it, and how people can contribute to it. Early on in the interview, you might be asked about your background. Tell people about yourself, and then tie that back into how your experiences laid the groundwork for the podcast, which works on the idea theme. Then talk about how you felt you could contribute to the Frisbee community, and how they can now contribute through your podcast, which works the contributions theme.

Be prepared

Have your own notes about important places, dates, and things you want to remember. Quotes are great, but they can be overplayed if you use them too often. Write out your notes in spoken format so that you remember to read out web site names and other facts slowly and clearly.

Hone your plug

If you are trying to convince people to listen to your podcast, you need to plug it. The plug should compel people to listen, or get them involved. And it should inform them as to what to do next.

Relax

It's very important to be relaxed during an interview. Don't schedule anything right before or right after. Don't drink anything caffeinated or use any alcohol or drugs. These can affect your ability to focus, and can add a stressed or slurry quality to your voice.

Being confident in your ability to nail the interview will help you relax. If you haven't done interviews before, ask a friend to throw some questions at you. This will help you feel more relaxed in the format, and will help you to hone your responses.

Large-small-large

A convincing method for making an argument is to present your point in the large, then provide a small illustrative anecdote, followed by an explanation of how this anecdote proves the larger point. Here is an example: "Westerns are the best type of movie. *The Good, the Bad, and the Ugly* was the best movie ever made. Movies like that make Westerns the best of all the genres."

During the interview, concentration matters most. Answering questions in a way that both informs and interests takes concentration. Professionals call this *being in the moment*, and it's important on both sides of the microphone. It's harder to get distracted with face-to-face interviews because the interviewer will be looking you in the eye most of the time.

With phone interviews, it's easier to be sidetracked by your computer, your kids, or your dog. Lock yourself in a quiet, comfortable spot with just you, your notes, and a pen or pencil to scribble notes during the interview. Turn off your cell phone.

You should consider having a library of *cuts*. Watch a movie actor appear on *The Late Show with David Letterman* to plug her movie. She will always have a clip from the movie that gets people excited about going to the theater to see it. You should do the same with your podcast, and bring along an iPod or CD with these select cuts, or point the interviewer to your site where you have a library of cuts to choose from. Each cut should have a transcript of what is in the cut. Give the interviewer a short list of the cuts that you think will fit the tone of the interview best.

See Also

- "Pick the Right Microphone" [Hack #13]
- "Assemble a Small Recording Rig" [Hack #69]

—*Jay Allison and Jack Herrington*

Record Telephone Interviews

HACK #34 Use hardware and software solutions that will give your phone interview a quality that is similar to what you would get in person.

When you can't get face to face with your subject for financial or scheduling reasons, your best bet is to interview him over the phone. This hack covers the legal issues and gives some technical solutions to get reasonable sound quality for remote interviews.

Keep It Legal

It's a fact of life that sometimes people will say one thing when they are being recorded and something else, probably more candid, when they are away from the microphone. In the U.S., it's illegal to record someone, particularly over the phone, without either one-party or two-party consent. Which of these standards applies to you depends on which state you are in and where you are calling. With one-party consent, only one of the people on the line, normally the interviewer, needs to consent to the conversation being recorded. In the case of two-party consent, all the participants, and that can be more than two people, need to consent.

Practically speaking, you should play it safe and always ask the person you are interviewing if she consents to being recorded. For more information on phone-recording laws, including those in other countries, check the Call Corder site (*http://callcorder.com/phone-recording-law.htm*).

Handset Tap

You can record a conversation over the phone in several ways. The simplest is the handset tap. This device fits between the phone and the corded handset. You disconnect the handset and connect the tap in its place. Then you connect the handset to the tap.

Next, using a microphone cable, you connect the tap to the microphone input on your computer or recording setup [Hack #12].

These are relatively inexpensive devices. The one shown in Figure 5-1, the QuickTap from JK Audio (*http://jkaudio.com/quicktap.htm*), costs around $60.

The audio recorded from taps is good enough for podcasting work. The downside of using a tap is that you cannot use your studio microphone in this setup. Also, the interviewer and interviewee's voices are mixed together on the same channel.

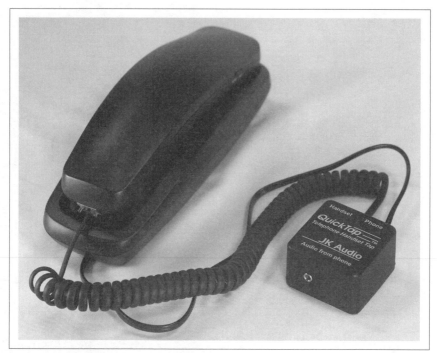

Figure 5-1. A handset tap from JK Audio

Coupler

A step up from the handset tap is the coupler, which fits between the phone and the wall jack. Couplers work like taps, but they have the additional feature of allowing output from the computer to be injected into the conversation through an input port.

Couplers are also handy when you don't have a corded handset to connect to.

The coupler shown in Figure 5-2 is the Voice Path (*http://www.jkaudio.com/voice-path.htm*) from JK Audio. It costs around $110.

The same disadvantages apply to the coupler as to the handset tap. Though in addition, you cannot use the coupler on multiline installations or on Voice over IP (VoIP) systems. However, a handset tap works in almost any situation.

Uncle Doug's hack. Doug Kaye, over at IT Conversations (*http://itconversations.com/*), recommends using two telephone lines and a coupler. The first line has the coupler attached and is the one you record off of. You speak into the sec-

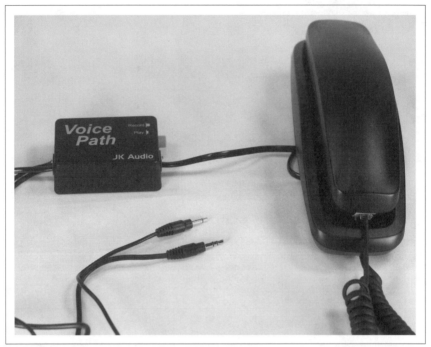

Figure 5-2. A coupler from JK Audio

ond line. When you have all three conferenced together, you will sound remote, just like the person you are talking to. This eliminates some of the volume issues associated with couplers.

Telephone Hybrid

At this point, you might be asking how your local radio shows do telephone call-ins, since those calls sound good and the announcer's voice is obviously coming through the studio microphone. They use a telephone hybrid. And in recent years, the cost of these hybrids has come into the affordable range for podcasters.

The Broadcast Host, shown in Figure 5-3, costs $495 and is available from JK Audio (*http://www.jkaudio.com/broadcast-host.htm*). The company also offers a lower-end version called the AutoHybrid (*http://www.jkaudio.com/ autohybrid.htm*), which is shown in Figure 5-4 and retails for $175.

Hybrids fit between the wall jack and the phone. They have an output for the sound of the caller and an input for the sound of the microphone [Hack #13]. These inputs are usually XLR jacks suitable for use with a mixer or preamp.

Figure 5-3. The Broadcast Host telephone hybrid

Figure 5-4. The AutoHybrid telephone hybrid

To receive a call with a hybrid, just use the call button to take the call off the hook. You will hear the caller in your headphones and be able to talk with him through your microphone.

To start a call, you use your handset to dial and then you press the call button to take the hybrid off the hook. Next, hang up the handset and communicate using your microphone and headphones.

Of all the options I will present in this hack, the hybrid offers the highest sound quality and the most control. You can have the hybrid mix signals into a single channel for recording, or you can record both interviewer and interviewee on separate channels. The two-channel recordings allow for maximum flexibility.

Record Through a Modem

Call Corder (*http://callcorder.com/callcorder.htm*), $49.95, and Modem Spy (*http://www.modemspy.com/*), $24.95, are Windows applications that record audio from the phone line using an internal or external modem that supports voice mode. Using a Y connector, you attach a handset to the modem, then you dial manually or have the computer do it for you, and you talk over the phone as you normally would. The software records the conversation to an audio file.

On the Macintosh, the voice modem-recording situation is not so good. OS 9 and earlier versions allowed you to use the modem audio as an input channel for recording. Unfortunately, Mac OS X has not allowed for this as of this writing. So, while it is possible to take the modem off-hook indefinitely and to hear the audio through your system speakers, it is not possible to record that audio internally.

Teleconferencing Systems

Another option is to use one of the many teleconferencing services available on the Internet. An example of this is Conference Call (*http://conferencecall. com/*). When you sign up, you will get access to a phone number that all your participants can call. You can request that the conversation be recorded and that the recording be sent to you.

Editing these types of recordings is limited because the sounds of all the callers will be mixed equally in stereo.

Conference Calling Your Blog

Audioblogger [Hack #38] (*http://audioblogger.com/*) can record podcasts from a phone call. You can use this feature to record your interviews. Using the conferencing feature on your phone, you call the interviewee and your Audioblogger account, and then conference the two together.

Once the call is over, Audioblogger will post a link to the audio in your blogger account. Then you can download the file to your machine, make any edits you please, and post it on your blog in its finished form.

As with the other teleconferencing solutions, the audio will be mixed together across the mono or stereo signal. This will reduce your ability to make edits exclusive to an individual participant.

Audioblog (*http://www.audioblog.com/*) also supports this feature and works with a variety of different blogging packages.

Cell Phones

In a pinch, you can use the call-recording feature on a cell phone to record a call. However, the space is usually limited and the quality of the recording is very low. Use the Bluetooth, infrared, or Universal Serial Bus (USB) cable support on your phone to download the recorded conversation to your computer.

Recording the Speakerphone

If all you want is the voice for dictation purposes and you have no hardware to speak of, you can record a speakerphone. Use the internal microphone on your computer to record while you talk over the speakerphone. Be sure to turn off the speaker on the computer to avoid feedback. Keep the computer relatively close to both you and the phone. And turn the volume on the phone to its highest level before it starts to distort.

If you have a good omnidirectional microphone on hand, you can place it between you and the speakerphone. If the speakerphone has reasonable sound, you should be able to get a signal quality that approaches that of a teleconferencing system.

Skype

Still another option is to get away from phones altogether and use the Skype service [Hack #35] to make and record calls.

Two-Enders

Even the best recordings of phone interviews can be difficult to listen to. A phone line removes components below and above the content portion of the voice's tonal spectrum. Unfortunately, the removed sections add depth and character to the sound of our voices, so we end up sounding very grating and harsh. All of us have learned to live with it out of necessity, but when we listen to a whole interview conducted over the phone, it can get so bad that even with the most interesting content it becomes something we want to turn off.

Broadcasters have been dealing with this problem for years and have developed a simple solution. It's called a *tape sync* or a *two-ender*. The idea is simple. You have your phone conversation as you normally would, but at both ends you also record the conversation with a high-quality microphone [Hack #13] and recorder [Hack #69]. Then the interviewee sends the interviewer his side of the conversation using email or FTP. On the editing side, the interviews are placed in different tracks, and the alignment is adjusted until the interview questions and responses line up properly.

In the old days, when recording was done on tape, getting the two conversations to line up could be problematic. The tape would stretch, or one tape would run slightly faster or slower than the other would. Now, with digital recording, it's easy to get the two conversations to line up. Though in practice, the 44.1 kHz rate on one recorder is not the same as the 44.1 kHz rate on another, so over a long interview you will have to do some manual addition or subtraction of silence in one signal or the other to line them up.

If the person you are interviewing has a decent microphone and a computer or portable recorder, this should not be a problem to set up.

If he doesn't have a microphone, you have a couple of options. The cheap route is to use Skype or iChat recording [Hack #35], but to have the interviewee use Audio Hijack Pro on his side of the session as well. Then he sends you his file after the interview and you can line up the two. This way, you get a clean microphone sound on both sides of the fence. You record the incoming Skype signal only as a backup. This method will scale to multiple participants in a Skype conference call, but lining up each signal is more time consuming.

If you have the money and you are serious about getting a high-quality sound, you can also hire an independent recordist to go on location to record your interviewee while you talk with her on the phone. The recordist sends you the file with the high-quality sound. You can find independent recordists through your local public radio affiliate.

ISDN

If you have the money and the time, you can use ISDN [Hack #61] to get professional quality for your remote interview. Broadcast studios have ISDN lines to each booth and you can rent an hour or two in the booth at your local station and at a remote station if you know to request the rental of a broadcast booth with ISDN access. It will be expensive, but the sound quality will be spotless.

See Also

- "Record Interviews on Skype" [Hack #35]
- "Edit Your Interviews" [Hack #36]
- "Set Up a Home Studio" [Hack #61]

Record Interviews on Skype

#35 A cheap way to get a phone interview is to use Skype and to record the session digitally.

Recording Skype calls and conferences can be a cheap way to get an interview that sounds reasonably good, without having to travel to meet the person face to face. This hack covers methods for recording Skype calls on both Macintosh and Windows.

Recording Skype on Macintosh

To set up this hack, you will need the following:

Skype (http://skype.com/)
    This is the Skype application, which you probably already have.

Audio Hijack Pro (http://rogueamoeba.com/)
    Audio Hijack Pro [Hack #50] is an excellent audio recording application for the Macintosh that can record from any input source as well as any open application. After installing Audio Hijack Pro, you also need to install the Instant Hijack option using the Install Extras... option on the Audio Hijack Pro menu.

Soundflower (http://www.cycling74.com/products/soundflower.html)
    This is a virtual audio driver for routing audio between applications.

USB headset
    I use a USB headset [Hack #12] for recording, but you can just as easily use your studio microphone and the headphone port on a Mac.

What initially stymied me, and what I was unable to convey for quite a while correctly to the fine people at Rogue Amoeba tech support, was that I wanted to accomplish two separate goals:

- Mix the input from the USB headset's microphone with the output from the Skype application and record it to a file.
- Monitor the output from Skype in the USB headset's earphone.

Because the Macintosh treats each sound stream as a separate item, hijacking the audio from Skype records only what the other person is saying; your microphone input is not mixed into that output. This is very nifty for separation and quality, and for full duplexing of sound; but was not so nifty for my purposes.

Soundflower was part of the solution, allowing me to pass sound through from both input and output to a single audio stream that I could record, but monitoring it was a problem: I heard myself in a slightly delayed echo in the headset earphone.

Rogue Amoeba finally gave me a solution: its pro software includes a number of audio effects, and one of them was the ticket to making this work. Read on for the details.

Putting it together. Download and install Soundflower, which requires a restart, and then Audio Hijack Pro and Skype, which do not. Buy a headset and plug it in. The demo version of Audio Hijack Pro allows 10 minutes of recording per file, after which it inserts noise, so it's fine for testing.

Before running Audio Hijack Pro or Skype, go to the Sound tab in System Preferences. Set the input and the output to your USB headset.

Launch Skype, select Preferences from the File menu, and click the Audio tab. Set the input to your USB headset and set the output to Soundflower (two-channel), as shown in Figure 5-5.

Figure 5-5. Configuring Skype's Audio tab

Launch Audio Hijack Pro. We're going to set up three separate hijacked streams, which is slightly complicated, but makes this work as expected. Select New from the Session menu to create a new audio stream, and select Rename from the Session menu to rename it. Create three streams. To keep them at the top of the list and in order, name the streams as follows: "1 USB in to Soundflower 2ch," "2 Soundflower 2ch to file," and "3 Skype to monitor."

For "1 USB in to Soundflower 2ch," select Audio Device from the Source menu. Select your USB headset from the pop-up menu as the input device. Select Soundflower (2ch) as the output device. Click Hijack. The result should match Figure 5-6.

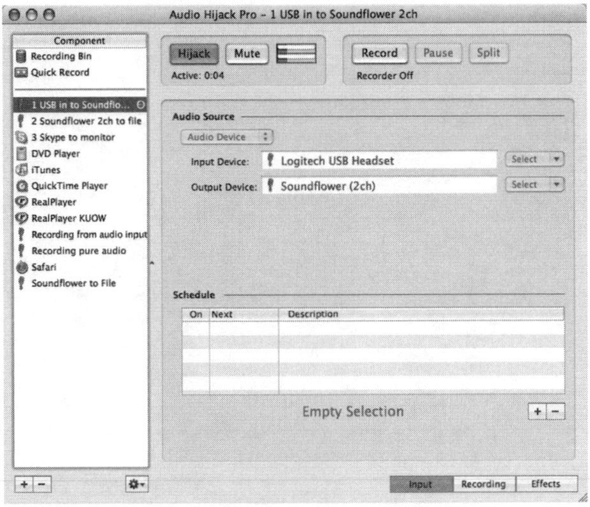

Figure 5-6. Creating the USB-headset-to-Soundflower session

For "2 Soundflower 2ch to file," select Audio Device from the Source menu. Select Soundflower (2ch) as the input device, and select Soundflower (16ch) as the output device. This last step means that the output of this mix isn't played back at all; it's just a dummy method to record a file. Now click the Recording tab and set up the options. Typically, you want a small MP3 file; I'll provide more details on your choices here in a moment. Click Hijack. The result should match Figure 5-7.

For "3 Skype to monitor," select Application from the Source menu, and choose Skype from the list of applications, as shown in Figure 5-8.

Finally, click the Effects tab at the lower right of the screen. Click the upper-left blank spot that reads Click Here to Insert Effect. Choose the Auxiliary Output submenu from the 4FX Effect menu. From the Editor that appears, choose Built-in Audio as the device; leave Source as default. Click Hijack. This should look like Figure 5-9.

Running the hack. To test this setup, make a Skype call to someone you know who won't be annoyed by you testing the service, or use *echo123*, which is a simple echo program that will record what you say and play it back to you. You shouldn't hear yourself, but you should hear the sound of the Skype phone ring and the other person. They should hear you, too. Note that you will need to keep the "3 Skype to monitor" set to Hijack as long as Skype is set to Soundflower (2ch) for output; otherwise, you won't be able to hear the other party.

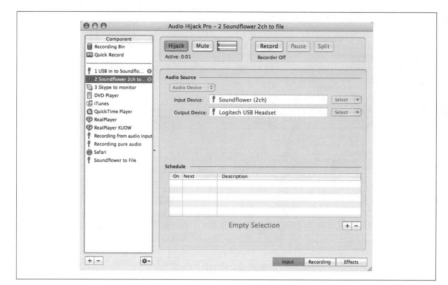

Figure 5-7. Creating the Soundflower 2ch–to-file session that we will record

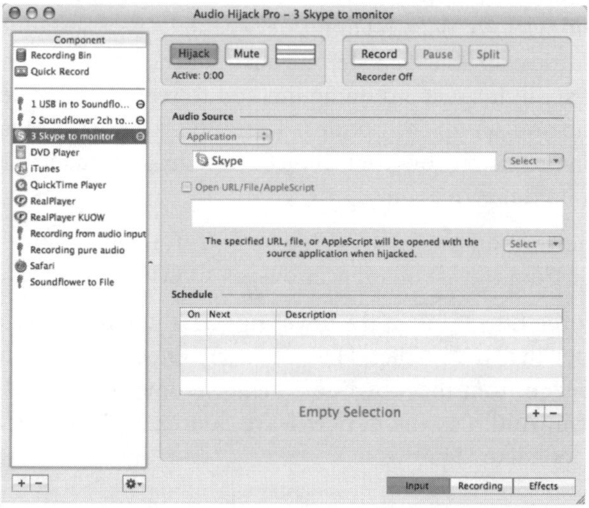

Figure 5-8. Creating the Skype monitor session

Click Record in the "2 Soundflower 2ch to file" stream to record while you speak. Just record a few seconds of both of you talking to each other, and click Record again to stop the recording.

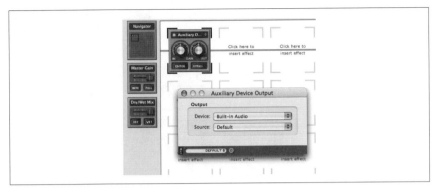

Figure 5-9. Setting up the Auxiliary Output Device plug-in

To listen to the playback, click the Recording Bin item in the left pane of Audio Hijack Pro. You can select the file you just recorded and click Preview to have it played from within the program.

If you cannot hear the other person or if the recording lacks both parties, try quitting Audio Hijack Pro and Skype, and launching them again. Occasionally, the audio settings lag behind the choice in a program, but relaunching seems to clear the state and enable your choice.

Recording Skype on Windows

Of all the options for recording Skype on Windows, the HotRecorder application (*http://hotrecorder.com/*) is the easiest to set up and use. It's a freeware application that records directly from Skype. Figure 5-10 shows the main HotRecorder screen.

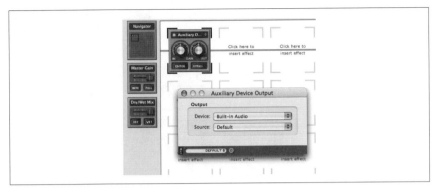

Figure 5-10. Recording Skype with HotRecorder Premium

Simply select Skype as the Source, and then hit the Record button. The recordings are stored in the *PhoneCalls* subdirectory, just below where you installed the application.

There are two problems with the application. The first are the ads that surround the application—you can dispatch these if you pay $14.95 for the Premium version. The second is that the recordings are stored in the impenetrable *.elp* file format, which no sound program understands. The

only way to decode the *.elp* format is to use the Audio Converter application that you can get as a download after you pay the money for the Premium version.

The Audio Converter for HotRecorder application, shown in Figure 5-11,
converts *.elp* files to either *.wav* or *.ogg* format for use in your podcasts.

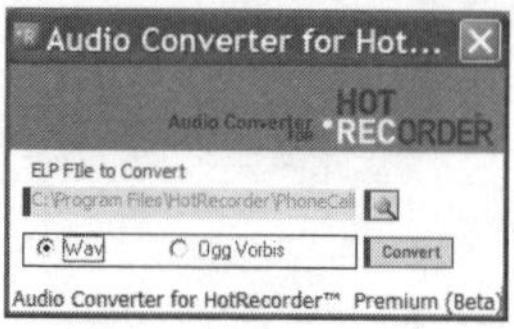

Figure 5-11. Audio Converter for HotRecorder

Other options that record Skype on Windows involve using the NTONYX
Virtual Audio Cable 3 system (*http://ntonyx.com/vac.htm*) to channel the
Skype output directly into Windows Sound Recorder or Total Recorder Pro.
Stuart Henshall and Bill Campbell cover this in depth at *http://henshall.com/
blog/archives/001056.html*.

Testing Out Your Recording

You can test your Skype recording setup by calling a friend and recording
the conversation, or by using the echo123 account.

See Also

- "Edit Your Interviews" [Hack #36]
- "Mix Multiple Tracks" [Hack #60]

—Glenn Fleishman and Jack Herrington

Edit Your Interviews

Learn how to edit interviews to build an interesting story for your listeners.

Scoring the right interview and asking the right questions is just the beginning of the art of the interview. Some interviews contain up to 10 hours of
raw material [Hack #33]. Finding the essence of the story and editing it down to
something that conveys that theme is an art.

I'll discuss four basic types of interview editing in this hack. Categorizing
them this way makes it easier to explain the techniques. But you should not
feel bound by these categories. There are no hard and fast rules. You can
mix and match as you like.

Bare-bones edit

In the bare-bones case, you chop off the silence at the beginning and end of the interview, and normalize the gain; that's it. It's the podcast equivalent of a live interview. Whatever you or the other person said is what you get.

Basic editing

The most basic form of editing involves removing unnecessarily long pauses in speech, large numbers of "ums" and "ahs," and *retakes*. A retake occurs when the person decides during or after a reply that he would rather phrase his answer in a different way. If you told the person you would "clean up the interview," you are obliged to do at least a basic editing pass to remove the gnarly bits.

Artful editing

This is a more substantive overhaul of the material. Segments are edited out completely or are rearranged to provide a better narrative flow. The editing takes into account the position of breath sounds and the natural cadence of the person's speech, and leaves in silence where it implies contemplation.

News editing

Another category altogether is the news interview. In this form, segments of the interview are placed within the context of a studio-recorded story. So, the editor needs to account for the difference between the dead silence of the studio and the ambient sound of the recorded segments.

Each form of editing has different tools and techniques that can help you shape the interview the way you want it. While it's easier to explain the different techniques of editing in groups such as this, you should not feel limited by them. If you want to use techniques mentioned in the upcoming "Artful Editing" section when you are doing a news story, use them. There are no hard and fast rules. You should do what you need to do to create the compelling story that you want.

Basic Editing

The most basic edits start with removing any noise from the signal [Hack #15]. A clean signal is much easier to edit than a signal with periodic background noise.

The next step is to even out the volume across the interview. This involves using the gain envelope feature in your editor to remove any dips in the signal or to cancel out any jumps in volume. You can also use a compression or normalization filter [Hack #56] to do some of this work for you.

After normalizing the volume and removing any noise, chop off the silence at the beginning and end of the file and save the file with a different name. This new file will be the new master copy for the interview.

After the initial cleanup, it's time to do any basic content edits. That means removing extra "ums" and "ahs." A general rule in the broadcast industry is to retain a few "ums" and "ahs" to give a feel for the person's manner of speech. To err is human, very human. All of us talk with "ums" and "ahs," so removing them all will make the person sound like a robot.

With the "ums" and the "ahs" removed, it's time to take out any retakes. Hopefully, you will have some space before the person started her response again. You should coach her to do that before the interview. With the blank space in there, it's easy to simply select the faulty reply and delete it.

That's it for a basic edit of an interview. You might want to fade in at the front and fade out at the back so that when you drop it into your show after the introduction, it won't start abruptly at full volume.

Artful Editing

Artful editing occurs when you take a raw interview and shape it like clay until you have it tell the story you want. It starts not in the editor, but with transcribing the interview with a word processor. In the word processor you can copy, paste, and rearrange the original interview as you please. This document becomes the interview script.

After you have the script, the next step is to clean the interview, as discussed in the "Basic Editing" section. Naturally, you don't have to clean the passages you won't be using in the script, but it might be easier to clean the entire script.

The next step is to take the cleaned interview file and to cut out the segments that you need. Leave some silence before and after each cut so that you can preserve the cadence of the speakers and the natural silence between the segments.

With the cuts in hand, you can rearrange them in the scripted order in a new audio file. Fade in at the beginning, and fade out at the end, and you have your completed interview in the order you want.

There is certainly an art to the structure and the arrangement of the interview, but there is also an art to the way the sound is shaped. The subsections that follow detail what you should be aware of when you are editing to this extent.

Breath sounds. In general, people start a sentence with a short breath in, and then speak fairly loudly, getting progressively softer until the sentence ends. This also works at a macro level with paragraphs of speech: people take a larger breath in the beginning and the sentences tend to start louder and get softer as they expend their breath.

Though the effect varies by individual, it's something you should account for in your editing. Ideally, you should remove entire phrases between the end of the expenditure of breath at the end of a sentence, and the intake of air for the new sentence. If you account for the breath sounds, the effect of the edit should be imperceptible.

Figure 5-12 shows what you would think would be the correct selection to remove a word from some audio. You bracket the word and then remove it. But it turns out that Figure 5-13 is the correct edit.

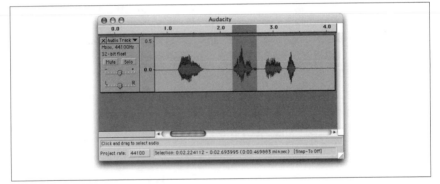

Figure 5-12. A tight cut around a word

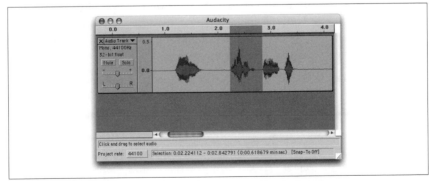

Figure 5-13. The correct cut for a word that accounts for the breath

The edit in Figure 5-13 selects the breath between the two words so that you don't get a double breath or an absence of breath where there should be a natural breath.

Cadence of speech. Some people talk very fast and others speak more slowly. It's almost musical in form, with a beat and a tempo. When you cut between the two speakers, you need to cut the new speaker in at the beat point where the first speaker would have started again. This means that for a fast speaker, the pause between where he finishes his sentence and where the next speaker starts should be short. For a slower talker, the delay should be a little longer.

While this level of detail in editing isn't strictly necessary, it will result in an interview that's easier to listen to if you pay attention to it.

Contemplative silence. Any musician will tell you that the notes you don't play are just as important as those you do play. Sometimes we stop and think, and the result is silence. And sometimes that silence says more than the words we could fill it with. When a person spends some time thinking about an answer, sometimes the delay is, in itself, noteworthy.

This type of delay is effective particularly with big life questions: "Do you regret what you did?" or "Would you do anything differently in hindsight?"

It goes almost without saying that it would be unethical to add silence that would imply contemplation if there was none to start with.

News Editing

Editing for a news story is similar in form to artful editing. The difference is in the role of the interview. In the artful edit, the interview was paramount. With editing for news, the story is paramount and the samples of interview are used as quotes within the body of the story.

The editing starts the same way as in the artful edit. You begin with a transcript of the interviews that you have available for the story. Then you write a story with call-outs for the cuts of the interview that you need.

Once you have the interview cleaned, you extract the cuts you need for the story. Then you record the story using a studio setup, and leave gaps for the quotes from the interview. To smooth out the sound, you should apply a short fade-in effect at the beginning of each cut and a fade-out at the end [Hack #58].

With an editing program such as Audacity [Hack #50], you create a two-track setup and place the studio sounds in one track and the interview cuts in another track. Remove the spaces from the studio sounds, and position the interview segments in those gaps.

Figure 5-14 shows three tracks: one for the host and one each for two guests. At this point, you can save the interview as a multitrack project. Then you mix-down to stereo or mono for the MP3 export of the finished story.

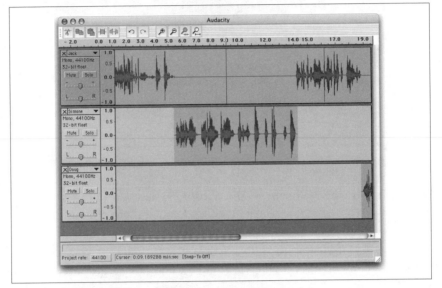

Figure 5-14. A multitrack interview

Ambience. The sound of a studio is dead silence. A friend of mine calls this the "disembodied voice phenomenon," and finds a pure voice arriving as if out of a noise-free vacuum very disturbing. Regardless of whether you find it disturbing, there will be a difference between the background noise of the studio and the noise of the interview cuts. This is evident particularly if the interview was done in the field, as they so often are.

To account for this difference, you should take at least a minute of blank sound recording [Hack #64] before the start of the interview. Then you can loop this blank sound underneath the interview segments with a fade-in and a fade-out at the beginning and the end of the interview clip.

People usually do this by creating a third track for the ambient noise. They use the gain envelope feature to accomplish the fade-ins and fade-outs for the ambient track (as shown in Figure 5-15).

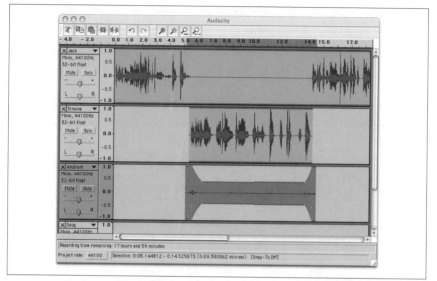

Figure 5-15. The multitrack interview with an ambient track

Done properly, this will smooth the transitions between the studio sound and the interview sound and will make for a much more pleasant listening experience.

Is it worth the effort? It is, because you want your listeners to concentrate on the story's content and the interview quotes, and not be distracted by jarring audio effects.

Up cuts. When people put two thoughts together into a single sentence using a conjunction such as *and*, *or*, or *but*, they tend to finish the last word before the conjunction stronger than normal. If you were to cut it there, the sentence would end going up in volume, not going down, as it normally would. This is called an *up cut*, and it's a sign that someone was cut off before they could finish their thought.

Because time is not so critical with podcasts, there should be no reason to cut someone's quote so short as to create an up cut.

Editing Ethics

With today's technology, it's all too easy to turn an interview that said one thing into an interview that says something else. You need to watch out for two things. First, don't rearrange an interview such that it ends up saying something the interviewee did not intend to say. Second, never rerecord your questions. A subtle change of inflection, or worse, a change in the content of the question, can color the answer in a new light. It's unethical to change the question to alter the meaning of an answer.

It's important to keep in mind as you are editing that you want the result to appear seamless to your listeners. You should make your edits as imperceptible and natural as possible. The interview is what's important, not the edits that you make to clean it up.

See Also

- "Choose the Right Audio Tools" [Hack #50]
- "Add Special Effects" [Hack #58]
- "Mix Multiple Tracks" [Hack #60]
- "Record and Add Background Ambience" [Hack #64]

Blogging
Hacks 37–43

It's all about reaching out to people of a like
mind about things they care about.
—Adam Ritenour

Podcasts start with a blog. The blog will have some entries for the podcasts as well as entries with just text or pictures. You can start a blog in two ways. The first is to use a blog service, and the second is to install blog software on your ISP. Blog services [Hack #38] are the easiest route. With these services, you concentrate on the content, and they do all the infrastructure work. If ultimate control is your thing, or if you already have one or more web sites set up, I recommend the second option of installing your own blog software.

HACK #37 Podcast Without a Blog

Use Podcastamatic or DirCaster to build a podcast from just your MP3 podcast files.

At its core, a podcast is a set of MP3 files and the RSS 2.0 XML file that catalogs them. You don't really need a blog, though there are advantages to having one. In fact, you can start with just the basic set of MP3 files and the RSS 2.0 feed, and add the blog later if that suits you.

A Short Introduction to RSS 2.0

You need to know a little about RSS and, in particular, RSS 2.0, to be able to get your podcast off the ground. RSS stands for Really Simple Syndication. I kid you not. There is some confusion around the different standards and their numbering. Suffice to say they all are XML and all are used primarily to summarize and syndicate the most recent postings (articles, photos, audio recordings, and more) on a web site.

Web browsers such as Firefox and Safari understand RSS, which allows them to treat certain bookmarks as live bookmarks: instead of having to visit a site several times a day to see if anything's new, you can glance at your bookmarks to see if the web page has been updated. Suppose you subscribe to Apple's Hot News feed. If you're all caught up on the recent items, the live bookmark will appear as "Apple Hot News." But if the site contains three new articles you haven't read yet, the bookmark might appear as "Apple Hot News (3)." Specialized applications called *aggregators* are dedicated RSS readers. For example, Bloglines (*http://www.bloglines.com/*) is a web-based aggregator, and NetNewsWire (*http://ranchero.com/netnewswire/*) is an RSS aggregator that runs on the Macintosh.

The only RSS standard that matters for podcasting is RSS 2.0. The podcasting equivalent of an RSS aggregator is called a podcatcher [Hack #1].

Here is an example RSS file from Adam Curry's Daily Source Code show:

```
<?xml version="1.0"?>
<!-- RSS generated by UserLand Frontier v9.0.1
 on Sun, 20 Feb 2005 20:29:52 GMT -->
<rss version="2.0">
 <channel>
  <title>Adam Curry&apos;s Weblog</title>
  <link>http://www.curry.com/</link>
  <description>There are no secrets, only information you don&apos;t yet
    have...</description>
  <language>en-us</language>
  <pubDate>Sat, 19 Feb 2005 23:00:00 GMT</pubDate>
  <lastBuildDate>Sun, 20 Feb 2005 03:30:04 GMT</lastBuildDate>
  <docs>http://backend.userland.com/rss</docs>
  <generator>UserLand Frontier v9.0.1</generator>
  <category domain="http://www.weblogs.com/rssUpdates/changes.xml">
    rssUpdates</category>
  <managingEditor>adam@curry.com (Adam Curry)</managingEditor>
  <webMaster>adam@curry.com (Adam Curry)</webMaster>
  <cloud domain="live.curry.com" port="8080" path="/RPC2"
    registerProcedure="manilaRss.pleaseNotify" protocol="xml-rpc" />
  <item>
   <title>Daily Source Code for February 17th 2005</title>
   <link>http://homepage.mac.com/dailysourcecode/dsc/dsc-2005-02-17.mp3
     </link>
   <description>...</description>
   <category>Daily Source Code</category>
   <guid>http://www.curry.com/2005/02/18#a2742</guid>
   <comments>http://www.curry.com/comments?...</comments>
   <enclosure
     url="http://static2.podcatch.com/blogs/gems/dscedit/DSC20050217.mp3"
     length="19643677" type="audio/mpeg"/>
  </item>
  <item>
   <title>Ssales bonanza!!</title>
```

```
    <link>http://www.curry.com/2005/02/16#a2704</link>
    <description>...</description>
    <category>Blog Posts</category>
    <guid>http://www.curry.com/2005/02/16#a2704</guid>
    <comments>http://www.curry.com/comments?...</comments>
   </item>
  </channel>
 </rss>
```

I've put the important parts in bold. At the top of the file is the title of the
podcast, the author, a short description, and so on. Each entry is listed in its
own <item> block, with the URL of the entry, the time it was made, and a
description. And, in the case of a podcast entry, the enclosure tag points to
the MP3 file of the podcast using a URL. The length and MIME type (i.e.,
audio/mpeg) of the media item are also listed.

Podcasting works because of RSS 2.0's normalized XML format. The feeds
are always structured the same way so that aggregators and podcatchers can
read this XML to see what media are available for download by looking at
the <enclosure> tags. And they can make sure they don't download it twice
by looking at the <guid> or <pubDate> (not shown in this example) for each
entry.

The open nature of the <enclosure> tag means that this mechanism can be
used to transmit audio, video, images, or any other type of attached content.

Blogless Podcasting Alternatives

You have three alternatives for podcasting without a blog: writing your own
RSS file, using Podcastamatic to write the XML file for you, and using Dir-
Caster, which is a PHP script that you run on your server.

Writing your own RSS file.   Copying an existing RSS 2.0 file makes writing one
a lot easier. First you need to find one that is valid to start with. FEED Validator (*http://feedvalidator.org/*) will tell you if a feed is valid when you give it
the URL of the feed. In a pinch, just use a copy of Adam Curry's RSS 2.0
feed at *http://www.curry.com/*.

Once you have an RSS 2.0 file in hand you will want to cut it down to just
the description and a single entry:

```
<?xml version="1.0"?>
<rss version="2.0" xmlns:dc="http://purl.org/dc/elements/1.1/">
<channel>
 <title>My Blog Title</title>
 <link>http://myblog.com</link>
 <description>A description of my blog.</description>
 <language>en-us</language>
 <copyright>(c) Copyright 2004 - 2005.</copyright>
```

```
<lastBuildDate>Sun, 20 Feb 2005 18:35:21 GMT</lastBuildDate>
<ttl>60</ttl>
<item>
 <title>First podcast</title>
 <link>http://myblog.com/podcasts/firstpodcast.mp3</link>
 <description>My very first podcast!</description>
 <pubDate>Sun, 20 Feb 2005 18:34:50 GMT</pubDate>
 <enclosure url="http://myblog.com/podcasts/firstpodcast.mp3"
  length="680734" type="audio/mpeg"/>
</item>
</rss>
```

Replace the title, link, description, and lastBuildDate fields with the appropriate information. For date fields, follow the format shown here *exactly*.

Next, add your first podcast in as the first item, then copy, paste, and change the information for all the subsequent MP3 files. The length field is simply the size of the MP3 file that you can get from a directory listing.

I recommend naming the file *rss.xml* and putting it in your site's root directory. This is one common place podcatchers look when people only specify a site's domain name. The podcast entries should be in their own directory, called *podcasts*, right below the root directory.

With all of this set up, use your FTP or SFTP client to upload the files to your server. Then validate the URL using FEED Validator and start publicizing your podcast.

As you add new podcasts, you will have to add another <item> tag group and change the <lastBuildDate> tag to the current date.

Use Podcastamatic to write the RSS file for you. Podcastamatic (*http://bradley. chicago.il.us/projects/podcastamatic/*) is a small Perl script that uses a directory of MP3 files as source material to create the RSS 2.0 file. It also creates a nice HTML file to act as the site's frontend. You can customize the HTML using the HTML template.

The first step in using Podcastamatic is to download and unpack it. From there, you will need to download ActiveState Perl on Windows (other platforms, including Mac OS X and Linux, include a copy of Perl). Next, make sure you have the MP3::Info Perl module [Hack #7]. More details are available on the Podcastamatic site.

You can check if you have MP3::Info already, and if Perl is installed correctly, by typing this on the command line:

```
% perl
use MP3::Info;
```

After you press Return on the use statement, Perl will complain if it can't find the module. If Perl does not complain, you should be able to use Podcastamatic. Press Ctrl-D to finish your Perl session.

The next step is to configure your Podcastamatic installation. This starts with creating the configuration file.

Copy *example_podcastamatic.conf* to *podcastamatic.conf*. Then open *podcastamatic.conf* in your favorite editor. About 20 variables can be tweaked, but only 7 really need adjustment in the beginning:

Title
> The title of your podcast

Description
> A description of your podcast

AudioPathServerSide
> The path to the MP3 files on your computer

AudioPathWebSide
> The base URL of where the MP3 files will be located on the server

HTMLServerSide
> The path where you want the generated HTML file to go on your computer

XMLServerSide
> The path where you want the RSS file to go on your computer

XMLWebSide
> The URL of where the RSS file will go on the server

Remember, all you need when you show up to this party are the MP3 files. The Perl script will create the RSS 2.0 and HTML files for you. You just need to tell it where the MP3 files are, and where you want to put the RSS and HTML files both on your machine and on the server. The script will do the rest.

To run Podcastamatic, use this command:

```
% perl podcastamatic.pl
Reading configuration file "podcastamatic.conf" ... Done.
Looking for audio files...
   Found bc/bc_0805074562.mp3
   1 audio files were found.
Building XML file "bc/rss.xml"
   Adding "Revolution in the Valley"
   XML file is done.
Building automatic HTML file "bc/index.html"
   Adding "Revolution in the Valley"
   Automatic HTML file has been created.
Note: No template driven HTML file to be generated per config file.
```

The output files, located in the *bc* directory where I configured the output to go, are now ready for uploading to your web server with FTP or SFTP. Once the files are uploaded, use FEED Validator (*http://feedvalidator.org/*) to make sure the feed is valid before you publicize it. You should also subscribe to your feed with your favorite podcatcher to make sure everything is created properly.

Use DirCaster to podcast a directory on the server. I saved the easiest tool for last. DirCaster (*http://www.shadydentist.com/wordpress/software/dircaster*) is a PHP script that you download into a directory on a PHP-enabled web server. For example, you might choose a directory called *podcast*. You upload your MP3 files into that directory as well. When you access the *dircaster.php* script through your web browser, you will see that the script has read all the MP3 files in the directory and has created a properly format-ted RSS 2.0 feed. How simple is that? To add more podcasts, you simply upload another MP3 file to the directory.

Before you upload the script, you will want to make a few changes to it with your favorite text editor. At the top of the file, you need to set the `$titleTAG` variable to the title of your podcast, the `$linkTAG` variable to the URL of your home page, and the `$descriptionTAG` variable to a description of your pod-cast.

Once you make these changes, you should upload the *dircaster.php* file, and your MP3s, and then try it out. Always make sure you use FEED Validator (*http://feedvalidator.org/*) to test your feed. Then use your podcatcher to sub-scribe so that you see what your audience will see.

See Also

- "Blog Your Podcast" [Hack #38]
- "Manage Bandwidth" [Hack #39]
- "Tag Your MP3 Files" [Hack #40]

HACK #38 Blog Your Podcast

Blog your podcast with a hosted blogging service, or with software on your ISP.

By far, the most popular method for podcasting is through a blogging ser-vice or through blog software installed on your hosting provider. This hack walks you through all the different options that are available to you.

Podcast with Blogger

Blogger is a free blog service, and that's a wonderful thing. It means you can get into podcasting with no financial commitment. The first thing to do is to set up your Blogger blog. Surf over to Blogger (*http://blogger.com/*) and follow the three-step process to set up your account.

After setting up your account, go to the Settings tab and the Site Feed section and select Yes in the box next to Publish Site Feed. That will set up your Atom feed.

Next, go to the Formatting section of the Preferences tab and select Yes in the box next to Show Link Field. Now you will have a place to put the URL of your MP3 podcast file.

Create a new blog entry that has a link to your podcast MP3 file, and publish it. You can't host your MP3 files on Blogger, so you will have to find another place to put them that is accessible to the Internet [Hack #39].

To save your sanity, check the blog home page to make sure the entry was posted. Then check the *atom.xml* file located at *http://yourblog.blogspot.com/ atom.xml* just to make sure it's reasonable and seems to have the right entries in it.

FeedBurner. The *atom.xml* file is a good start, but to be a valid podcast feed it has to be RSS 2.0. The next step is to use FeedBurner (*http://feedburner. com/*) to create the RSS 2.0 feed for the site from the *atom.xml* feed.

Surf over to FeedBurner and type the URL of your *atom.xml* file into the Feed URL field. From there, you will need to describe your blog and set up an account. Not to worry, though; it's free.

To turn your Atom feed into RSS 2.0 [Hack #37], you need to check the Smart-Cast button. Now you will have a new RSS 2.0 feed hosted by FeedBurner. Even better, FeedBurner also gives statistics for each burner feed so that you can see how popular your podcast is.

Use your podcatcher to subscribe to your new RSS 2.0 feed to make sure everything is in order. Then use the Template tab in Blogger to add a link to your FeedBurner RSS 2.0 feed.

Audioblogger. Audioblogger is a very cool service for Blogger clients. When you hook it up to your Blogger account, it will give you a phone number and a PIN. You can call that number, enter your primary phone number and PIN, and then talk for as long as you want (long-distance charges might apply). The audio will be stored on their server as an MP3 file and your Blogger blog will be updated with a new entry pointing to the file.

Since Blogger and Audioblogger accounts are free, nothing can stop non-Blogger podcasters from using the service. Just download the saved MP3 file from Audioblogger and start editing it.

This service makes it very easy to record phone interviews [Hack #34] for later podcasting. Simply conference in your Audioblogger account and it will record the entire conversation. Then download the audio, and delete the blog entry from Blogger.

Podcast with Radio UserLand

Radio UserLand is a commercial blogging service with an easy-to-use client for Windows and Macintosh. It costs $39.95 per year, though there is a 30-day trial period during which you can experiment and see if it's right for you. The first step is to download the client from Radio UserLand (*http://radiouserland.com/*).

Start up the application on your Windows or Macintosh computer and you will be presented with your web browser pointing to a page on your machine. From here, you can set up your blog. I suggest making a blog entry or two just to get a feel for the interface. The fact that your local blog and your remote blog are kept in sync can take a little getting used to.

Once you have your blog set up, click the Prefs button on the bar along the top of the web browser window. Then select RSS Configuration. Around the middle of the page is an entry for language; make sure your language is selected there. Then go back to Prefs and select "RSS enclosures." Check the last box on the page, the one that talks about adding enclosures to your RSS output channels.

Now go back to the Home tab and edit one of your previous posts. You will see that you now have an Enclosure item along with the blog text field. Use this field to enter the URL of your MP3 file.

If your podcast MP3 files are smaller than 1 MB, you can have Radio User-Land host a few of them for you. To do this, move your MP3 file into the *www/gems* folder in the Radio UserLand application's directory. This file will be uploaded to the server automatically, and you can put a link to it in the *enclosures* field.

If your files are larger than 1 MB, you will need to host them somewhere else [Hack #39].

Before you go out to the world with your podcast, make sure you test it using your favorite podcatcher [Hack #1]. In addition, you should validate the RSS feed using FEED Validator (*http://feedvalidator.org/*).

Podcast with Movable Type

Movable Type (*http://movabletype.org/*) is an extremely popular, commercial, Perl-based blogging system from Six Apart. A single-user, noncommercial license is free.

Getting started with Movable Type is straightforward. You upload it to your web server, unpack it, and then run an installation script. The Movable Type site provides a full walk-through of the installation. The requirements are Perl support and MySQL, which are satisfied easily by any reasonable hosting provider.

Movable Type 3 comes with RSS 2.0 support preinstalled, but it does not support the enclosure extension. To get enclosures in your RSS 2.0 feed, you will need to install a Movable Type plug-in.

Using the enclosure plug-in. Movable Type has a cool plug-in infrastructure that allows you to add everything from surveys to weather reports to your blog. Brandon Fuller's MT-Enclosures plug-in (*http://brandon.fuller.name/ archives/hacks/mtenclosures/*) allows you to add <enclosure> tags to the RSS 2.0 template. Installing the plug-in is a snap. Simply unpack the archive and upload the *Enclosures.pl* file to the *plugins* directory within Movable Type.

Now when you look at your Movable Type administration home page, you should see MT-Enclosures listed with the active plug-ins. That's a good sign. You are halfway home.

The next step is to add an MTEntryEnclosures tag to your RSS 2.0 Index template:

```
<item>
<title><$MTEntryTitle remove_html="1" encode_xml="1"$></title>
<description><$MTEntryBody encode_xml="1"$></description>
<link><$MTEntryPermalink encode_xml="1"$></link>
<guid><$MTEntryPermalink encode_xml="1"$></guid>
<category><$MTEntryCategory remove_html="1" encode_xml="1"$></category>
<pubDate><$MTEntryDate format_name="rfc822"$></pubDate>
<$MTEntryEnclosures$>
</item>
```

After saving the revised template, you will need to rebuild the RSS 2.0 page.

With this plug-in installed, you will get enclosure tags for any media that are in the body of the blog posting. That includes audio, images, and movies. One potential gotcha is that many podcatchers will get only the first enclosure tag. So, if your blog entry has an image tag included before the link to the sound, you will get the image enclosure tag first.

I encountered this enclosure ordering problem on my site, so I edited the plug-in to remove any code that looked for GIF or JPEG images. It was easy just to comment out the lines that looked for these tags.

Podcast with WordPress

WordPress 1.5 (*http://wordpress.com/*) is a free PHP-based blogging system that you download to your ISP web account. Any hosting service that supports PHP and MySQL should be compatible with WordPress. Thankfully it already has support for RSS 2.0 and enclosures baked right in. Any time you include a reference to a media file within a blog entry, WordPress will create the appropriate enclosure tag automatically. Now that's service!

If for some reason you want don't want to add a link in the entry itself, you can add the enclosure tag through the custom fields mechanism. When you edit your blog entry, click the Advanced button and scroll down to the custom field area. Add a new custom field with the key named enclosure. Then type the URL of the enclosure into the value field, its size in bytes, and its type, on three consecutive lines separated by returns:

```
http://www.boundcast.com/podcasts/bc_0131465759.mp3
760465
audio/mpeg
```

It's ugly, but it works out of the box. Obviously you will need to get the size of the MP3 file for this to work. Any directory listing should give that to you.

Podcast with Drupal

Drupal (*http://drupal.org/*) is a PHP-based blogging application. The 4.6.0 version of Drupal supports RSS 2.0 enclosures natively, but you need to configure the application properly. You start by enabling some additional modules. Use the Administer menu and select the Modules submenu. Enable the aggregator and upload modules by selecting the corresponding checkboxes on the righthand side of the window. From there, select the Blocks submenu and enable the Syndicate checkbox.

With these configuration items enabled, an attachment field will appear for new blog entries. Click the Choose File button to select a media file to attach to the blog entry, and then click the Attach button to complete the upload and attachment. If you just press Preview or Submit, you won't get the attachment on the blog entry.

Your blog's readers will see an XML icon above the blog's navigation menu. This is an RSS 2.0 feed, which any podcatcher can use.

Podcast with Libsyn, AudioBlog, or Odeo

Three new dedicated podcasting services are available on the Web. The first is Liberated Syndication, the second is AudioBlog, and the third is Odeo. These provide podcast hosting for accounts for a monthly fee.

Liberated Syndication. Liberated Syndication (*http://www.libsyn.com/*), or Libsyn, is a hosted service designed specifically for podcasting. The company has a unique billing model. You sign up for a certain number of megabytes per month. The basic rate is $5 for 100 MB per month. This means you can upload 100 MB of new podcasts per month, regardless of how much you have uploaded in the past. If you figure that every podcast you make will be around 5 MB, that's 20 podcasts. You are not charged for any bandwidth fees.

To set it up, you surf to the Libsyn site and click the "sign-up for service" link. Follow the registration and payment steps, and within a few pages you will be editing your blog. To create a new entry, click the Podcast/Blog tab. You will get a blog entry form with a button on the bottom that allows you to upload your podcast file. You can also make a text-only blog entry if you want.

The service manages the RSS 2.0 feed for you automatically, with the appropriate enclosure tags.

As of this writing, you can control the blog's look and feel through templates. You can change the blog's fonts and styles by altering the CSS, and you can change the contents of the sidebar by using a simple Wiki-style syntax.

Libsyn is the easiest way to start podcasting if you currently don't have a web site or a blog.

Libsyn has a directory of all its podcasts at *http://directory.libsyn.com/*. You can subscribe your aggregator to them by following the RSS links of the main directory page.

Audioblog. Audioblog (*http://audioblog.com/*) provides a service similar in form to Audioblogger, but extends the reach to all the various blogging platforms and services. For $4.95 you have a hosting service for your media that you can attach to your hosted blog (e.g., your *http://blogger.com*) account, or the Movable Type or WordPress blog you have on your ISP.

You can add sound to your blog through Audioblog in three ways. The first is by uploading your podcast MP3 file. The service also provides a Flash extension that you can use to record directly to the site, as well as a phone number you can call where you can leave messages that will be posted to your account. Disk space and bandwidth are unlimited. However, the size of any one media file is limited.

When you post through Audioblog, the system automatically will contact your Blogger account, or the blog on your ISP, and post the blog entry with the associated media link. It also posts a sexy Flash player that readers can use to listen to your podcast without leaving the page.

Audioblog also provides an RSS 2.0 feed for your audio that you can link to from your home page. This means you don't have to hack Movable Type to get it to put enclosure tags in the RSS 2.0 XML.

You can think about Audioblog as an extension service for your existing blog. If you already have a blog, and you want to add audio and are willing to pay a monthly fee to have someone deal with that for you, Audioblog is a service you should look into.

Odeo. As this book went to press, the Odeo (*http://www.odeo.com/*) podcasting service was in beta and preparing for its launch.

Odeo is similar to AudioBlog (*http://audioblog.com/*). There is a Flash recorder tool to record your podcasts. You can also upload podcasts as MP3s, and phone them in on a phone number hosted by the service. Pricing specifics had not yet been worked out as this book went to press.

One innovative new feature is the OdeoSyncr application that you can download to your Windows machine or Macintosh. This is a very easy-to-use podcatcher that works specifically with Odeo podcasts.

Podcast for Free with Ourmedia

Ourmedia (*http://ourmedia.org/*) is the podcasting service of the Internet Archive (*http://archive.org/*). As long as the material you upload is licensed under a Creative Commons license, you can podcast on their service free of charge.

To begin using the service, simply request a new account by clicking the Register link on the home page. Follow the instructions and a new account will be created for you. Your password will be sent to the email account you specify.

Once you have your password, log in to the service and click "my page." From here you can put up a picture of yourself and flesh out your biographical information. To upload your first podcast, click the "post to my blog" link.

The top portion of the blog form contains the subject and an edit box for the entry. The bottom portion of the page is where you specify attached media files using the Attachments area. Once you have your blog entry and the attached MP3 podcast file, press the Submit button to post it to the Web.

There are some downsides to the service. The upload can be fairly slow, particularly if you have a slow connection to the Internet, and you don't get any progress information as it's going. In addition, you don't have much control over the look of the blog. But, free is a great price, especially when you just want to try out podcasting.

Categorize Your Podcast Feeds

Organizing your podcasts by category can help your listeners navigate to the shows that interest them. Both Movable Type and Word Press have category management built in. You can assign one or more categories to each post. The number and organization of the categories are completely up to you.

With Movable Type, you will need to create a new RSS 2.0 template for each feed. First copy the contents of the RSS 2.0 Index template. Then create a new template and paste in the contents from the original template. Alter the MTEntries tag to add a category filter using the category attribute, like so:

```
<MTEntries lastn="15" category="fun" >
<item>
<title><$MTEntryTitle remove_html="1" encode_xml="1"$></title>
<description><$MTEntryBody encode_xml="1"$></description>
<link><$MTEntryPermalink encode_xml="1"$></link>
<guid><$MTEntryPermalink encode_xml="1"$></guid>
<category><$MTEntryCategory remove_html="1" encode_xml="1"$></category>
<pubDate><$MTEntryDate format_name="rfc822"$></pubDate>
</item>
</MTEntries>
```

You can also filter on author if you have multiple blog authors. And you can filter on number of days if you want to restrict it to the last couple of days or longer.

Once you have created your new template, you should rebuild the site and use your podcatcher to check out the feed. If that works, add some links to the category feeds to your Main Index template, which is your blog's home page.

WordPress has the category feed capability built in. Simply add a category qualifier to your RSS 2.0 URL, like this:

```
http://localhost/wordpress/wp-rss2.php?cat=1
```

This is the RSS 2.0 URL with a category filter on it. To get the full feed, simply remove the ?cat=1 portion. To change the category, just tweak the value from 1 to the ID of the category you want. Category IDs are listed in the Categories section of the Manage tab.

You can add links to these category-specific feeds to your Sidebar template or Links template in the Theme Editor portion of the Presentation tab.

Hacking the Hack

To make it easier for your audience to listen to the show straight from your blog, you can use a free embedded Flash player, called MusicPlayer (*http://musicplayer.sourceforge.net/*). Download and unpack the player you want. You can choose the wide version or the slim version. I've used the slim version in this example.

First upload the *xspf_player_slim.swf* Flash player movie to your site in a directory that is visible to the web server. The next step is to create an *XML Shareable Playlist Format (XSPF)* file that references just the podcast. These files are given the extension *.xspf*, and their format is defined on the format's home page (*http://xspf.org/*).

Here is an example XSPF file from my site:

```
<?xml version="1.0" encoding="UTF-8"?>
<playlist version="0" xmlns="http://xspf.org/ns/0/">
 <trackList>
  <track>
   <location>http://boundcast.com/podcasts/intro.mp3</location>
   <annotation>Boundcast Introduction</annotation>
  </track>
 </trackList>
</playlist>
```

The important details are the URL of the MP3 file for the podcast, and the name of the podcast. Since it's a playlist file, you could have multiple tracks, one with every podcast on the site. It's up to you.

Upload the *.xspf* file to your site in a place that is accessible from the web server, perhaps in the same directory as the podcasts.

The final step is to add the player to your web page. Here is some example code that you can drop in your blog entry or page template, depending on how you want to use the player:

```
<object classid="clsid:d27cdb6e-ae6d-11cf-96b8-444553540000"
codebase="http://fpdownload.macromedia.com/pub/shockwave/cabs/flash/swflash.
cab#version=7,0,0,0"
id="xspf_player_slim" align="middle" height="15" width="400">
 <param name="allowScriptAccess" value="sameDomain"/>
```

```
<param name="movie"
  value="http://www.boundcast.com/podcasts/xspf_player_slim.swf"/>
<param name="quality" value="high"/>
<param name="bgcolor" value="#e6e6e6"/>
<embed
src="http://www.boundcast.com/podcasts/xspf_player_slim.swf?playlist_url=/
podcasts/040105.xspf"
  quality="high" bgcolor="#e6e6e6" name="xspf_player_slim"
  allowscriptaccess="sameDomain" type="application/x-shockwave-flash"
  pluginspage="http://www.macromedia.com/go/getflashplayer"
  align="center" height="15" width="400">
</object>
```

The two places you need to tweak are the movie tag, which is a URL to the location of the player on your site, and the src attribute, which is the same but has the playlist_url argument added with the relative URL of the playlist. In this case, I chose to use the filename *040105.xspf* for the playlist, and to put it in the same directory as the movies and the rest of the podcasts.

See Also

- "Podcast Without a Blog" [Hack #37]
- "Manage Bandwidth" [Hack #39]
- "Tag Your MP3 Files" [Hack #40]

HACK #39   Manage Bandwidth

Obviously it's great to get a lot of listeners, but it's not great if you get a big bandwidth bill at the end of the month. Find out several approaches to avoiding monster bandwidth bills.

> Well folks here's a story about a man name Jed, / He wrote a funny blog and was Slashdot-ted, / When he first got the news he was one happy dude, / Then he opened his ISP bill, and was totally screwed.
>
> —The Ballad of Slashdotted Jed

Bandwidth is a serious problem for people with popular blogs. And considering that the average HTML page is 30 KB and the average podcast size is 5 MB, it quickly can become a big problem for you, too.

Let's do a few calculations, starting with an example monthly bandwidth limit of 100 GB. If my average podcast is around 5 MB, I can get 200 shows in 1 GB (roughly). With a 100 GB monthly limit, I can get 20,000 total downloads before I go over the limit. In practice, I would hit that limit before that because of the transfer protocol cost and the RSS feeds.

For a single podcast, 20,000 downloads a month sounds like a lot. But this is a subscription service, and if you figure on 20 podcasts in a month, the number of downloads drops to 1,000 per podcast, which looks a lot like a small fan base.

What's worse is that many hosting sites have far less than a 100 GB bandwidth limit on their accounts. This means the size of the audience you can support will drop dramatically.

The troubles aren't going to come from your fan base, though. When you look at your server logs, you will be able to see well ahead of time if you are going to go over your bandwidth allocation from the day-to-day downloads of your fan base. The problem comes from the spike in bandwidth caused by services such as Slashdot.

Slashdot is the geek capital of the Internet, and it's the reason you want to be sure of what happens in an overage situation. Any site referenced from an article off the Slashdot home page invariably will be hammered with hundreds of thousands of requests in the first few hours. The effect is so well known that it has been dubbed *Slashdotting*. Sites brag about being Slashdotted and withstanding the load.

If you say something interesting enough to get on Slashdot, chances are good that your podcast will have a sudden and dramatic rise in the number of downloads. And the only thing you will notice is that your site is responding much slower, or not at all. If you are lucky, your site will be disabled due to bandwidth overage and that will be the end of it. If you haven't planned for this and checked out your ISP contract, you could be in for a nasty surprise.

There are four solutions to the bandwidth problem: using a free content hosting service, using a pay-for file service, using your own ISP, and having your own server and a dedicated connection.

Free Content Service

You can avoid bandwidth and storage problems altogether by using a free content service such as the Internet Archive (*http://www.archive.org/*). They will pay the hosting costs and the bandwidth charges for you, and will give you a link that you can use in your blog. In exchange, you need to conform to the Creative Commons license and use their minimum MP3 encoding format (64 Kbps).

You start with getting an account on the Internet Archive. Then download ccPublisher from *http://mirrors.creativecommons.org/software/publisher/*. Use ccPublisher to upload your file to the server. At the end of the process, you will get a link to the content description page. And from that page you get a link to the media itself. You will use that link on your blog and in your RSS enclosure tags.

The Ourmedia service (*http://ourmedia.org/*) is a free blogging and podcasting system built on top of the Internet Archive storage system [Hack #38].

At the time of this writing, none of the top 10 podcasts was using this technique for file storage.

Hosted File Services

For $99.95 a year, you can get a 250 MB file store on .Mac, which you can use to store your podcasts (for $50 more per year, you can get 1 GB). The fine print on the contract states that bandwidth overages will result in the site being disabled, though it doesn't mention the exact bandwidth restrictions. To create a .Mac account, go to *http://www.mac.com/*.

This solution is ideal if you already have an account on a service such as .Mac. But with more than 1 GB of file space going for around $7 a month, you can do better with other ISPs, and have complete control of your hosting environment.

At the time of this writing, two of the top 10 podcasts were using .Mac for hosting, including Adam Curry's Daily Source Code.

Using Your ISP

The dreaded scenario I painted at the beginning of the hack referenced a hosted ISP service. With this type of service, you pay a small monthly fee to get a portion of a server on the Internet, and a small amount of disk space and bandwidth. DreamHost (*http://www.dreamhost.com/*) and BlueHost (*http://www.bluehost.com/*) are two examples of this type of service.

So, what happens when you go over the bandwidth limit with an ISP? That depends on the hosting service. Some will allow reasonable overages. Others will warn you and then start denying the transactions. Still others will charge you for overages on a per-megabyte basis. The lesson is, read the fine print before signing up with a hosting company. And if the company doesn't specify anything, get something in writing from an authority at the company about how bandwidth overages will be handled.

When interacting with the hosting company, be clear what you intend to do with the service; you plan on hosting a blog, that blog will reference MP3 files, created by you, on the server, and it's likely that people will be downloading them quite often. If you go way over and you were cagey or deceptive about your intentions with their service, you could be held in breach of contract anyway. Honesty is the best policy.

If you plan to do just a few podcasts a month, you will probably be fine. But if you plan on podcasting exclusively and often, and you are a popular person with a popular topic, you will need to take steps to ensure you don't run into bandwidth problems.

Staying under the limit. One way to combat excessive traffic is to reduce the number of items in your RSS feed. If you feed only the 3 most recent podcasts, when new subscribers show up they will download just those 3 and not the 10 you might have listed on the home page. To get more they would have to go to the home page and click the links manually.

Another way is to host your MP3s on a different server. There is no hard and fast rule that says the blog server also has to serve the MP3s. If you can find a hosting site that will host just the audio, you can use a link to that in the blog and in your enclosure tag.

In an emergency, pull this lever. If you do go over your bandwidth limit and you want to stop traffic yourself, simply rename the RSS feed file, and rename your podcast files temporarily. The server will start responding with "Resource Not Found" responses, which are a lot smaller than your podcasts.

Find a hosting service. If you don't have a hosting service and you are going to start looking for one, I recommend spending a least a couple of hours on the task. Keep some notes on what hosts have what plans. Shop around. In particular, make sure you know the bandwidth limits and overage policy. If you have the time, ask for a recommendation on a podcast forum or mailing list. Sometimes it's only after a few months that a service's flakiness becomes apparent. You can leverage the community to get some honest feedback about good services.

When people ask me, I recommend DreamHost (*http://dreamhost.com/*), BlueHost (*http://bluehost.com/*), or WebIntellects (*http://webintellects.com/*). All of these provide a great service at competitive rates.

At the time of this writing, most of the podcasts in the top 10 were hosted using an ISP service. However, no particular ISP service dominated the field.

Hosting Your Own Servers

When it comes to hosting your own servers, you have two choices. You can get a commercial-grade DSL connection with a static IP address to host your web server. Commercial DSL lines have a guaranteed bandwidth and have a fixed monthly fee. With this, you can set up a server and publish as many podcasts as you want, without worrying about bandwidth overage charges.

If you are looking for something even larger, you can do what ISPs do. What is an ISP after all? It's a company or co-op that has leased some T3 or larger lines from a larger network provider. Then it set up shop with some firewalls, routers, and server hardware. Some individuals have done this for themselves and they donate or rent space very cheaply to their friends and family.

On the upside, the costs look appealing if you have a very large web service in mind. You can put as much cheap equipment as you want behind the firewall as a one-time cost, and the only monthly cost is the connection.

The downside of both methods is that maintenance is a nightmare. Worms, viruses, denial-of-service attacks—all of these things that once fell on your ISP's plate now fall on yours. This leaves you less time for podcasting.

If you only want to get better bandwidth rates for your podcasts, this is not the avenue to take. However, if in your travels, you find a person or co-op that is doing this as a friendly service, you should try to see if you can get involved. As with an ISP, you should be up front with what you are going to do with the service, and have your current bandwidth numbers in mind to give them a sense of the impact you will have on their service.

BitTorrent

BitTorrent is a peer-to-peer (P2P) file-sharing network. The value of posting your podcasts on the BitTorrent network is that you will share the bandwidth load with everyone who seeds a copy of your file. Unfortunately, using BitTorrent is not as simple as just uploading your file to a server. First you have to understand the basics.

Using a BitTorrent client, a user can download a *.torrent* file to start the Bit-Torrent download. This *.torrent* file contains a pointer to a tracker application hosted somewhere on the Internet that the client then logs into. The tracker tells the client that several other clients are *seeding* that file. The download client then connects to those seeding clients to get chunks of the file.

You have several BitTorrent clients to choose from. On the Macintosh you have the Tomato Torrent (*http://sarwat.net/bittorrent/*) and original BitTorrent (*http://bittorrent.com/*) clients. On Windows you have the original Bit-Torrent among other native clients. But the one that seems to get the most praise is the cross-platform Java client named Azureus (*http://azureus.sf.net/*).

One particularly nice feature of Azureus is the graphical display that shows you what portions of the file are still left to download.

This file chunking is one of the reasons BitTorrent is so fast. You don't download the entire file from one source. You download segments of the file from a variety of hosts and assemble them into one big file as you go.

The moment you download a segment of the file your client is also seeding that segment to the rest of the world. That's how BitTorrent distributes the bandwidth load. Every client that has a copy of the file distributes portions of that copy to everyone else.

The downside is that at least one client must be seeding the whole file for it to be downloadable. This is why *web seeding* is so important. In the web seeding model you have a server on the Internet that both holds the *.torrent* file and acts as a continuous seed for the whole file. If some clients come along and get the file, they too will act as seeds, but in the meantime, at least the file will be on the network. Some web hosting services such as Hurricane Electric (*http://he.net/*) provide web seeding services.

If you don't have a web seeded file, you will have to host that seed yourself by having a computer on the network that runs the BitTorrent client continuously. Unfortunately, this is not so easy. Most people don't even notice when their client isn't seeding the file it's downloading. And in most cases, for home machines connected through a router, your client will not be able to seed for two reasons: the BitTorrent ports are blocked by the firewall in the router or in the operating system of the computer; and the host is on an internal IP address provided by the Network Address Translation (NAT) system in the router (in other words, your broadband provider's network configuration renders your computer effectively invisible to the outside world).

Now that you understand the basics, let's talk about how to put this into practice.

Finding a tracker. You can't BitTorrent a file without first having a tracker to assign the file to. Trackers on the Internet come and go, primarily because they are being used to exchange copyrighted material. But some are restricted to material where there is no copyright infringement, and one in particular, *http://downloadradio.org/*, is designed specifically for podcasting.

Another option is to use a hosting service that provides tracker and torrent services such as Hurricane Electric (*http://he.net/*). And still another option is to use a machine that is always on the Web on your home network to provide tracking services. This will require altering your firewall and installing tracker software. Look for the tracker software on *http://bittorrent.com/*.

One last option is Blog Torrent (*http://blogtorrent.com*), which is a PHP-based tracker. As of this writing, the home page advertises that the software will support web seeding *soon*. There are potential security issues with this software, so make sure you read the documentation fully when you install it.

Creating the torrent. Once you have a tracker, you can create a *.torrent* file to reference your podcast *.mp3* file. In the File menu of your BitTorrent application, select Create Torrent File. Then specify the location of the *.mp3* file and the URL of the tracker.

Upload the *.torrent* file to the tracker. Then reference the *.torrent* file in the enclosure tag of your RSS 2.0 file:

```
<enclosure url="http://www.mytracker.com/bit/mypodcast.torrent"
  length="12782" type="application/x-bittorrent"/>
```

Notice that the length of the file is the size of the *.torrent* file and not the size of the target *.mp3* file.

Podcatchers that support BitTorrent (e.g., iPodder) will initiate a torrent session to download the file when they see this MIME type or extension.

Seeding the file. The podcatcher won't get very far with downloading the file unless that file is being seeded actively by a client somewhere. An ISP that does web seeding can do that seeding, or you, the podcaster, can do it, keeping your BitTorrent running with a copy of the podcast. If you remove your computer from the network, and you are the only one seeding the file, no client will be able to download the file.

Another problem is that you might not be able to seed the file from your computer. This happens when you are behind a firewall or have an IP address provided by NAT. To configure your router properly, you will need to do three things. First, get a static IP address from your broadband provider, or set up an account with a dynamic DNS service such as DynDNS (*http://www.dyndns.org/*), which allows you to have a permanent hostname, even when your IP address is shifting constantly. Second, assign that static IP address to a set of ports on the server—this is called *port forwarding*. Third, disable any filtering of the forwarded ports on your own computer.

Another option that doesn't require a static IP address is to combine port forwarding with *port triggering* if your router supports it. With port triggering, the act of attaching the client to the BitTorrent tracker triggers the router to open the forwarding ports and assign them to your computer dynamically. This has the advantage of being more secure, since the ports aren't opened until you are serving files, and when you stop serving files the ports are closed.

The manner of configuring your router is specific to the router's make, model, and even firmware version number. Full details on configuring each type of router are available on *http://portforward.com*.

Is it worth the time? BitTorrenting your podcasts has several significant downsides. First, it's hard to set up. Second, in the case where only you are seeding your file from your personal computer on your home network, you will have to hack your firewall and it will eat your bandwidth. Third, not all podcatchers are compatible with BitTorrenting. Fourth, not all blog software and RSS tools support building BitTorrent feeds. So, you might have to do some hacking.

On the upside, if your podcast is *very popular*, you will save on bandwidth.

Trackerless BitTorrent. As this book was going to press, the BitTorrent client was being upgraded to work without a tracker application. This 4.1 beta version is certainly worth looking at, though it remains to be seen how long it will take for this to become ubiquitous and be supported by podcatchers.

The Future

Podcasting is developing rapidly, and as it grows, so do the bandwidth problems that podcasters face. Wherever there are problems, there are going to be people looking to make a dollar from solving those problems. An example is Liberated Syndication, which created a whole new business model around the requirements of podcasters.

Keep subscribed and current with some podcasting mailing lists, and with the forums on the major podcasting sites (*http://ipodder.org/* and *http://podcastalley.com/*), to watch for announcements from hosting services.

See Also

- "Construct Your MP3s" [Hack #18]

HACK #40 Tag Your MP3 Files

Make sure your filename and ID3 tags are formatted properly for your listeners.

MP3 files have internal tags that store information about the title of the song, the artist, the name of the band, the genre, and more. These are called *ID3 tags*. Programs such as iTunes rely on these ID3 tags to navigate and categorize your music library. Ensuring that your ID3 tags are formatted properly makes life easier for your listeners, and it is simple to do.

Here are the fields that are relevant to podcasters and what those fields should contain:

Title

> This should contain the name of the show, and its date in short form (mm/dd/yy) or its episode number.

Album

> Put the name of your podcast here.

Artist

> Put your name here.

Year

> This is the year the podcast was first released.

Track

> This is the episode number of the podcast, if you release by episodes.

Genre

> Set this to be "Podcast." Or if you can't, just choose "Other."

Comments

> This item is free-form. I recommend the URL of the blog entry for this podcast, or the home page for the podcast. You should also include information about how the listener can comment on the show—either an email address or a phone number [Hack #62].

Now that you know what the ID3 tags should contain, how do you go about setting the values? The following applications [Hack #18] allow you to set the ID3 tags of MP3 files:

iTunes

> iTunes has an excellent built-in ID3 tag editor. If you store your podcasts in iTunes before uploading, you can use the Get Info dialog and the Info tab to set the ID3 tags of your podcast.

Audio Hijack Pro

> The Tags section of the Recording tab is where you can set the ID3 tags for the output file, if you are recording to MP3.

Audacity

> When exporting to an MP3 file, Audacity will prompt you for the ID3 tags. Unfortunately, the genre is set from a pick list, which currently doesn't include "Podcast," so you can use "Speech" or "Other." The ID3 Tags dialog is also available from the Edit ID3 Tags command on the Project menu.

MP3 Tag Tools (http://massid3lib.sf.net/)

> This is an open source Windows application that edits the ID3 tags on MP3 files.

On Windows, you can install a free shell extension that adds ID3 editing to the Properties window in the File Explorer. To install the extension, download it from *http://softpointer.com/AudioShell.htm* and follow the simple installation instructions. Then just right-click any *.mp3* file and select Properties. You will see the AudioShell Tag Editor tabs that you can use to edit the ID3 tags on the file, as shown in Figure 6-1.

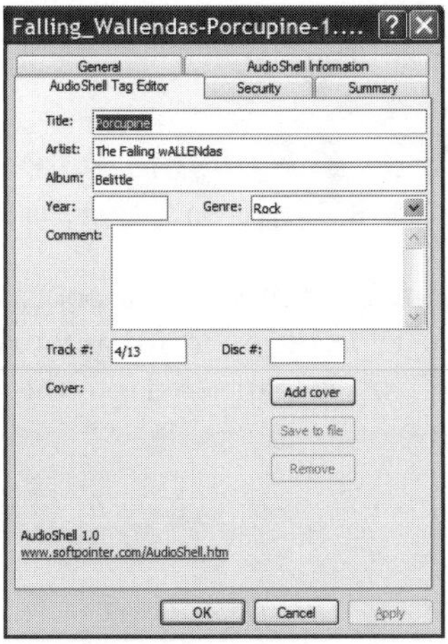

Figure 6-1. The AudioShell Tag Editor

Naming the podcast file. The name of the podcast file is also important. Some podcatchers put all the downloaded files into one directory. So, if your filename isn't unique, these podcatchers might have collision problems between your file and another.

The best bet is to come up with a combination of two parts for the filename. The first part should be a three- or four-letter prefix, most likely some abbreviation of the name of your show. Adam Curry of the Daily Source Code uses "dsc."

The second can be the date, the show or episode number, or some other number that will be unique over the lifetime of your show. For an episode number, use leading zeros. For example, episode number 33 of This Strange Life would be tsl00033. This leaves room for an additional 99,967 shows, which would be a good run in anyone's book. If you were to go by date, and you assume that you won't do more than two shows in one day, the filename for February 20, 2004 would look like this: tsl20040220 with a long year, or tsl040220 with a short year. You should always use year (2004), month (02), and day (20), in that order, to make it easier for people to sort the audio files by date of release, since you can't count on the file-creation date being preserved across various file transfers.

There is no set standard for filenames or ID3 tags yet. But these simple conventions should keep your files safe from collision and your podcasts visible in listeners' MP3 players.

See Also

- "Construct Your MP3s" [Hack #18]

H A C K #41 Feed Your MP3s to Movable Type

Use Movable Type's XML-RPC support to podcast your MP3s automatically.

Perl makes it easy to create a script that will podcast an MP3 for you automatically, using Movable Type's support for automatic blogging through its XML-RPC mechanism. This is partnered on the Perl side by the Net::MovableType module [Hack #7].

The Code

Save this file as *ap.pl*:

```perl
use Net::MovableType;
use MP3::Info;
use Net::SFTP;
use strict;

# The specifics of your MovableType blog

use constant MT_XMLRPC_SERVICE => "http://myhost.com/mt/mt-xmlrpc.cgi";
use constant MT_LOGIN => "Melody";
use constant MT_PASSWORD => "Nelson";
use constant MT_BLOGID => 1;

# The base URL of the directory where the podcasts go

use constant PODCAST_URL_BASE => "http://myhost.com/podcast/";

# The remote directories for SFTP to use to login and upload
# the file

use constant REMOTE_DIRECTORY => "html/podcast/";
use constant REMOTE_HOST => "localhost";
use constant REMOTE_LOGIN => "username";
use constant REMOTE_PASSWORD => "password";

# Post an entry to the blog using MovableType's XML-RPC mechanism
# through Net::MovableType
```

```perl
sub postToBlog($$$)
{
  my ( $title, $comment, $podcastURL ) = @_;

  my $mt = new Net::MovableType( MT_XMLRPC_SERVICE,
    MT_LOGIN, MT_PASSWORD );
  $mt->blogId( MT_BLOGID );

  my $description = $comment;
  $description .= "\n\n";
  $description .= "<a href=\"$podcastURL\">Listen to '$title'</a>";

  my $entry = { title => $title, description => $description };

  $mt->newPost( $entry, 1 );
}

# A progress indicator for SFTP

my $g_last_percent = -100;

sub progress
{
  my($sftp, $data, $offset, $size) = @_;
  my $percent = int ( ( $offset / $size ) * 100 );
  if ( $percent - $g_last_percent > 5 )
  {
        print "   ".$percent."%\n";
        $g_last_percent = $percent;
  }
}

# Post the MP3 file by uploading it to the site and then adding
# the blog entry

sub postMP3($)
{
  my ( $fileName ) = @_;

  # Get the title and comment of the MP3

  my $info = new MP3::Info( $fileName );
  my $title = $info->title();
  my $comment = $info->comment();

  # Upload the podcast using SFTP

  print "Uploading podcast file...\n";

  my $sftp = new Net::SFTP( REMOTE_HOST,
        user => REMOTE_LOGIN, password => REMOTE_PASSWORD );
  $sftp->put( $fileName, REMOTE_DIRECTORY.$fileName, \&progress );
```

```
    print "Done.\n";

    # Post the blog entry

    print "Posting the blog entry\n";
    postToBlog( $title, $comment, PODCAST_URL_BASE.$fileName );
}

# Check to make sure that the user has specified an MP3 file

die "You must specify an MP3 file" unless ( $ARGV[0] );

# Post the MP3 file to the site as a podcast

postMP3( $ARGV[0] );
```

You can get the title and contents of the blog entry from the title and comment files of the ID3 tags in your MP3 file. After that, all you need to do is upload the file, and you can use Net::SFTP to do that using the SFTP protocol.

To start using the script, you will have to change the constants at the top that specify the location of the blog, and the login parameters for the server where it uploads the podcast.

The script uses three modules: MP3::Info to get the tag information from the MP3 file, Net::SFTP to do the SFTP upload, and Net::MovableType to post the blog entry. All of these modules are available through CPAN, and you can use this command to install them automatically on Unix machines:

```
% perl -MCPAN -e "install Net::MovableType"
```

Replace the module name with the one you want to install, and the CPAN module will download and install it automatically [Hack #7].

Running the Hack

To test the script, I built a simple sound file in Audacity and set the title and comment tags to something meaningful before I exported it as MP3. I saved the file as *test1.mp3* and ran the script this way:

```
% perl ap.pl test1.mp3
Uploading podcast file...
  0%
  35%
  70%
Done.
Posting the blog entry
```

After the script executes, you can check your blog to make sure it was posted properly. If you want to alter the text format of the posting, just change the section of the `postToBlog` subroutine that builds the description string.

This script depends on the `MT::Enclosure` plug-in being installed to function properly [Hack #38].

Podcast by Email

#42

Use an email parser on your ISP server to automate podcasting to Movable Type.

Wouldn't it be great if you could email your podcasts to your weblog and have them posted automatically? The text content of the message becomes the podcast entry, the subject becomes the title, and any attachments are put into the right spot and are linked into the body of the blog entry.

This simple Perl script does just that.

The Code

Save this code as *poster.pl*:

```
use FileHandle;
use MIME::Base64;
use strict;

# The base MovableType directory

use constant MT_DIR => "/Library/WebServer/CGI-Executables/mt/";

# The blog ID to post to

use constant BLOG_ID => 1;

# The blog login and password

use constant BLOG_LOGIN => "Melody";
use constant BLOG_PASSWORD => "Nelson";

# The UNIX directory where the podcasts should go

use constant PODCAST_DIR => "/Library/WebServer/Documents/podcast/";

# The base URL to use for the podcasts

use constant PODCAST_URL => "http://myhost.com/podcast/";

BEGIN {
    unshift @INC, MT_DIR . 'lib';
    unshift @INC, MT_DIR . 'extlib';
```

```
    }

    use MT::XMLRPCServer;
    use SOAP::Lite;

    $MT::XMLRPCServer::MT_DIR = MT_DIR;

    use constant WAITING_FOR_BOUNDARY => 1;
    use constant IN_HEADER => 2;
    use constant IN_BODY => 3;

    my $boundary = undef;
    my $state = WAITING_FOR_BOUNDARY;
    my $header = "";
    my $body = "";

    my $subject = undef;
    my $textbody = undef;
    my $podcasturl = undef;

    sub process($$)
    {
      my ( $header, $body ) = @_;

      if ( $header =~ /text\/plain;/ )
      {
        $textbody = $body;
      }

      if ( $header =~ /audio\/mpeg/ && $header =~ /filename=(.*?)$/ )
      {
        my $filename = $1;

        $podcasturl = PODCAST_URL.$filename;

        $body =~ s/\n//g;
        $body =~ s/\r//g;
        my $out = new FileHandle( PODCAST_DIR.$filename, "w" );
        binmode $out;
        print $out decode_base64( $body );
        $out->close();
      }
    }

    while( <> )
    {
      if ( !$boundary && /Content\-Type\: multipart\/mixed; boundary=(.*?)$/ )
      {
        $boundary = "--".$1."\n";
      }

      if ( !$subject && /^Subject:\s+(.*?)$/ )
```

```
  {
    $subject = $1;
  }

  if ( $state == IN_HEADER )
  {
    $state = IN_BODY if ( $_ eq "\n" );
    chomp;
    if ( /^\s/ ) { s/^\s+//; $header .= $_; }
    else { $header .= "\n".$_; }
  }

  if ( $_ eq $boundary )
  {
    process( $header, $body ) if ( $header && $body );

    $state = IN_HEADER;

    $header = "";
    $body = "";
  }

  if ( $state == IN_BODY ) { $body .= $_; }
}

$textbody .= "\n\n<a href=\"$podcasturl\">Listen to '$subject'</a>";

my $item = {
  title => $subject,
  description => $textbody
};

MT::XMLRPCServer::newPost( "", BLOG_ID, BLOG_LOGIN,
  BLOG_PASSWORD, $item, 1 );
```

Running the Hack

This script is meant to be called by Sendmail or Qmail when new mail is sent to an account. With Sendmail, you create a *.forward* file in the home directory of your ISP account. With Qmail, the file is *.qmail*. Either way, the content is the same, and it looks like this:

```
| perl /myhome/myscripts/poster.pl
```

The pipe symbol (|) means the mailer should run the script and pipe the contents of the message into it through STDIN.

After you have uploaded the script, you need to change the variables at the top to match your setup. The first variable, MT_DIR, is the full path to the Movable Type installation directory. It's important because the script will use that installation to post the blog entry using the XML-RPC newPost handler.

The PODCAST_DIR constant is the Unix directory where podcast audio or video files should be stored on the server. The PODCAST_URL constant is the corresponding URL for that directory.

The other interesting part of this script is the code that decodes the Base64-encoded attachment. The binmode call is important here because it throws the file handle into binary mode so that the MP3 file isn't corrupted as it's built.

To test the script, send your email account (the primary account associated with your hosted site) a message with an MP3 file as an attachment. Normally your Unix email address will be separate from your POP3 email boxes. So, you can use this script on your Unix email address. You should check with your ISP to make sure this configuration can work for you.

The great part about this script is that it can take email from any source and post it. You can upload podcasts from your PC. On newer phones, you can record sound and then send it as an attachment over email and podcast directly from your phone!

See Also

- "Blog Your Podcast" [Hack #38]

Syndicate Your Podcasts to the Radio

HACK
#43

Using the PRX service, you can play your podcasts on National Public Radio (NPR).

The revolution is not yet complete, and in fact it doesn't necessarily ever have to be. Commercial radio might have started to sound stale through relentless consolidation, but public radio in America makes a point to look for new voices and innovative ways of producing audio. A motivated podcaster can contribute a lot to the community of listeners around a local public radio station, and there's a lot—production tricks, a community of producers—that the station can give back.

And think of the exposure you'd get for your podcast by broadcasting just a single audio segment on a national program. More than 113 million Americans still drive to work, and there's still an FM radio in every car.

How do you do this? You can start at the Public Radio Exchange (*http://prx. org/*). PRX is a web-based marketplace for public radio work. Independent audio producers use PRX to make high-quality audio features and documentaries available—through standardized licensing terms—to public radio stations. In return, the stations, when they choose to air your work, pay a royalty back out to you through PRX.

Benjamen Walker, a public radio producer (who used to be a comic-book artist), began podcasting his experimental weekly half-hour audio show, The Theory of Everything (*http://toeradio.org*), in September 2004. In April 2005, he was looking at 7,500 downloads a week, but also was reaching hundreds of thousands of additional listeners through a couple of public radio stations, including Chicago Public Radio, which started airing him, through PRX, a half hour after This American Life.

And yes, he noticed a traffic spike after his Chicago broadcast debut.

Here is a step-by-step guide to getting started:

1. Open up a PRX account at *http://www.prx.org/membership*. A producer's starter account gives you a free hour of audio space.

2. Encode your audio. PRX stores pieces as broadcast-quality MP2 files, a standard that stations use. An MP2 survives up and down the broadcast chain a little better than an MP3 does.

   To create an MP2, start with the original audio as a *.wav* file. Most higher-end audio editing tools allow you to save to *.wav*; if yours doesn't, you can used the free and open source Audacity **[Hack #50]** (*http://audacity.sf.net/*) to load an MP3 and save it to *.wav*. Once you have a *.wav* of your podcast, use the free PRX encoder tool (*http://www.prx.org/help*) to convert it to an MP2.

3. Upload your audio to PRX. PRX has built a free tool to manage this, too; the uploader tool comes with your encoder download. Enter your account info, drag and drop, and move your audio up to your "loading dock" on the PRX server.

4. Create a *piece listing*. Log in to PRX, click My PRX, and then Add a piece. Take the time to fill out all the information here; the more thoroughly you describe your piece, the more likely a station is to pick it up. About 30 seconds' worth of suggested intro text makes it easy for a broadcast host to introduce your piece.

You're published! A public radio station can pick up your audio and put it on the air.

Producing to Time

That's not it, of course. As with any other market, you need to look at what the demanders are demanding. Podcasters have the luxury of producing their work as long or as short as the content merits; public radio producers have to fit a clock.

Here are some guidelines to follow:

Half-hour series
> Benjamen Walker reports that a single human can't possibly produce more than a half hour of high-quality radio a week, so it might be the upper limit of regular productivity. Keep in mind, though, that public radio program directors, while open to inserting half-hour shows into their schedules, find it difficult to shuffle things around to fit a new half hour.

Periodic one-hour specials
> Many stations—for example, Seattle's KUOW—leave one-hour slots open on the weekends for specials on current topics. If you have a lot of material or interviews on a single topic, consider producing it to 57 minutes (leaving time for transitions to make it broadcastable).

Three-and-a-half-minute drop-ins
> Most public radio stations run NPR's morning and evening news programs, Morning Edition and All Things Considered. Both of these feed out to local stations with optional three-and-a-half-minute holes for local essays or news. Many stations broadcast exactly what they get from the national stream; offer them something from their own region for their own air.

Seven 15-minute segments
> National shows, such as WNYC's The Next Big Thing, shop on PRX to find short segments for use in their weekly hour-long shows.

Get in Touch with Your Local Station

Public radio is largely a donation-driven business that relies heavily on volunteers and the love of the game. Check in with your local public radio station and let them know you have your own studio and are wandering around with a microphone, recording interviews. Tell them you want to produce a series of stories about a local housing development, or contribute a regular essay on local politics. It's harder to volunteer to be a part of the driven, professional staffs of large-market stations such as Boston's WBUR or New York's WNYC, but if you live in a small town, who knows? You might end up with your own show.

—Brendan Greeley

Publicity
Hacks 44–49

> *The worst thing about podcasting is also the best thing: the saturation of the medium. There are so many podcasts out there, and new ones springing up everyday, that finding shows you like can be a crapshoot. But there are so many shows out there, there's something out there for everybody.*
> —Brian Ibbot

What's the point of having a podcast if nobody listens to it? Standing out in the crowd is a challenge. At the time of this writing, more than 3,000 podcasts were available. Having your podcast listed in all the directories is the first step. From there, you will need to market your podcast continuously to keep the energy going. This chapter contains ideas that can help you build the size of your audience.

HACK #44   Get Listed

Listing your podcast in public directories is the cheapest and easiest way to connect with and build your audience. Find out what directories are available and how to get signed up.

Any reasonable podcatcher will have support for browsing OPML directories [Hack #45] of podcasts. Users don't need to search for new podcasts; they see new podcasts listed in the New Podcasts portion of the directory every day.

A bunch of OPML directories of podcasts are available to listeners. You should sign up with all of them. The process varies from site to site, but usually it involves putting the basics of the show, the name, and the feed URL into some form fields and hitting Submit. The listing time can vary from site to site. So, it's best to do it as soon as your first show goes live.

Here is a short list of the directories open to submissions at the time of this writing:

iPodder (http://ipodder.org/)
> This is the original podcast directory. Use it to find the category in which you think your podcast belongs, and use the "Suggest a link" button to add your podcast.

iPodderX (http://www.ipodderx.com/)
> Add your podcast with the "Submit this Podcast" link on the Podcast Directory page (*http://ipodderx.com/directory/add*).

All Podcasts (http://www.allpodcasts.com/)
> This is possibly the simplest submission form. It takes just your RSS 2.0 feed URL. Follow the Add A Podcast link on the home page.

Podcasting News (http://www.podcastingnews.com/)
> You need to register with the site. Then you can surf the directory to the category where you think your podcast fits, and use the Link Submission button.

podCast411 (http://www.podcast411.com/)
> Click the Add Your Podcast button on the lefthand side of the home page.

Podcast Alley (http://www.podcastalley.com/)
> These guys have a link right on the home page that takes you to a simple submission form.

Podcast Network (http://podcast.net)
> They have a podcast submission page with a fairly elaborate form (*http://www.podcast.net/addpodcast*).

Digital Podcast (http://www.digitalpodcast.com/)
> This has a link right on the home page for adding a podcast through a simple form.

The Podcast Bunker (http://www.podcastbunker.com/)
> Use the big Submit Podcast button and follow the instructions, which have you write a small blurb about the site and then send it through a simple submissions page.

Audio Weblogs (http://audio.weblogs.com/)
> This has a very simple ping form for adding new podcasts (*http://audio.weblogs.com/pingform.html*).

PenguinRadio (http://www.penguinradio.com/podcasting/)
> Click the Add your Feed form to go to the Podcast Directory to add your feed.

Podcasting Tools maintains a list of podcast directories that will be more up-to-date than the preceding list. Visit *http://www.podcasting-tools.com/submit-podcasts.htm.*

Mailing Lists and Bulletin Boards

In addition to adding your podcast to all the directories, you should become a member of the mailing lists and bulletin boards [Hack #48]. From there, you can post about your new show and point people to the site and feed. Some podcasters go as far as posting about every new show.

Open Podcast

Open Podcast (*http://www.openpodcast.org/*) is an open mic for anyone who wants to say, well, almost anything. There are a few guidelines about not using copyrighted material, but in general, as long as your segment is interesting, you are in.

You can mail in an MP3 to *submit@openpodcast.org*, or phone it in to (206) 984-1190. Submissions vary in length, from 15–30-second promos to full podcasts. I recommend that you put together a little teaser promo about your first podcast, with some choice cuts from the show, and use that as the submission. This will also help you with Adam Curry's Daily Source Code.

Daily Source Code

Adam Curry is one of the driving forces behind podcasting. His very well-produced Daily Source Code (*http://www.curry.com/*) is required listening because it has daily podcasting news and plugs for new shows. Adam is good about getting new-show information out there. Just send him a promo spot at *mp3feedback@gmail.com* and he likely will get it on the air in a day or two.

I suggest that you listen to more than a few of the most recent Source Codes to get a feel for what promos were interesting and well received. Then put something together that is short, funny, and compelling and send it up to him.

Podcast Networks

Even by podcasting standards the phenomenon of podcast networks [Hack #49] is relatively new. But the concept of a network of related shows isn't. The value to listeners is that they get a series of shows that reinforce a particular style or philosophy. It's a one-stop shop for shows that key around topics that interest them. The GodCast Network (*http://www.godcast.org/*) is a good example of this idea. The network presents several shows from a variety of podcasters on a daily basis. But listeners need to subscribe to only the single service.

Each show in the network remains an individual show, with its own production, host, and site. But it also contributes to the network and references other shows on the network in a cooperative fashion.

There were three networks at the time of this writing:

TechPodcasts (http://techpodcasts.com/)
    A set of podcasts, all working the IT and technology angle

The GodCast Network (http://www.godcast.org/)
    A Christian network with around 12 different shows

The Podcast Network (http://www.thepodcastnetwork.com/)
    A set of related shows with a central production staff

Keep your eyes and ears open to Open Podcast (*http://openpodcast.org/*), the mailing lists, and forums to look for new networks that you can contribute content to.

Regular Old RSS

If you are running your podcast off your blog [Hack #38], be sure to register your blog with blog search engines. The two I use are Feedster (*http://www.feedster.com/*) and PubSub (*http://www.pubsub.com/*). These two services monitor your blog for new entries and allow subscribers to search your blog's content using keywords. This is another reason to make sure you use text content in your blog entry to augment what you talk about in your podcast.

See Also

- "Launch a New Category" [Hack #45]
- "Market Your Podcast" [Hack #46]
- "Make Money with Podcasts" [Hack #47]
- "Connect with the Community" [Hack #48]
- "Join or Build a Podcast Network" [Hack #49]

Launch a New Category

The world of podcasting is expanding rapidly, and new categories are continuously being added to the public directories. These categories are maintained by individuals just like you, and you can propose and maintain categories for topics that interest you.

When the Internet first started, one of the biggest problems people faced was finding new pages. O'Reilly's Global Network Navigator was the first directory of web pages, a concept that was later refined by Yahoo! and the Open Directory Project (*http://dmoz.org/*). These directories contained a set of categories and subcategories with web site links at each level. It broke the Web wide open for people.

Podcasting has grown so fast, in part because of the immediate availability of the list of all the podcasts through use of an OPML directory. OPML stands for *Outline Processor Markup Language*. It's an XML syntax for a nested hierarchy of outline elements. In the case of podcasting, it's used for links to the podcast feeds.

Here is an excerpt from the OPML that is maintained for Australian podcasts:

```
<?xml version="1.0" encoding="ISO-8859-1"?>
<!-- OPML generated by Radio UserLand v8.0.8 on Sun, 09 Jan 2005 11:52:09
GMT -->

<opml version="1.1">
  <head>
    <title>Australia.opml</title>
    <dateCreated>Sun, 14 Nov 2004 11:41:36 GMT</dateCreated>
    <dateModified>Sun, 09 Jan 2005 11:52:09 GMT</dateModified>
    <ownerName>Podcast Australia</ownerName>
    <ownerEmail>toby@podcast.com.au</ownerEmail>
    <expansionState></expansionState>
    <vertScrollState>1</vertScrollState>
    <windowTop>55</windowTop>
    <windowLeft>0</windowLeft>
    <windowBottom>483</windowBottom>
    <windowRight>744</windowRight>
    </head>
  <body>
    <outline text="Beer">
      <outline text="Australian Craft Brewers" type="link"
        url="http://rss.oz.craftbrewer.org/"/>
      </outline>
    <outline text="Current Affairs">
      <outline text="triple j's Hack" type="link"
url="http://www.abc.net.au/triplej/hack/podcast/podcast.xml"/>
      </outline>
```

```
    <outline text="Photos">
      <outline text="lookANDsee" type="link"
  url="http://las.new-england.net.au/feed/rss2/"/>
      </outline>
    <outline text="Technology">
      <outline text="A Random Act of Podcasting" type="link"
  url="http://feeds.feedburner.com/ARandomActOfPodcasting"/>
      <outline text="G'day World" type="link"
  url="http://www.gdayworld.com/rss_mp3.xml"/>
      </outline>
  <outline text="G'day World" type="link"
    url="http://www.gdayworld.com/rss_mp3.xml"/>
      <outline text="A Random Act of Podcasting" type="link"
  url="http://feeds.feedburner.com/ARandomActOfPodcasting"/>
      <outline text="triple j's Hack" type="link"
  url="http://www.abc.net.au/triplej/hack/podcast/podcast.xml"/>
      <outline text="lookANDsee" type="link"
  url="http://las.new-england.net.au/feed/rss2/"/>
      <outline text="ABC's Dig Radio" type="link"
  url="http://abc.net.au/dig/podcast/dig_rss.xml"/>
      <outline text="Australian Craft Brewers" type="link"
  url="http://rss.oz.craftbrewer.org/"/>
      </body>
  </opml>
```

The header section describes some of the biographical elements of the outline: what it is, who made it, and when it was last touched. The visual elements are optional and are used only by editors.

Within the <body> tag of the OPML are outline elements. Each outline element has the text of the element and optionally a type field and a URL.

More information about the OPML standard is available at the OPML site (*http://www.opml.org/spec*). The standard is very loose. Most of the elements and attributes are marked as optional. And the semantics of some of the attributes, such as type, are so loosely defined that they are meaningful only by convention. A DTD that describes the format is available through the site. An example of the laxness in the spec is that all the elements in the header section might or might not be present. A title is not strictly necessary.

Yahoo! Groups hosts the almost inactive opml-dev group (*http://groups.yahoo.com/group/opml-dev/*) that talks about the OPML standard and its continuing development.

Radio UserLand is the original interface for editing OPML. Simply open the file using the Open File command in the File menu. Edit using the Outline menu.

If you don't have Radio UserLand and you want to edit or maintain one of these files, you can use your favorite text editor, or an XML editor such as oXygen (*http://www.oxygenxml.com/*) or XMLSpy (*http://www.altova.com/*).

If you are going to write OPML by hand, I recommend that you at least have the title, dateCreated, dateModified, ownerName, and ownerEmail in the outline's header section. I also recommend that you run the XML through an XML validator to make sure it's minimally valid. An OPML validator is available at *http://www.kbcafe.com/rss/?guid=20041030111147*.

URLs inside of OPML can point to anything. That includes the RSS 2.0 feed of a podcast, or the OPML of another directory. In this way, a single directory can be hosted on multiple servers and maintained by multiple authors.

For example, the Australia directory shown earlier is referenced in the iPodder directory using this element tag:

```
<outline text="Australia" type="link"
    url="http://www.podcast.com.au/gems/Australia.opml"/>
```

This flexible directory architecture makes it very easy to maintain large distributed directories of podcasts.

Proposing a New Category

You can help the podcasting community [Hack #48] by maintaining a leaf of the larger podcast directory tree. In the example here, the OPML author is maintaining the section on podcasts in Australia. To start your own leaf, first you create the OPML file with the section of the original outline, or an entirely new outline. Then you validate it using an OPML validator.

Next, you contact the maintainer of the parent directory and propose maintaining the subdirectory, or creating a new directory leaf. If the maintainer agrees to this, he will hook your URL into the directory using an outline node, such as the one shown earlier that links in the Australia node.

As a maintainer, it's up to you to handle requests for additions to your podcast directory through email in a timely manner. The amount of work required depends greatly on the popularity of the directory that you pick.

See Also

- "Market Your Podcast" [Hack #46]
- "Connect with the Community" [Hack #48]

Market Your Podcast

HACK #46

Visibility is critical to building a listener base. Find out how to plug and get plugged effectively.

Marketing in the podcast world isn't as overt as it is in commercial radio, but it's definitely being done. With an increasing number of both listeners and podcasts, you need to grab listeners and hold them. This will be especially true as people start making money at podcasting.

After the initial directory listings have gone out, people get the word out about their podcasts in several ways. These are detailed in the sections that follow.

Trading Plugs and Promos

When you trade plugs with another podcast, you produce a short promo for them that offers your podcast to their listeners, and vice versa. The duration, style, and content of the promos should be negotiated between you and the other podcaster.

I recommend that you contact the shows that you like and that you think you share an audience with. Their listeners should be interested in your podcast, and vice versa. Obviously the topics of the two shows should be tangentially related, but they should not overlap. There is little reason why two competing shows would want to plug each other.

Once you have the right show, just contact the host and see if she is interested in trading plugs. If she is interested, work out the details of how long the spots should be and what (in general) they should say.

You can use a service such as Podcast Promos (*http://podcastpromos.com/*) to find promos for other podcasts, and to upload your own podcast promo.

Another option after you trade plugs is to trade links.

Trading Links

Your podcast should refer people to your blog and your blog should link to your podcast. The blog should provide extra material for your listeners. You should include links to the resources you talked about in the show, and any supporting material.

The blog should also link to other sites or podcasts that you think will be of interest to your listeners in the permanent links section of the blog. These links usually appear on the home page as part of the navigation system.

Just like you trade plugs with another show, you can also trade links. They link to your show on their site, and you link to theirs. You will be able to check the referrer logs on your web server to see whether people are coming from the other podcast site.

Conference Presence

Go to the conferences related to your topic. See and be seen. Have a bunch of cards printed up with the name of your podcast and a link to the site so that when you talk with people about the podcast, you have something to give them.

If they are new to podcasting, be sure to tell them that your site is a good starting point for podcasting because it has links to all the fundamental podcast sites.

Giving a talk is another way to make your presence known at a conference. Be sure to plug your podcast during and at the end of your talk.

The parties before and after each group of sessions are a wonderful time to mingle and drop off some cards with people. Cards are cheap, and if people are interested in the topic at the conference, and your podcast relates to it, you have a captive audience. Make use of it.

Interviews are another relatively cheap way to cross-market and get great content for your show. If the conference relates to your podcast, lots of people should be around whom you can talk with.

Podcasting is so new that for larger conferences, you should be able to contact the conference coordinator to get a press pass. Not only does this get you in free, but also you should have the opportunity to get the podcasts you publish about the conference linked off the conference's site.

Interviews

People and companies love to talk about what they do. It's both a boost to the ego and good publicity. It's also an excellent opportunity for cross-marketing. You interview them [Hack #33] and talk about what they are doing. Then they link to your interview with them on the public relations portion of their site.

Always make sure that the people you are going to interview do this cross-marketing if they have a web site. Ideally, in addition to a link to their interview, they should include a small description of your podcast with a link to the home page. To make this easy on them, you should have example copy of such a blurb on hand.

Advertising

When all else fails, you can buy marketing through search engine ads. Google AdSense (*http://www.google.com/adsense*) makes it easy to register your advertisement for various keywords. Pricing is highly variable and depends on the value of the word. You can cap the money you are willing to spend on advertising on a daily basis.

Smart marketing and search engine submissions should keep your ranking high in the search results if you understand the basics. A recent Pew study showed that surfers couldn't distinguish between paid ads and free ones. So, why buy the placement when you can get it free by doing the legwork to get your page designs right and trade links appropriately?

Voting

Podcast Alley (*http://podcastalley.com/*) maintains a comprehensive list of podcasts, partly because it's also where people go to vote on their favorite podcasts. Make sure your podcast is listed on Podcast Alley, and encourage your listeners both in your podcast and on your blog to vote for your podcast.

Pinging

Another way to get noticed is to *ping* the Audio Weblogs site (*http://audio.weblogs.com/*) each time you post a new podcast. This site has a list of the most recent podcasts that people can subscribe to. You can add your podcast to the list simply by filling in the ping form at *http://audio.weblogs.com/pingform.html*. Blog software such as Movable Type [Hack #38] can do this automatically for you by specifying the URL of the ping form.

Another option in a similar vein is the MSN Alerts service (*http://alerts.msn.com*). This service monitors your RSS feed and then updates subscribed listeners via instant messaging when new posts and podcasts are available.

HACK Make Money with Podcasts
#47
Google ads are an easy way to generate revenue that will offset your bandwidth costs. Learn to use this effective advertising mechanism.

Monetizing podcasting is a hot topic in the podcast community. People are trying to make money on all aspects of podcasting, including the hosting, software, networking, and audience itself. Podcasters are trying to see if they can cover the costs, or more, of podcast production and hosting through advertising.

The most direct way to do this is through ads placed in the show itself. There is no standard for this yet. I recommend that you develop an ad policy that covers ad duration, format, and content. You will also need to add a spot for ads in the format of your show.

If this podcast is an individual work, you will need to come up with a payment method. PayPal (*http://paypal.com/*) or a similar service can work well for this. You will also need to work out the tax details on your own or with an accountant. Payments from other companies will need either corporate billing information or a Social Security number that they can register in their books if you are in the U.S.

Traditionally, making money on the Web meant selling ad space on your web site or blog. This means driving people to your site both before and after they listen to your podcast. You should always mention your blog in the show and encourage your listeners to visit the site to find additional materials that supplement the show. I also recommend using full-text RSS feeds. With these feeds, the blog entry text is included in full and is not truncated. In addition, you can use services such as RSS Ads (*http://www.rssads. com/*) to monetize your RSS feeds directly.

You can monetize your web site using several methods. These are listed in the sections that follow.

Google's AdSense

Google provides an easy-to-use ad service that puts ad links on any of the pages of your site. Local tax considerations are handled through the interface. You request an account by going to the AdSense home page (*http:// www.google.com/adsense*).

Once you have an account, you change your blog templates to add the AdSense JavaScript into the page to download the ads. You have a variety of shapes and sizes to choose from. Google does some magic to deduce what your topic is from the page contents, and customizes the ads to suit.

It's critical that your blog is more than just a set of links to your podcast. Your blog should augment your show with links and commentary. And the podcast should reference the blog to encourage your listeners to look at your site and to click your ad links.

Amazon Associates

If your podcast is about technology products, books, DVDs, music, or anything else that Amazon sells, you should use the Amazon Associates program. With this program, you can earn a commission on any product that is sold through Amazon that was referred from a link on your site.

The first step is to sign up as an associate. Then you get an associate ID that you tack onto the end of any Amazon product URL that you place on your site. Amazon does the rest of the tracking for you. You can get the referral money as either a check, direct deposit, or Amazon gift certificate.

Amazon provides several formatting options, including the usual text links. Amazon also has a handy wizard-style creation mechanism that builds the HTML for your page for you.

Tip Jar

Another option is to put a tip jar on your home page and on each individual blog entry page. One of the easiest ways to do this is to use your PayPal (*http://paypal.com/*) account. Under the Merchant Tools tab is an option for donation, which is a factory for creating HTML for your page. Use the tool to create the HTML, and then copy and paste it into your page templates for your blog.

Amazon also supports a tip jar–style service it calls the Amazon Honor System (*http://s1.amazon.com/exec/varzea/subst/fx/help/payor-faq.html*). Your listeners who are Amazon customers can pay you through their Amazon accounts and you will receive payment by check. Amazon takes a small percentage of the donation amount as a processing fee. Handling the tax ramifications of these payments is left to you.

Commercial Status

You should be aware that once you start making money from your podcasts, you have become a commercial entity. This might change your ability to use licensed material [Hack #68] where that license distinguishes between commercial and noncommercial entities, such as the Creative Commons license.

See Also

- "Grab Audio Legally" [Hack #67]
- "Use Copyrighted Music Legally" [Hack #68]

Connect with the Community

#48 Keep in touch with the podcast community through newsgroups and message boards.

The best way to keep up on what's happening in the podcasting world is to be an active part of it. You should subscribe to these two message boards and mailing lists:

iPodder (http://iPodder.org/)
> The iPodder site discussion board consists primarily of postings from Adam Curry about additions to the iPodder directory. The real discussions happen on ipodder-dev.

Podcast Alley (http://podcastalley.com/)
> This is an excellent site for both its podcast directory and its bulletin board. Topics on the board include new podcast listings, technical talk, news, and article listings.

Yahoo! Groups

A number of Yahoo! Groups (*http://groups.yahoo.com*) mailing lists discuss podcasting. A sampling of the bigger ones are listed here:

ipodder-dev
> The iPodder development Yahoo! Group. Ostensibly this group is about the development of iPodder, but in reality, it's a high-traffic list that talks about everything podcasting.

Podcasters
> The second biggest podcasting list. It's almost indistinguishable in content from ipodder-dev.

Podcastrevolution
> A smaller and newer podcast mailing list.

Videobloggers
> This is an older mailing list that focuses on video blogging. But recent postings cover podcasting topics.

podcast-review
> A small but growing mailing list that reviews the new podcasts on the block.

Registration on all of these is required, but it's free. That helps keep down the spam. Some of these require a free Yahoo! account to register. With others, you can register by email.

What You Can Offer

Podcasters are regular people who have day jobs just like you and me and everyone else. Most are not radio or audio professionals. So, by engaging in and contributing to these groups, you can work with all of us to raise our common skill level. Topics include everything from which microphones to choose and how to debug RSS, to how to tell great stories. Then there is the inevitable periodic war over where podcasting is going, or how, and even if, it can be commercialized [Hack #47].

I suggest that you hang back on the boards for a while; lurk, if you will. Get a sense of the proper form and how you can add value to the conversation. Then get in there and get involved.

Keeping Up-to-Date

Adam Curry's Daily Source Code (*http://curry.com/*) is the primary way to stay up-to-date on the world of podcasting. He plugs new podcasts regularly and is generally in the center of the storm. Dave Winer (*http://www.scripting.com/*) is another great resource for tracking new developments in podcasting.

Using Google's News service (*http://news.google.com*), you can subscribe to email alerts on words such as *podcast* and *ipodder* and receive email updates when stories appear on the newswires about these topics.

Blog aggregators such as Feedster (*http://www.feedster.com/*) and PubSub (*http://www.pubsub.com/*) are useful in tracking blog mentions of podcasting. These create custom RSS feeds that you can use in your aggregator or in newer versions of the Safari and Firefox browsers that support RSS. When new blog entries come up that match your search criteria, they are listed in the composite RSS feed that comes from the service.

Join or Build a Podcast Network
#49
There's strength in numbers when it comes to podcasting, and by joining or building a podcast network, you can benefit from increased numbers in a variety of ways.

Podcasting's ability to target niche markets can be both a strength and a weakness. It's a strength because podcasting is uniquely able to provide content where it doesn't make economic sense for other forms of media to do so. It's a weakness because those niche markets aren't always large enough to make it practical for podcasters to promote themselves efficiently or to provide the listener base necessary to attract advertisers.

Podcast networks provide a solution to the niche dilemma by grouping podcasts together, either informally, most likely centered on a common theme; or formally, for commercial purposes. This grouping offers a number of advantages for listeners, podcasters, and advertisers.

Informal Networks

An *informal network* is defined as one that is formed for the primary purpose of increasing the visibility and therefore listenership of its members. By grouping together podcasts of a similar theme or a complimentary variety, an informal network can promote itself using the combined listener base of its member podcasts. This gives it the ability, for example, to have the same voting power in online directories as larger podcasts. It also has the advantage for the listener of making it easier to find content of a specific nature.

The first podcast network was an informal one, formed way back (in podcasting time) on December 7th, 2004, and it serves as a model example for the purpose and style of an informal network. The GodCast Network was created when the host site, *http://godcast.org/*, received a mention in an article on podcasting in *Time* magazine, and site owner (and author of this hack) Craig Patchett decided to share the publicity with other similar podcasts. The network currently hosts 11 shows, 7 of which are produced externally. The simple techniques used for building The GodCast Network, which you can easily use to build your own informal network, will be covered later in this hack.

Typically an informal network will offer a mirrored RSS feed for each of its member podcasts, along with a combined RSS feed that offers all the podcasts in one subscription. The member podcasts will still maintain their own sites and the network will link back to those sites. (See *http://www.godcast. org/* for an example.)

Commercial Networks

While a commercial network is also interested in increasing visibility and listenership of its member podcasts, its purpose for doing so is to make money. The larger the listener base, the greater the number of advertisers that will be interested in advertising, and the more money they will be willing to pay. In addition, a well-designed and marketed commercial network will draw traffic to its site and can generate additional income from banner ads placed on its web pages.

The first commercial podcast network launched on February 14, 2005. The Podcast Network was founded by Mick Stanic and Cameron Reilly of the G'day World Podcast and is designed to present a "best-of" collection of podcasts in a variety of categories. Podcasts are offered as network "channels" and each one covers a different topic, such as mobile phones, tablet PCs, jazz music, etc.

Due to the nature of commercial networks, all RSS feeds for the member podcasts will typically be offered through the network host, along with the hosting for the podcast sites themselves. This gives the network full control over access to the podcasts to be able to track advertising statistics effectively. (See *http://www.thepodcastnetwork.com/* for an example.)

Joining a Network

Each network will have its own criteria for joining, based on the type of network, the subject matter it's trying to cover, and the idiosyncrasies of its owners. The best general approach to joining a network is to consult its home page for information on joining or for contact information. While membership in most networks is free once you're accepted, you might have to agree to terms regarding things such as advertising, content limitations, etc.

Building a Network

While joining a network has its benefits, building one can have even more and will certainly be an enjoyable venture. Although building a commercial network could be the topic of a book of its own, building an informal network can be remarkably easy, thanks to features offered in popular blogging applications used by podcasters to build their sites, such as WordPress [Hack #38] (*http://www.wordpress.org/*) and Radio UserLand (*http://radiouserland. com/*). In particular, both of these applications offer a category feature that allows you to assign each blog entry to one or more predefined categories. Since each category has its own RSS feed, this feature is perfect for supporting a network. Simply create a category for each podcast in the network, along with a primary feed (if desired) to carry all the shows. This is exactly how The GodCast Network was set up.

Using this technique gives you a separate web page for each podcast in your network. If you have your own domain, this allows you to set up subdomains for each podcast and forward them to the appropriate page if you want. For example, *http://rachel.godcast.org/* and *http://tlw.godcast.org* each point to separate podcasts at The GodCast Network.

One final option, if you're the enterprising sort, is to purchase a dedicated server or virtual private server and become your own web host for your network as well, becoming a digital landlord and renting out space and bandwidth [Hack #39] to the members of the new podcasting community you're creating.

See Also

- "Rebroadcast Your Favorite Feeds" [Hack #2]

—*Craig Patchett*

## CHAPTER EIGHT

Basic Editing
Hacks 50–60

*I don't know that I'm doing it so much as a
protest against radio as I am to develop the
radio show I always wanted to hear.*
—Brian Ibbot

Broadly speaking, audio production software falls into one of four categories: recording, editing, mixing, and plug-ins. Recording tools sample audio from one or more inputs and store it to disk. Editing programs allow you to rearrange or delete sections of previously recorded audio. Mixing tools take sounds collected from various sources and mix them together into a final produced piece. And plug-ins [Hack #51] are used throughout the process to add or remove distortion, noise, and echo, and to create sonic effects.

If all you plan to do is record a mono track of speech, make some small edits, and then encode it to MP3, all you need is one program, Audacity [Hack #50]. For more complex audio work, professionals use a combination of multiple programs, each of which specializes in one of these tasks.

In addition to these basic tools, other types of specialized applications can be useful to podcasters. Small audio routing applications, such as Soundflower, can make it easy to reroute audio within your system from applications that might not have elaborate sound input and output options.

Cart applications [Hack #54] and [Hack #55] can be a handy way to organize the samples and sounds that you will use throughout your show. These applications preload the sounds for easy access and then present a grid of buttons; you press a button to play the corresponding sound.

An altogether new type of tool is the podcasting application. This tool performs a number of functions, from holding the show notes, to providing cart application functionality, to recording and playing back segments.

Choose the Right Audio Tools

Download free audio software, and spend your money wisely on the right commercial audio software.

A wide variety of free and commercial audio tools are available for podcasting. But that doesn't mean it's easy to find the right software. You can spend a lot of money on an application that is great for musicians but doesn't have the right functions for podcasters.

In this hack, I cover both the free and commercial tools, explaining which ones are good for podcasting, and why.

Audio Editors

Audio editing applications allow you to edit sound as though you're using a word processor. You can cut, copy and paste, delete, and arrange sound in any way you choose. Most of these applications allow you to work with multiple tracks that you can think of as sonic layers. You can use these tracks to work with each sound in isolation, and then mix down to a single mono or stereo signal at the end. In addition, many of these applications allow you to apply effects to the volume or the character of the sound.

Audacity. Audacity (*http://audacity.sf.net/*) is a free sound editing program that runs on Windows, Mac, and Linux. You should download Audacity and install it *right now.* It's an excellent starter program and it's possibly the only editing program you will ever need. Figure 8-1 shows the Audacity main window.

On the recording side, Audacity supports mono and stereo recording from any sound input source on your machine. It even has meters in the document window to show when you are *clipping* (cutting off a portion of the signal). Unfortunately, plug-ins [Hack #51] are not supported during recording. So, you will need to do all the filtering work after the recording.

Audacity has excellent editing capabilities. You can zoom and scroll on both the time axis and the amplitude axis. The keyboard controls for navigating around the document and then creating and extending your selections are easy to use. Cut, Copy, and Paste all work as if you were in a word processing document. However, copying and pasting between documents of different sampling rates can get tricky.

Audacity supports envelope editing. With this feature, you can manually boost or reduce the amplitude of parts of the recording using simple visual cues. This is very handy when you have sections of audio that drift from very soft to very loud.

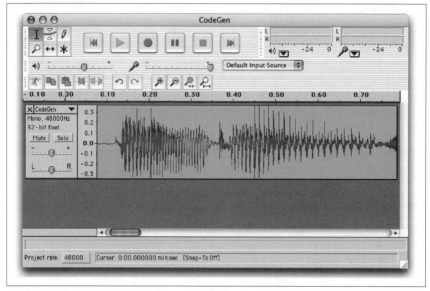

Figure 8-1. Audacity's main window

When you download Audacity, you should also grab the LAME MP3 encoder and the Virtual Studio Technology (VST) plug-in support module. VST is a plug-in standard that is supported by a number of sound applications on both Windows and Macintosh. Audacity has a variety of filters already baked in, but the VST plug-in support expands your sonic toolkit tremendously.

Pro Tools free. Digidesign (*http://www.digidesign.com/*) is so cool that it released one of its earlier versions of Pro Tools completely free to the public. Pro Tools is a commercial-quality recording application that, in its current version, is coupled with the company's Mbox hardware [Hack #12].

Unfortunately, this version works only on Windows 98 and Mac OS 9. It does not work on the Classic emulator on OS X. If you are running on Windows 98 or OS 9, this is a heck of a bargain. Some Macintoshes can dual-boot between Mac OS X and OS 9 to save you a lot of money.

Peak 4. BIAS's (*http://www.bias-inc.com/*) Peak 4 ($499) is one of the premier sound editing tools on the market. It has a remarkably intuitive interface that allows you to find the samples you are looking for quickly in the alien world of waveform display. Peak is shown in Figure 8-2.

Sections of audio can be delineated into regions and exported separately automatically. There is also an interface for batch edits to multiple files.

Figure 8-2. Peak on Macintosh

Perhaps the most appealing feature is the Vbox, which allows you to arrange multiple effects [Hack #51] together and stream the currently selected audio through them over and over until you get the sound you are looking for. You then bounce the signal through the Vbox to apply the filter to the signal.

Peak also has a recording feature that shows the stereo input waveform as it's being recorded.

Peak's sister application, Deck ($399), is a studio-quality recording application that supports mixer functionality with unlimited virtual software mixer channels. It's overkill for podcasters, but if you are creating a home studio for podcasting and music, you should check it out.

DSP-Quattro 2. Another high-end sound editing package for Macintosh is DSP-Quattro 2 (*http://www.i3net.it/Products/dspQuattro*). The list price is around $149. It supports region editing as well as both VST and AU effects plug-ins, and has an intuitive interface for making your edits. For the price, this is an awesome sound editor.

Audition. On the Windows side of the recording and mixing cycle is Adobe's Audition. Audition was originally Cool Edit, and then Cool Edit Pro, before it was acquired by Adobe. It's a professional's product at an amateur's price that has had years of honing.

With Audition, shown in Figure 8-3, you can multitrack record and edit. It offers a reasonable set of built-in effects, and you can extend the processing using VSTs. It has a high-quality tunable noise filter built in. On the output side, a number of formats, including MP3, are supported.

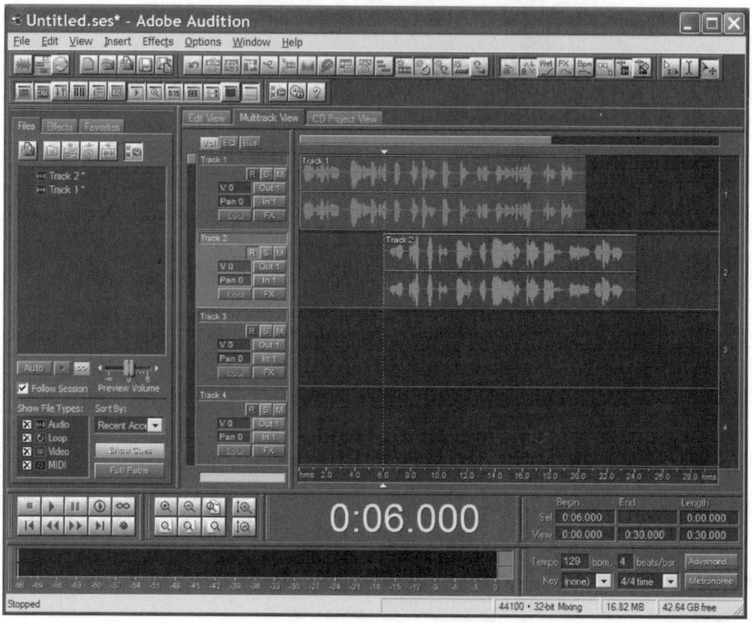

Figure 8-3. Adobe's Audition, which used to be Cool Edit

On the downside, the interface is initially very complex and will be familiar only to those with experience in multitrack recording systems. On the upside, the documentation that comes with the product is an excellent introduction not only to the software, but to the science of audio recording as well.

Sound Forge. Sony's Sound Forge (http://soundforge.com), which is pictured in Figure 8-4, is a full-featured, multitrack recording and editing application for Windows.

A full complement of effects is built in, but it also supports the VST plug-in standard so that you can add your own effects. An audio editor is built into the product, as you can see in Figure 8-4 in the lower righthand corner of the main window. The package includes noise reduction tools that will help you clean up sub par recordings.

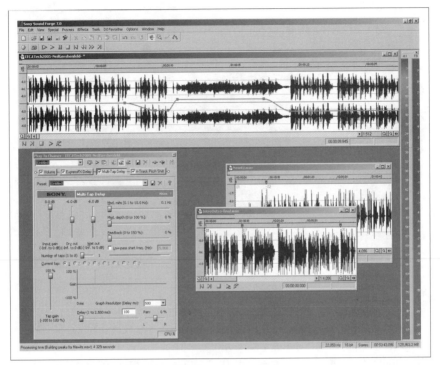

Figure 8-4. Sony's Sound Forge application

If video is your thing, you can import video and sync up your audio editing with it. If creating music loops is more your style, this program integrates with Sony's ACID program. You create the loops here [Hack #63] and then use ACID to choreograph them into a song.

At the time of this writing, Sound Forge sold for $299.95.

n-Track Studio. n-Track Studio (*http://fasoft.com*), written by Flavio Antoni-oli, is a multitrack recording and mixing program for Windows. It's rela-tively inexpensive at $49 for the limited edition and $75 for the full version. n-Track Studio is shown in Figure 8-5.

A demo is available online that you can use for a limited time, to get a sense of its features. It has a pretty daunting interface, but once you get the hang of it, you can get to recording and arranging pretty quickly. It does not have a built-in signal editor, so you will need Audacity or Sound Forge to edit your recordings directly.

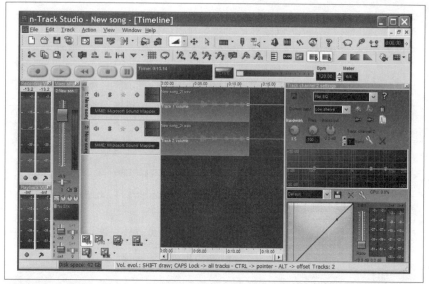

Figure 8-5. n-Track Studio

GarageBand 2. GarageBand 2, pictured in Figure 8-6, comes bundled with Apple's $49 iLife 5 suite. It's a steal alone at that price. The inclusion of the other iLife applications makes it just that much sweeter. GarageBand is good for both recording and mixing sound.

Figure 8-6. GarageBand 2

Along the right side of the window are the tracks of the recording. Each row contains little blobs of audio. You can change their duration as well as their placement in time.

GarageBand doesn't support robust sound editing. So, you will still need an application such as Audacity or Peak to do your editing. However, Garage-Band's ability to string together audio loops makes it ideal for making musical melodies for intros, outtros, bumpers, and stingers.

Logic Express 7. Logic Express 7 (*http://www.apple.com/logicexpress/*), $299, is the Apple product that is one step up the scale from GarageBand 2. It's a sophisticated multitrack recording, editing, and production tool. Logic Express is shown in Figure 8-7.

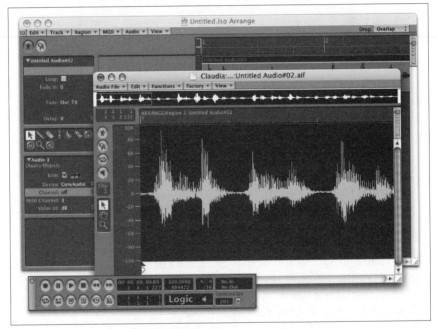

Figure 8-7. Logic Express on Macintosh

The multitrack recording and editing capabilities are ideal for a home studio music recording setting. For podcasting, it will have way more functionality than you require, but at $299, it's hard to say no.

Sound Recording Applications

A few applications specialize just in the recording of sound. Some of these subspecialize in taking sound directly from applications in addition to traditional sources, such as microphones.

Audio Hijack Pro. Audio Hijack Pro (*http://rogueamoeba.com/audiohijackpro/*), $32, is a Macintosh podcaster's best friend. It's an application that can record audio from any sound input, or any running application. This means you can integrate music or sound from iTunes directly into your recording. Figure 8-8 shows the Input tab of an Audio Hijack Pro session.

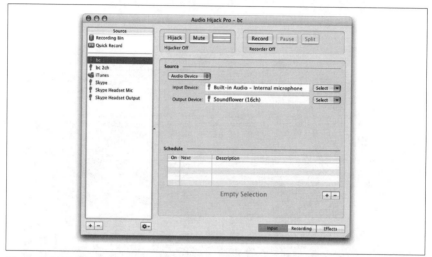

Figure 8-8. Audio Hijack Pro's Input tab

On the lefthand side of the window is the list of sessions. Each session, as specified on the righthand side of the window, has an input and output source, details about where the output file is supposed to go (in the Effects tab shown in Figure 8-9), and the grid of effects.

Audio Hijack supports a set of effects to alter the sound of your recording as you make it. These effects are strung together in an intuitive graphical format.

Through the Voice Over effect, you can bring audio from iTunes into your recording in real time. It's this ability to *hijack* sound from other applications—along with the application's incredible stability—that makes Audio Hijack Pro a very popular recording tool for Macintosh podcasters. Rogue Amoeba, the publisher of Audio Hijack Pro, has noticed this, and subsequent versions of the software are being built with podcasting in mind [Hack #52].

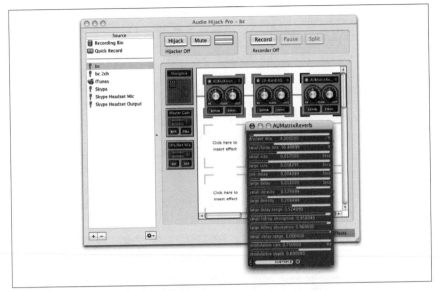

Figure 8-9. Audio Hijack Pro's Effects tab

Total Sound Recorder. The inexpensive Total Sound Recorder (available at: *http://highcriteria.com/*) is a favorite of Windows podcasters. The standard edition costs $11.95, and the professional version costs $39.95.

You can use the Total Sound Recorder Pro main window, shown in Figure 8-10, to record audio from all the standard input sources, as well as from applications.

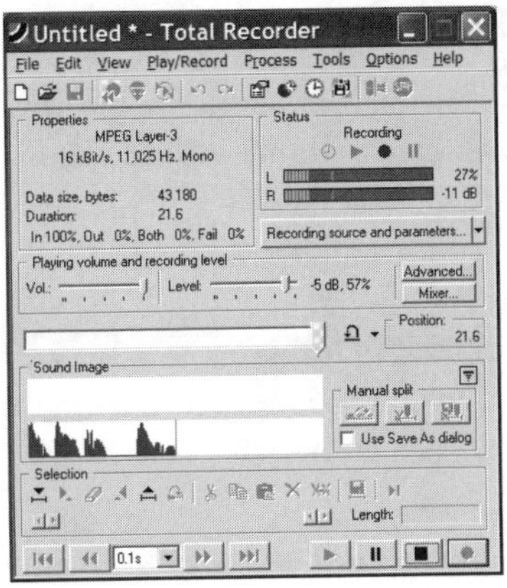

Figure 8-10. Total Sound Recorder Pro

Audio In. Another freeware recording tool is Audio In (*http://home3.swipnet. se/~w-34826/*). This is a nicely put together application that does one thing, record sound from any input, and does it well. As you record, an attractive oscilloscope display shows the signal.

Podcasting Applications

With the advent of podcasting have come specialized podcasting applications. These applications combine sound recording, rudimentary editing, and mixing, and also automate the encoding and uploading process.

iPodcast Producer. iPodcast Producer is an all-in-one podcaster application for Windows. Figure 8-11 shows one recorded segment of audio.

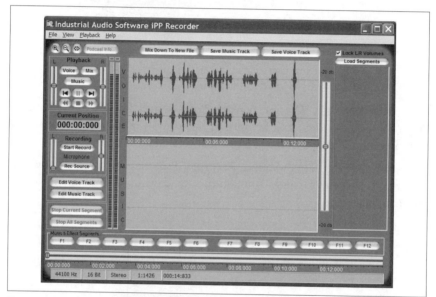

Figure 8-11. iPodcast Producer

Using this application, you can record your voice segments and drop in prerecorded effects and sounds that you can assign to hotkeys. A companion application enables you to edit the individual sound files to add some effects or to remove "ums" and "ahs" from your voice track.

Once you are done developing the podcast, the application will mix it down to MP3 or WAV format for you. It will even go as far as to upload the mixed file using FTP, and update your RSS 2.0 feed [Hack #37] to add the podcast with the correct enclosure tags.

iPodcast Producer is available for $149.95 at *http://industrialaudiosoftware.com/.*

Winpodcast. One of the first podcast authoring applications is Winpodcast (*http://podcast.scon.de/*). It has a recorder, show notes, and a cart interface, all built into one application. This application is still in its early days, but it looks promising for simple podcast productions.

MixCast Live. MixCast Live (*http://mixcastlive.com/*) is the first Macintosh podcasting application. It has a show notes area, a cart for samples, and a recorder built into the application. It was prereleased at the time of this writing. The purchase price was $59, but you could get a $20 discount if you wanted to take the leap early.

Propaganda. The oddly named Propaganda (*http://www.makepropaganda.com/*) from MixMeister Technology is a Windows podcasting application that costs $49.95. Segments can be recorded and multitrack mixed in the application. Then the show is encoded and uploaded to your site using a built-in file transfer mechanism. The application also handles creating the RSS 2.0 XML file for the podcast and uploading it to your site.

Cart Applications

Radio studios used to have racks of specially designed audio tapes called *carts* that held spots and commercials. Today these units are digital and are controlled with a special control surface that the DJ or engineer uses to trigger the sample or sound effect.

Several PC- and Mac-based cart applications are available for injecting sound into your show on demand. These applications are listed in the sections that follow, as are hacks that cover building your own cart application for Macintosh **[Hack #54]** or Windows **[Hack #55]**.

JazlerShow. JazlerShow (*http://www.jazler.com/products/JazlerShow.asp*) is a freeware cart application for Windows. You can place up to 30 samples in a grid and then play them on request with the click of a mouse.

Sound Byte. The options for Macintosh cart programs are limited. Sound Byte (*http://www.blackcatsystems.com/software/soundbyte.html*) is a $24 sound cart application that can preload an unlimited number of sounds into a grid. To play the sound in the cart, you simply click the button.

Helper Applications

Here are a few more applications that will help you develop your podcasts.

Soundflower and Soundflowerbed. Soundflower (*http://cycling74.com/products/soundflower.html*) is a handy sound routing utility for Macintosh. It creates two virtual sound drivers: Soundflower 2Ch and Soundflower 16Ch. These drivers support 2 and 16 channels, respectively.

The value of Soundflower is that you can specify a Soundflower port as the input or output of any application and then route sound through to it from another application. For example, you can route the output of Skype or iChat through Soundflower and into a recording application, thus recording the output of a Skype call [Hack #35].

Soundflowerbed, available on the same site, is a handy helper application that allows you to monitor your Soundflower channels.

FuzzMeasure. FuzzMeasure (*http://www.supermegaultragroovy.com/products/FuzzMeasure/*) measures the noise in your signal path and environment. It's a $49.99 application, but the company has a demo download that you can use to get some results if you are merely curious. The application actually simulates the environment using white noise and then calculates the response from the signal path and the environment.

Frequency. Frequency (*http://home3.swipnet.se/~w-34826/*) is a freeware application for Macintosh that provides an image of a sound source of the frequency domain. When editing sound, we normally look at audio in the amplitude domain. We see the audio signal as it moves up and down in waves over the time axis.

Another way to look at sound is in the frequency domain. We do this when we look at a graphic equalizer. Each bar represents a frequency and the height of the bar is the amount of volume present at that frequency.

Working with Frequency is like looking at a graph of these graphic equalizers laid out along the recording's time axis. The darkness of the band indicates the intensity at that frequency. Figure 8-12 shows the Frequency main window.

Through the miracle of really tough math, you can also edit in the frequency domain, literally removing or adding sound by frequency rather than by changing the signal itself.

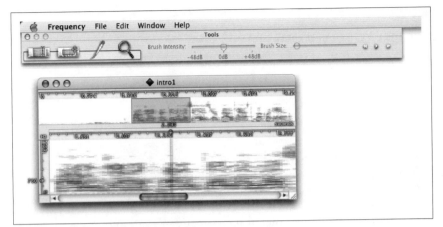

Figure 8-12. Frequency main window

Practical applications for a podcaster working with just her voice and some effects are somewhat limited. But you can use the tool to determine the frequency of particularly nasty transients and noise, and even remove them.

Another free application that works in the frequency domain is FFTea (*http://oomz.net/FFTea/index.html*). At the time of this writing, the 1.0 version had been released but a bunch of features still were missing.

Demos

Most of the software products listed here have evaluation downloads that are good for a certain period of time. My suggestion is that you always try before you buy. It's easy to get an application that is overkill for podcasting, and then get lost in the complexity. If you can't figure out how to get a track or two recorded within five minutes of installing the application, you should probably look for something that you are more productive with.

When it comes to recording, you will get the same result from all of these applications. Since the source of noise [Hack #15] is in your equipment and your environment, your recordings will have the same amount of noise no matter what you choose. So, there is no benefit to going up-market on the recording side. The same cannot be said of effects, plug-ins, and filters. There are variations in quality there, and you should test them with your own ears before you buy.

The best advice I have ever heard about digital recording is that you put the money in the microphone, and then work back along the signal path to the software. You can always get better software, but it's impossible to get better source recordings after you have made them.

See Also

- "Juice Your Sound" [Hack #51]
- "Build a Simple Sound Cart for Macintosh" [Hack #54]
- "Build a Simple Sound Cart for Windows" [Hack #55]
- "Maintain the Gain" [Hack #56]
- "Build a Sweet Sound" [Hack #57]

H A C K   Juice Your Sound
#51   Pick from a world of free and commercial audio plug-ins to get the right sound for your show.

Plug-ins are self-contained digital filters that can snap into any application that supports their particular plug-in standard. Several plug-in standards are available, but the most popular is the cross-platform Virtual Studio Technology (VST) standard, and the Macintosh-specific Audio Unit (AU) plug-ins.

Plug-ins usually install themselves or have a *README* file attached, which will walk you through the installation. Once you've installed them, you can use them in several ways. In Audacity, they are run against the current selection of audio, and the result is placed back into the file, replacing the selection. In mixer and recording programs, the plug-ins snap into the signal path so that you can hear their effect immediately as you record, though some will cause a delay in the signal.

Programs such as Peak allow you to set up a series of plug-ins and then run the signal through it while tweaking the parameters until you get the sound you want. The input and output of each plug-in is shown with a graphical meter.

In Figure 8-13, you can see the original input of the lefthand side going through a set of three VST filters and popping out on the righthand side. With the *e* button on each effect, you can edit the effect's parameters to tweak the sound.

Vboxing with Audio Hijack Pro

If you want the dynamic effect processing ability of the Vbox, where you can tweak the settings and then run the sound again and again, you can do that with Audacity and Audio Hijack Pro [Hack #50]. Use Audio Hijack Pro to hijack the signal from Audacity. Then hold down the Shift key when you press Play on Audacity. That will set Audacity into loop play mode.

Figure 8-13. The Vbox in Peak

Now, in Audio Hijack Pro you can add, remove, or edit effects to your heart's content while listening to the effects through your headphones or speakers. When you are done with the settings, you can record a playback from Audacity through the settings and import the recorded file.

Plug-In Sites

Plug-ins range from traditional effects such as compression, reverb, and flanging to synthetic instruments and visualizations. Here are some sites where you can find free or commercial plug-ins:

KVR Audio (http://www.kvraudio.com/)
> An outstanding searchable database of VST plug-ins. The site includes a forum as well as categorized RSS feeds.

OSXAudio (http://osxaudio.com/)
> A new site that covers the AU plug-in market. Both commercial and free plug-ins are listed here. An RSS feed is available to keep you up-to-date.

MadTracker (http://www.madtracker.org/)
> A searchable plug-in database.

Plugzilla (http://www.plugzilla.com/)
> A huge database of VST plug-ins.

Steinberg (http://www.steinberg.net/)
> The originator of the VST standard has links to a bunch of VST developers and plug-ins.

The Music Womb (http://www.musicwomb.org/)
> A searchable database of plug-ins of various flavors, including VSTs.

Recommended Plug-Ins

Here is a set of plug-in vendors I have found in my travels that you should have a look at:

Freeverb (http://www.dreampoint.co.uk/)
  An excellent cross-platform free reverb plug-in.

Fillet of Fish plug-ins (http://www.digitalfishphones.com/)
  These three plug-ins provide gating, compression, and de-ess'ing (removal of the long "s" sound).

Green Oak plug-ins (http://www.greenoak.com/)
  Free phaser, chorus, delay, excitifier, and more.

MDA VST Effects (http://www.mda-vst.com/effects.htm)
  A huge library of free VST plug-ins.

Voxengo (http://www.voxengo.com/)
  Has a bunch of commercial and free VST plug-ins for Windows.

RubyTube (http://www.silverspike.com/rubytube.html)
  A free plug-in for Mac and Windows that simulates a tube amp.

SoundSoap 2 (http://www.bias-inc.com/)
  A high-quality commercial noise filtering plug-in.

Pluggo (http://www.cycling74.com/)
  A set of around 100 VST and Real Time Audio Suite (RTAS) plug-ins that you can download and play with in demo mode and purchase if you want.

Kjaerhus Audio Classic Series (http://www.kjaerhusaudio.com/classic-series.php)
  A free set of VST plug-ins for the PC that covers all of your basic needs.

Ohm Force (http://www.ohmforce.com/)
  One free and a bunch of commercial plug-ins. Damned if I know how to use them, but they look really cool.

SmartElectronix (http://www.smartelectronix.com/)
  A group of plug-in developers that has built a wide variety of free plug-ins.

Develop Your Own Plug-Ins

The VST plug-in standard is maintained by Steinberg (http://www.steinberg.net/). The site includes an API reference as well as mailing list links. The AU standard is part of Apple's new Core Audio interface. Documentation and developer tools are available on http://developer.apple.com/.

There are other plug-in standards as well. MOTU has the MOTU Audio System (MAS) plug-ins. Pro Tools has two standards: RTAS plug-ins, and expensive Time Division Multiplexing (TDM) plug-ins. Microsoft is also on the scene with its own DirectSound plug-ins.

See Also

- "Build a Sweet Sound" [Hack #57]
- "Add Special Effects" [Hack #58]
- "Fix Common Audio Problems" [Hack #59]

HACK #52 Automate Audio Hijack Pro

Automate your Audio Hijack Pro recording sessions with its support for AppleScript.

Audio Hijack Pro [Hack #50] is the premier low-cost audio recording solution for podcasting. It integrates nicely with the audio from other applications, such as iTunes, making it easy to do a one-shot recording of a show that's fairly complex in structure.

In its latest release, Audio Hijack Pro (AHP) includes extensive support for AppleScript. This make it possible to automate AHP individually and to choreograph your recording with other scriptable applications such as iTunes or QuickTime Player.

You can script AHP in four different ways:

External scripting
> Using Apple's Script Editor or AppleScript Studio, you can control AHP from outside the application. For example, you can create buttons to start and stop recording AHP from an AppleScript Cart application.

Menu scripts
> AHP has a script menu where you can add your own custom scripts. To add a script, simply save your script file from Script Editor in the *Library/Application Support/Audio Hijack Pro/Menu Scripts* directory.

Post recording scripts
> These scripts are attached to sessions and run when the recording finishes. The AHP help has information on how these scripts are structured and where they go. AHP is preinstalled with a script that automatically imports the recorded file into iTunes.

Recording Bin script
> AHP has added AppleScript support to the Recording Bin. It is preinstalled with scripts that export the media to your iPod or to iTunes, or that re-encode the audio in various forms. Information about how to create your own Recording Bin script is included in the AHP help.

Sample Scripts

I've included some example scripts to get you started with your own AHP automation. Simply type the code into the */Applications/AppleScript/Script Editor* application in a new AppleScript document.

Start recording a session. This script finds the session named *bc* and starts hijacking it, then recording it:

```
tell application "Audio Hijack Pro"
    start hijacking the session named "bc"
    start recording the session named "bc"
end tell
```

You need to start hijacking before you can start recording.

Stop recording a session. This script will stop the recording on a session named *bc*:

```
tell application "Audio Hijack Pro"
    stop recording the session named "bc"
    stop hijacking the session named "bc"
end tell
```

Start and stop two sessions. Sometimes you will want to start and stop two sessions almost simultaneously. Here is the script to start the two-session recording. This will start the hijacking and recording of Skype Headset Output and Skype Headset Mic as close together as you can get:

```
tell application "Audio Hijack Pro"
    set chan1 to the session named "Skype Headset Output"
    set chan2 to the session named "Skype Headset Mic"
    start hijacking chan1
    start hijacking chan2
    start recording chan1
    start recording chan2
end tell
```

To shut them down, simply reverse the script:

```
tell application "Audio Hijack Pro"
    set chan1 to the session named "Skype Headset Output"
    set chan2 to the session named "Skype Headset Mic"
    stop recording chan1
    stop recording chan2
    stop hijacking chan1
    stop hijacking chan2
end tell
```

Set the ID3 tags. AHP gives you full access to the session's ID3 tags. Here is an example script that sets all the different ID3 tags:

```
tell application "Audio Hijack Pro"
    tell session named "bc"
        set title tag to "my title"
        set artist tag to "my artist"
        set album tag to "my album"
        set genre tag to "my genre"
        set track number tag to "10"
        set year tag to "2005"
        set comment tag to "my comment"
    end tell
end tell
```

You can use a script like this to set the ID3 tags with some information that AHP might not have, such as the ISBN number of the book you are reviewing in your podcast.

Set the output directory. Another handy thing to set automatically is the output directory:

```
tell application "Audio Hijack Pro"
    tell session named "bc"
        set output folder to "~/Desktop/bc"
    end tell
end tell
```

By automating both the Finder and AHP, you can have the script create the output folder you want, and then set the session output folder in AHP to that new folder. More recent versions of AHP will automatically create output folders if they are not found when the recording session starts.

Set the output filename. AHP has a wide variety of options for output filenaming, but you might have reasons to automate this yourself. Here is a simple script to set the output filename format:

```
tell application "Audio Hijack Pro"
    tell session named "bc"
        set the output name format to "%date %index"
    end tell
end tell
```

Set the input or output device. When AHP can't find a device, it sometimes sets the input and output devices back to something safe, such as the system-standard input and output devices. This first script sets the input device to whatever you want. In this case, I'm setting the input device of the session named *bc* to the internal microphone:

```
tell application "Audio Hijack Pro"
    set inputChannel to the audio input named ¬
        "Built-in Audio: Internal Microphone"
    set input device of session named "bc" to inputChannel
end tell
```

A script that sets the output device is just as simple. Here I'm setting the output channel to the two-channel Soundflower device:

```
tell application "Audio Hijack Pro"
    set outputChannel to the audio output named "Soundflower (2ch)"
    set output device of session named "bc" to outputChannel
end tell
```

Inspect the Recording Bin. You might want to have a script look through your Recording Bin to remove, process, or move recorded files. This small script walks through the entire Recording Bin and prompts you with the path-name of each recorded file:

```
tell application "Audio Hijack Pro"
    repeat with recording in audio recordings
        display dialog (path of recording as string)
    end repeat
end tell
```

The important parts are the repeat statement that iterates through all the recordings, and the path of recording portion that gets the path to the recorded file. The name of the file is also available as name of recording.

See Also

- "Record Interviews on Skype" [Hack #35]
- "Timestamp Your Show Notes" [Hack #53]
- "Build a Simple Sound Cart for Macintosh" [Hack #54]
- "Build a Simple Sound Cart for Windows" [Hack #55]

HACK #53 Timestamp Your Show Notes

Use Audio Hijack Pro's AppleScript interface to mark important interview moments in your show notes.

During the course of an interview or show, you will find that you want to take note of the current time so that later you can make some edits relative to that point. Thoughtfully Audio Hijack Pro [Hack #50] has included an AppleScript interface that you can use to get the current time of the recording.

In this hack I provide an AppleScript fragment that takes the current recording time from Audio Hijack Pro and places it into the clipboard so that you can paste it into your show notes.

The Code

Create a new file in the Script Editor, with this code:

```
tell application "Audio Hijack Pro"
    repeat with sess in sessions
        if sess is hijacked then
            set theTime to current recording time of sess
            set minuteCount to theTime / 60 as integer
            if (minuteCount * 60) > theTime then
                set minuteCount to minuteCount - 1
            end if
            set secondCount to theTime mod 60 as integer
            if secondCount < 10 then
                set secondCount to "0" & secondCount as string
            end if
            set theTime to minuteCount & ":" & secondCount
            set the clipboard to (theTime as string)
        end if
    end repeat
end tell
```

Running the Hack

Pressing Play in the Script Editor will run the code. This takes the time of the current recording and puts it into the clipboard.

The important bits are where I get the current recording time, which is returned in seconds (and even fractions thereof). Then I convert that into a string in a really roundabout process that is convoluted only because of AppleScript's horrendous support for math. Then I put it into the clipboard as a string.

Hacking the Hack

If you want to send it directly to an application, here is another derivative script that adds the time to the current document in TextEdit:

```
tell application "Audio Hijack Pro"
    repeat with sess in sessions
        if sess is hijacked then
            set theTime to current recording time of sess
            set minuteCount to theTime / 60 as integer
            if (minuteCount * 60) > theTime then
                set minuteCount to minuteCount - 1
            end if
            set secondCount to theTime mod 60 as integer
            if secondCount < 10 then
                set secondCount to "0" & secondCount as string
            end if
            set theTime to minuteCount & ":" & secondCount
```

```
        end if
    end repeat
end tell
```

```
tell application "TextEdit"
    set currentText to the text of the front document as string
    set the text of the front document to currentText &
        return & (theTime as string)
end tell
```

This script takes the front document of TextEdit and adds the record time to it.

Ideally this type of marking procedure would be a single keystroke. Using an application such as Keyboard Maestro (*http://keyboardmaestro.com/*), you can bind this script to an unused hotkey.

See Also

- "Control Your Recorder with Your Mobile Phone" [Hack #17]

Build a Simple Sound Cart for Macintosh

#54 Use Xcode on Macintosh to build a sound cart application with AppleScript Studio.

Having sample sounds close at hand is important for podcasters. Using AppleScript Studio, you can quickly build a standalone application with whatever interface you want to control your recording application (e.g., Audio Hijack Pro [Hack #50]) and play your samples at the touch of a button.

First I start with Xcode, which is available to Apple Developer Connection members (online membership is free) from *http://developer.apple.com/tools/ download/*, and quite possibly on your Mac's hard drive in */Applications/ Installers/Xcode Tools*. With Xcode, I create a new AppleScript Application project using the New Project command. For this example, I'll use the name SampleCart for the project.

Now I want to build the interface, so I double-click the *MainMenu.nib* file, which launches Interface Builder (shown in Figure 8-14). Using the controls from the Cocoa-Controls palette, I drag three buttons onto the window and change their titles to Start Recording, Stop Recording, and Sound 1, respectively. Start Recording will start Audio Hijack Pro's recording, Stop Recording will stop it, and Sound 1 will play a sample sound.

Next I select Show Info from the Tools menu. This brings up the information palette, which tells me all about the windows and the buttons. I click the first Start Record button and change the info palette, now named NSButton Info, to display the AppleScript section. Then I select the `clicked`

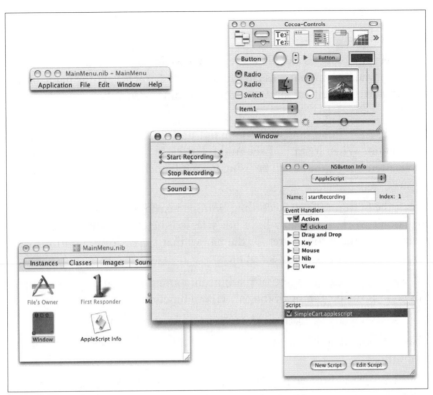

Figure 8-14. Editing the cart application's UI in Interface Builder

item under the Action section and select *SimpleCart.applescript* down in the script section.

This links the clicking of the button to the AppleScript file. I do that with all three buttons. I also give each one a unique name. For this example, I called them startRecording, stopRecording, and sound1, respectively.

By clicking the Edit Script button, I am taken back to Xcode to write the script for these buttons.

```
on clicked theObject
    if the name of theObject is "startRecording" then
        tell application "Audio Hijack Pro"
            start hijacking session named "bc"
            start recording session named "bc"
        end tell
    end if
    if the name of theObject is "stopRecording" then
        tell application "Audio Hijack Pro"
            stop recording session named "bc"
            stop hijacking session named "bc"
```

```
        end tell
    end if
end clicked
```

The preceding code is the click event handler for the script. It takes as an argument the button that was clicked, called theObject. I get the name of the button and then either start or stop recording, depending on what was clicked.

Next I use the Build and Run command under the Build menu to run the application. When it starts, I see Audio Hijack Pro opening up as well. The application knows that I will be using it, so it launches Audio Hijack Pro just in case.

I click the Start and Stop Recording buttons just to make sure they work. If they don't work, I probably have not selected the click event or the Apple-Script file in the Info palette. Or the names that I used for the buttons vary from the names I put in the script file.

If I want to check the name of the button coming into the script file, I put this code at the beginning of the on clicked function:

```
display dialog the name of theObject as string
```

That will pop up a dialog with the name of the button before the rest of the script runs.

Now I need to support the Sound 1 button, which means first getting a sound. Really any sound will do. I call mine *testsound.aif*. First I copy the sound file into the project directory. Then I click the SampleCart item in the project and select Add Files…from the Project menu. From here, I select the sound file. When it asks me if I want to add the file to all the projects, I just click OK.

With the sound file in the project, I can add this code to the on click handler:

```
if the name of theObject is "sound1" then
    set theSound to load sound "testsound.aif"
    play theSound
end if
```

Wow. That was easy. This loads the sound file from the *resources* folder into a variable called theSound and then plays the sound. I run the application again, and lo and behold, clicking the Sound 1 button plays the sound. But there is a slight delay, and that's a problem.

What I would like to do is have the sound file loaded when the program starts up and then just play the copy loaded in memory when I hit the button. So, I need to go back to Interface Builder, click the main window, and select the awake from nib event from the Nib section of the AppleScript items in the Info window. Then I assign that to the *SimpleCart.applescript* file and select Edit Script again.

Now I have a new event handler called awake from nib where I put this code:

```
on awake from nib theObject
    set theSound to load sound "testsound.aif"
end awake from nib
```

Those with a keen eye will realize that I'm setting a local variable in this function. So, how do I get the variable theSound to show up in the click handler? I define it as a property at the top of the file, like this:

```
property theSound : ""
```

Then I change the click handler to play theSound:

```
if the name of theObject is "sound1" then
    play theSound
end if
```

Now when I run the program again, the sound plays instantly when I hit the button.

The complete script looks like this:

```
property theSound : ""

on clicked theObject
    if the name of theObject is "startRecording" then
        tell application "Audio Hijack Pro"
            start hijacking session named "bc"
            start recording session named "bc"
        end tell
    end if
    if the name of theObject is "stopRecording" then
        tell application "Audio Hijack Pro"
            stop recording session named "bc"
            stop hijacking session named "bc"
        end tell
    end if
    if the name of theObject is "sound1" then
        play theSound
    end if
end clicked

on awake from nib theObject
    set theSound to load sound "testsound.aif"
end awake from nib
```

Going on from Here

This is a simple AppleScript Studio application. AppleScript is a very complete language and the Studio environment allows you to create fully featured and beautiful applications.

One expansion idea is to allow the user to select the sounds at runtime for the various buttons. Another is to allow users to choose which Audio Hijack Pro session to use for recording dynamically.

You can even display HTML show notes in a web browser window that is easy to integrate into your application.

While developing this hack, I took it to the extreme and made myself a nice little AppleScript Cart application. It was too much to document in this hack, but all the code is available on the O'Reilly site in the example code section associated with this book. Then end result looks like Figure 8-15.

Figure 8-15. The finished AppleScript cart

The top panel controls Audio Hijack Pro, and you can select which session you want to use from the drop-down list. The bottom section is a list of sounds that you can add to and remove from with the + and - buttons. To play the sound, you either double-click the list entry or press the Play button. The files are selected from anywhere on your machine using the File Open panel.

See Also

- "Build a Simple Sound Cart for Windows" [Hack #55]

Build a Simple Sound Cart for Windows

#55

Using ActiveState Perl on Windows, you can build a quick cart program to play WAV files on demand.

ActiveState Perl comes with Tk (see *http://www.tcl.tk/*) support built in for creating reasonably good-looking Windows interfaces quickly. It also comes with the Win32::Sound module [Hack #7], which makes it simple to play WAV files with a single command. So, I figured I would take these two packages and slap them together to make a simple Windows sound cart program. The result is this script.

The Code

Save this file as *perlcart.pl*:

```perl
use Tk;
use Tk::Button;
use DirHandle;
use Win32::Sound;
use strict;

sub play($) { Win32::Sound::Play( $_[0] ); }

my $main = new MainWindow( );

my $dh = new DirHandle( "." );
while( my $filename = $dh->read( ) )
{
        next unless $filename =~ /[.]wav$/i;
        my $buttonname = $filename;
        $buttonname =~ s/[.]wav$//i;
        my $button = $main->Button( -text => $buttonname,
                -command => sub { play( $filename ); } );
        $button->pack( -fill => "x", -padx => 2, -pady => 2 );
}

MainLoop;
```

Running the Hack

Add a couple of *.wav* files to the directory where you placed *perlcart.pl*. Then run this command:

```
C:\> perl perlcart.pl
```

It doesn't come a whole lot simpler than this. I create the main window, then iterate through the files in the current directory looking for *.wav* files. Each time I find one, I add a new button with a command handler that will play the file using the play subroutine. I then pack the button into the main window, which is Tk's simplest way of doing layout. Then I run in the infinite MainLoop subroutine.

The result is Figure 8-16.

Figure 8-16. The Perl cart

I could have added a Quit button, but I figure the Close button on the window is just as good.

Where you go from here with this little script is up to you. Tk has the ability to show HTML in windows, so you can display your show notes along with the cart buttons. If you find a recording application that supports automation through COM, you can even drive that from the script using Win32::OLE and create a complete podcasting application.

See Also

- "Choose the Right Audio Tools" [Hack #50]
- "Build a Simple Sound Cart for Macintosh" [Hack #54]

HACK #56 Maintain the Gain

Use gain controlling filters to maintain a consistent level throughout your podcast.

When you start your sound editing application and open a sound file, the display that you see is an *amplitude graph*. The horizontal axis of the graph represents time, and the vertical axis of the graph represents the amplitude of the signal. If the signal almost reaches the top and bottom of the graph, it will be loud, if it's close to the center of the graph, it will be soft.

Figure 8-17 shows a sound sample in Audacity [Hack #50]. The selected portion is loud, and the other half is relatively quiet in comparison.

The amplitude of a signal is rated in decibels (dB). A soft signal is in the –20 dB range, a loud signal approaches –6 dB, –2 dB signals are very loud, and 0 dB signals are clipped in the digital world.

Using sound tools, you can alter the amplitude of a signal with various filters and effects. You need to keep two key things in mind when you are

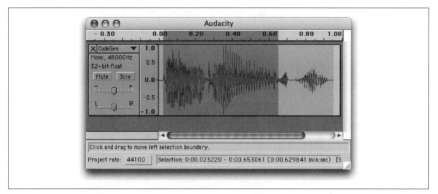

Figure 8-17. A loud portion of a signal selected in Audacity

working the amplitude of a signal. First, you should have a target dB range in mind. For music, I recommend somewhere between –6 and –2 dB. For the spoken word, I recommend –6 to –12 dB. This means that your loudest signal should be no more than –6 dB, and your softest signal that isn't silence should be at least –12 dB. Of course, these are personal preferences and you should come up with a range that's comfortable for your show.

The second thing to keep in mind is that 0 dB in the digital world is where signals clip. This means that sound above 0 dB will be clipped to 0 dB as a flat line. This creates nasty noise artifacts. Don't clip digital signals. Analog tapes can be overdriven to create an appealing, powerful sound; digital signals sound bad when they clip.

It's interesting to note that approaches to amplitude management differ between genres. Classical music, as an example, uses the full recording dynamic range from very soft to extremely loud. This is because absolute fidelity to the music is of paramount importance. Talk shows take the other extreme: signals are boxed into a zone (e.g., -12 dB to -6 dB) so that the listener can concentrate on what someone is saying and not worry about the volume of his iPod.

Gain Enveloping

A good sound editor provides a mechanism for editing the gain of an individual track over its duration. This is called *gain enveloping*, or just *enveloping*. With this feature, you draw a curve over the signal. Where the curve is high the sound will be at 100% gain, where you draw the curve down toward the bottom the sound will fade to 0%. Most envelope features allow you to draw either lines or curves: lines are a steady drop, and curves give you a smoother fade feel.

Figure 8-18 shows the example signal flattened by *attenuating* the first portion of the signal and letting the rest of the signal go out at 100%.

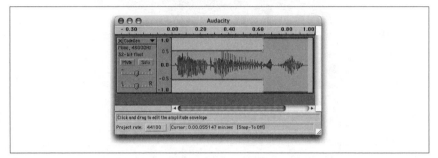

Figure 8-18. Using Audacity gain enveloping

In Audacity, enveloping is one of the editing modes on the signal window. You adjust the envelope first by creating a new control point by clicking the current envelope. Then you drag the control point around to squeeze and expand the signal as you see fit.

Automation. Old-school sound engineers use the term *automation* to describe *enveloping*. The old mixing consoles [Hack #14] with lots of faders could record the positions of those faders over the course of the song and then replay them during playback. The feature is called automation and it does exactly the same thing that we now do in software with gain enveloping.

If you want to use faders to control the levels on a signal during playback, Behringer (*http://www.behringer.com/*) and others sell inexpensive Musical Instruments Digital Interface (MIDI) mix boxes such as the BCF2000 (~$239). This box has a set of eight faders, among other controls, that you can attach through software to the amplitude of any track in your session. As you play back the mix, adjusting the fader will set the gain envelope in the software. If you play the mix again, you will see the fader move during playback, just the way you did it before.

Compression and Limiting

Working with enveloping either by drawing the lines yourself or through MIDI controls is a time-consuming process. Compression filters do this gain management automatically for you. The function of a compressor is to attenuate signals that go over a set threshold. Loud signals are compressed by a user-settable ratio to bring them in the target dB range if they go over the threshold.

There are four basic compression parameters:

Threshold

The dB cutoff above which the signal will be compressed.

Ratio

The amount of compression to be applied to the signal. At a setting of 2:1 it will take 2 dB of signal to create 1 dB of output. A low compression such as 2:1 is a fairly soft compression; 10:1 compression, or limiting, brings the signal down a lot faster.

Attack

A time value that specifies how quickly the compressor will work when the signal goes above the cutoff.

Release

The amount of time to hold the signal after the signal dips back under the cutoff level.

Figure 8-19 shows the compressor that's built into Audacity. The Threshold control defines the level above which the signal will be compressed. Here I have it set to –7 dB, so anything between –7 dB and 0 dB will be compressed. The ratio is 2:1, so anything above –7 dB will be cut in half.

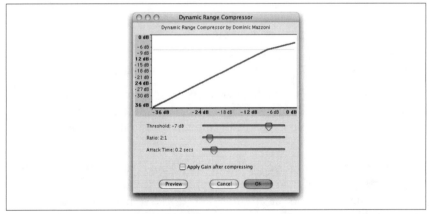

Figure 8-19. The Audacity Compression filter

Some people find compression confusing because it seems to both compress and expand the signal. That's because compression is a two-stage filter. The Threshold and Ratio controls will only ever attenuate signal. But most compressors have an output gain that will boost the entire signal after the compression. You control Audacity's compressor with the "Apply Gain after compressing" checkbox.

For spoken-word work in podcasts, I recommend a fairly fast-attack time of around 5 ms. A slower release of 50 ms gives you a natural feel coming out of the compression. A ratio of around 2:1 is not too harsh, but it will avoid clipping. Set the cutoff level to the top end of your ideal gain box. For example, if your ideal signal goes between −12 dB and −6 dB, set it to around −6 dB. Compression levels of 8:1 or 10:1 sound squashed and unnatural.

Limiters. A *limiter* is a simple compressor that has a ratio of 10:1 or above. It's used as a last resort to avoid clipping the signal.

Expanders. A less common filter is an *expander*, which is the inverse of a compressor. An expander will boost signals that fall below a certain threshold. This is handy when you have a signal that fluctuates between too quiet and just right.

Hardware. Compression and limiting are the effects that you should think about getting hardware for, even in a home studio. A software compressor will help you tone down a bright signal in post-processing, but it won't help you fix signals that were clipped by the audio input device. If you put a hardware compressor between the microphone and the digital conversion device, you can avoid unnecessary clipping.

Some digitizing devices, such as the Edirol UA-25 [Hack #12], come with an optional limiter built in to avoid clipping.

Maximizing and Normalization

A *normalizing* or *maximizing* filter seeks to take all of the signal, both the highs and the lows, and compress them into a boxed range of dBs. It's a useful last step in processing to get the overall level of the show to be where you want it.

Maximizing is used by music producers who want a very *loud* sound. If you look at some music in a sound editing program, it will look like one enormous box that peaks out at around −2 dB to leave headroom for stations that don't have their levels set properly. This boxing effect leads to distortion that can feel unnatural for spoken-word podcasts.

Noise Gate

A *noise gate* is a simple filter that reduces the signal to silence if there is no significant input. When you talk into your microphone, the gate reads the presence of a signal and opens up, letting the sound pass. As you stop talking, the filter sees that there is no input and closes the gate, which returns the signal to absolute silence. This can be a very handy filter in noisy conditions.

There are several controls on noise gate, and they vary from gate to gate. In general, you will have a cutoff control that tells the filter what it should consider a significant signal. You will also have a speed control that affects the speed at which the gate closes after you stop speaking. In noisy environments, you will want to set that to a fast setting to block out as much noise as possible. In quieter environments, set this to a slower setting to maintain a smoother sound.

Noise gating is not strictly a gain control feature, but using a noise gate can eliminate background noise between voice segments, allowing you to add more gain to the overall recording without increasing the noise.

See Also

- "Set Up a Basic Home Studio" [Hack #12]
- "Reduce Noise" [Hack #15]
- "Juice Your Sound" [Hack #51]
- "Build a Sweet Sound" [Hack #57]

HACK #57 Build a Sweet Sound

Use frequency filters to adjust your recording to get the tone you want.

You can look at sound in two ways: either in the amplitude domain, or in the frequency domain. Frequencies are measured in hertz (Hz). The lower the frequency, the lower the pitch, and the higher the frequency, the higher the pitch. All sounds have a frequency, or a set of frequencies, with an amplitude at that frequency. Amplitude filters can alter the level of your sound, and frequency filters alter the character of your sound.

Human voices are strongest between 200 Hz and 3 kHz. Men's voices tend to have more amplitude in the low end and center a little lower in the spectrum than women's voices. Boosting the low frequencies will add more depth and warmth to a voice, and boosting the high frequencies will add detail and make the sound more crisp.

Voices also have under- and overtones that extend into the 15 kHz range and down to 50 Hz. Cutting the frequencies to between 500 Hz and 5 kHz results in boxy, phone-style sound that feels processed and unnatural. You can attenuate signals outside of this range to reduce rumble in the low end and hiss in the high end, but you shouldn't remove them altogether unless you are going for that boxy sound.

Table 8-1 shows a short list of the different frequencies in the human voice and the effect you get when you up the graphic equalizer (EQ) in that range.

Table 8-1. Vocal characteristics at certain frequencies

Frequency	Characteristic
200 Hz	Enhances the bass in the voice
3 kHz	Adds extra clarity in the voice
5 kHz	Enhances vocal presence
7 kHz	Brightens vocals for lower voices
10 kHz	Brightens vocals for higher voices
15 kHz	Increases the breath sounds

Keep these ranges in mind as you are using equalizers to adjust your sound.

Graphic Equalizers

The most familiar frequency mechanism is the EQ. This filter breaks up the frequency spectrum into bands. You can add or remove amplitude in each band by changing the position of the slider. Most equalizer plug-ins **[Hack #51]** come with settings for common scenarios, adding or removing bass, adding detail, or cutting off the high end.

Figure 8-20 shows the 10-band equalizer from Audio Hijack Pro.

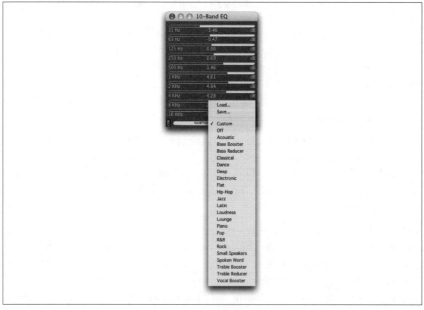

Figure 8-20. The graphic equalizer in Audio Hijack Pro

You can change the settings manually or pick from a handy drop-down list of predefined settings.

Parametric Equalizers

Parametric equalizers have a similar function to graphic equalizers, but they are more flexible. They usually have between two and ten control points that you can set to any frequency. You shape the equalizer by moving the control point up and down to add or remove amplitude at that frequency.

Figure 8-21 shows the Freq4 parametric equalizer from BIAS.

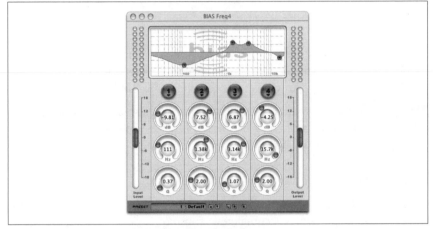

Figure 8-21. The BIAS Freq4 parametric equalizer

A Q value allows you to control the spread of the effect. A large Q value means that the effect will be centered strictly on the control point, and a smaller Q value means that the effect will be spread over a wider portion of the frequency spectrum.

In Figure 8-21, the first control point is centered around 100 Hz and has a low Q value, which is why the effect is spread out. The second control point is centered around 1.3 kHz and has a tighter Q value.

Low-Pass Filter

A simpler form of EQ is the low-pass filter that trims off the high frequencies and lets low frequencies "pass." You control the cutoff frequency, above which all frequencies will be attenuated. Some filters have a roll-off control that allows you to control the ramp of the cutoff, so frequencies that are closer to the cutoff aren't dropped as sharply as frequencies that are farther out.

This filter is ideal for cutting high-frequency noise such as the whine of a computer or the hiss from an air conditioner.

High-Pass Filter

The inverse of the low-pass filter is the high-pass filter. This filter lets high frequencies pass. Like the low-pass filter, you control a cutoff frequency. Below the cutoff, all frequencies will be reduced in strength.

A high-pass filter is good for reducing low rumbling noises such as the wind noise in a field recording, or the 50 Hz or 60 Hz cycle noise of a recording with ground loop noise.

Band-Pass Filter

A band-pass filter has two cutoffs, one for low frequencies and one for high frequencies. Frequencies in the band between the low and high cutoffs are allowed to pass. That's how this filter gets the name *band pass*.

This is more a description of a filter than an actual piece of software. You can use an EQ to implement a band-pass filter by notching down the low and high ends above and below your cutoff frequencies.

Tunable Noise Filtering

Frequency filters are often used to remove noise, such as hums or hisses, which occur at particular frequencies using *notch filters* (EQ filters set to very tight bands). Simple noise, such as the 50 Hz or 60 Hz hum from a power line, can be attenuated with a notched EQ filter. But complex noise, such as the sound from an air conditioner, is actually a multilayered noise source. You hear the whoosh of the wind moving, as well as clanking and rattling that come from the mechanism itself. As humans, we simplify this noise and reduce it, but microphones pick it up well.

A new advancement in digital noise reduction is the *tunable noise filter* that can tune itself to periodic noise, such as that of an air conditioner, and set up frequency filters to remove it. The trick is to reduce the noise without adding distortion to the original signal.

To use a tunable noise filter, you need a sample of just the noise from the environment. Usually this is the few seconds after you hit Record but before you start talking. Opinions vary on just how much of this sample noise is required, but to play it safe, you should record at least five seconds of it. However, you might want to record up to a minute of the environmental noise to use when editing [Hack #64].

BIAS SoundSoap 2 (*http://www.bias-inc.com/*), $99, is an excellent tunable noise reduction filter. You can run the filter in standalone mode or as a VST plug-in. When in standalone mode, select the input file with the noise sample at the front of the file. Then click the Learn Noise button and press Play. Figure 8-22 shows SoundSoap filtering the noise from a signal.

Figure 8-22. The SoundSoap sound reduction application

You can tune the filter using the controls to adjust the amount of reduction from the signal. Sometimes you don't want to block it all out because there is an ambience that you want to keep. When you have everything the way you want it, click the Apply button to apply the filter to the signal. Then use Save As to save the cleaned-up file with a new name.

The quality of tunable noise filters varies greatly. I wasn't able to get Audacity's [Hack #50] noise filter to remove noise without distorting the signal. Adobe's Audition sound editor for Windows has a high-quality tunable noise filter built in.

Tunable noise filters are similar in function to the noise reduction headphones popular with airline travelers. These microphones sample the outside noise and then create an antisignal to block out the noise selectively.

See Also

- "Choose the Right Audio Tools" [Hack #50]
- "Juice Your Sound" [Hack #51]

HACK #58 Add Special Effects

Use plug-ins to create unique sonic effects in your podcast.

Today's digital editing tools [Hack #50] make creating sound effects or altering the feel of your sound a snap. How many or how much of each effect you use depends on the type of sound you are going for. For a voice podcast, you should probably go with just a slight reverb to add some depth to your voice or to simulate a larger space. A music show might use all of these effects at various times.

Understanding effects starts with understanding *wet* and *dry*. An effect is referred to as wet when it's fully applied to the target signal. It's dry when it's applied sparingly. A signal that's processed heavily is often referred to as wet.

Reverb

When you talk, your voice is reflected back at you off the walls, the floor, and the ceiling. The shape and size of the room, as well as the texture and materials of the walls and the floor, all add to the room's sonic character. For example, your shower is very active and has a lot of reflectivity because of the tight space and the materials on the walls. A closet will be less reflective because the clothes will deaden the sound.

This effect is known as *reverberation*, or *reverb* for short. Using a software reverb adds a simulated space to a signal. Simple filters allow you to control just the size of the room, and more complex commercial filters actually simulate complex spaces such as Carnegie Hall. Specialized packages even include hardware that can sample a space and then reproduce it as filter settings.

Reverb can easily be overdone. It's an effect that you should use sparingly. An overly wet reverb effect sounds very unnatural. Just a little can add depth and warmth to a voice.

> Doug Kaye from IT Conversations (*http://itconversations. com/*) recommends having a friend do your reverb and compression settings for your voice. This will keep you from building a filter that ends up making your voice sound unnatural.

Flanger and Chorus

Reverb, flanger, and chorus are all in the *delay effects* family. Each takes a running copy of the signal and then plays it back, sometimes with the gain altered, later in the signal. The amount of this delay, between a peak in the signal and when the copy of the peak in the signal occurs, is what delineates each effect. Reverb, which simulates the acoustics of a room, has a very short delay. Flanger, which is a rock 'n' roll guitar effect, is a little longer. Chorus, which simulates multiple voices, is longer still.

Flanger and chorus are useful when you are doing a music show and you want to make some of your own music or do some fun effects stuff with your vocals.

Diffing

Diffing takes a copy of a signal from a portion of one track and copies it onto another track slightly shifted in time. This has the effect of fattening up the sound of particular words or phrases.

Figure 8-23 shows the signal in Audacity that I diffed. I started by creating a second track and copying the portion of the signal that I wanted to accentuate. Using the Move tool, I positioned this copied version just a bit ahead of the original signal. To make that process easier, I used the Zoom tool to zoom in on the two signals.

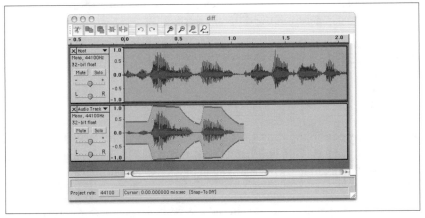

Figure 8-23. Diffing in Audacity

In addition to varying the position of the copy to add more or less of a sonic doubling, you can also use gain enveloping, as I have here. This enveloping allows me to change the intensity of the effect at various points in the word. In this example, I accentuated the start of the word and let the effect trail off toward the end.

Diffing is very time consuming to get it to sound the way you want. It's an ideal effect to add some more punch to promos.

Pitch Shifting

You can lower the pitch of your voice and sound like James Earl Jones, or raise the pitch of your voice and sound like The Chipmunks, by using *pitch shifting*. Audacity's Change Pitch effect gives you control by percentage, or you can raise or lower by semitones.

Changing Speed

If someone talks too fast or slow, you can use a speed filter to speed them up a little or slow them down. Audacity supports this with two filters. The Change Speed effect has a percentage change going up to speed up a sound, or down to slow it down. The tone will change as you speed it up or slow it down. The other effect, named Change Tempo, speeds up or slows down the signal without altering the tone.

Excitifiers

The *aural exciter* is a single effect that uses a set of filters to brighten up a dull sound. This is done by adding harmonics so that it is more acoustically interesting to listen to. This is one effect that I recommend simply sitting down and playing with. Run the effect over and over on a short sentence to see what you can get from the different settings.

Excitifiers are a bold journey into the murky realm of *psychoacoustics* where signal differences are not always quantifiable but are in the ear of the beholder.

Silence

Every sound editor supports the Silence function that replaces the selected signal with silence. This is a handy tool for manually removing noise segments from individual tracks that you are going to merge into a single mono or stereo track.

The last word in altering sound should always be to compare what was there before with what you have now. Listen to the two and make sure you made an improvement. It often helps to have someone else listen to both for the first time, without letting them know which has been altered.

See Also

- "Choose the Right Audio Tools" [Hack #50]
- "Juice Your Sound" [Hack #51]
- "Maintain the Gain" [Hack #56]
- "Build a Sweet Sound" [Hack #57]

Fix Common Audio Problems
#59 Advice from the experts on how to fix common problems in recorded sounds.

I've rounded up some solutions to common audio problems. In audio you always have many ways to do a single thing. You can use these as a starting point on the way to finding your own solution.

Reduce Wind Noise

Wind noise creates a loud rumbling that is below the 100 Hz level in recordings. You can use a low-pass filter or EQ [Hack #57] to attenuate this effect. However, it's unlikely you will be able to remove the noise entirely. You should aim to reduce it to an unobtrusive background level and go from calling it *noise* to calling it *ambience* instead [Hack #64].

The ideal solution is to resample the sound with a windscreen and a filter on the microphone to take out wind noise.

Give Your Voice a Phat Sound

Starting with a good clean signal, you can add some depth by using an EQ to boost the mid and low ranges from about 1.5 kHz down. A slight reverb helps, though you will want to dial this in to make sure you aren't adding so much that the sound feels over-processed. Set the reverb to a small room and set the wet/dry mix very low [Hack #58]. You don't want to hear the delayed signal, you just want to double the existing sound to phatten it out a little.

If you have the chance to do a retake on the sound, have the person move much closer to the microphone. This will make use of the proximity effect, and the microphone will pick up more of the natural depth of the voice.

Obscure a Voice

If you want to preserve someone's anonymity, you can layer a series of effects [Hack #58] on their voice to give them a completely different sound without it becoming too distracting. I recommend first doing a pitch change to drop the person's voice by several whole notes. That will take her out of her normal pitch range.

People talk with a signature cadence. Think of William Shatner in *Star Trek*. His cadence was so peculiar that imitators don't even go after the voice— they just tweak their cadence. You need to obscure that. So, use a Change Tempo filter to speed up or slow down the pacing, and then take some of the clear recording at the beginning of the file or in between the words and randomly add or remove small segments from the spaces between the words.

Fix a Muffled Voice

If a person moves his mouth away from the central axis of the microphone, his voice will drop and become muffled. Try boosting the signal in ranges between 5 kHz and 7 kHz with an EQ to boost up the clarity of the voice. Then use a gain envelope to boost the signal to the level of the rest of the podcast.

Make Someone Sound Far Away

A person who is far away will sound faint, so reduce his levels. He won't be close enough to a mic to get the proximity effect, so you should cut the low end of the frequency range that would be there if he were up close. In addition, you can add some reverb to make him sound as if he is in the corner of the room.

Remove Hum

Low-frequency hum at around 50 Hz or 60 Hz is caused by ground loops coming from your power source. It's worth finding and removing the source of this signal [Hack #15]. To eliminate the noise from signals you already have, try a parametric EQ with a notch filter at 50 or 60 Hz.

Another option is a tunable noise filter [Hack #57]. Some of these filters, such as BIAS's SoundSoap, have filtering code to handle these power leakage problems specifically.

Remove Hiss

Hiss is high-frequency periodic noise. The high frequency gives it the annoying high pitch. Thankfully, this also moves it away from the voice spectrum so that you can remove it without too much distortion to the original signal. Use an EQ to remove frequencies above 7 kHz. Use less EQ in the closer frequencies and be more aggressive in the higher frequencies.

Simulate a Phone

When you have one side of an interview recorded through the phone and the other side on a clean studio microphone, the result can be jarring to the ear. It helps to take a little of the quality out of the studio microphone recording by dropping off the low end below 60 Hz and reducing the high end above 3.5 kHz. Don't kill them entirely because then you will sound like you are on a phone; instead, reduce them a little to lessen the jarring difference in quality between the two sounds.

Another technique is to use a coffee mug on its side to trap part of your voice [Hack #32].

Simulate a Radio

Growing up in the mid-'80s, one of my favorite songs was Wall of Voodoo's "Mexican Radio": "I wish I was in Tijuana, eating barbequed iguana." At several points in the song, the singer sounds like he is talking through an AM radio, severely boxed and distorted.

You can use digital effects to simulate this by doing a hard chop of the frequencies below 500 Hz and above 3 kHz with an EQ, and then over boosting the top end of the vocals around 3 kHz to add some distracting gritty clarity. Adding in another track of toned-down white noise will also add a little sonic grit.

If you have the time, another solution is to record through an actual radio. Put your recording on your iPod, and then use a Griffin iTrip to broadcast it on an FM band. Tune your radio close to that band. Analog tuners are better, since you can get them close but not quite there. Move the iPod around until you get some randomly slight cut-outs. Then record the signal coming out of the radio with your microphone. Using the internal microphone on your computer will add another level of grit and boxy compression.

Simulate Rewind and Fast-Forward

You can simulate rewind and fast-forward in two ways. The easiest is to use the Change Speed effect in Audacity to speed up the sound for fast-forward. Or reverse the signal using the Reverse effect and Change Speed to simulate rewind.

Another option is to record from iTunes as you rewind using the song position control. Use Audio Hijack Pro [Hack #50] to hijack and record the iTunes output, and then fast-forward and rewind to your heart's content. An advantage of this approach is that it sounds like a person honing in on a piece of content when the rewind slows as you approach the target.

The Voice of God

Apparently God has a deep voice, or sounds like George Burns. I'll take the easy route and go with the deep voice, which is just a *change pitch* effect. Additionally, drop your own voice and try to talk out of your chest and not your mouth. Your chest gives you a deeper pitch and a fuller sound. Slow down your cadence as well, or use *change tempo* to slow it down in post. But not too much—God's voice is deep but not ponderously slow.

See Also

*   "Choose the Right Audio Tools" [Hack #50]
*   "Juice Your Sound" [Hack #51]
*   "Maintain the Gain" [Hack #56]
*   "Build a Sweet Sound" [Hack #57]

HACK #60   Mix Multiple Tracks

Use multiple tracks in your audio editor to combine multiple elements into complex shows easily.

Multitrack editing [Hack #50] allows you to combine multiple sounds together into a single stereo mix. With Audacity and all the other editing programs, you can create an unlimited number of virtual tracks. Each track can contain one or more sounds that are positioned in the track at various points in time.

A multitrack sound project is not an audio file that can be played by a standard MP3 player. To do that, you need to perform a *mix-down* operation that flattens all the tracks into either a mono or stereo output file. This is the final stage of any project. You should always retain the multitrack project and consider the output mixed-down file as throwaway.

If you are familiar with Photoshop, Fireworks, or other image editing programs, you can think of a multitrack project the same way as you do an image file with multiple layers. A Photoshop file is the equivalent of a multitrack project with multiple layers. And the exported JPG or GIF file that has the flattened layers is the equivalent of the mixed-down MP3 file.

A track in a multitrack editing system has several key features:

Name
> You can rename a track to something meaningful, such as *voice*, *music*, or *ambience*. Sometimes these are abbreviated as *ax* or *acts* for *voice*, *mus* for *music*, and *abl* for *ambience*. This will make it easier to manage your tracks.

Position
> A track can be mono, stereo left, or stereo right.

Stereo pan
> Stereo tracks can be located somewhere within the stereo field, from absolute left to dead center to absolute right. An interview that was

recorded with two separate microphones might be mixed with one signal slightly left and the other slightly right to give a feel of separation
between the interviewer and interviewee.

Gain

Each track is assigned a master gain, which is the level at which it will
be mixed into the final stereo or mono mix-down.

Effects

Some editing programs, such as Apple's GarageBand and Adobe's Audition, allow you to assign effects to each channel, including reverb, chorus, and delay. This is in addition to any effects [Hack #58] that you have
applied to the signals within the channel.

Figure 8-24 shows an example of a two-track interview project in Audacity.

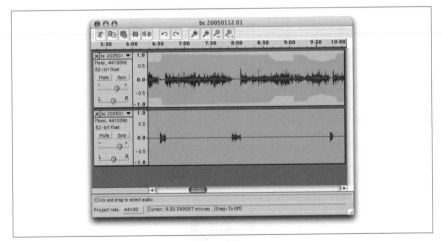

Figure 8-24. An interview multitrack mix

The top track is the interviewee and the bottom track is the interviewer. The
gain of the interviewee has been enveloped using Audacity's gain enveloping feature [Hack #56]. You can see the differences in the gray background of
the track: where the gray pinches in, the sound level is reduced; where it
reaches the top and bottom of the window, the signal is at full strength.
Enveloping and the master gain of the track work together to control the
overall gain of the signal.

Figure 8-25 is a close-up of a stereo project. You can see the controls for stereo pan and gain in the sidebar of each channel.

Notice how the top channel is assigned to the left output channel, and the
bottom channel to the right. You are free to have as many left, right, and

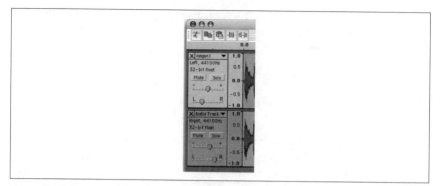

Figure 8-25. Stereo multitrack mix in Audacity

mono channels as you like, and Audacity will handle mixing them properly during mix-down.

At the bottom of each channel are the gain and pan controls. The gain is the slider with the minus and plus indicators. The pan is the slider with the L and R indicators.

You can also mute the channel during playback with the Mute button. Listen to just one track by pressing the Solo button. Please note that the Mute button in recent versions of Audacity is ignored for mix-down.

A mono project, as shown in Figure 8-26, looks similar.

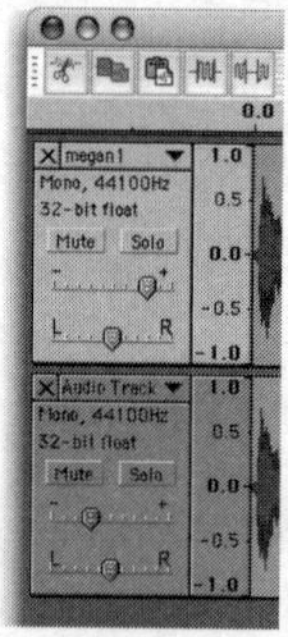

Figure 8-26. Two mono channels in Audacity

The two channels are marked as mono, with the master gain of each set to the appropriate levels.

You can test your mix and tweak it as you work by hitting the Play button on the document. Audacity does this mix to the left and right on the fly, and presents you with the sound of the finished product. If you want to remove a track from the mix, temporarily hit the Mute button on the track. Or if you want to check a particular track, hit the Solo button on the track.

At any time, you can export the project to MP3, which will flatten the mix down to what you hear on the left and right during playback. If you want to preview that in Audacity before you export to MP3, use the Quick Mix command to flatten the project down to a stereo or mono track.

See Also

- "Mix Your Podcast in Hardware" [Hack #14]
- "Choose the Right Audio Tools" [Hack #50]
- "Maintain the Gain" [Hack #56]
- "Set Up a Home Studio" [Hack #61]

Advanced Audio

Hacks 61–68

Well, it's one louder, isn't it? It's not ten.
You see, most blokes, you know, will be
playing at ten. You're on ten here, all the
way up, all the way up, all the way up,
you're on ten on your guitar. Where can you
go from there? Where?
——Nigel Tufnel, *This Is Spinal Tap*

This chapter takes your audio expertise to the next level. You'll see the benefits of a higher-end studio, and then get into advanced audio techniques for multitrack editing, adding music and effects, and more. You'll also learn about the legal side of things so that you can use music from your favorite artists safely.

HACK #61 Set Up a Home Studio

Use a combination of quality hardware and software to produce high-quality shows suitable for both podcast and broadcast.

Podcasting makes for a great entry point into the wider world of audio production. That can include more complex podcasts, or producing music or stories for radio. You can upgrade your audio production in two ways. First, you can buy better audio hardware and software, and second, you can improve the dynamics of the space you record in. Of course, you can do both at the same time.

Better Hardware and Software

This section deals with improving your hardware and software setup so that you get a cleaner sound, as well as more flexibility in terms of the sound you can produce.

Build a Digital Audio Workstation. Whereas before you got by with some basic recording and editing software, now you will need studio automation software. These systems control the mixer during playback and allow you to route and record audio from multiple sources and destinations. The result is what is called a *Digital Audio Workstation* (DAW).

Digidesign's Pro Tools [Hack #50] software and hardware combinations is one of the industry leaders in DAWs. Its current line, starting with the Mbox, and moving up to the 001 and 002, provide flexible and affordable solutions for home studios. In terms of price, these systems start in the low hundreds and go well into the thousands. Other software options include Mark of the Unicorn's (MOTU) Digital Performer, Apple's Logic, and Steinberg's Cubase. If you decide to go with a non–Pro Tools option, you will need to invest in an audio interface, for getting audio in and out. Some of the hardware manufactures in this space include MOTU, Apogee, Edirol, and TASCAM, just to name a few.

Your next choice concerns the type of mixing surface [Hack #14] that you want to use. You can use a dedicated mixer such as those from Mackie or TASCAM. Mackie's higher-end boards now support FireWire for recording and control. The benefit of buying a mixer is the ease of routing options, and the availability of preamps for your mics [Hack #13] and card slots for effects. The downsides to using a mixing board are that you are limited to the board's bandwidth and you have to wire it all up to your digital-to-analog (DAC) converters, patch bays, etc. That can take a lot of time and money. Mixers also provide phantom power for your microphones.

Control surfaces, on the other hand, look and feel just like a mixing board, but usually only a couple of cables come out the back and connect to your computer. The control surface lets you control any aspect of the DAW (level, pan, aux, bus) via a FireWire or Universal Serial Bus (USB) connection. Make sure your DAW software fully supports the control surface you choose.

At Cedub Studio, we use Digital Performer with multiple MOTU DACs running through patch bays and a Mackie D8B mixing board. The Mackie D8B offers HUI, so you can use it as a mixing board and as a control surface.

Better microphones. You should buy a variety of microphones [Hack #13] to suit your audio work. All the microphones you buy should use the XLR cabling format. For vocal work on podcasts, we recommend the studio-standard Electro-Voice RE20. Other options include the Shure SM57 and SM58. These are cheap and almost indestructible.

If you plan on recording music, you should get microphones that accentu-ate the acoustic properties of the instruments.

Better wiring. With more equipment comes more wiring. You can buy qual-ity cabling or build it yourself. The one thing you should not do is skimp on interconnect quality. Building your own cables allows you to use better materials by leveraging your own time. Home-built cables are 20% of the price of store-bought cables. The result is having a set of cables cut to length, which means less chance of noise. Belkin, Mogami, Switchcraft, and Neutrik will sell you cabling and parts so that you can make your own cables.

Microphone preamps. Preamps [Hack #14] take a mic-level or instrument-level signal and convert it to line level. Preamps also provide phantom power for condenser microphones. Mixing consoles provide mic preamps, but exter-nal preamps provide more headroom and a cleaner sound.

We recommend that the first preamp you buy be a very clean, Class A design because this will give you the most flexibility. A low-noise mic and a clean line allow for more effects and processing. We recommend the AMEK 9098. It's clean, and it provides two channels for two separate microphones.

Other preamps, such as tube-based preamps, offer input color and warmth that can be great for defining your sound. The options for microphone preamps are limitless.

Hardware effects processors. Between the preamp and the board is where effects will go. Effects [Hack #51] can be hardware or software devices that manipulate the sound (e.g., reverb, flange, equalization, compression). A popular hardware unit is the APHEX 320A Compellor, which is a combina-tion compressor and limiter. The compression helps manage the overall input level and the limiter keeps the signal from peaking.

You should avoid external effects hardware, for two reasons. First, most of these effects are now available in software. Software effects are often plug-ins that you can integrate into your DAW, such as Native Instruments' Gui-tar Rig or the Waves (*http://waves.com/*) series of plug-ins. You can also use off-board DSP processors such as the Universal Audio UAD-1 or the TC Electronic PowerCore.

Second, introducing effects boxes into the signal path can increase noise even if they aren't switched on. Reducing signal path complexity is one way to reduce noise and avoid ground loops. Make sure that as you set up your studio, you make it easy to modify the signal path between the microphone and the mixer.

Studio hybrids. In [Hack #34], we covered the use of a telephone hybrid to allow listeners to call in to your show, or for you to call out. The hybrids we mentioned in that hack are personal devices meant for a single line. Studios that host call-in shows have much more elaborate systems that combine special phones, rack-mounted hybrids, rack-mounted control systems, computer monitor hookups, and keyboards.

The result is a system that can automatically prompt callers for topic information, queue them up, and feed them audio from the show. The board operator and call screener monitor the incoming calls and feed them into the host. The host can also have a list of who is available.

Vendors of such systems include Telos Systems (*http://telos-systems.com/*), ClearOne (*http://clearone.com/*), and JK Audio (*http://jkaudio.com/*).

ISDN audio. Another feature of professional studios are ISDN links that feed CD-quality audio direct into the board from ISDN lines. Sonifex (*http://sonifex.co.uk*) makes a variety of ISDN hardware devices that can go studio to studio or studio to transmitter. With these, you can conduct an interview with someone in another studio, and make it sound as though you are sitting right next to the person. You will get studio-quality sound on both sides of the conversation.

If you want to go remote and connect with your home studio, Plain Old Telephone Service (POTS) adapters send high-quality audio signals back to the studio over a standard phone line. Telos Systems, Sonifex, and others sell these POTS codecs.

Recording systems. Instead of using a computer-based DAW, you can use dedicated CD recorders or solid-state recording systems [Hack #69]. Computers in the studio can generate fan noise as they are recording. Dedicated standalone systems generate no noise. This can be an advantage in a small studio setting where the microphones are in the same room as the computer.

Examples of these dedicated CD recorders include the Tascam CC222MKII and the Denon DN-C550R.

Rack systems. Most processing hardware devices are built to fit into rack mounts. If you have an information technology (IT) background, you will recognize the four screws or screw holes at the right and left edges of the hardware device. These are standard form factor mountings meant to fit into a rack system.

Rack systems come in a variety of forms to meet your needs. Middle Atlantic Products (*http://www.middleatlantic.com/*) has a line of office rack mount

furniture that looks at home in any office. The line of hard cases from Anvil
Cases (*http://www.anvilcase.com/*) is what you would find backstage at an
Aerosmith show. These are handy if you want your setup to be portable.
Odyssey (*http://odysseygear.com/*) even offers rack mount bags that you can
sling over your shoulder. Odyssey also makes carpet-lined rack mounts.

Monitoring systems. To hear what is being recorded, you will need monitoring speakers in your control room. These special speakers accurately represent audio, without any coloration. Two popular and well-respected near-
field monitors are the Genelec 8000 series and the Dynaudio BM5As.

Picking monitors is a matter of personal taste. Take CDs you know well to a
pro shop and compare a number of speakers. Choose the set you think is the
most accurate. Sweep an equalizer through the spectrum and make sure the
monitors provide the clarity necessary to hear the changes.

You will need headphones as well. For an interview studio, you need to have
one set of headphones for each microphone, driven by a headphone mixing
system that allows gain control on a per-channel basis. Use the same make
and model of headphones at each station.

Upgrade Your Space

A studio setting allows you to record a sonically clean signal that is free from
noise, where noise is defined as unwanted signals, such as hums, hisses, or
the sound of planes flying overhead. For podcasting, you might not want a
completely clean sound—the natural character of your office or a café could
be just what you want. But if you want something clean to use in voiceovers,
promos, or spots, or you just want your show to be free from noise, you will
need to work on your space.

Sound design. To get a clean sound [Hack #15], you need to understand the
dynamics of how a particular space will color the recorded sound. The primary component is the shape of the room. The worst shape for a studio
room is a square or a rectangle. Square and rectangular rooms are bad
because sound waves reflect off the walls and ceilings and create *nodes* (two
waves combine and increase the sound), *antinodes* (two waves collide and
decrease the sound), and *early reflections* (bits of the sound reach your ears
first).

The materials in the room can also affect the sound. Flat reflective surfaces
such as books or the coating on walls can reflect sound and create problems. These sound anomalies can play havoc on your mixing.

Fixing these problems is called *sound treatment*, and it's a science. Angles, sound pressure, velocity, and room length all play a role in treating a room. Just running out and buying a room treatment package might not help your specific room. Take some time to research what you need for your room.

One thing to keep in mind is that you can also go too far. Don't try to create a dead room by covering every inch of wall in foam and curtains. Having some life in a room is important to create a more sonically interesting mix.

Room equalization. A cheap but effective room equalization technique comes from Doug Kaye of IT Conversations (*http://itconversations.com/*). It starts with positioning the microphone where you want it and recording about a minute of speech. Then run the sample through a spectrum display in Audacity. Because you have averaged your voice by speaking for a minute, the peaks you see will be artifacts of the room resonance. Use a parametric equalizer to reduce these nodes and save that preset. In Doug's case, this translates into a preset with a 70 Hz high pass, a 12,000 Hz low pass, and a –12 dB notch that's 0.4 dB wide, centered at 152 Hz.

Now you can apply that preset any time you use that microphone in that position. If you change the microphone position, you will need to make another preset. You can also use a hardware noise gate or parametric equalizer to reduce some of the ambient noise.

Sound treatments. You can try to create a silent space in your office by using some acoustic treatments such as foam, T-diffusers, and bass traps. Other options include actually changing the shape of the room by building a room in a room, removing 90-degree angles, etc. Even a little treatment can make a huge difference in your room. Auralex (*http://auralex.com/*) makes a wide variety of acoustic treatments. Even if you build your own studio, you will need some of these treatments in specific locations to deaden selected frequencies.

If you don't want to spend money on specialized foam treatments, which can be pricey, try some blankets and throw rugs. Hard surfaces will reflect sound, so you want to cover those in something soft that absorbs sound.

With a few treatments and some experimentation with positioning, you can create a mini-studio with a low noise floor [Hack #15] in your home office. Gregg McVicar produces the Earthsongs radio show (*http://earthsongs.net/*) out of his home office. He uses two sheets of studio foam and four Sunburst-360 acoustic dampeners to create a nearly silent space.

Buy a booth. Acoustic Rooms (*http://acoustic-rooms.com/*), WhisperRoom (*http://whisperroom.com/*), Acoustic Systems (*http://acousticsystems.com/*),

ClearSonic (*http://clearsonic.com/*), and other companies sell literal "rooms in a box." But these aren't just any rooms: these are mini recording booths that keep external noise out while permitting few reflections in. The smallest starts at around four feet square and goes up to office-size space.

Building your own studio. If you want total control and you take your sound very seriously, you can build your own studio. As with any building, you need some free space on your property (usually in the backyard) a permit from the county, a good design, some contractors, and a lot of money.

In the next section, we will explain how we created Cedub Studio in our backyard.

Building Cedub Studio

Both of us are musicians and we wanted to build a studio that would allow us to get high-quality recordings, and to play as loud as we wanted without disturbing the neighbors. So, we decided to build another building in Chris's backyard to house the studio.

The first step in building the studio was to read some books on the subject. These included *Sound Studio Construction on a Budget* (McGraw-Hill) and *How to Build a Small Budget Recording Studio from Scratch...With 12 Tested Designs* (Tab Books). Chris measured the gear and then began plotting the rooms' layout. The design we settled on reduced the number of parallel walls, and separated the control and live rooms.

Figure 9-1 shows Chris's final drawing.

We hired a studio designer to go over the drawings. It was a huge eye opener. He suggested that heavy, thick, and rigid walls, ceilings, and floors are what keep sound in (and out). All openings have to be totally sealed or doubled. He also suggested building a bass trap into the room design by having the back walls of the room come together at specific angles. This kind of construction is tricky and expensive. Ideally, you'd want to build a room inside a room. With our meager budget, there was no way we would get close to ideal.

We decided on a larger control room than live room, given the amount of gear we had and the need for a couch. (We also spend more time mixing than recording, so it had to be comfortable.)

To save money we did much of the work ourselves. We handled the foundation trench, the electrical wiring, and the internal finishing, including the inside/outside painting. See Figure 9-2.

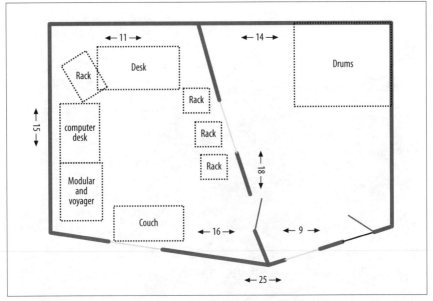

Figure 9-1. Final layout diagram of Cedub Studio

The foundation is slab concrete. It's thick and solid, and with a few carpets, it warms right up. The framing was 2×6 bases and offset studs. The ceiling slants from 8 feet in the back to 12 feet in the front with 2×12 joists. We put in a 3×5 double-pained window between the rooms so that we can see into the live room from the control room. The door between control and live is a single door, and the exterior door is double-layered.

The 100-amp service to the building splits into six different circuits: lights, computers, guitar amps, power amps, racks, and one more for good measure. We installed two mic jack panels on either side of the live room (Figure 9-3) that feed into the control room (Figure 9-4). These lines carry 12 mic jacks each and a combination of line-level and speaker cables so that we can plug directly into the wall and then route to the board via the patch bay in the control room.

We filled the internal walls with insulation, followed by Auralex SheetBlok (in the live room), sound-deadening board, and 5/8-inch sheet rock. We decided on the final layers partially based on our budget. The ideal would have been insulation, plywood, and two layers of sheet rock. Plywood is expensive stuff, and at the end, we had to go with what we could afford at the time.

The final phase of the project—wiring the studio from scratch—took three months. With the wiring done, the "burn in" period began. We had to test every line and iron out the ground loops. Then we began another round of

Figure 9-2. View of the studio during framing

sound reinforcement. We hung four sheets of 4-inch foam behind the mixing console. We placed six T-diffusers above the mixing console with 2-inch foam between and then Venus bass traps in the back of the room.

There are a lot of options to choose from when it comes to upgrading your home studio to suit your needs. If you are considered in your use of time and money you will find the right option for your needs and your budget.

See Also

- "Set Up a Basic Home Studio" [Hack #12]
- "Pick the Right Microphone" [Hack #13]
- "Mix Your Podcast in Hardware" [Hack #14]
- "Reduce Noise" [Hack #15]
- "Choose the Right Audio Tools" [Hack #50]
- "Juice Your Sound" [Hack #51]
- "Maintain the Gain" [Hack #56]
- "Build a Sweet Sound" [Hack #57]

—*James Polanco and Chris Walcott*

Figure 9-3. The live room

Figure 9-4. The control room

Integrate Audio and Email Feedback

Engage your audience in a conversation by integrating their audio feedback and email into your podcasts.

One of the distressing elements of podcasting is that you never know if you are talking to an empty room. You can check the logs and see the downloads. But did they listen? And more importantly, what did they think of the show? This is why feedback is so important, and why you should spend the time making it easy for people to interact with you.

The first thing to do is to build several feedback mechanisms that listeners can use. I've included several ideas in the sections that follow. Once you've set these up, you need to encourage people to comment and send feedback on every show you produce.

Blog Comments and Bulletin Boards

The easiest feedback mechanism is the one you already have on your blog: the comments system. Both the Movable Type and WordPress blogging systems **[Hack #38]** support Really Simple Syndication (RSS) feeds that include comments. You should create these feeds and subscribe to them so that you are notified when people post feedback. In the early days of your show, the feedback will be minimal, so you need to jump right on it.

If you get too many comments or the comment system is not easy enough to use from your listeners' perspective, you can switch to a bulletin board system such as phpBB (*http://phpbb.com/*). Then you can link the blog to the bulletin board and shut down the comment system in the blog. Regardless of which way you go, you should always have comments enabled so that listeners can tell you what they like and don't like about your show.

Once you get your text feedback, you should read the most interesting ones in your podcast. People are encouraged to give you more feedback when they hear others mentioned on the site. To mix it up a little, you can have someone else read your mail and turn the response into a full-fledged conversation.

MP3 Email Feedback

For listeners who are also podcasters, or who want to hear their comments aired on the show, you should accept audio comments encoded as MP3s. These can get quite large, so check your web hosting account, if you receive mail that way, to make sure the quota is set large enough to handle at least 100 MB of messages.

If space is an issue, you can get an account with one of the leading Internet mail providers. Google's Gmail (*http://gmail.com*) has 2 GB of storage space, and Yahoo! Mail's Plus account has 2 GB of storage space for email messages.

Phone Messaging

To make it even easier for your listeners to give audio feedback, you can set up a voice mail account that will send the messages directly to your email as audio files. Here are a few of these services:

RingCentral (http://ringcentral.com/), eVoice (http://evoice.com/), and j2 (http://j2.com/)
> These services have free voice mail via email accounts, with phone numbers provided in your local area code. The messages arrive in your email account as attachments, or you can check them on the Web. Upgrade options enable you to send and receive faxes. Other handy services also are available.

MaxEmail (http://maxemail.com/)
> The basic MaxEmail voice mail-to-email service is around $15 a year, with a 30-day free trial period. This service can also receive faxes.

Vonage (http://vonage.com/)
> Vonage is an Internet-based Voice over IP (VoIP) solution whose basic service ($14.99 per month) includes voice mail that you can forward to your email.

Onebox (http://onebox.com/)
> This service provides voice-mail-to-email routing using a toll-free number. The basic service starts at $12.95 per month. Fax services are also included, as is a new email address that you can use.

Frankly, having one of these accounts, particularly one of the free ones, is a benefit even if you don't use it for your podcast work. You can use it when you have to supply a phone number to companies that you suspect might sell your information, and then dump it if you get too much unwanted solicitation.

Another phone option is to use your home answering machine to take messages, but there are two downsides to this. The first is that you are giving away your home number, which removes a level of privacy and might have you startled awake at all hours of the night.

The other problem is getting the messages off the machine. To fix that, you can buy a voice modem that supports an answering machine feature. If the machine doesn't come with software that supports it, try EzVoice 3.0 ($26.80) from *http://internetsoftsolution.com/*.

See Also

- "Record Telephone Interviews" [Hack #34]
- "Record Interviews on Skype" [Hack #35]
- "Blog Your Podcast" [Hack #38]

HACK #63   Add Top, Bottom, and Bumper Music

Cut and use tops, bottoms, and bumpers to give your podcasts a professional feel.

You can use copyrighted material [Hack #68] from your favorite band to add music to your podcast, but the licensing issues can cost you time, money, and frustration. With today's music tools, you can create the top, bottom, and bumper music for your podcast very easily, and own the rights to the material.

Tops, *bottoms*, *bumpers*, and *stingers* are music segments placed at the beginning, ending, and middle of your show. In the commercial radio world, bumpers bring you in and out of commercials. Stingers sit in between segments in a news show to delineate between stories.

Whether these short music segments have vocals is up to you. For a mellower, more thoughtful show, you might go with only acoustic material and for a music show with a hard edge you might pick up something with vocals for the top and bottom. Generally the bumpers and stingers, because they are shorter, will not contain vocals.

From a music standpoint, you want something that makes its presence felt and presents its theme in about four bars. If you are going to use a song, you should look at the beginning segments of a song for the tops, and the ends of songs for the bumpers. In any case, you should prefade the start and end portions of these segments to ease the transition from spoken word to music.

Building Your Own Music

Apple's GarageBand and Sony's ACID [Hack #50] make it very easy to construct songs that sound good simply by dragging and dropping loops. *Loops* are portions of sound that repeat. They are categorized by instrument, genre, and beats per minute, and can contain raw sounds or repeating phrases of notes.

Figure 9-5 is an example of something I threw together very quickly in GarageBand. To create your own song, start up GarageBand and then select New from the File menu to create a new song. Use the Show Loop Browser in the Control menu to show the loops you have available. To preview a loop, click the sound icon next to the name. To add it to your song, simply drag and drop it onto the track surface and position it wherever you like.

Figure 9-5. The loop window in GarageBand 2

Use the mouse to click the righthand side of the loop to extend it for as many bars as you like. Then use the volume controls on the track to set the volume for that instrument. For loops where the content comprises notes, such as the one at the top of the example song shown in Figure 9-5, you can set the instrument by double-clicking the icon of the instrument.

This is a fun and very addictive activity. You can create good sound—I swear it—simply by dragging and dropping, even if you have no musical background.

GarageBand comes with a wide variety of loops preinstalled. You also can buy packages of loops from Apple to supplement the loops in GarageBand, and you can find free sets of loops on the Web. To install new loops, simply drag the folder containing the loop files onto the loop browser from the Finder.

Once you have your song, use the Export to iTunes command in the File menu to save the file in AIF format to your iTunes. At the time of this writing, Audacity had issues reading AIF files directly, so I had to use Quick-Time to export the file as a *.wav* file that Audacity could read before bringing it into my podcast.

If you want to find free music that you can get off the shelf without creating your own, check GarageBand.com (*http://garageband.com/*). Many of the songs on the GarageBand site are licensed under Creative Commons [Hack #68]. Although that is not a guarantee that you can use the song in your podcast, it's a good sign that you can. In particular, you should ensure that the license grants you the right to create derivative works. If you are a commercial entity, or are using this material for profit, you should check to make sure the license allows for commercial use.

Incorporating Effects

If you're looking for a particular sound effect, such as the roar of a lion or the thrum of a motorcycle engine, you can usually find these on the Web. I've had good luck finding decent free sound effects at Partners in Rhyme (*http://partnersinrhyme.com/*). This company offers a wide selection of sounds and royalty-free music.

In Figure 9-6, I took some boring intro vocal work and snazzed it up with an effect in another track. To do this, I used the Import Audio command to bring in the *.wav* file I downloaded from *http://partnersinrhyme.com/*. Then I used the Envelope tool to fade in the beginning a little bit, and to do a smooth fade out toward the end.

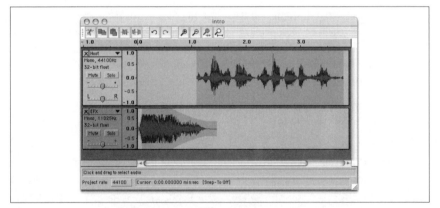

Figure 9-6. Adding an intro sound in a different track in Audacity

I recommend two additional sites for sound. Sounddogs.com (*http://sounddogs. com/*) has a wide variety of effects sounds, all of which are relatively inexpensive. MovieWavs (*http://moviewavs.com/*) contains sound samples from popular movies that vary in sound quality from very good to barely passable. Many have a high-frequency hiss that's caused by poor sample; using a low-pass filter, you can remove the hiss easily and create a sound that is fine as background material.

If you can't find the sample you want from a movie, just use Audio Hijack Pro on your Macintosh or Total Recorder Pro on Windows to grab the audio directly from the DVD playback application.

FindSounds *(http://findsounds.com/)*, AltaVista Audio *(http://altavista.com/audio/)*, WavSite *(http://wavsite.com/)*, Analogue Samples *(http://analoguesamples.com/)*, and Lost & Found Sound *(http://npr.org/programs/lnfsound/)* have sounds that you can download and play with, though you will have to account for permissions.

As always, with copyrighted material you should be aware of copyright infringement issues [Hack #67].

Making Your Own Sound Effects

All you need to create your own sound effects are a portable recorder, a microphone, and some creativity. David Filskov maintains a list of sound effects recipes on his site *(http://sfx.davelab.com/)*. Here is a sampling:

Body and face hits
> Rolled-up newspapers hit with a soft wooden stick. Hitting real meat also works, as does using a baseball bat to hit leather jackets wrapped around baseball gloves, or breaking chicken bones.

Car crashes
> A scrap yard and a sledge hammer: heaven for crashing effects.

Explosions
> A lion roar with a flange effect to beef it up.

Lava
> Bubbling sound from a hot radiator tank on a car.

The seashore
> Pouring a fizzy drink onto tarmac, or any floor. At least that's what they used in *Jaws*.

A spear piercing flesh
> Biting into an apple.

A stone coffin opening
> Sliding off the top of a toilet tank.

As you can see, you often can get something that sounds genuine from something other than the actual activity.

See Also

- "Produce Great Audio Theatre" [Hack #32]
- "Choose the Right Audio Tools" [Hack #50]
- "Juice Your Sound" [Hack #51]
- "Maintain the Gain" [Hack #56]
- "Build a Sweet Sound" [Hack #57]
- "Add Special Effects" [Hack #58]

HACK #64   Record and Add Background Ambience

Using background ambience can add a sense of place and time to your podcasts. Learn to record these sounds and mix them effectively into your sonic landscape.

You can talk about the rain, or the howl of the wind, but to *hear it* brings the listening experience to a whole new level. These sounds, which can be the muted conversation in a restaurant, the wails from a crowd, or the chirps of birds in trees, are lumped into the term *ambience*.

> It's a joke among sound engineers in the broadcast industry that any noise in shoddy recordings that can't be removed is ambience.

Creating the ambient sound you hear in well-produced radio shows is a real art. Knowing how to create quality ambient sound can mean the difference between a show that draws you into a theatre of the mind, and one that feels flat, like a voice in a can. The technical aspects involve choosing the right microphone and finding the right location to get the sound. But the real art is in knowing what you want and having the time and patience to find it. Atmospheric effects, such as thunder, you simply have to wait for; when it's so loud that it clips, or so soft that it's indistinguishable from noise, you will just have to wait some more.

Ambient sounds serve two main purposes. The first is to provide background material for the story. An example is the crunch of leaves underfoot accompanying the voice of the narrator telling listeners about a recent hike. The second purpose for ambient recordings is to provide smoother transitions between studio segments and field recordings. Ideally you should record a minute of background ambience before an interview [Hack #36] for this purpose.

Recording Ambience

To record ambient sound you will need a portable recording unit, such as an iPod with a Griffin iTalk, an iRiver, and a mini-disc, DAT, or solid-state recorder [Hack #69]. You need something that is small and light enough so that you can chase the sound around a bit and record from multiple angles. Your microphone [Hack #13] options will be limited to a dynamic microphone that requires no power, or a self-powered condenser microphone.

For the ambience of a room where you want to get a wide field of sound, I recommend a handheld dynamic microphone such as a Shure SM57, Shure SM58, or Electro-Voice RE-50. These are all relatively cheap and almost indestructible.

For a more contained sound, such as the rustling of the wind in trees or the crunching of feet in a forest, I recommend a short shotgun microphone. Examples include the Sennheiser K6/ME66 and the Audio-Technica 835B and 897.

These are general recommendations. What really counts is getting out and looking for creative ways to get the sound you want. Once again, the key is in knowing what you want and finding any means it takes to get it. You can capture the sound of howling wind in the small crack in a window; you can find the sound of crunching snow in a box of packing peanuts.

Editing the Sound

With the sound in hand, use your editing program to create multiple tracks in your show recording. Always put the ambient sounds in their own track so that you can control their volume independent of the voice and music tracks.

Getting the right volume for the ambience is critical. You might want it to start strong and then fade away completely. Or you might want it to start soft, fade to strong, fade away, and then come back again. It all depends on the story you are trying to tell. Using your program's gain-enveloping feature is the easiest way to control ambience levels.

For a very complex mix of voice, music, and ambient sounds, you might want to invest in a Musical Instruments Digital Interface (MIDI) control surface [Hack #61] such as the Behringer BCF2000 ($239.99). This is a MIDI controller that you can use in conjunction with applications that support automation (e.g., Pro Tools) to control gain, stereo pan, and other effects during playback using sliders and knobs.

See Also

- "Pick the Right Microphone" [Hack #13]
- "Choose the Right Audio Tools" [Hack #50]
- "Set Up a Home Studio" [Hack #61]
- "Assemble a Small Recording Rig" [Hack #69]

HACK #65 Speech Synthesize Your Podcast Introduction

Placing a small introductory segment with the name of your podcast and the episode number or date at the beginning of the show is becoming standard. Learn how to use free or cheap speech synthesis tools to do this.

Playback devices such as the iPod Shuffle, which have no screen, make it difficult to recognize what podcast you are listening to. Songs have different introductions that you can clue in on immediately; but a podcast has the same introductory material at the beginning of every show. This leaves listeners having to fast forward through the introduction to get to the show so that they can see if they have listened to it already.

One solution is to place a few seconds of identifying material at the front of the show, with the name of your show and the episode number or date. To do that, podcasters have used both their voice and speech synthesis to record the segment. This hack shows how to get synthesized speech on demand on Macintosh, Windows, and the Web.

Speech Synthesis on Macintosh

Mac OS X has had speech synthesis built in from the start. The easiest way to invoke it is to select a piece of text in a document and then select the Start Speaking Text command from the Speech item in the Services menu (shown in Figure 9-7). The Services menu is that strange section of the application menu that nobody ever seems to use.

In this case, I used TextEdit, the text editor that comes with the system, to write my introduction. Then I selected it and ran the Start Speaking Text command. You'll hear a slight delay the first time. Then you will hear the synthesized voice. To record this, use the System Audio sound source in Audio Hijack Pro.

To change the timbre of the voice, use the Speech panel in System Preferences, as shown in Figure 9-8.

You have 22 different voices to choose from, ranging from male and female voices to computer-sounding synthetic voices to voices that are fanciful in nature.

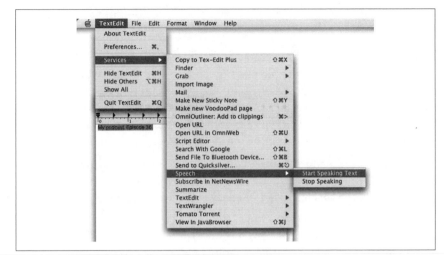

Figure 9-7. The Speech service on Mac OS X

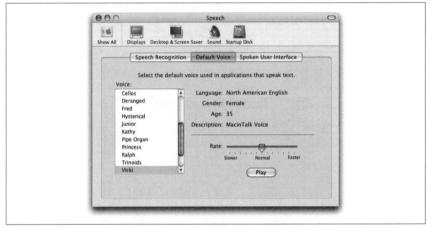

Figure 9-8. Choosing a default voice on Mac OS X

Apple has gone a step further and embedded speech synthesis verbs into its AppleScript language. Open the Script Editor application (*/Applications/ AppleScript*) and type in this code:

```
say "My podcast. Episode 36."
```

Then press Run and you'll hear the synthesized sound. You can have the speech synthesizer speak any string you want. You even can specify the voice if you want:

```
say "My podcast. Episode 36." using "Agnes"
```

If you don't specify the voice, you will get the system default voice that you set in the Speech System Preferences panel.

In addition, you can have the system save the speech output to a sound file, like this:

```
say myString using "Agnes" saving to ":Users:jherr:Desktop:foo.aif"
```

Outputting the sound to the file takes much less time than it would take the system to play the file and record it in Audio Hijack Pro [Hack #50]. If you are going to edit your podcast in a program such as GarageBand, Logic Express, or Pro Tools, you should have the speech synthesizer save it to a file. Then you can just drag-and-drop it into your project where you want it.

Certain commands allow you to control your Macintosh through speech with AppleScript, or through the Speech preferences panel. Although we don't cover that in this hack, it's still neat and is worth playing with.

Cepstral Text-to-Speech (*http://cepstral.com/*) has several speech synthesizer voices for both Windows and Macintosh. These voices are relatively inexpensive at around $30 apiece. The quality of the sound is far superior to the MacinTalk sounds you get with the Macintosh built-in voices.

Speech Synthesis on Windows

To get your Windows machine to talk to you, use the Speech control panel, as shown in Figure 9-9.

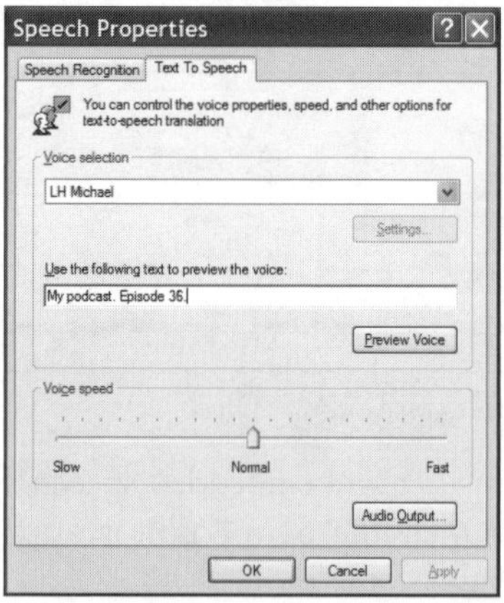

Figure 9-9. Setting the default voice on Windows XP

Type the text you want the synthesizer to say into the "Use the following text to preview the voice" text box. Then press the Preview button to hear the voice. You can alter the type of voice by clicking the first drop-down menu and selecting from one of the three available voices. You can speed up or slow down the speech by using the slider at the bottom of the dialog.

Recording the voice is a little trickier. I was able to use Total Recorder Pro to grab the output stream of the voice synthesizer by clicking the Audio Output button on this dialog, selecting "Use this audio output device," and then selecting Playback through Total Recorder in the drop-down menu. Total Recorder [Hack #50] saved the speech in the output file to the location I wanted in the format I specified.

Speech synthesis from code. Microsoft is supporting both speech synthesis and speech control through its speech APIs. You can download the SDK at *http://microsoft.com/speech*. Click the link for the Microsoft Speech Application Software Development Kit 1.1 Beta (or a more recent version), follow the instructions, and get a huge download.

Once you have downloaded this monster, you unpack it into *C:\SpeechSDK*. Within that folder is the *Redistributable Installers\Speech Add-in for Microsoft Internet Explorer* folder. That contains the speech extension for Internet Explorer. Launch the *setup.exe* program in that folder to install the speech extensions.

With that installed, you should be able to write small web pages that synthesize voice on your computer. This code sample, which I found on the Web, drives the engine from a web page:

```
<html xmlns:salt="http://www.saltforum.org/2002/SALT">
<object id="speech-add-in"
 CLASSID="clsid:33cbfc53-a7de-491a-90f3-0e782a7e347a">
</object>
<?import namespace="salt" implementation="#speech-add-in"/>
<salt:prompt id="prompter"></salt:prompt>
<body>
<h2>SALT: Speak Field Contents</h2>
<input type="text" id="iptext" name="iptext"
 value="Type some text here" size="40">
<input type="button" name="speak" value="Speak" onClick="dospeak( )">
</body>
<script>
function dospeak( )
{
  var pfield=document.getElementById("iptext");
  var pprompt=document.getElementById("prompter");
  pprompt.Start(pfield.value);
}
</script>
</html>
```

Save this file anywhere on your drive as *speech.html*. Then view it (Figure 9-10) with Internet Explorer. It will not work properly in Firefox or any other non-IE browser.

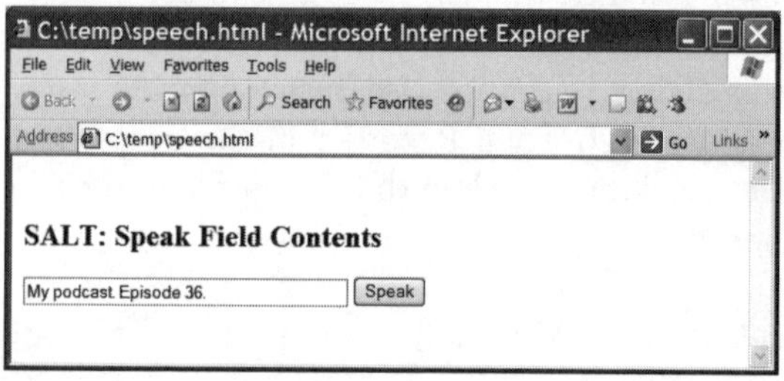

Figure 9-10. A simple Speech Application Language Tags (SALT)–enabled web page

The object definition at the top of the page creates a new control for the speech add-in. Then there is a text field where you type the text to be spoken, and a button labeled Speak that you click to activate the synthesizer. This calls the dospeak JavaScript function, which in turn calls Start on the speech engine with the value of the text field.

Type your text into the text field and then press the Speak button to have the synthesizer say your words. The output will go out the sound driver set in the Speech control panel. You can use Total Recorder to capture the sound to a file.

The Speech SDK also contains APIs that you can use from any of the .NET languages to drive the speech engine. A good example is AutoCast (*http:// autocastsoftware.com/*), which reads RSS feeds and then uses the Speech API to turn the text into speech [Hack #6] that is stored as MP3 files for a podcast aggregator. Full source code for AutoCast is included on the site.

Windows voice synthesis programs. VoiceMX Studio 4 (*http://www.tanseon. com/*), $19.95, is a text-to-voice application for Windows that has a much smoother voice than the Windows API driver does. VoiceMX Studio 4 is pictured in Figure 9-11.

Type the text you want read into the text field and then hit the SPEAK button to play it, or the FILENAME button to save the output directly to a *.wav* file.

Speech Synthesis on the Web

Good-quality text-to-speech is one of the Holy Grails of computer science. IBM has an ongoing research program in this field with a demo that is available on the Web (*http://www.research.ibm.com/tts/coredemo.shtml*), as shown in Figure 9-12.

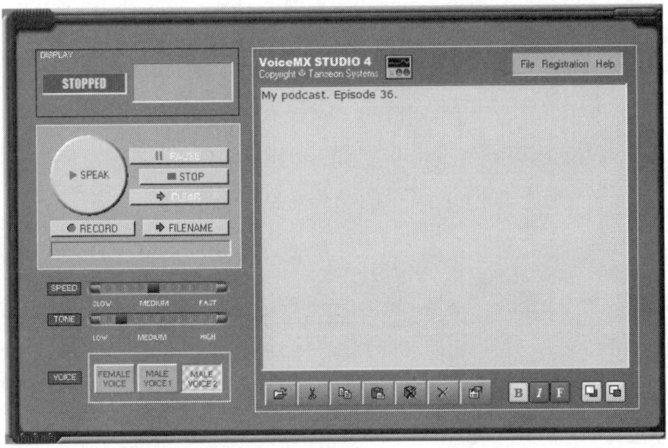

Figure 9-11. VoiceMX Studio 4

Figure 9-12. The text-to-speech page at IBM Research

To have the system synthesize some speech for you, type your sentence into the box and press the SPEAK button. You will get a file of the audio in response that you can save to your local drive and use in your podcast. You have four different voices to choose from. In my opinion, all of them sound better than Macintosh and Windows voice drivers. The result is a lot smoother and more natural.

You are limited in terms of the number of times per day you can access the site. But I didn't see anything on fair use of the generated audio.

Lucent Technologies' Bell Labs also offers a demo of its speech synthesis system (*http://www.bell-labs.com/project/tts/voices.html*), as shown in Figure 9-13.

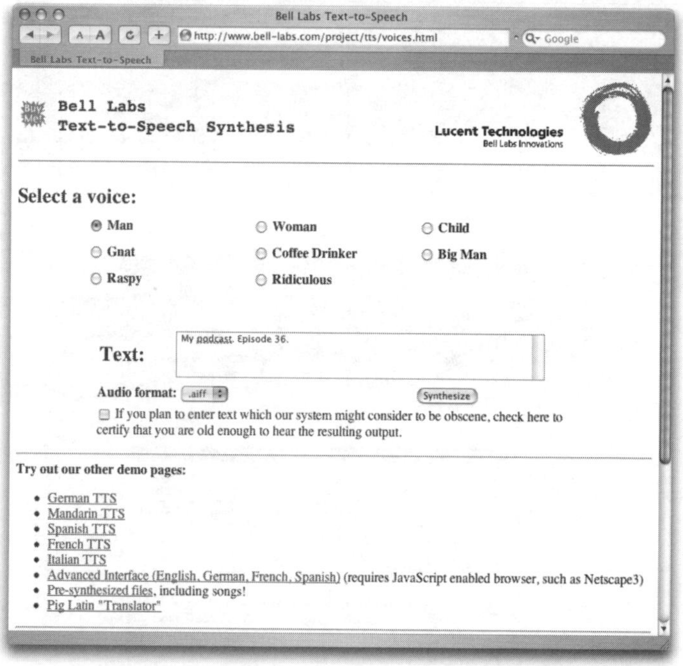

Figure 9-13. The text-to-speech page at Lucent

When you press the Synthesize button, you will receive an audio file in the format you specify. You can save this to a file on your disk and use it in your podcast by opening it in your mixing or editing application.

The footer on the bottom of that page says that this engine is restricted to "noncommercial" uses, though there is no definition of what that means.

See Also

- "Convert Text-Based Blogs into Podcasts" [Hack #6]

Make a Mash-Up

Mash-ups of music and voice are an exciting way to liven up your podcast.

Mash-ups or *bootlegs* are two or more tracks that you combine to create a third different track. They started as a genre with hip-hop DJs doing mixes for radio and live performances in the late 1970s and early 80s, but the revival started in 2001 with "Stroke of Genius" by Freelance Hellraiser and Girls on Top (a.k.a. Richard X).

Anyone with access to a home computer can make mash-ups, which is one of the reasons they have become so popular over the last four years. Mash-ups come in several types, but the one most people have heard is the *A versus B* type, in which you combine two tracks—say, a track from Christina Aguilera and one from the The Strokes. Another type of mash-up is a *glitch*, in which you cut tracks into small pieces, and distort and warp them.

Mash-ups can comprise more than two tracks: mash-up artists such as DJ Earworm and Loo & Placido combine up to 10 tracks into 1 in their crazy mash-up juggling acts. I'll be focusing on just two tracks in this hack.

Good Mash-Ups

Creating mash-ups, like all audio cut-up and musical culture, is an art; as such, deciding what is good or bad is subjective. Certainly, some mashes and bootlegs don't work on a technical or musical level, but something to regard is what type of audience your mash is for. Are you creating it purely to listen to, as comedy, or to prove a musical point (e.g., these tracks are the same!), or for the dance floor? Many mashes are for the feet (i.e., for use on the dance floor), but don't neglect the heart or the head.

What I like to do in a mash-up is take the source materials as far from their era or genre as possible. A good but rather complex example of this is DJ Earworm's "Stairway to Bootleg Heaven," which takes a whopping eight tracks from Dolly Parton to Pat Benatar to the Beatles and makes them work together in one happy mash harmony. I like it because it is the musical mash equivalent of juggling about eight things at once, and amazingly, DJ Earworm does not let anything drop.

But don't worry, simpler A versus B mash-ups such as the one I'll discuss also rock. One of my all-time favorites is the classic "Lisa's Got Hives," by Conway, which was one of the early rock/rap mash-ups mixing Lisa "Left Eye" Lopes' "Block Party" with The Hives…still an ultimate party good-times record.

Mash-Up Software

To create a mash-up, you need software that can time stretch or create looped *segments*.

Most sequencers can do time stretching, but can't easily do much more than simple mash-ups without a lot of tiresome loop creation. So, for an audio-sketchpad approach, most mash-up artists use Sony's ACID Pro [Hack #50]. This is currently PC-only, so Mac mash-up artists use Ableton Live (*http://ableton.com/*).

The examples I use here apply to ACID Pro 4 and Music Studio 5, but a lot of the principles should work for other programs. A free version is available, called ACID Xpress, but it doesn't have the beatmapping functions, so it isn't used for mash-ups.

Five Easy Steps

For a simple A versus B, you need an instrumental, an a cappella recording, and the original track the a cappella is from.

It's probably best to start with a rap vocal from an artist such as Eminem or Missy Eliott, as they rap on the beat and thus are quite easy to match to another track. For an instrumental, choose another hip-hop instrumental or slow house or trance track, something around 100–120 beats per minute (BPM) with a defined kick drum, which will be easy to see.

Although an important part of mash-ups is genre clash (rock versus R & B, rap versus polka, etc.), the goal here is learning how to make a mash-up instead of amazing the world with your eclectic taste in music. I'd avoid rock to start with, as the tempo usually varies during the song. Once you've learned the basics, you can go on and do that Big Black versus Shania Twain bootleg you've always wanted to do.

To create a new mash-up, follow these steps:

1. Create a new ACID document.
2. Import the source tracks.
3. Beatmap the imported tracks (see the "Hit That Perfect Beat(map)" section, later in this hack, for more information). Note the original track's BPM value.
4. The program will ask you if you want to match the ACID song tempo to one of the tracks. Unless they are widely different tempos, it's probably

best to match the tempo of the instrumental you're using. You can change this later if your vocals start sounding like chipmunks.

5. Change the track type of the a cappella to Beatmatched in the General tab, click the Stretch tab, and plug the BPM value from the original track into the Original Tempo field. Hopefully they'll match; if they don't, see the upcoming "Timing Problems" section.

That's a very simple description of how to make a mash-up. Invariably you'll have issues with tuning, timing, or sequencing, which I'll go into next.

Take Me to the Bridge

It's likely that you'll have an instrumental breakdown just where the a cappella chorus kicks in, or that the instrumental will end too early. One of ACID's great features is the Split at Cursor function, which lets you chop and change tracks until you're happy with the result. First make sure that Snapping is on (in the Options menu, or right-click in the Context menu). Then select any part of a track, right-click, and select Split at Cursor. Move that track segment around as a separate chunk (ACID calls them *events*), to the rest of the track.

If you need to shorten your intro, move the chorus, repeat, or copy chunks to make sections longer, make sure you're cutting accurately in *bar* segments that loop nicely (otherwise, you'll get audible jumps), and that your beatmapping settings are correct (otherwise, you'll have to tweak these edits later).

Timing Problems

If you're having trouble with the samples lining up, do the following:

- Make sure Snapping is on.
- Check that the beatmapping is correct.
- Make sure your a cappella is starting on the right beat. Sometimes singers and rappers start just before the first beat in a bar, or later for that dub/swing effect. Listen to the original track.

What if your track has breaks in it, or it changes tempo? Well, you have several additional advanced techniques that you can use if you're dealing with a rock track or a track that changes tempo over the length of the song:

- You can beatmap several duplicates of the same track, starting at different points within the track (intro, middle, end, etc.).

- You can cut up a rock track into one- or two-bar segments in a sound editor and import them as loops. Then ACID will vary the playback and keep it in time. Beware: this can kill the groove and excitement of a rock track.

- You can cut the vocal to the guitar track. Sometimes the groove is more important than slight differences in timing, especially with slow tracks.

> If you're having difficulty matching an a cappella recording, here's a handy tip: put the original track and the a cappella recording on adjacent tracks. Make sure the original track is synced accurately with your instrumental, and then roughly match the a cappella to the original track.
>
> Alter the BPM value and start point of the a cappella gradually, until the phasing and echo are at a minimum. Now you have the correct BPM value for the a cappella.

Tuning and Pitch Shifting

If there's a pitch difference between your tracks, you can alter the pitch of each track within the General tab in semitone values, either positive (for higher pitch) or negative (for lower pitch). I suggest changing the value of the instrumental first, as people tend to notice pitch changes in the vocals before the backing.

This verges into music theory and there isn't enough space here to go into lots of detail, but remember these brief points:

- Pianos, wind instruments, and guitars don't sound very good when they are pitched up or down more than a few semitones. Avoid doing this, if possible.

- If you have problems with a particular section clashing, you can pitch each event by using "Split to cursor," and then altering the pitch by selecting it and right-clicking Properties. Then enter a semitone value the same as you can for the track.

Hit That Perfect Beat(map)

Beatmapping is the key to making a mash-up in ACID Pro and ACID Music Studio. When you import a track into ACID, it will ask you whether you want to beatmap it. First, you will need to tell it where the downbeat is (the first kick drum if there is one). It will try to auto-detect where this is, but it won't always get it right. Don't worry if this start point is quite a way into the track (see Figure 9-14).

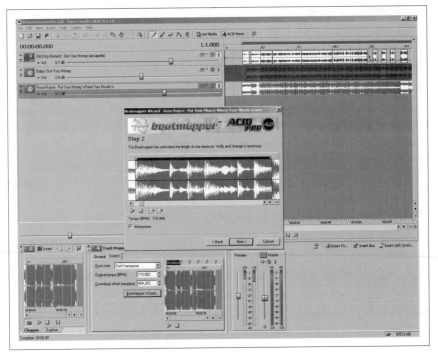

Figure 9-14. Lining up the beatmap in ACID

Then it will ask you to define the length of one measure. Zoom in (by pressing +) to make sure this is accurate. Press the Play icon and listen to the loop. Make sure it sounds fluid, and then press Next.

If it's electronic music (i.e., not rock) that was recorded to a click track or was studio produced after 1985, it should beatmap closely across the whole track. Check each mapped bar from the start, and try to map each start point of each bar to match the start of the bar of music. You might have to click back and adjust the length of the measure and start again if it isn't working.

Finding or Making A Cappellas and Instrumentals

So, how do you find these juicy a cappellas? Well, you can find them in several places. The first place is on white label or DJ 12-inch vinyl records and promo CDs.

This might seem amazing to those who've heard about Dangermouse and his run-in with EMI (having received a cease and desist order for his Grey Album that mixed Jay-Z and The Beatles), but record companies actually issue a cappellas and instrumentals to encourage DJs to remix their tracks as a form of "focus group" research to see which tracks are hot. So, if you pick up these promo releases, they sometimes come with an instrumental or an a cappella track.

Other places are peer-to-peer services such as Soulseek, and web sites such as *http://www.acapellas4u.co.uk/*.

The final, and more difficult, solution is the do-it-yourself (DIY) approach. You can extract an a cappella recording digitally from a track (usually called *pseudo* or *DIY pellas*) with varying amounts of success.

This requires digital techniques such as phase inversion, noise reduction, or even EQ to create an a cappella or instrumental. A good place to start with these is Adobe Audition (formerly Cool Edit), which has good noise reduction and center-channel extraction tools.

The same applies for instrumentals, but instrumentals tend to be easier, as you can make those yourself, either from craftily cutting up an existing track, using phase inversion and EQ to mute a vocal, or finding an extended DJ remix to use.

A good Virtual Studio Technology (VST) plug-in that makes real-time phase inversion and center-channel extraction possible is Waves S1 Imager (*http://www.waves.com/content.asp?id=159*). Few people know about this plug-in. It's not cheap, but you can select any part of the stereo field to isolate it. Very useful!

Copyright and Copyleft

Officially it's illegal to release mash-ups unless you have rights or permissions to all the included material [Hack #68], but in reality it's much more complicated. Some record companies don't mind them, especially in the hip-hop and R & B genres, but others, as we've seen with EMI and Disney, take a dim view of mash-ups.

Unless you are making money out of your mash-ups and are releasing them on CD, it's unlikely you'll have problems. But you certainly should be careful how and where you use the mash-ups you create (unless you're willing to fight a few legal battles; check out the links in the next few paragraphs for more information!).

Shouldn't we have the right to mash up the music or media we buy? Musicians and artists have been "stealing" from each other since the dawn of time; in this case, mash-ups are called *influences* and *appropriation*. The thing to remember is to bring something of your own to the party; make it yours.

New initiatives such as Creative Commons are bringing this issue of creativity versus commerce to the fore. I think we should be able to "play" with the media we've bought, as long as no commercial transactions take place; in this case, we'd be playing with it for fun, and for art. Check out Creative Commons (*http://www.creativecommons.org/*) and Illegal Art (*http://illegalart.net/*) if you want additional information on legal issues, and how people are fighting them.

This is the reason I like mash-ups. Their very existence makes them unsellable, which makes the art form vibrant and necessarily underground (you can't really sell out when they are unsellable!); but it also resists the current music industry's commercial model and reveals as archaic the old copyright laws that are supposed to protect artists.

Have Fun

The important thing is to have fun. By producing mash-ups, you can learn a lot about the structure of songs and audio production, and it can lead to offers of official remixes or DJ sets. Furthermore, you can use a lot of the tricks and tips you learn creating mash-ups when you create your own podcasts and songs.

See Also

- "Mix Multiple Tracks" [Hack #60]
- "Add Top, Bottom, and Bumper Music" [Hack #63]
- "Use Copyrighted Music Legally" [Hack #68]

—*Tim Baker*

Grab Audio Legally

HACK
#67

Can you legally grab audio from another source and use it in your podcast? Find out the dos and don'ts of copy and paste podcasting journalism.

In the text blogosphere, you copy and paste text from one source and comment on it in your own blogs. Can you do the same with audio? To understand the implications, you need to understand the issue of copyrights, and the Creative Commons license [Hack #68], which is often used to supplement copyrights. This hack applies to U.S. copyright code. Check the legal statutes for your country before using copyrighted or licensed material.

Caveat Emptor

Do not use the material in this hack as a substitute for legal advice specific to your situation. We did our research and what we are presenting is a good basis of understanding the law. But the law is applied on a case-by-case basis. So, getting good legal advice that is specific to your situation is critical to avoiding legal troubles and big damage bills.

Copyright

When a person creates a unique work of art—a podcast, a book, a movie, something tangible—he can protect that work with a copyright. A copyright owner has certain rights, and so do people that consume the copyrighted material. Sections 106 and 107 of the U.S. copyright code (*http://copyright.gov/title17/92chap1.html*) cover the rights of the owner and the consumer, respectively. If you are curious, section 102 covers what material can by copyrighted. This is all plain English stuff and is well worth the read.

The copyright owner's rights are straightforward. The copyright owner maintains the exclusive right to copy the work, to create derivative works, to distribute copies, and, depending on the medium, to perform the work. In the case of podcasting, we can assume it's the same as a song, which means to play the song publicly.

The really important bit is the derivative work part. If you incorporate some of someone else's podcast into your podcast, you could be creating a derivative work under the copyright code—or not; it could be *fair use*.

Fair use is covered by section 107 of the code. In a nutshell, it says that you can use the work if you critique it, if you comment on it, if you use it as part of a news story, if you use it as part of a teaching exercise, or if you are using it in a research capacity.

But this isn't as clear as it sounds. If you just say, "This is good," and then play an hour of another podcast, is that really criticism? To judge whether this is so, the court can take into account four things:

- The purpose and character of the use (in particular, whether you profited financially from that use)
- The work itself
- The amount of material you used
- The effect your podcast had on the marketability of the original work (in other words, did you steal customers or have an impact on the product's bottom line?)

Damages. If you used copyrighted material and the copyright owner decides that you infringed on his copyright, you could end up in court. The law holds that the copyright owner doesn't even need to notify you first. The first notification you could get would be a notice to appear in court. Hopefully, however, you will get a letter instructing you to cease and desist, which you should take seriously.

To receive damages, the copyright owner must register the copyright with the copyright office. This is a process of proving that the copyright owner owns the material and has a valid claim to the copyright. Once that is in hand the copyright owner can claim damages on copyright infringement. Just because a work isn't a registered copyright today doesn't mean it can't be tomorrow. In fact, the law holds that the copyright owner has up to three months to register the copyright after the first transmission of the material.

Permission. At this point, I should mention that the best way to get around all of this is simply to ask the owner for permission to use his material. If he says no, you'll be in less of a position to claim fair use by virtue of your asking permission. If you're unsure whether fair use applies and you're thinking of asking permission, it would be worth seeking legal advice.

The Recording Industry Association of America (RIAA) and the American Society of Composers, Authors and Publishers (ASCAP) are agencies that hold the copyright for music and performances and are famously vigilant in their protection of copyrights for their artists [Hack #68].

Creative Commons

Creative Commons (*http://creativecommons.org/*) is a relatively new organization that maintains a set of easy-to-use licenses for audio, video, software, text, and other material. The basic idea is to allow content producers to retain some control over the material's use in commercial or noncommercial settings, but to leave the door open for people to freely use the work and derive new works from it.

Technically, a Creative Commons license is still a copyright; it's just more lenient in form than the traditional *all rights reserved* licensing form.

You can select several alternatives when creating a Creative Commons license. In particular, you can disallow commercial use or derivative works. It's important to know which Creative Commons license you are dealing with and how it will affect your use of the material.

Creative Commons licenses are particularly concerned with whether the use is commercial or noncommercial. Obviously using material in a podcast for a company is commercial use. But things become less clear if you are using it for your personal podcast, particularly if you have advertisements in the podcast, or advertising on your site. If the advertising covers costs and you claim it as personal income, it's unclear whether you are a commercial entity in the Creative Commons sense. According to the Creative Commons Frequently Asked Questions (FAQ), the use is commercial if it is for "monetary compensation or financial gain." I talked with someone at Creative Commons who gave me another definition: "if you intend to profit from it," which also can help clarify the issues surrounding commercial use.

If it's unclear whether you can legally use the Creative Commons licensed material, just contact the content owner.

Unlicensed Material

If you find that the material you want to use is in the public domain, you can use it in your podcast as you please. You should check the ID3 tags [Hack #40] in the MP3 file, the page that references the material, as well as the site's home page and About Us page. To check even further, you can search on the terms *copyright* and *license* within the site using Google, by adding the *site:domainname.com* restriction to the search.

That said, the copyright law is clear that copyright information should be displayed prominently with the material (section 401 of the copyright code). It doesn't need to be in the podcast sound itself. But it should be in the tags, in the RSS feed, and on every blog page.

Most of the material I have found that is expressly unlicensed is described as such boldly on the page containing it. In fact, it's a feature of the material.

Avoid Libel and Slander

Another legal issue to be aware of when you are creating your podcast is libel and slander. The harsh words you say can have harsh ramifications, as your target can sue you for libel or slander. And while with a blog all they would have against you is what you wrote, with a podcast they will have your spoken word to hold against you.

Libel occurs when you write something defamatory about someone, and *slander* occurs when you say it. For someone to claim that you made defamatory statements, the statements cannot be the truth or be spoken as an opinion. This is why you hear a lot of talk show hosts say "in my opinion" before they say something particularly nasty.

There are process and timing issues as well. For example, you need to be notified with a request to remove or retract the offending material in a timely manner (around 20 days after the posting). An overall time limit often is imposed by a statute of limitations. This means that around a year after posting, the party might not be able to sue you at all.

All this being said, the best policy on saying something nasty is not to say it. If you have to say it, state clearly that it is your opinion, unless you know and can prove that it's absolutely true.

See Also

- "Use Copyrighted Music Legally" [Hack #68]

Use Copyrighted Music Legally

Keep lawsuits away by making sure that any music you use in your podcasts is properly licensed or is license free.

At some point in the process of putting together a podcast, you'll run into the need (or desire) to use music. Whether it's for an intro [Hack #63], a *sound bed* (music that plays in the background while you're talking), or a featured part of your show, music can improve the way a podcast sounds significantly. Unfortunately, you face a huge obstacle when it comes time to distribute to your listeners a podcast that includes music. It's known as "the law."

Know Your Rights

Most of us, when we work, expect to get paid for what we do, and artists are no exception. Both composers and musicians have the right to be paid for the songs they create and those rights are protected by copyright law. As someone who wants to use those songs, you need to make sure you understand those rights, because the failure to do so can result in some hefty fines (up to $150,000 per song, as of this writing).

For the sake of keeping things simple, this hack focuses on how song rights are handled in the U.S. Because it can be a full-time job to manage the rights to a song, most composers will assign the responsibility to someone else. In the case of a composer, this would be a performing rights organization. In the case of an artist, this would be a record label. For you, the podcaster, this means that to obtain legal permission to use a song, you must not only obtain the composer rights from the appropriate organization, but also the performer rights from the label.

Composer Rights (ASCAP/BMI/SESAC)

Three primary performing rights organizations in the U.S. handle *composer rights* (also known as *public performance rights*): ASCAP (The American Society of Composers, Authors and Publishers at *http://www.ascap.com/*), BMI (Broadcast Music, Inc. at *http://www.bmi.com/*), and SESAC (The Society of European Stage Authors and Composers at *http://www.sesac.com/*). Membership in these organizations is free; the organizations take a percentage of the licensing fees they collect on behalf of the composers.

As a podcaster, you need to apply for an annual license from one or more of these organizations to be able to use songs written by the composers they represent. (Each organization offers a search feature on their web site to help you determine which organization represents a given song.) This license gives you the right to use the organization's songs in your podcasts during the year. When the license expires, you must either renew it or remove any podcasts that use the organization's songs from your server.

While the licensing costs vary from organization to organization and year to year and depend on a variety of factors, for most noncommercial podcasts the 2005 cost is around $300 per year each for ASCAP and BMI and around $170 for SESAC. This means that even if you use one ASCAP song in one podcast, you will have to pay a $300 licensing fee for each year you make that podcast available on your server. On top of that, you also have to report the number of times your podcast is downloaded. If it ended here, you'd be relieved. Read on for the rest of the story.

Performer Rights (RIAA/SoundExchange)

While paying for a license from one or more of the performance rights organizations might make the composers happy, it does nothing for the performers if you're using a recording of a song instead of performing the song yourself. As mentioned previously, the performer's rights are handled by the record labels, which are represented by the RIAA (*http://www.riaa.com/*). The licensing arm of the RIAA is called SoundExchange (*http://www.soundexchange.com/*), and SoundExchange is where the podcast licensing story hits the proverbial dead end.

There are actually two different types of performer rights: *mechanical rights* and *master use rights*. Mechanical rights cover the right to record and distribute a song for private use. Master use rights are the rights to use previously recorded material. Mechanical rights (and the digital equivalent) are handled by the Harry Fox Agency (*http://www.harryfox.com/*) and master use rights are handled by the individual record companies. So, how does SoundExchange fit into the picture?

Obtaining mechanical and master use rights is done on a per-song basis and is expensive, time consuming, and in some cases impossible. (Record labels don't have to grant master use licenses, and since they are against file downloading, you can imagine what their attitude is toward podcasts.) So, SoundExchange (at the not-so-gentle nudging of the government) offers what is known as a statutory license that is specifically designed to bypass these potential licensing roadblocks for Internet webcasters and offer blanket performer rights at a reasonable annual rate ($500 for 2005).

Several podcasters have rejoiced upon discovering the statutory license and thought it to be the answer to their licensing woes. Unfortunately, the terms of the license are worded in such a way as to limit the license to streaming media; therefore, podcasts don't qualify, which brings us right back to where we started. In other words, there is currently no way to legally license your podcast to play RIAA music, no matter what you've heard to the contrary.

What About Fair Use?

"But what if I don't play an entire song?" you might ask. "What if I play just a short excerpt? Isn't that covered under fair use?"

In short, no. Urban myths are floating around the podcast community, which say you can play excerpts from songs as long as they are less than 30 seconds long. This is simply not true. The "fair use" aspect of copyright law is very complicated, but generally, it is limited to use for teaching, research, news reporting, comment, criticism, and parody. However, even the context of these uses is limited, and if you're even thinking of trying to get away with something under fair use, you should probably consult a copyright attorney or spend some time studying fair use online (see *http://fairuse.stanford.edu/*).

The Alternatives

If at this point, the whole situation looks hopeless, you've assessed it properly. Until the RIAA reevaluates its position on downloadable media and comes up with a form of licensing that covers podcasts, there is no way to use RIAA-licensed songs legally in a podcast, unless you are able to negotiate a licensing agreement directly with an individual record label (and even that falls into a gray area).

Fortunately, alternatives are available. The RIAA does not license all music. Plenty of independent record labels and bands produce excellent music and are more than happy to have their songs featured on podcasts. Web sites such as GarageBand (*http://www.garageband.com/htdb/index.html*) and Indieheaven (*http://www.indieheaven.com/*) allow you to explore many of these artists and preview their music. In GarageBand's case, a free licensing agreement is available that allows you to use any song in its catalog in your podcast. In the case of Indieheaven and most other independent artist/label web sites, you should contact the artist/label directly for permission. (Even if an artist provides a downloadable MP3 of a song on her web site, you still need permission.) I have yet to be turned down for such a request and usually receive a very enthusiastic and appreciative response.

Your other option for legal music, especially for instrumental music and sound effects, is to do a web search for royalty-free music. Royalty-free music can be completely free, but usually it involves paying either a one-time fee or an annual fee for the right to use it, regardless of how many listeners you have. Three examples of web sites that offer this type of service are:

- Freeplay Music (*http://www.freeplaymusic.com/*), which has a wide variety of themed tracks to pick from on an a la carte basis, with an annual usage fee

- IB Audio (*http://www.ibaudio.com/*), which offers a library of tracks on an annual "all-you-can-eat" subscription basis

- Sounddogs.com (*http://www.sounddogs.com/*), which offers music and sound effects tracks on an a la carte basis, with a one-time usage fee

If you decide to go the royalty-free route, make sure you read the fine print to determine exactly what fees are involved.

The Bottom Line

As complicated as all this might seem, the bottom line is simple: make sure you have permission to use any content in your podcast that you haven't created (and written) yourself. In the case of recorded music, the only way to get permission at this point in time is to use songs from independent bands and/or labels. The good news is that the Internet is a rich resource for finding these songs, and they are just as good as or better than the songs that you won't be able to use!

Protecting Your Podcasts

The thought of protecting your podcasts might never occur to you. Until, that is, the day someone figures out a way to make money marketing them, without your permission, and you realize that you can do little or nothing about it. In the short history of podcasting, this scenario has already happened, as people have started scrambling to find a way to make money.

One idea that has shown up several times involves streaming podcasts sequentially in a variation on Internet radio, with commercials playing between them. In an ideal environment, podcasters would receive part of the proceeds from these commercials. If you haven't taken steps to protect your podcast, however, you might not have the right to claim anything. Fortunately, there is an easy and free solution to this potential problem.

Creative Commons licenses. While all creative works have an implicit copyright from their moment of conception, putting a work into public distribution without spelling out terms of use is risky at best. Creative Commons is an organization that was founded in 2001 with the specific intention of offering free copyright tools for those creating and distributing digital works. These tools build on the basic "copyright by default" and allow you, the creator, to have full control over how your creations are used, without sacrificing any of your rights.

Using the legal groundwork Creative Commons has put into place, you can make sure it is easy for others to understand exactly how they can use your podcast, without having to guess or contact you for permission. Just as importantly, the process of doing this is simple and straightforward for you also.

License conditions. In short, Creative Commons licenses allow you to grant blanket permission for your podcasts to be used under certain conditions, while retaining your copyright. You select those conditions from the following list:

Attribution
> You let others copy and distribute your podcast—and derivative works based on it—but only if they give you credit.

Noncommercial
> You let others copy and distribute your podcast—and derivative works based on it—but for noncommercial purposes only.

No derivative works
> You let others copy and distribute only unedited copies of your podcast, not derivative works.

Share alike
> You allow others to distribute derivative works, but only under a license identical to that which governs your podcast.

These descriptions are based on those given at the Creative Commons web site and are used with permission under a Creative Commons license with an attribution condition.

You have 11 Creative Commons licenses to choose from, in addition to a public domain license that releases all your rights to a podcast and makes it freely available for public use.

Taking and using a license. Once you've decided which conditions you want to apply to your podcast, you simply choose a license using the online form at *http://creativecommons.org/license/*. Submitting this form will generate the appropriate license code that you can then copy and paste into the HTML for your web site. The result will look something like Figure 9-15.

Figure 9-15. The Creative Commons notice

Clicking the icon will take you to a Creative Commons page, also known as the Commons Deed, which spells out the terms of the license. Figure 9-16 is an example.

It's important to note that, because of the license code, your license has been expressed in three ways (these descriptions are again taken from the Creative Commons web site):

Commons deed
    A simple, plain-language summary of the license, complete with the relevant icons

Legal code
    The fine print that you need, to be sure the license will stand up in court

Digital code
    A machine-readable translation of the license that helps search engines and other applications identify your work by its terms of use

Now your podcast is protected.

Tagging MP3s. Having the Creative Commons licensing information on your web site is fine, as long as people visit the web site before subscribing to your podcast. Since that's often not the case, it's obviously useful to have some way to embed the licensing information in the podcast MP3 files themselves [Hack #40]. Creative Commons has developed a method for doing this that includes a verification link back to your web site and the license info

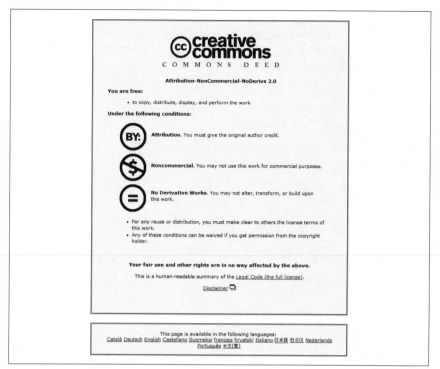

Figure 9-16. The Creative Commons license for a particular work

page that includes the license metadata. This link is stored in the copyright ID3 tag. For example:

```
2005 The GodCast Network. Licensed to the public under http://
creativecommons.org/licenses/by-nc-nd/2.0/
verify at http://www.godcast.org/cclicenses.html
```

Creative Commons provides two tools, ccLookup and Publisher, that make it easy to tag your MP3s and generate the corresponding verification metadata. You can find these tools, along with more information about the tagging process, at *http://creativecommons.org/technology/nonweb*.

Tagging RSS files. You can also tag RSS files to indicate that the contents of the RSS file or the contents of a particular item within the file are covered by a Creative Commons license (or any license, for that matter). Here's an example of the RSS element that allows you to do this:

```
<creativeCommons:license>
    http://www.creativecommons.org/licenses/by-nc/1.0
</creativeCommons:license>
```

You can use this as a subelement of <channel> to indicate that the content of the entire RSS file is available under the license referred to by the specified URL. You can also use it as a subelement of <item> to limit the license to the contents of that particular item.

See Also

- "Tag Your MP3 Files" [Hack #40]
- "Add Top, Bottom, and Bumper Music" [Hack #63]

—Craig Patchett

On the Go
Hacks 69–72

*Anyone with a marginally decent tape recorder
can chronicle a moment in their lives...*
—Jay Allison

*Rules for Field Recordists: 1) Use only
equipment you're completely familiar with.
2) Test and new equipment thoroughly before
your trip. These are the rules I should have
followed. If I had, I wouldn't be in the fix I am.*
—Barrett Golding

Podcasting is a way of bringing your listeners closer into your life. But, unless your life is really dull, you aren't in your studio all the time. So, to bring people along with you means recording on the road. In this chapter, you'll find out how to do that, and have it sound great.

HACK #69 Assemble a Small Recording Rig

Podcasting on the road opens up a whole new realm of interesting and engaging content. Learn how to build a small audio rig that will give you sound that sounds as good on the road as it does at home.

To get quality field recordings you need to start by getting a good recording device that fits into your budget. Next you need to put the right microphone [Hack #13] on it and understand a little about how to use it. I'll walk you through these steps, and then I'll give you a few tips at the end of the hack.

This hack is not just about field recording, though. Solid-state recorders, such as the Marantz and the Edirol, can do a better job at recording than a computer with hardware at the same price point. Plus they have the advantage of being portable, so you can take them anywhere. They are dedicated to the task, so you never get glitches or missing samples, and they inject no noise into the environment. So, if you are thinking about a studio with just you and a microphone, you might want to look into one of these rather than an adapter for your computer.

When it comes to audio recording, you get what you pay for. If you're doing lots of critical recording, it makes sense to spend the money on a professional machine. A recorder with XLR connectors, good mic preamps [Hack #14], reliable metering, and digital inputs and outputs or data transfer capabilities will make your life easier.

Consumer-level recorders have some downsides: the microphone inputs are usually mini-jacks, which can make unreliable connections; the built-in mic preamps are often noisy or not strong enough to record loud, clean signals from dynamic microphones; and there's a risk of losing your audio if the unit loses power while recording. The input volume controls are often problematic, sometimes offering only automatic gain control (AGC), which makes it easy to get a decent recording level quickly, but sudden loud sounds will often create distortion or unpleasant pumping artifacts.

AGC can be very useful for untrained recordists, especially nonprofessionals making audio diaries. It can also be a lifesaver in uncontrolled, "run and gun" situations where there's no time to twiddle with settings and you just need to get sound on tape. But in most cases, a stable recording level sounds better than one that's constantly adjusting to the input, so ideally, you want to set the levels manually and be able to turn them up or down as needed.

Here are some of the commonly used recording devices, and information about them:

iPod and iRiver

> You might be able to record with the MP3 player you already own. Some small MP3 players allow audio recording, sometimes with optional add-ons. But check the specs carefully. Often the sample rate or bit depth is low, resulting in grainy or muffled sound, or the gain control is minimal, resulting in low-level or distorted audio. If your only option is recording to a compressed format such as MP3, you could have quality problems down the line if your audio is converted multiple times.

> The iPod in particular produces low-quality audio. The standard sampling size is 8 bits and the sampling rate is 8 kHz. This doesn't result in quality audio. But there is an alternative. You can install Linux on your iPod (*http://ipodlinux.org/*) and boost the sampling rate to 96 kHz.

> The small iRiver (*http://iriver.com/*) devices with line inputs are the choice of Greg Narain for his Beercasts [Hack #30]. These units are

cheap—they cost around $100–$200—and they have a variety of memory and input configurations. They can record up to 44.1 kHz to MP3.

Solid-state recorders

The newer flash media or hard-disc recorders offer the advantage of a direct connection to the computer. Plug in a Universal Serial Bus (USB) or FireWire cable, or put the flash memory in a card reader and the drive will just appear as a volume on your computer's desktop. Then you can copy those files easily to your computer's drive for editing or archiving.

Several digital recorders offer professional or semiprofessional operation, ranging from about $400 to several thousand dollars. Edirol, Marantz, and Sound Devices make recorders with good mic preamps, some of them with XLR connectors for use with professional mics, prolevel sample rates and bit depths, and full-bandwidth recording of *.wav* files for maximum quality.

Digital dictation machines

Tiny digital dictation machines are tempting due to their size and ease of transferring recordings to a computer, but the sound quality is sometimes marginal.

DAT

DAT recorders avoid the hiss, *wow* (alternations between fast and slow), and flutter of analog tape, but they're expensive to buy and maintain, and still are subject to the vagaries of tape: occasional breakages, tangles, crumples, and head-wrap problems. And the format is increasingly rare these days, so finding parts, tapes, and repairs will be increasingly difficult and expensive.

Some portable DAT recorders require a special cable for digital output, and it's sometimes just easier to use the analog outs. Even if you're forced to do an analog transfer, you still have the sonic advantages of recording to a digital medium, with less noise and wider bandwidth than older tape-based media. And when done carefully, analog transfers can have minimal negative impact on sound quality.

Mini-disc

Mini-discs are still a popular choice, especially the portable consumer recorders. They are inexpensive, tiny, and easy to use, and while there is some data compression in the recording process, the sound quality is still very good.

Sony Minidiscs make it difficult or impossible to change the record level while recording, other machines beep when the record level is adjusted, and some have no manual record level at all, relying on the AGC to set the record level based on the input strength.

It's worth noting that despite the ambiguous terminology in product descriptions, the USB connections on the small mini-discs, except for the HiMD (High capacity MeDia) models, support only moving audio from the computer to the mini-disc, not the other way around, as most sound recordists would like. If you're using a recorder like that, the way to get sound to the computer for editing is via the analog outputs, in many cases the headphone out. That analog output is connected to an audio-in on your computer, built either into your soundcard or on an external interface.

MiniHD

The newer HiMD recorders allow uncompressed *.wav* recording, and even allow you to move the files as data to your computer over USB, but the process is unduly complicated and restricted, and not possible on all operating systems.

Pocket PC PDAs

Core Sound (*http://core-sound.com/*) has a card for Pocket PC PDAs called the PDAudio CF. The card is capable of recording 24 bits per sample at up to 192 kHz. At the sane rate of 16 bits at 44.1 kHz you can get 94 minutes on a 1 GB card, according to the vendor. There is a 1/8-inch stereo jack input for a microphone. The card sells for $199.

The equipment is changing everyday; in the end it's up to your ears what's "good enough." But keep in mind the recording format and the level of control. Full bandwidth is best, and the more control over recording levels, the better. Always record with the lossless pulse code modulated (PCM) or AIF formats, if possible.

It depends on what you need: if all you are looking for is intelligible audio, the size, price, and convenience of recording into an iPod or solid-state dictation machine might outweigh any quality compromises. A compelling story will overcome any technical limitations, and plenty of good productions have started from less-than-ideal field recordings. But a high-quality recording can more effectively transport listeners, and distortion or background noise can distract from the audio environment you're creating.

The small or nonexistent meters on consumer devices can create a problem, so experiment a bit to find what they really mean. You might need to record what appears to be slightly louder or softer than you would normally to get good levels. As with most digital recorders, "overs" sound really terrible, but very low record levels will sound bad in a different way—hissy and coarse—

once they are brought up to the proper volume at the mixing stage. Get somewhere in the middle.

Get a Good Recording

To get started, use a good mic, which will probably make the biggest difference in your sound quality. If you're interviewing people in the field, a dynamic omnidirectional mic, such as the Electro-Voice RE50 or the Beyer M-58, is a reliable, easy-to use industry standard. If you know any musicians, a Shure SM58 is bound to be nearby, and can be a good interview microphone. If you need to isolate your subject from background noise, or record from further away, a shotgun mic such as the Sennheiser K6/ME66 combination is the best tool.

If you're recording environments or events, stereo can be a powerful tool. A small stereo mic with a mini-connector such as the Sony ECM-MS907 is a decent starting place, but more elaborate mics such as the Audio-Technica AT822, the Rode NT4, and the Shure VP88 can give better results with some practice. Simple voice interviews rarely benefit from stereo mic use; in fact, the changing soundstage can be distracting, even nauseating, if the mic is moved around rapidly. If the background sound is interesting while your interview subject is talking, stereo might be good. Just be careful to keep your mic as still as possible, with the main subject in the center of the stereo image.

Use the best recorder you can. Almost any recorder can do in a pinch, but the better the input connectors, controls, and metering, the more likely you'll be to get intelligible and pleasing sound. Practice with it before you go on an important interview.

Some recorders have built-in mics, and this can be fine for note-taking or transcriptions, but not as good for high-quality sound. It's rarely practical to hold the recorder up in an ideal position for any length of time, and an external mic is almost always of better quality than the tiny mics that are built in. On the other hand, the ease of use and speed of setup can outweigh any sonic compromises in some circumstances.

Get a good-quality microphone cable of an appropriate length (a little longer than your arm is a good rule of thumb). Then get another one as a backup.

You'll need a good converter cable if you want to connect a professional mic to a mini-jack mic input on the recorder. Broadcast supply houses have cables made for this specific purpose. You might want a right-angle mini-jack to maintain a better connection. Those jacks are notorious for wearing out, so if practical, leave the cable plugged in to reduce damage. Don't build a conglomeration of adapters and converters, since every added connection increases the potential for noise and short-circuits.

You might have trouble getting enough volume into consumer recorders from low-impedance dynamic microphones, such as the Electro-Voice RE-50. You can try a mic with a louder output, such as a condenser mic, but be sure you can provide "phantom power" with a battery in the mic, since the small consumer recorders that have mini-jack inputs cannot supply the needed charge for condenser mics. Another choice is to get the $50 Shure A96f cable, which raises the impedance of a low-impedance microphone a bit, giving you some more volume without requiring extra power (it also converts from XLR to mini, so it might be the only cable you need).

One of the most important elements of a recording rig is a good set of headphones. Listening to what's coming into your microphone allows you to place the mic better, notice background noise you might otherwise miss, and verify that you are actually getting clean audio into your recorder. Any headphones are better than no headphones, but ideally you want a set that will isolate you from outside sound. The professional standard is the Sony MDR7506.

Tips from the Pros

Bring extra media, whatever you're recording to. Extra cassettes, DATs, mini-discs, or flash media can be a lifesaver. You never know when an interview will go longer than you thought, and you don't want to run out of recording time right as the interesting stories are flowing. Bring extra batteries, for both your recorder and your mic, if it needs batteries.

A good bag that will hold everything in an organized way can be a huge help, especially if you can leave it stocked with all your accessories so that you never get caught short. A camera bag is good to keep everything together and protect your gear from damage.

When you record people on the street, be sure to ask if it's OK to record them and to post the result on the Internet. It's best to get that in the recording and then cut it out for the released version, but keep it on your master copy.

Finally, observe the most important rule of field recording: listen! Don't trust that you're recording a good sound. Use your headphones and listen to what's coming into your mic.

See Also

- "Pick the Right Microphone" [Hack #13]
- "Mix Your Podcast in Hardware" [Hack #14]
- "Reduce Noise" [Hack #15]
- "Podcast in Surround Sound" [Hack #16]

—Jeff Towne

HACK #70 Podcast from Your Car

Podcasting from a car can be fun and interesting for your listeners, but it can be unsafe and potentially illegal. Learn how to do it safely, cheaply, and legally.

With today's recording technology, you can podcast from anywhere. MP3 recorders are even built into cell phones and watches. This makes it possible to take your listeners along with you as you drive around town.

To get quality sound in a car, first you need to understand what you want. Do you want to concentrate the sound on your voice? Or do you want to pick up everyone in the car to capture the whole experience?

It also depends on who is going to control the microphone. Is it the person who is driving, or a passenger? If it's a passenger, he can use almost any microphone he wants. However, I recommend one such as the Shure SM58 [Hack #13], which has excellent noise rejection to block out road and engine noise.

If you are the driver *and* the podcaster, things become more interesting. You need a solution that keeps your focus on driving safely, while getting the sound you want. Here are three different approaches.

Mounted Shotgun Microphone

For a podcast with a strong singular voice presence, I tried several approaches and found that the best solution involved a shotgun microphone mounted just above the dashboard.

I took two cable holders with adhesive backs and put them on the center of the console, as you can see in Figure 10-1. Those cable holders held in place an Audio-Technica 837 short shotgun microphone. On this car, a Civic Hybrid, I had to bring the wheel down a little so that it wouldn't interfere with the microphone. I connected the shotgun microphone through an XLR cable to a Marantz 660 portable recorder [Hack #69].

Figure 10-1. A dashboard-mounted microphone

The resulting sound quality from this rig was excellent. My voice was very present and strong, and the road noise was present as background ambience but wasn't overwhelming. As with all of these solutions, I recommend keeping the windows rolled up and the air conditioner set to a low setting to cut down on background hiss.

Mounted Lavalier

I used a similar method to mount a lavalier microphone and connect that to the portable recording rig. A lavalier is a much smaller omnidirectional microphone that is often used in hands-free aftermarket kits. These microphones have clips on them so that you can attach them to various points in a car. It takes some experimentation to find the best spots.

The mounted lavalier solution has the advantage of picking up a lot more of the sound in the car. You can use it to get several voices with generally the same level. The shotgun will get the person it's aimed at, and the other voices, but at a lower level.

Lavalier on Yourself

The mounted solutions share a single problem. Your recording rig is stuck in the car. So, wherever you want to take your listeners, you need to drive them there. The alternative is to put a lavalier microphone on yourself and attach it to a portable recording unit such as an iRiver, an iPod, or the Marantz 660. This way, you can drive around, and then get up and walk around after you have parked, without having to stop and disassemble the mounted rig.

It's worth spending some time to find the right position for a lavalier microphone on your shirt. T-shirts have limited positioning options. A button-down shirt will give you some more flexibility so that you can find a point where the microphone doesn't rub constantly against fabric and create a grating noise.

Legal Matters

If you intend on podcasting while driving, you should study the traffic laws of your state or country. It should be possible to equate podcasting with talking on a cell phone with a hands-free set. I strongly recommend against attempting to hold a microphone and drive simultaneously.

Then there is the question of what you are recording to. If you intend to use a laptop computer, you should read the laws regarding the location and direction of video screens within the view of the driver. It's very possible that operating a computer while driving or even having one pointed at you is illegal.

Having a portable recorder is an ideal alternative to using a computer. The Marantz 660 I used when I was researching this hack is perfect. It's a solid-state recorder that uses CF cards for storage of MP3 or WAV files. It has handy meters that show your signal level, it generates no sound or heat, it takes XLR inputs for two microphones, and it provides phantom power.

On the Content

Most of us drive or are driven on a regular basis. So, listening to someone drive is not inherently interesting. If your driving podcast is a soundseeing driving tour [Hack #72], here are some recommendations:

Be descriptive
> Describe the colors and shapes of what you see. Use lots of adjectives and nouns. Never rely on abstractions that you think your listeners will relate to. Your words are painting pictures for their imagination. So, the more you describe, the better the experience will be for them.

Hook into stories

Driving isn't interesting on its own. Stories about where you are driving can be interesting. Personal vignettes about events in your life keyed to various locations can be very interesting.

Add some history

If you live in a historic area, bring some of that into your drive. Use the text portion of your blog to point to links where the listener can find out more about where you toured in your car.

Talk with folks

Stopping to talk with the drive-through café attendant, or a neighbor, can be an interesting diversion for your listeners.

Expect pauses

Sometimes there isn't much to talk about, so there will be a natural silence. If it goes on for a while, be sure to start the next section with something such as "I'm back, not much to talk about there." Then cut the long silence to something smaller in the editing later. The road noise will vary from section to section, so the hard cuts to remove the silence will sound awkward unless you explain them.

Car culture, particularly in the U.S., is central to our way of life. As kids, we drive the strips on Friday and Saturday nights looking for the next beer bash. As we get older, we carpool or go to car conventions. Americans love their cars and we have a lot of stories to tell with and about them. All it takes are a little technical know-how and some creativity to set your inner car enthusiast free.

See Also

- "Pick the Right Microphone" [Hack #13]
- "Reduce Noise" [Hack #15]
- "Build a Beercast" [Hack #30]
- "Build a Sweet Sound" [Hack #57]
- "Create a Soundseeing Tour" [Hack #72]

Podcast at an Event
#71

Find out what's legal and ethical when recording at a live event, and how to record effectively so that your listeners get a sense of place and intensity.

Podcasting an event such as a concert, parade, sports event, or other activity with lots of excitement and a big crowd is a great experience to share with your listeners. Surprisingly enough, very often it's legal as well as fun. For public events, such as parades, you can record as much as you want (unless taping is expressly forbidden).

For ticketed events, such as concerts, the policy is a combination of the performer's taping policy and that of the venue. Phish and The Grateful Dead were well-known taper-friendly bands that even had taper sections at performances. This is called *taper access*. The tradition didn't stop there, though, as other bands learned the value of the free publicity of taping. Taper-friendly bands include the Indigo Girls, the Dave Matthews Band, the Black Crowes, Little Feat, Blues Traveler, and many others. GWAR allows taping, but I'm not sure what you would get. A complete list of bands that support taping is available at *http://btat.wagnerone.com/*.

Other ticketed events, in particular professional sporting events, are very protective of their copyrights and are not amenable to taping.

With taper access you can bring recording equipment with you to the show. There is often a policy against "pro" equipment, with some specification as to what defines "pro."

Particularly when bringing recording equipment to a concert, you should bring along a printout of the taper policy from the band's web site. This is handy for handling the private security at the door who might not know the policy.

Getting Good Sound

If you want to record the band itself, the best sound from an event is *board access*. This is the feed directly from the performers. Check the band's web site or contact their management to see if board access is available at the event and what the format is. Usually it's either XLR or RCA pairs [Hack #69].

Without board access, if you want to get a good recording of the concert, I recommend a stereo pair of cardioid microphones on a boom. Often these rigs are allowed in special taper sections where they won't obstruct the view of the band.

A podcast that's just a band playing is just a recording. If you want to personalize the podcast with your own voice, I recommend using a small lavalier omnidirectional microphone with proximity effect [Hack #13]. That will bring in the ambience of the event but give your voice good presence when you speak. These can work in combination with an iPod or iRiver, a minidisc recorder, a DAT recorder, or another solid-state recorder [Hack #69]. Another option is a short shotgun microphone or dynamic cardioid microphone that you can point at the band to record the songs and then back at yourself to give your live reviews.

Interviews

One way to add some color to your event podcast is to interview [Hack #33] the people you went to the event with about what they are looking forward to before the show, and what they liked about the show afterward.

If it's a lesser-known band, or the concert is a small venue, you should consider contacting the band's management to see about getting an interview before or after the show. It's always worth a try.

HACK #72 Create a Soundseeing Tour

Bring listeners with you on a tour through your world with vivid verbal imagery.

Soundseeing podcasts are walking tours around neighborhoods, events, or special places. What makes them unique is the medium. If the tour were video, we could simply sit back and watch the pictures of the scenery in a very passive manner. By using audio, our podcasting tour guide creates a "theatre of the mind" [Hack #32] by painting images with words that we must then interpret in our own minds.

Examples of soundseeing tours are available at *http://soundseeingtours.com/*. This is a Really Simple Syndication (RSS) feed you can use in your podcatcher.

This use of imagery means your listeners become much more active participants. And the podcaster is free to guide the listeners' attention as to what they think is the essence of the scene. That's not to say that the background audio isn't important. You couldn't do a fun soundseeing tour from a studio. The chants of the crowd at a game, the clink of glass in a café, or the creaking of floorboards in an old house all add detail to the vision painted by the podcaster's words.

A successful soundseeing tour comprises three critical pieces. The first, somewhat obvious one is that you should tour someplace interesting. Your house could be an interesting tour if you are famous. But those of us not burdened with fame might choose a walk around a historic town, a carnival, an event, or a tourist destination.

The second critical element is interaction. Talk with the hot dog vendor. Ask the crazy guy with the sign on the street corner what the sign means. Have a chat with some tourists to see where they come from and what they like about this spot. Interaction drives the narrative and gives listeners a reason for taking the journey.

The third is not so obvious until you hear it for yourself in a good soundseeing tour. It's *detail*. Detail is the essential element that lets listeners create the theatre of the mind. The more detail, the more clues they can use to construct their vision of what you are saying in their own minds.

Here is a quick example of why detail is important. Let's say I tell you "I'm walking up to my old house." OK, I see a house, maybe it's old, or maybe it's a place I rented last year. Who knows?

Now how about this; "I'm walking up to the house I grew up in. The snow is crunching under my boots the way it used to when I was a kid. The house is painted green now. It used to be white when I was a kid. Here that creak? That's the old porch. I remember hiding under that porch with my brother when we were young."

That's why detail is so important. You know ages, you know colors, and you know the season. And in your mind you create a picture, which is different for every person. This is why audio is so compelling. With video, all the work of building the imagery is done for your listeners. With audio, they become active participants in the storytelling. The next time you listen to a soundseeing tour, or to a story on the radio, pay attention to how much detail they use to draw with words what would take 1,000 frames of video to convey.

One last thing on content before I get into technique: never think of the audience; just imagine a single listener walking along with you. Because that is what's happening. You are talking to an individual, alone in their headphones. You aren't talking to a group. And your soundseeing tour is a private moment for them to walk with you in a very intimate and friendly way.

Getting Your Rig Together

Since a soundseeing tour involves walking around, you can cross your laptop computer off the list of good recording rigs. This leaves the mobile options: an iPod or iRiver, a mini-disc recorder, or a solid-state recorder such as the Marantz 660, among others [Hack #69]. With the iPod you can use a device such as Griffin's iTalk to record from a microphone, although you might want to experiment first to make sure you are happy with the 8 kHz record rate at 8 bits.

With the recording device in hand it's time to get the right microphone or microphones [Hack #13]. If you want something you can set once and forget about, you will want an omnidirectional microphone that picks up sound from anywhere and has a proximity effect that will emphasize your voice. For this purpose I recommend a single lavalier located about 6 inches down from your chin, or a binaural microphone [Hack #16] set that will give a unique surround sound experience for your listeners.

If you want more control over the sound and a richer presence, you can use a handheld microphone such as a small dynamic omnidirectional microphone. This will emphasize your own voice and still will pick up a lot of ambient sound. If you are more interested in what you intend to say and in getting a clear sound from your talks with other people, you should use a shotgun microphone such as the Audio-Technica 897.

By far, the preferred mechanism is the lavalier microphone. The first reason is convenience, since it's generally set properly and forgotten. The second is that it's not threatening to people since it's either hidden or is reasonably small. If people on the street think anything about you, it will be that you are a nutcase talking to yourself.

Preparing a lavalier microphone. Like other microphones, lavaliers come in both cardioid and omnidirectional shapes. Omnidirectional is better for this purpose because it will pick up sound from all around you, which adds ambience. And it's not as prone to handling noise [Hack #15] as a cardioid microphone is.

In addition, you will want a lavalier that has a proximity effect. This means that closer sounds will be louder so that when you speak, your voice will stand out from the background.

Thankfully omnidirectional lavaliers with proximity effect are very common and inexpensive. RadioShack sells a wired lavalier for around $25. Wireless systems are also available, but those can run into the $200 to $700 range.

Setting up a lavalier properly is a bit of an art. The microphone wire is small and delicate. So, you should loop that around twice, at about a 1-inch diameter, and fasten it to the clip. That will act as a strain relief on the connection to the microphone.

If you wear the lavalier on the outside of your shirt, it should have a windscreen on it. That's the little ball of black fuzz that usually comes along with the microphone. This will cut down on wind noise significantly.

Positioning the lavalier is very important. It should be around 6 inches below your chin, and dead center on your body. That way, when you move your head from side to side, the volume loss will be consistent.

Handling noise is a real problem with these small microphones, particularly from the material of your clothing. Do your best to tack the microphone down so that your clothes and the microphone move in unison. If they can separate, there will be bunching and rubbing, which will cause noise.

Use some tape and a matchbook cover to insulate your body from the microphone if you are wearing it on the inside of your shirt.

Editing Your Soundseeing Tour

The accepted practice for soundseeing tours is to add the usual top and bottom segments for the show. In addition, a small introductory segment recorded using the studio rig is placed at the front to describe the when, where, and how of the tour.

The amount of editing you do to your tour audio is up to you. Editing varies from none at all, all the way to an edited set of vignettes that is more of a sonic collage than a tour. I recommend only that you keep an ear out for the background noise. As you walk, the noise will change dramatically, and listeners are used to these subtle changes in noise from place to place. If you edit, you will need to recognize the transitions between the background noise from one location to another. Either insert some silence between the edits, with fade-ins before the next segment, or record some ambient noise before each segment and fade in the noise for the next segment at the end of the current segment.

Once you have your soundseeing tour posted to your own podcast, be sure to contact Adam Curry (*adam@curry.com*) with an announcement. He will post a link to the podcast on *http://soundseeingtours.com/*.

Using the Blog

Don't forget to use the HTML portion of your blog to augment your soundseeing tour. A few still pictures of what you saw can provide more detail for the imagery without completely spoiling the effect of the theatre of the mind. Links to more information about the location or the event make it easy for listeners motivated to re-create your experience.

The real technogeek should bring along a GPS unit and use it to track the tour and superimpose it on a map using HTML. Several products will even merge GPS data with the timestamps of your digital photos (if you sync the two) and provide links to the images taken at various points on your walk. These products include QuakeMap (*http://earthquakemap.com/*), OziPhoto-Tool (*http://oziphototool.alistairdickie.com/*), and GPS-Photo Link (*http://www.geospatialexperts.com/gpsphotolink.html*). For the truly hardcore, the Ricoh Pro G3 digital camera has an optional GPS receiver that can embed GPS data in the data stored with the image.

Check out PodGuides (*http://www.podguides.net/*) to see how far the linkage between audio, photography, and GPS can go. This service is creating iPod guides to cities using a combination of all of these technologies.

The Las Vegas Soundseeing Tour

Perhaps one of the most compelling podcasting stories is Tim Dressen's Las Vegas soundseeing tour. Tim was on one of his usual trips to Vegas. He likes to stay and gamble at the Venetian as well as at the Barbary Coast.

One morning he decided to supplement his regular podcast (*http://fivehundybymidnight.com*) with a soundseeing tour of his walk between the two casinos. He had walked that way many times before and knew there would be lots of interesting sounds. His only planned stop was at O'Shea's to catch some of their announcements.

He popped his Belkin microphone into his iPod [Hack #69] and went on his walk. He talked a little about what he saw along the way. But he mainly let the sounds of the strip do the storytelling for him. The result was a soundseeing tour about 20 minutes in length that became a huge hit.

He received a lot of enthusiastic email, but one in particular struck him. Here is a quote from that email:

> Most people get to look at pictures to remind them of their trips. This was the first time that I had a reminder of Las Vegas that I could enjoy and experience in a way that was meaningful to me.

The last time the woman had been to Las Vegas she paid extra attention to remember the rich sites and sounds, because she knew she was going blind. For her, Tim's spur-of-the-moment iPod soundseeing tour evoked all the sites and sounds she had strained so hard to remember.

With that kind of feedback, it's no wonder that Tim plans several more soundseeing tours.

See Also

- "Pick the Right Microphone" [Hack #13]
- "Assemble a Small Recording Rig" [Hack #69]

## CHAPTER ELEVEN

Videoblogging
Hacks 73–75

Videocasting opens up another dimension to podcasting. Well, several actually. You can use the enclosure extension to Really Simple Syndication (RSS) 2.0 [Hack #37] to add any type of file to a blog. So naturally, QuickTime movies or Windows Media files are fair game. Find out more about how to videocast with the hacks in this chapter.

HACK #73 Start a Videocast
Use your camcorder and some inexpensive editing and compression tools to build movies to add to your blog.

Creating a videocast is very similar to creating a podcast. The same mechanism—the enclosure [Hack #37]—is used to distribute the videocast as in the podcast. So, once you create a video file for syndication, you upload and publish it in the same way as you publish a podcast. The attributes in the enclosure element are the same as well. Easy? Not so fast! While the format for audio files in a podcast is fairly standardized, the video in a videocast is not. A wide variety of video formats and encoding parameters are available. The major components to choosing a format are the video compression codec, video bit rate, video frame rate, audio compression codec, audio sample rate, and audio bit rate. In some cases, it is useful to calculate the total bit rate (audio plus video) as well.

The Source Format

Your source format will depend on the equipment you have or can obtain. Probably the highest convenient quality for most people is a video camera with *FireWire*—also called *iLink* (Sony), or *IEEE-1394*. Since many computers are coming with FireWire jacks in them, with the right software this can be a very convenient method to get your video into your computer (some cameras come with Universal Serial Bus [USB] as well, or you can get a FireWire add-on adapter). Once the video is in your computer, you can edit it if necessary and convert it to a format suitable to your audience. *Mini-DV* (a type of digital video tape) video cameras with FireWire generally output in *.mov* or *.avi* format using a mini-DV codec. You can post this "raw" file in your videocast, but it likely will be bigger in pixel size, bigger in file size, and higher in quality than is really necessary.

A wide variety of portable video devices are available, from mobile phone cameras that create video, to digital cameras that create video, to video cameras that store video on Secure Digital flash cards, to video cameras that store video on full-size or mini-DVDs. Some of these produce video that, depending on your audience, can be perfectly suitable to post as a videocast without further conversion if you don't want to do additional editing. Other devices, such as those that output on DVDs, will likely produce bigger videos than you reasonably can expect your audience to download. These files will need to be compressed into the destination format.

The Destination Format

You have lots of video formats to choose from when it comes to exporting your videocast. As far as I know, there is no *.wmv* player for Palm, nor is there a QuickTime player. I have been able to find a *DivX* player (which is one of the encodings that can hide in an MP4 or AVI). A RealPlayer is available for Palm, though. If you care about supporting Palm, you should consider DivX encoding. DivX requires an additional application to be installed on both the Palm and Pocket PC [Hack #8]. This is probably the closest to a standard that we have, aside from Real.

Nokia by default includes the RealPlayer on its phones, though some people have complained of its quality. You have at least one option for downloading a player that supports some type of AVI file (although I can't discern exactly which encoding, except that it supports DirectShow plug-ins).

For the Pocket PC (and Windows Mobile smartphone) you should choose WMV. Note that the Windows smartphone resolution is 176×220. The Pocket PC resolution (QVGA) is 320×240. You should choose 320×240 or a simple multiple (160×213 or 120×160). You should consider a nominal bit rate (for the higher resolutions) from 200 kbps–300 kbps, a maximum of 400 kbps (for variable bit rates), and 10–20 frames per second with an audio sample rate of 22,050.

Many people believe that the *H.264 encoding format* will become ubiquitous and playable on a large number of devices. This format is designed to play at high quality with a wide range of compression ratios and sizes, from mobile phone to HDTV. It would be wise to consider publishing in this format as it becomes more popular (unless the winds of technology have changed between when this book was printed and when you are reading it).

From the H.264 Frequently Asked Questions (FAQ):

"H.264 is the next-generation video compression technology in the MPEG-4 standard, also known as MPEG-4 Part 10. H.264 can match the best possible MPEG-2 quality at up to half the data rate. H.264 also delivers excellent video quality across the entire bandwidth spectrum—from 3G [third-generation wireless] to HD and everything in between (from 40 Kbps to upward of 10 Mbps)."

The Portable Videocast

Pocket PCs suitable for watching videocasts will likely have 256 MB or greater storage capacity. It might be reasonable to have a file size of 50 MB or even 100 MB with such a client, but probably not much more. Keep this in mind when creating your videocast. The playback capabilities on modern portable devices are suitable for high-quality playback.

Portable media players, such as the Archos PMA400, have large amounts of storage, 30 GB in the case of the Archos. Although these media players cannot download videocasts directly like a Pocket PC can, when one is combined with a desktop-based aggregator, a user can transfer videocasts to a portable media player and watch them while mobile.

Creating a Videocast

First, shoot the video. Once you have the video on your recorder, you need to get it into your computer. One way is via FireWire using Windows Movie Maker. In Figure 11-1, I've selected to capture parts of a video manually.

Now select the output quality, as shown in Figure 11-2. If you are taking the video directly from your video camera to your videocast, just select Pocket PC Full Screen at 218 kbps (this is a reasonable balance of quality and file size).

Once this is done, the Capture video screen appears, with video controls to play, pause, and rewind the tape in your camera. Use these buttons to capture video in the selected format on your hard drive.

Figure 11-3 shows the dialog that starts the conversion process.

Once you have the video encoded, you can upload the videoblogging file just as you would a podcast to your web server.

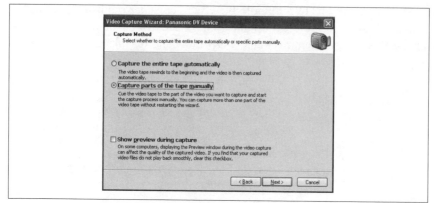

Figure 11-1. Setting the tape capture method

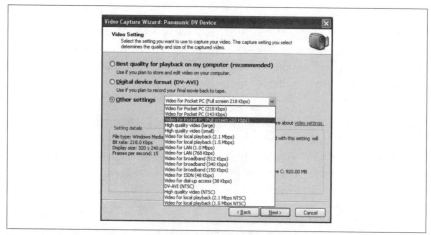

Figure 11-2. Setting the encoding method

Macintosh

On the Macintosh you can use iMovie and QuickTime Player Pro to produce and encode your movie in a variety of formats. iMovie allows you to break video recordings into smaller sections and arrange them just as you would sound in a sound editing program.

Final Thoughts

The wide variety of options for creating and watching videocasts virtually guarantees that videocasts will continue to be designed for different reasons and different audiences, and that these differing purposes will determine the format and quality (and therefore the file size, pixel size, and bit rate) of your videocast. As we see more specifications, and more client and

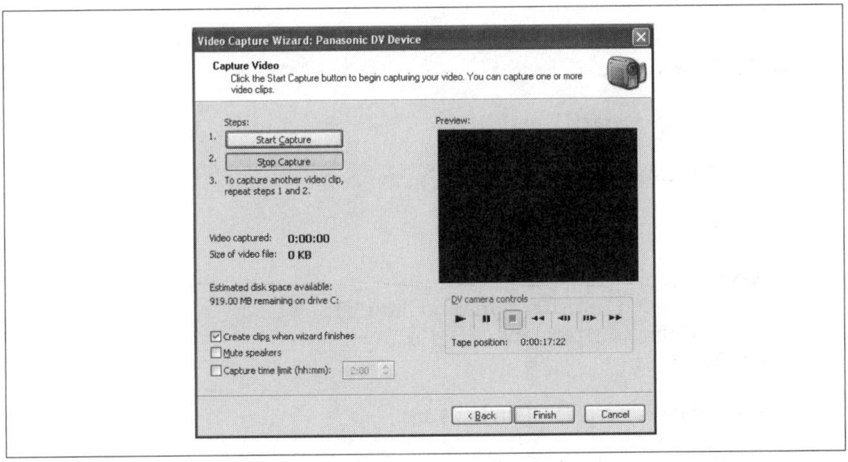

Figure 11-3. Starting the capture

production tools that take advantage of these specifications, we should be able to tailor our viewing of videocasts along with podcasts in the same way blogging and text RSS feeds have allowed us to tailor our reading and communication with others.

See Also

- "Listen to Podcasts on Your PDA" [Hack #8]
- "Podcast Without a Blog" [Hack #37]
- "Blog Your Podcast" [Hack #38]

—Greg Smith

Make a Quick-and-Dirty Prompter

#74

Use Perl CGI scripts to create a prompter that makes it easy to read from a script.

A *prompter* is a program that puts up the text of a script in large type and scrolls it on a timer. This makes it easy to concentrate on reading the script, instead of scrolling through pages of small type. In this hack I'll explain how to create a prompter that makes it easy to read from a script.

The Code

Save this code as *prompter.pl*:

```
#!/usr/bin/perl
use FileHandle;
use CGI;
```

```perl
use strict;

my $q = new CGI();

my $text = $q->param( "text" );

print "Content-type: text/html\n\n";

if ( $text )
{
  my $template = "";
  my $fh = new FileHandle( "prompter.html" );
  while( <$fh> ) { $template .= $_; }
  $fh->close();

  my @textitems = split /[\n+]/, $text;

  my $jsarray = join( ",", map { s/\n|\r//g; "\"$_\"" } @textitems );

  $template =~ s/\%\%lines\%\%/$jsarray/;

  print $template;
}
else
{
  my $fh = new FileHandle( "prompter_form.html" );
  while( <$fh> ) { print; }
  $fh->close();
}
```

Save this code as *prompter.html*:

```html
<html>
<head><title>Podcast Prompter</title>
<script language="Javascript">
var lines = [
%%lines%%
];
</script>
<script language="JavaScript">
var wordDelay = 300; // The average time per word in milliseconds

function getwordcount( str )
{
  words = str.split( /\s+/ );
  return words.length;
}

var currentPrompt = 0;
var timeoutId = 0;

function prompt( index )
{
  if ( index >= lines.length )
```

```
    index = lines.length - 1;

  currentPrompt = index;

  if ( index > 0 )
    line0.innerHTML = lines[ index - 1 ];
  else
    line0.innerHTML = "<br/>";

  line1.innerHTML = lines[ index ];

  if ( index < lines.length - 1 )
    line2.innerHTML = lines[ index + 1 ];
  else
    line2.innerHTML = "<br/>";

  clearTimeout( timeoutId );
  timeoutId = setTimeout( "prompt( "+(index+1)+" )",
    getwordcount( lines[index] ) * wordDelay );
}

function next( )
{
  clearTimeout( timeoutId );
  prompt( currentPrompt + 1 );
}
</script>
<style type="text/css">
.dim,.current {
  font-size: 48pt;
  font-weight: bold;
  padding: 20px;
}
.dim { color: #ccc; }
</style>
</head>
<body onload="prompt(0)" onkeydown="next( )">
<div id="line0" class="dim"></div>
<div id="line1" class="current"></div>
<div id="line2" class="dim"></div>
</body>
</html>
```

Save this file as *prompter_form.html*:

```
<html>
    <head><title>Prompter Form</title>
    </head>
    <body>
        <form method="post">
            Text for the prompter:<br/>
<textarea name="text" rows="20" cols="80">
</textarea>
            <br/>
```

```
            <input type="submit" />
        </form>
    </body>
</html>
```

Install all of these files in the *cgi-bin* directory of your web server, either on your hosted server or on your local machine [Hack #7].

Running the Hack

After the scripts are installed on your server, use your browser to navigate to *http://localhost/cgi-bin/prompter.pl* (if you're running on a remote server, replace *localhost* with the hostname). Once there, you will get the form shown in Figure 11-4.

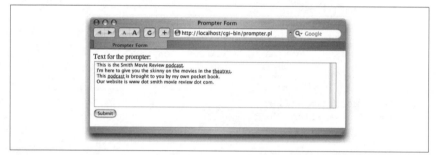

Figure 11-4. Entering the text for the prompter

This is the form from the *prompter_form.html* file. Put the text of your speech in the big text box and hit Submit.

Figure 11-5 shows the prompter in action. The text of the speech, now split into lines, is shown in three rows. The center row is what you are reading. Above it is the previous line, and below it is the next line.

Hacking the Hack

The text will scroll by at a rate of 300 milliseconds per word. If you tend to speak faster than that, alter the *prompter.html* file to use a smaller value. If you speak more slowly, use a larger value. To jump to the next line before the time delay does it for you, just press the spacebar.

You can change the font size or font family of the display by adjusting the CSS values in the *prompter.html* file.

See Also

- "Build a Teleprompter" [Hack #75]

Figure 11-5. The prompter in action

Build a Teleprompter

HACK #75

Reading a script while talking into the camera is difficult without a teleprompter. Build your own prompter with MDF and window glass.

To engage with your viewing audience you sometimes need to look them straight in the eye. But how do you do that and still read scripted material? You can do what newscasters and presidents do: use a *teleprompter*. Teleprompters project your script on a sheet of clear or mirrored glass right in front of the camera. This means you can look straight into the camera and still read the script.

The downside is that the hardware and software for a teleprompter can cost big money. As always, however, where there is a will there is a way and cheap homemade solutions are available.

Do-It-Yourself Teleprompter

Using a small sheet of clear glass and some medium density fiberboard (MDF), you can build a simple teleprompter for around $20. Go to your local glass store and ask for clear glass, cut to your dimensions with the edges smoothed so that you don't cut yourself. Then go to your local hardware store to get some screws and a 4×4-foot sheet of MDF at ¾-inch thickness.

My design calls for three pieces of MDF. The two sides are 16.5×6.5 inches. The bottom is 15×14 inches, and the piece of glass is 10×16 inches. If you don't have access to a table saw, you can have your local hardware store make the cuts for you.

Use a saw to cut 45-degree slots for the glass. Then mount the glass and attach the base with four screws. If you have a table saw, this shouldn't take you more than an hour to put together. Using a handsaw it might take you a while longer to get the grooves wide enough to fit the glass. The completed project is shown in Figure 11-6.

Figure 11-6. The finished teleprompter

Once you have it completed, lay your laptop down with the screen facing the glass from underneath.

Place your video camera on the other side of the glass. Figure 11-7 is what it should look like when you have the proper software installed. Don't worry if the image is flipped from left to right. That's normal. This is the problem that custom software is supposed to fix.

Figure 11-7. Looking through the prompter

Prompter Software

Teleprompter software is not cheap. The cheapest I could find is Presentation Prompter 4 (*http://nextforcesw.com/*), at $65. It's a nice piece of software that (like all the prompter packages) handles both horizontal and vertical flipping. It also has a settable scroll rate to pan through the material. Other Macintosh alternatives include IntelliPrompter (*http://www.intellisw.com/intelliprompter/*) and ScriptQ (*http://script-q.com/*).

Prompter software is available for Windows as well. ScriptQ (*http://script-q.com/*) has a Windows version for $99. DRS Digitrax (*http://drs-digitrax.com/*) has several packages available.

Hacking the Hack

All of this commercial software, with no open source alternatives, got me to thinking that I could alter the code in the quick-and-dirty prompter [Hack #74]. The only modification I made was to the CSS style block, by adding these lines:

```
<style type="text/css">
body { background:black; color:white;}
.dim,.current {
```

```
      font-size: 48pt;
      font-weight: bold;
      padding: 20px;
      filter: fliph();
      width: 100%;
      color: white;
   }
   .dim { color: #666; }
   </style>
```

I changed the background of the page to black so that I could see through it.
To see the text, I added the color "white" to the `.dim` and `.current` classes,
as well as changed the dim color to something darker.

The real trick was in adding the `fliph()` filter to the text. This works only
on recent versions of Internet Explorer and it's a custom CSS style that flips
the HTML entity, in this case the text, horizontally. Other effects, such as
`flipv()`, flip the entity vertically. To make that work, I also had to add the
`width` field so that all the flipped text items would line up properly.

Unfortunately, I couldn't find any completely free solution for the Macintosh. However, $65 for Presentation Prompter 4 is a good deal for a nice
piece of software.

A less high-tech option is a cue card held just off to the side
of the camera.

A productized version of this hack, called the Pro Prompter, (*http://www.*
bodelin.com/proprompter/), is available for around $50.

Glossary

Audio has its own language. This short glossary provides definitions of some of the audio-specific terms found in this book:

AAC

Advanced Audio Coding, a synonym for the MP4 audio encoding standard [Hack #18].

ADC

An analog-to-digital converter that converts analog signals into digital bits.

AIFF

A lossless audio storage format [Hack #18].

Aliasing

When signals are under-sampled the higher frequencies are aliased, which creates distortion in the lower frequencies. To avoid aliasing, sample the signal at the *Nyquist frequency*.

Ambience

Background sound material [Hack #64] that augments the foreground audio.

Amplifier

Amplifiers [Hack #14] increase the input audio signal strength.

Analog

Before digital recording there was analog recording, where signals were stored on either tape or vinyl.

Attenuate

A synonym for *reduce* that is often used to explain the effect of a filter.

Audio Unit (AU)

The plug-in [Hack #51] standard from Apple Computer. It's a part of Apple's Core Audio subsystem in Mac OS X.

Automation

The feature in studio mixing boards [Hack #56] that tracks the position of each control on a channel in real time during recording and playback. In the digital world this is called *gain enveloping*.

Balanced

A cable is balanced when there are two signal cables and another cable for the shield. A cable is unbalanced when there are two cables and one is used for the shield as well as the signal. Always use balanced cables when you can to reduce noise [Hack #61].

Band-pass filter

A combination of high-pass and low-pass filters [Hack #57] that lets frequencies in the middle pass.

Bars

A measure of time in a musical score or song [Hack #66]. This is counted in beats. The length of time depends on the beats per measure and the tempo.

Bed

Music that you gain way down and put underneath [Hack #63] a spoken word track.

Bidirectional microphone

A microphone shape [Hack #13] with lobes to the left and the right, but that attenuates sounds to the front and rear. Also known as a figure-eight shape. It's used for radio theatre and single-channel interviews.

Binaural microphones

A matched pair of microphones [Hack #13] set to the sides of the ears, in the ear canal, that are recorded in stereo creating a surround sound effect [Hack #16].

Boomy

When a sound has too much bass.

Bottom

The sound for the end of the show [Hack #63]. The opposite of the top.

BPM

Beats per minute. A music measure of frequency [Hack #66].

Bridge

A long (15–30-second) segment of music [Hack #63] that is light in tone and allows listeners to reflect on what they just heard.

Bump

A 4- to 7-second section of music [Hack #63] that has the same volume at the start as it does at the end.

Bumper

A slightly longer version of a bump [Hack #63] (12–15 seconds) that starts and ends with the same volume. Also called a *buffer*.

Buzz

Synonymous with hum [Hack #15].

Cadence

The specific rhythm to a person's speech [Hack #36].

Cardioid microphone

A directional microphone shape [Hack #13] that favors sounds ahead of it while attenuating sounds to the side and to the rear.

Channel gain

The master gain for a single channel [Hack #14]. It applies to the entire signal on that channel.

Chorus

A long delay effect [Hack #58] that gives the impression of multiple singers from a single singer.

Clipping

Clipping occurs in digital audio when the amplitude of a signal exceeds the range of the analog-to-digital converter. All of the signal beyond that range is rendered as the same single clipped value. The result sounds very bad. In older analog systems it was possible to overdrive the system and create a reasonable, even appealing, sound. That is not the case in digital systems.

Codec

The software that encodes and decodes signals [Hack #18] from a file into a raw sound form that can be edited or played.

Cold

A psychoacoustic term that implies that a sound is harsh and unpleasant.

Color

A process that makes slight, but unintended, alterations to a sound.

Compression

Compression filters keep signals within the preferred output range

[Hack #56] by attenuating signals that go above a set value. For example, you can set the maximum level at -6 dB and signals above that will be attenuated so that they fall below that value.

Condenser microphone

A microphone [Hack #13] that uses a capacitive diaphragm to measure sound pressure. Thought to produce a more accurate and warmer sound than dynamic microphones. The downside is that they require *phantom power*. The other type of microphone is a dynamic microphone.

Cutoff point

The point in a high-pass or low-pass filter [Hack #57] above or below which the signal is attenuated.

DAC

A digital-to-analog converter. This converts digital signals back to analog for output in speakers or headphones.

DAW

A Digital Audio Workstation [Hack #61]. For podcasters this means your computer with some editing, mixing, and sound acquisition software.

Decibel (dB)

A measure of sound volume [Hack #56]. The higher the value, the stronger the sound. The lower the value, the softer the sound.

Decode

The act of parsing an audio file and turning it into a raw sound format suitable for editing or playback.

Delay effect

A class of effects that samples the current sound, delays it, and then feeds it back into the signal. These include reverb, echo, chorus, delay, and flanger [Hack #58].

Digital

The opposite of analog. Digital signals are discretely sampled at a set rate into data points of a set bit size.

DirectSound

The Microsoft audio standard. It's also a name applied to Microsoft's plug-ins [Hack #51].

Distortion

Anything that affects a signal. Reverb, chorus, and equalization apply a distortion to the signal [Hack #58].

Dry

When a signal is absolutely free of any effect or filtering [Hack #57]. Dry is on one edge of the spectrum. *Wet* is the opposite of dry, on the other edge of the spectrum.

DSP

Stands for digital signal processing. In its general form, it's used to describe filtering and effects applied to audio. It can also refer to hardware chips that perform this function.

Ducking

In a two (or more) microphone setup, the sound from the silent microphones can be ducked while the active microphone is brought up. This helps focus the listener's attention to the dominant speaker. It's also used in the political talk show format to tone down callers while allowing the host to talk over them.

Dynamic microphone

A microphone [Hack #13] that uses a voice coil and a diaphragm to measure sound pressure. Contrast this with a condenser microphone, which is less accurate but requires no power.

Dynamic range

The range between the softest sound a system can render and the loudest sound it can render.

Effect

A process that is applied to a signal to distort it by either adding or removing sound [Hack #51]. Examples include equalization, chorus, and reverb.

EFX

Short for *effects*.

Encode

The act of taking a waveform and converting it to an output format [Hack #18].

Equalizer

An effect applied in the frequency domain [Hack #57] to increase or decrease the amplitude at particular frequencies. Some equalizers have a set number of bands across the frequency spectrum, and others, called *parametric equalizers*, that allow complete freedom in tuning the frequency response curve.

Field recording

A recording made outside of a controlled studio setting [Hack #69].

Filter

Synonymous with an effect, but usually applied to processes that remove sound elements. Examples are low-pass, band-pass, and high-pass filters.

Frequency response

The curve that represents how a microphone reduces or enhances signals at particular frequencies. Some microphones have a flat frequency response, which is the most accurate. Others boost or attenuate the low or high ends.

FTP

Short for File Transfer Protocol. It is used to copy files from computer to computer. It's often used to transfer MP3 podcast files to a web server account.

FX

Short for *effects*.

Gain

The amount of boost applied to a signal [Hack #56]. The more gain, the louder the sound. The noise increases by the same amount.

Gain enveloping

The feature in editing programs which allows the gain to be adjusted over the time axis of the signal display [Hack #56].

Headroom

The number of dB between the 0 dB point and the maximum signal that you want in the recording. If the maximum signal you want is –2 dB, there is 2 dB of headroom between that and 0 dB.

Hertz (Hz)

A measure of frequency. Bass signals have a lower frequency in hertz, and higher pitches have a higher frequency. The human voice runs between 50 Hz and 5 kHz with overtones into the 10 kHz range.

High-pass filter

An equalizer set so that high frequencies pass [Hack #57] while attenuating low frequencies.

Hiss

A high-frequency periodic noise [Hack #15]. Sometimes caused by fans or fluorescent lights.

Hum

A low-frequency periodic noise [Hack #15] in the signal. Usually the result of a power bleed into the circuit, or a ground loop, which causes a 50 Hz or 60 Hz hum.

Hypercardioid microphone

A directional microphone [Hack #13] sound shape that favors signals in front much more highly than those to the sides or rear.

In the clear

A sound is considered in the clear when it's at full volume with no other samples layered on top or underneath it. This is most often used to refer to ambient sounds or songs that are either voiced-over when someone is talking over them, or "in the clear" if they are at full volume with nothing else playing.

Kid safe

Considered by the podcaster to be safe for kids to listen to. Usually implies no profanity or intense adult themes.

Kilohertz (kHz)

One thousand hertz.

Lavalier microphone

A small microphone [Hack #13] that is worn on a tie or lapel, or under a shirt.

Low-pass filter

An equalizer set so that low frequencies pass [Hack #57] while attenuating high frequencies.

MAS

The abbreviation for MOTU's Audio System plug-in [Hack #51] format.

Master gain

The gain [Hack #56] applied to the entire signal.

MIDI

Short for Musical Instruments Digital Interface. It's a digital interconnect standard for everything from musical keyboards to control panels to concert lighting.

Mini-disc

A smaller-format compact disc used for recording [Hack #69] and playback. It was supposed to be the next generation CD but never took off in the U.S. outside of audio buffs.

Mixboard

A synonym for mixer [Hack #14].

Mixer

A device that takes several stereo or XLR inputs and mixes them into a single stereo pair [Hack #14]. Often provides gain and filtering controls on a per-input basis.

Monitor speakers

Studio speakers [Hack #61] with a flat response curve that doesn't color the sound in any way on playback.

Mono

A single-channel signal. In stereo systems, a mono signal is rendered equally to the left and right channels.

MP2

A lossless compression standard for audio [Hack #18].

MP3

A lossy compressed format for audio [Hack #18].

MP4

Another lossy compression format for audio [Hack #18]. Also known as AAC.

Muddy

A psychoacoustic term that refers to a sound that lacks definition.

Noise

Unwanted sound [Hack #15] in a signal.

Noise floor

The decibel level of the softest possible signal [Hack #15] a system can render. The better the recording environment and sound system, the lower the noise floor.

Nyquist frequency

The frequency point where all of the recorded frequencies will be digitized without aliasing. This is four times the highest frequency. So, if you want to record sounds up to 10 kHz, you should sample at a minimum of 40 kHz to avoid aliasing.

Off axis

Used to indicate that you are speaking away from the diaphragm of the microphone [Hack #19]. Speaking off axis is one way to reduce plosives.

Off-axis rejection

A measure of the amount of sound recorded from areas out of view of the microphone's diaphragm [Hack #13].

Off the record

When a source is talking but the results are not recorded [Hack #21] and won't be used directly in the resulting story.

Omnidirectional microphone

A microphone sound shape [Hack #13] that weights all sounds around it equally.

OPML

The Outline Processor Markup Language (OPML) is an XML format [Hack #45] used to store hierarchal outline data.

Patch

A generic term that describes connecting a sound source to a sound input.

Parabolic microphone

A highly directional microphone [Hack #13] used at sporting events.

Parametric equalizer

A type of equalizer [Hack #57] that allows complete freedom in defining the frequency response curve of the filter using a number of parameters.

PCM (Pulse Code Modulated)

The storage format [Hack #18] for audio used on CD.

Peak normalization

Changes the amplitude of a signal to maximize its amplitude using the maximum amplitude of the signal [Hack #56]. This normalization technique cannot result in a signal that clips, but it will create uneven volume levels.

Periodic noise

Noise that repeats at a set frequency [Hack #15], such as the hum from a power source or the thrum of an air conditioning unit.

Phantom power

Power supplied through XLR cables to condenser microphones [Hack #14]. Some condenser microphones are self powered with batteries and do not require phantom power. Phantom power is supplied by preamps, amplifiers, and mixers.

Plosive

The sound pop that occurs when people speak the *p* or *b* sound directly into the microphone [Hack #19] without a pop stopper.

Plug-in

Software [Hack #51] that fits into a sound recording, editing, or mixing program to provide filters, effects, or virtual instruments.

Podcatcher

RSS aggregation software [Hack #1] that includes support for the enclosure tags in RSS 2.0 feeds.

Pod-safe music

Music that is completely unlicensed, or is licensed under Creative Commons or another license that allows the music to be used in "derivative works."

Proximity effect

The effect when a microphone [Hack #13] gets much louder as you move closer and falls off rapidly as you move away.

Psychoacoustic

A catchall term that applies to signal phenomena, or effects, that aren't easily quantified but can be felt by listeners.

Reverb

Short for reverberation [Hack #58]. The effect of sound hitting surfaces and bouncing back to the recording device. The amount of delay and the effect applied to the return signal gives a room its unique voice.

RMS normalization

Alters the gain of the signal [Hack #56] based on the Root Mean Squared (RMS) average for the signal. This can result in a signal that clips, but it will result in a signal of a consistent volume level.

RTAS

One of the two plug-in standards [Hack #51] for the Pro Tools software. It stands for Real Time Audio Suite. The other Pro Tools plug-in standard is TDM.

RSS

Short for Really Simple Syndication [Hack #37]. It's an XML format that gives a digest of recent entries on a blog. There are three popular versions of the format: 0.91, 1.0, and 2.0. The 2.0 standard supports the enclosure tag, which is what makes podcasting possible.

SFTP

The Secure File Transfer Protocol is the secure version of the older FTP protocol. If you have a choice, always go with SFTP.

Shotgun microphone

A highly directional microphone [Hack #13] used in field interviews and with video.

Sibilance

The hiss for the s sound [Hack #19]. This is removed using a de-esser filter.

Signal

Sound information organized as samples over time. The sampling rate defines how often samples are taken. The sample size, in bits, defines how much data is stored for every sample. A larger sample size can render a larger dynamic range of signal.

Solid-state recorder

A recording device [Hack #69] that stores the signal in solid-state memory. Since there are no moving parts, it cannot be a noise source.

Soundseeing tour

A recorded walking tour [Hack #72] where the speaker describes what he is seeing as he tours around.

SSH

The secure shell protocol allows you to connect to a command-line shell on a remote server machine securely.

Stereo

A two-channel signal that is rendered discretely into the left and right channels of a stereo system.

Stereo pan

The position of a signal in the sound space from left to right. A signal can be all the way on the left, where it will be exclusively in the left speaker, or centered in the middle, where it will apply equally to both speakers. If it's all the way on the right, it will apply exclusively to the right channel. Also, it can be positioned at some point in between.

Stings

A 4- to 7-second musical segment [Hack #63] that starts at one volume and ends at a different volume. Sometimes these have a sustained note at the end that fades out or reverberates.

Stinger

A longer version of a sting [Hack #63] (15–30 seconds). Has varied intensity throughout. The ending fades out so that sound can be placed over the top of it.

Studio microphone

Usually a large-diaphragm condenser microphone with a cardioid shape [Hack #13].

Studio recording

A recording made within the controlled environment of the studio.

Supercardioid microphone

A directional microphone shape [Hack #13] that favors signals from the front, and to a lesser degree from the sides, while adding some signal in from the rear.

TDM

The premiere Pro Tools plug-in format [Hack #51]. It stands for Time Division Multiplexing. The other standard for Pro Tools is RTAS.

Telnet

An older protocol to get remote terminal sessions on server machines over the network. It's nowhere near as secure as the more recent SSH standard.

Tempo

The speed of a song [Hack #66]. Usually measured in beats per minute (BPM).

Timbre

The quality of someone's voice.

Tinny

When something has too much treble, it sounds tinny.

Top

The sound for the introduction [Hack #63] to a show.

Unbalanced

The opposite of balanced. A cable has only two lines, where one is shared with the shield and is thus vulnerable to outside interference [Hack #61].

Up-cut

When a person's speech is cut during a rise in a sentence. Sentences tend to fade out. So, a cut when a sentence is rising in volume implies that the person was cut short [Hack #36]. This type of cut is an up-cut because the sound is going up and not down.

Virtual instrument

A musical instrument simulated in software.

VST

A plug-in standard [Hack #51] from Steinberg that works with many audio editing applications.

Walla

The distinctive cheer of a large crowd [Hack #32]. Sometimes used as ambience in sports stories. Each walla has a distinctive sound. The walla of a bar crowd sounds far different from a stadium walla.

Warm

A psychoacoustic term that implies that a sound is rich and deep and is pleasant to listen to.

WAV

The Windows lossless audio file format [Hack #18].

Wet

When an effect is fully applied to a signal [Hack #57], the result is called wet. *Dry* is at the opposite end of the spectrum from wet.

Work safe

Considered by the podcaster to be safe to listen to at work. Usually implies no profanity or intense adult themes.

XLR

The adapter used with microphones [Hack #13]. XLR cables fit into XLR jacks on the microphone and XLR jacks in the preamp. The jack has three connectors as opposed to two. This means that the cable is balanced, which reduces possible noise introduced by radio frequencies.

Index

Symbols

| (pipe symbol), 251

A

a cappellas, 348, 349, 350
A versus B mash-ups, 345, 346
AAC (Advanced Audio Coding)
    format, 31, 113
Ableton Live, 346
AC-3 format, 113
accent coaching, 118
ACID (Sony)
    beatmapping, 348
    creating music, 191, 277, 332
    mash-ups and, 346–349
    review podcasts, 166
Acoustic Rooms, 325
ActiveState Perl
    COM objects and, 22
    installing, 34–37
    Podcastamatic and, 225
    podcatchers and, 22
    Tk support, 299
ActiveSync program, 38, 40, 41
Adams, Doug, 13
Add or Remove Programs control
    panel, 35
Adobe (see Audition (Adobe))
Advanced Audio Coding (AAC)
    format, 31, 113
advertising, 110, 264
AeroPlayer player, 45

AGC (automatic gain control), 198,
    364, 365
aggregators
    defined, 223
    Libsyn directory and, 232
    Pocket PC devices and, 38
    RSS feeds and, 224
    tracking blog mentions, 268
"ahs", 216, 282
AIF files, 333
AIFF (Audio Interchange File
    Format), 113, 366
Air America Radio network, 147
AKG microphones, 76, 84, 86
Album field (MP3 files), 244
Alesis portable mixers, 90
Alexander, Gill, 167
All Music web site, 157
All Podcasts directory, 256
Allison, Jay, 193–201, 363
AltaVista Audio site, 335
Alto microphone preamps, 93
Amazon.com
    Associates program, 265
    Honor System, 266
    sports section, 168, 169
ambience
    adding background, 336–337
    interviews and, 219
    recording events, 373
    road noise, 370
    wind noise as, 313
AMEK microphone preamp, 322

We'd like to hear your suggestions for improving our indexes. Send email to *index@oreilly.com*.

American Press Institute, 132
amplitude
   graphic equalizers and, 306
   men's voices, 305
   parametric equalizers and, 307
   of signals, 300, 301
amplitude graph, 300
analog sound, 81, 301, 365
Analogue Samples site, 335
ANT client, 26
antinodes, 324
Antonioli, Flavio, 277
Anvil Cases, 323
Apache web server, 33, 37
APHEX 320A Compellor, 322
APIs, speech synthesis and, 341, 342
AppleScript
   Audio Hijack Pro and, 289
   automation toolkit, 32
   importing podcasts, 25
   speech synthesis and, 339, 340
   timestamping show notes, 292–294
AppleScript Studio, 294–298
appropriation (see mash-ups)
Archos portable media player, 381
Armstrong, Heather, 138
ART microphone preamps, 92
artful editing, 215, 216–218
Artist field (MP3 files), 244
ASCAP
   composer rights and, 154, 356
   copyrighted material and, 353
   podcast songlist and, 156
ASCII characters, 108
Atom syndication standard, 32, 228
ATRAC3plus format (Sony), 46
attack parameter (compression), 303
attenuating signals, 302
Audacity application
   AIF files and, 333
   beercasts, 180
   changing speed and, 312, 315
   compressor support, 303
   diffing signal, 311
   downloading, 48
   enveloping and, 302
   feeding MP3s, 248
   functionality, 272
   ID3 tags and, 244
   maintaining consistent levels
      and, 300

   multitrack editing and, 316, 317
   music podcasts, 159
   news editing and, 218
   overview, 273
   pitch shifting and, 312
   plug-ins and, 286
   political podcasts, 147
   review podcasts, 165
   room equalization, 325
   sports podcasts, 170, 171
   technology podcasts, 176
   tunable noise filters, 309
   Vbox feature, 286
   WAV format, 253
audience
   alternate commentary and, 150
   beercasts and, 179
   defining, 162
   keeping engaged, 126
   knowing the, 200
   respecting, 126
   soundseeing tour and, 375
audio
   background ambience, 336–337
   copyrighted material, 355–362
   digital, 49
   editing, 216, 273–279
   FireWire adapters, 71–72
   fixing common problems, 313–316
   grabbing legally, 351–355
   integrating email feedback, 330–331
   mash-ups, 345–351
   recording to files, 206
   saving files, 49
   setting up home studio, 320–328
   speech synthesis, 338–344
   tops/bottoms/bumpers, 332–335
   (see also quality sound)
audio bit rate, 379
audio compression codec, 379
Audio Converter for HotRecorder
      application, 213
Audio Hijack Pro application
   automating, 289–292
   building sound carts, 294–298
   cart programs, 189
   graphic equalizers, 306
   ID3 tags and, 244
   incorporating effects, 335
   interviews and, 208
   music shows, 156, 161

overview, 103–105, 280
review shows, 164
simulating rewind, 315
Skype and, 209–213
Soundflower tool and, 159
speech synthesis, 338
timestamping show notes, 292–294
Vbox feature, 286
Audio In tool, 282
Audio Interchange File Format
    (AIFF), 113, 366
audio sample rate, 379
audio theatre, 185–192
Audio Theatre.com, 191
Audio Unit (AU) plug-ins, 275, 286
Audio Weblogs, 256, 264
Audioblog
    conference calling, 207
    hosting MP3 files, 50
    overview, 232, 233
Audioblogger service, 206, 228
AudioPathServerSide variable
    (Podcastamatic), 226
AudioPathWebSide variable
    (Podcastamatic), 226
Audio-Technica
    condenser microphones, 80, 92
    field recording microphones, 82, 84
    mini-connectors, 367
    shotgun microphones, 80, 337, 369,
        376
    stereo microphones, 81
    studio microphones, 85
AudioTrak sound cards, 63
Audition (Adobe)
    Cool Edit and, 171
    encoding with, 180
    extraction tools, 350
    multitrack editing and, 317
    overview, 275, 276
    tunable noise filters, 309
aural exciter, 312
Auralex, 325, 327
AutoCast program, 31, 342
AutoHybrid, 204
automatic gain control (AGC), 198,
    364, 365
automation, 302
Azureus client, 240

B

back-announcing, 158
background chatter, 183
Baker, Tim, 345–351
band-pass filters, 112, 308
bandwidth, 232, 236–243, 270
bare-bones editing, 215
basic editing
    adding special effects, 310–312
    Audio Hijack Pro and, 289–292
    building sound carts, 294–300
    building sweet sound, 305–309
    defined, 215
    fixing audio problems, 313–316
    gain control, 300–305
    multiple tracks, 316–319
    selecting tools, 273–285
    sound considerations, 286–289
    timestamping show notes, 292–294
Basketball Babble, 168
bass traps, 326, 327
batteries
    checking, 198
    phantom power and, 368
    spare, 199, 368
Baty, Kit, 171
beatmapping, 346, 348
beats per minute (BPM), 108, 346, 348
Beercasting.com, 180
beercasts, 92, 177–181, 364
Behringer
    microphone preamps, 92, 93
    MIDI mix boxes, 302
    portable mixers, 90
    sound mixers, 87, 89, 141
    studio microphones, 85
being in the moment, 201
Belkin, 322, 378
Bellari microphone preamps, 93
Benge, Joel, 139
Beyer microphones, 367
beyerdynamic microphones, 80, 84
BIAS, 307, 309, 314
billboards, 125
binaural microphones
    explaining, 102
    soundseeing tours and, 375
    surround sound and, 100, 101

bit rates
   audio, 379
   defined, 107
   VBR, 107, 113
   video, 379
BitTorrent P2P network, 7, 240–243
blank sound recording, 219
Blankner, Brett, 170
Blog Torrent tracker, 242
Blogger service, 50, 228
Bloglines, 10, 16, 223
blogs
   ads and, 265
   bandwidth and, 236–243
   comments system, 330
   conference calling, 206, 207
   converting text-based, 27–31
   first podcasts and, 50
   MP3 files, 243–246, 246–249
   personal shows, 135
   podcasts and, 222, 227–236
   podcasts by email, 249–252
   podcasts without, 222–227
   political podcasts and, 145
   registering, 258
   soundseeing tours and, 377
   syndicating to radio, 252–254
   technology podcasts and, 176
   trading links to, 262
BlueHost service, 238, 239
Bluetooth
   call recording and, 207
   controlling applications and, 102
   hands-free headset, 62
   Logitech keyboard/mouse, 106
bluggcaster (Blugg.com), 10
Blugg.com, 10
Blythe, Erik, 166
BMI
   composer rights and, 154, 356
   podcast songlist and, 156
board access, 373
Bond, Stacy, 121–132
bookmarks, 10, 223
boominess, 59, 78
bootlegs, 345–351
bottoms, adding, 332–335
BPM (beats per minute), 108, 346, 348
breaking news, 127
breath sounds, 217, 306

Brigante, Richard, 141
broadband connection, 41, 42
Broadcast Host, 204
broadcasting
   coaches for, 117
   creating networks, 14–16
   defined, 124
   professional-quality, 52–60
   voice considerations, 114
browsers
   displaying HTML show notes, 298
   finding podcasts with, 1–13
   playing podcasts, 42
   RSS and, 223
   simulating, 31
BugCast podcast, 139
bulletin boards, 257, 267, 330
bumpers, 279, 332–335
Burwell, Keith, 146
buttons, checking names of, 296

C

CabInstl program, 38
cabling
   analog sound, 81
   DAT recorders, 365
   microphones and, 67, 70, 82, 367
   recommendations, 322
   signal path noise and, 98
cadence of speech, 218, 313
Call Corder site, 202, 206
Callahan, Karen, 193
call-ins
   alternate commentaries, 147
   political podcasts, 146
   sports podcasts, 168
   telephone hybrids and, 204, 323
Campbell, Bill, 214
capsules, pick-up patterns and, 76
cardioid microphones, 77, 80, 373
Caribbean Free Radio podcast, 160
cart applications
   example code, 298
   functionality, 272, 283
   sound effects and, 189
carts, 283
category management, 234, 259–261
ccLookup tool, 361
ccPublisher tool, 237, 361

Cedub Studio, 321, 326–328
cell phones
    beercasts and, 179
    BugCast podcast, 139
    call-recording feature, 207
    controlling recordings with, 102–107
    data connections, 41
    hands-free headsets, 62
    MP3 recorders and, 369
    video devices and, 380
Cepstral Text-to-Speech, 340
Cepstral Voices, 30
cgi-bin directory, 34, 386
change pitch effect, 315
change speed effect, 312, 315
change tempo effect, 312, 313, 315
channels
    defined, 87
    microphone preamps, 93
    mixers and, 92
    surround sound and, 101
chorus
    mixers and, 89, 91
    overview, 310
    SoX tool, 112
Cinecast podcast, 165
civic journalism, 128
ClearOne, 323
ClearSonic, 325
click event handler, 296, 297
clipped signals, 89, 301, 304
CNN network, 143
Code Generation Network, 53
COM objects, 22
commentary, 148–152, 166
comments, 139, 330
Comments field (MP3 files), 244
commercial networks, 269
commercial status, 266, 268, 334, 354
commercials, 332
composer license/rights, 154, 356
composure, host role and, 57
compression
    filtering, 215, 302–304
    hardware effects processors and, 322
    mixers and, 89
    signals and, 94
compression rate (MP3 files), 49

compressors
    Audacity support, 303
    clipping and, 89
    limiters and, 304
    music shows, 156
    noise from, 99
    recommendations, 59, 322
    signals and, 88, 302, 304
computers
    mash-ups and, 345
    noise from, 56, 62, 96, 323
    podcasts from car, 371
    portable mixers and, 91
    speakers on, 207
    USB standard, 67
    VNC and, 106
concentration, host role and, 57
condenser microphones
    audio theatre, 188
    functionality, 76
    interviewing and, 198
    moisture and, 74
    power to, 66, 68, 80, 92, 322, 368
    recording ambience, 337
    sample setups, 73
Conference Call, 206
conferences, attending, 263
confidence, host role and, 57
contemplative silence, 218
content
    creating elements, 124–125
    importance of, 50
    listening for, 51
content elements (see segments)
contests, 168
ControlFreak, 105
Cool Edit, 171, 275
(Cool) Shite on the Tube podcast, 164
copyrighted material
    fair use, 357
    grabbing audio legally, 352–353
    infringement issues, 335
    legal considerations, 350, 355–362
    licensing and, 332, 353
    taping and, 373
Core Sound, 100, 366
countdowns, 168
couplers, 203–204
Coutin, Sam, 167–171

Coverville, 2
Coverville podcast, 153
CPAN module library
    feeding MP3s, 248
    functionality, 32
    importing podcasts into iTunes, 25
    installing Perl modules, 31
crash box, 190
Crazy Dog Audio Theatre, 191
Creative Commons
    commercial status and, 266
    free content service and, 237
    GarageBand.com and, 334
    grabbing audio legally, 351–355
    Internet Archives and, 143
    legal issues and, 351
    Obi Show and, 140
    Ourmedia and, 233
    overview, 353, 354, 359–362
Creative Labs, 63, 67
credits, placement of, 125
cron jobs, 17
C-SPAN Archives, 143
cues, 187
Curry, Adam, 127, 267
    (see also Daily Source Code)
cutoff frequency, 307, 308
cuts, library of, 201
cyberjournalists, 127
Cygwin Perl, 22, 34

D

DAC (digital-to-analog) converters, 321
Daily Source Code
    games and, 137
    hosting for, 238
    overview, 2, 257
    RSS file example, 223, 224
    soundseeing tours and, 377
    staying up-to-date and, 268
Dailysonic MP3zine, 181
damages, copyrighted material, 353
DAT recorders, 337, 365, 373
Data::Dumper module, 32
dateCreated field (OPML), 261
dateModified field (OPML), 261
DAW (Digital Audio
        Workstation), 321, 322

The Dawn and Drew Show, 2
De Blieck, Augie, Jr., 165
debates, 168
debugging Perl scripts, 32
decibels (dB)
    clipped signals, 301
    compression parameters, 302
    defined, 300
    maximizing filters and, 304
Deck application, 275
delay effects, 310
deleting
    podcasts, 8, 38, 43
    portions of recordings, 49
    videoblogs, 26
Denon recording systems, 323
derivative works, 352
Description field (Podcastamatic), 226
description field (RSS), 225
$descriptionTAG variable, 227
destination formats (videocasting), 380,
        381
detail
    soundseeing tour and, 375
    in storytelling, 136, 195
dictation machines, 199, 365
diction, 115
diffing, 311
Digidesign
    Mbox device, 70, 274, 321
    Pro Tools, 274, 288, 321
    USB sound adapters, 68
Digigram PC Card adapters, 67
digital audio, 49, 301
Digital Audio Workstation (DAW), 321
digital cameras, 377
Digital Performer, 321
Digital Podcast, 256
digital rights management (DRM), 114
digital-to-analog (DAC) converters, 321
DirCaster, 50, 222, 224, 227
directors, audio theatre, 189
DirectSound plug-ins (Microsoft), 288
distortion, 99, 364
DivX encoding, 380
DIY pellas, 350
DJ Earworm, 345
DNS service, 242
documentary interview, 194

Dolby compression standard, 113
domains, podcasts and, 50
Donahoe, Emily, 114–120
Dooce, 138
Doppler Radio podcatcher, 8, 12, 13
dospeak function (JavaScript), 342
downloads
　Audacity application, 48
　BitTorrent support, 7
　demos, 285
　displaying, 43
　enclosures, 39, 43
　FeederReader application, 38
　file chunking, 241
　Flash players, 235
　length as deterrent, 153
　multithreaded, 8
　Net::SFTP module and, 32
　to PDAs, 41
　photos, 46, 47
　resuming, 8, 42
　scripting, 17, 22
　sound effects, 334, 335
DreamHost service, 238, 239
Dressen, Tim, 378
driveway potential, 133
DRM (digital rights management), 114
drop-ins, 254
Drupal blogging application, 231
dry signal, 58, 310
DSL connections, 239
DSP-Quattro 2 package, 275
DTDs, 260
duration, 122, 153
DVD output, 380
dynamic microphones
　field recording and, 367
　functionality, 76
　interviewing and, 198
　microphone cables, 67
　recording ambience, 337
　recording events, 373
　sample setups, 73
　soundseeing tours and, 376
　volume and, 368
Dynaudio BM5As monitor, 324
DynDNS service, 242

E

early reflections, 324
Earthsongs radio show, 325
eating the mic, 117
Echo
　FireWire audio adapters, 72
　PC Card sound cards, 67
　PCI sound cards, 64
echo effect, 112
echo123 program, 211, 214
EDGE data service, 41, 42
Edirol
　digital recorders, 365
　FireWire audio adapters, 72
　solid-state recorders, 363
　UA-25 device, 69, 304
　USB sound adapters, 68
editing
　artful, 215, 216–218
　Audacity support, 273
　audio production software, 272
　Audioblogger and, 207
　bare-bones, 215
　conference calls, 206
　envelope, 273, 302
　ethics in, 220
　ID3 tags, 165
　interviews, 195, 197, 214–221
　multitrack, 316–319
　news, 215, 218–220
　recordings, 49, 89
　sound, 337
　soundseeing tours, 377
　SoX tool, 112
　talking naturally and, 120
　(see also basic editing)
editor, role of, 59
Edwards, John, 147
effects
　adding, 310–312
　Audio Hijack Pro support, 280, 287
　audio theatre, 187, 189, 191
　delay, 310
　fixing audio problems, 313–316
　hardware/software processors, 322
　incorporating, 334
　microphone preamps, 93
　mixers and, 89
　multiple, 275

effects *(continued)*
  multitrack editing and, 317
  music shows, 156
  portable mixers, 91
  recording, 199
  signal amplitude and, 300
  SoX utility, 112
  technology podcasts, 176
  voice over, 280
Egress program, 41
Electronic Musician web site, 87
Electro-Voice
  dynamic microphones, 76, 80, 161,
      321, 337, 367, 368
  field recording microphones, 83
  studio microphones, 86
elements, 123, 124, 125
elevator pitch, 53
.elp format, 213
email
  integrating audio feedback, 330–331
  mailing list registration, 267
  podcasts by, 249–252
emotional interview, 194
emotions, storytelling and, 134, 136
E-MU sound cards, 64
enclosures
  adding tags, 224, 230
  building podcatchers, 22
  downloading, 39, 43
  Liberated Syndication and, 232
  podcasting applications, 282
  resume capability, 42
  RSS readers and, 10, 11, 44
  videocasting and, 379
  WordPress and, 231
encoding
  audio theatre, 191
  defined, 107
  H.264 format, 380, 381
  LAME software, 108, 110
  technology podcasts to blogs, 176
  VBR, 107, 113
  video formats, 380
ender, 124, 125
engineer, role of, 56
enunciation, 115, 117
envelope editing, 273
enveloping, 301, 302
environmental noise, 94, 96–97

EQ (see graphic equalizers)
ESPN, 169
ethics, editing, 220
event handlers, 296, 297
events, podcasting at, 372–374
excitifiers, 312
expanders, 304
experience, host role and, 57, 59
exporting
  show notes, 55
  videocasts, 380
eye contact, 196
EzVoice, 331

F

fade ins
  blank sound, 219
  editing and, 216, 218
  as effect, 112
fade outs
  blank sound, 219
  editing and, 216, 218
  as effect, 112
  example, 334
fair use, 143, 151, 352, 357
Fairness and Accuracy in Reporting web
      site, 132
Fairness Doctrine, 142
Fantasy Focus podcast, 171
fast-forward, simulating, 315
FCC (Federal Communications
      Commission), 142
FEED Validator, 224–227, 229
feedback
  beercasts, 181
  importance of, 126
  integrating audio/email, 330–331
  opinion and, 166
  personal podcasts, 139
  phone-message-to-email service, 139
  sound quality, 170
  technology podcasts, 174
FeedBurner, 228
FeederReader application, 38–40, 43
Feedster service, 258, 268
FFTea application, 285
field recording
  assembling recording rig, 363–368
  bringing spares, 368

high-pass filters and, 308
microphones listed, 82–85
MP3zines, 183
podcasting from car, 369–372
podcasts at events, 372–374
recommendations, 97
soundseeing tours, 374–378
file chunking, 241
File Explorer, 42
file management, 38, 42, 43
File::Find module, 23
filenames, 245, 291
Fillet of Fish plug-ins, 288
Filskov, David, 335
filters
   Audacity support, 274
   consistent levels with, 300–305
   editing and, 215
   frequency, 305–309
   headphones and, 156
   LAME software and, 109
   low-pass, 313
   maximizing, 304
   Movable Type support, 234
   noise gates, 304
   noise training, 99
   normalizing, 304
   Smart Playlist, 12
   software, 99
   speed, 312
   teleprompter and, 390
   for wind noise, 313
Final Cut Pro, 161
FindSounds site, 335
Firefox browser
   listening to podcasts, 2, 4, 10
   RSS and, 223
FireWire (IEEE-1394) standard
   DAW and, 321
   functionality, 70
   sample setups, 73
   solid-state recorders and, 365
   sound cards and, 65
   sound mixers and, 321
   videocasting and, 379, 381
Fireworks program, 316
FLAC (Free Lossless Audio Codec)
   format, 113
flanging, 89, 91, 310
flash cards, 380

Flash devices, 232, 233, 235
flash memory, 72, 365
Fleishman, Glenn, 209–214
fliph( ) filter, 390
flipv( ) filter, 390
flutter, 365
FOIA (Freedom of Information
   Act), 131
fonts, manipulating for
   teleprompter, 386
format elements, 51
formats
   adopting for podcasts, 121–127
   audio theatre, 185–192
   beercasts, 177–181
   defined, 121
   interviewees knowing, 199
   MP3zines, 181–185
   music podcasts, 153–161
   Mystery Science Theater, 148–152
   news podcasts, 127–132
   personal shows, 135–142
   political shows, 142–148
   review podcasts, 162–166
   sports podcasts, 167–171
   story shows, 133–135
   technology podcasts, 172–176
   videocasting, 379–381
.forward file, 251
Fox News network, 143
free content hosting service, 237
Free Lossless Audio Codec (FLAC)
   format, 113
Freedom Forum, 131
Freedom of Information Act
   (FOIA), 131
Freeplay Music, 358
Freeverb plug-in, 288
frequency
   band-pass filters and, 308
   boosting, 305
   characteristics of, 305
   editing process and, 284
   graphic equalizers and, 306
   high-pass filters and, 308
   hiss and, 314
   hum and, 314
   low-pass filters and, 307
   parametric equalizers and, 307
   simulating radio, 315

Frequency application, 284
FTP (File Transfer Protocol), 32, 225, 227, 282
Fuller, Brandon, 230
FuzzMeasure application, 284

G

gain control
    automatic, 198, 364, 365
    basic editing and, 300–305
    MIDI and, 337
    multiple tracks, 318
gain enveloping
    Audacity support, 317
    diffing and, 311
    editing sound and, 337
    overview, 301
games, 137, 145
GarageBand
    audio theatre, 191
    building music, 332–334
    functionality, 278–279
    multitrack editing and, 317
    music podcasts, 155
    political podcasts, 148
    previewing music, 357
    review podcasts, 164
Genelec 8000 monitor, 324
Genre field (MP3 files), 244
genres
    amplitude management and, 301
    customizing feeds by, 16
    forcing, 12
    ID3 tags and, 108
    mash-ups and, 346
Geoghegan, Michael, 2, 162–166
GIF images, 231, 316
GigaDial service, 16
Glass, Ira, 121, 194
glitch, 345
Global Network Navigator, 259
God, voice of, 315
GodCast Network, 257, 258, 269, 270
Golding, Barrett, 363
Google
    AdSense, 264, 265
    Alerts, 169
    Gmail, 331
    News, 143

GPO Access, 143
GPRS, 41, 42
GPS units, 377
GPS-Photo Link, 377
graphic equalizers
    creating a cappellas, 350
    frequency and, 284
    muffled voices, 314
    overview, 306
    recommendations, 313
    reducing wind noise, 313
    removing hiss, 314
    removing hum, 314
graphical user interfaces (GUIs), 32
Greeley, Brendan, 252–254
Green Oak plug-ins, 288
Griffin Technology
    iMic USB adapter, 70
    iTalk recorder, 337, 375
    iTrip FM transmitter, 315
ground loops
    high-pass filters, 308
    hum and, 314
    ironing out, 327
    noise and, 98
GUIs (graphical user interfaces), 32
Guitar Rig plug-in (Native Instruments), 322
Gunn, Moira, 175
gverb effect, 176

H

H.264 encoding format, 380, 381
half-hour series, 254
Hallgren, Sam, 165
hand signals, 188
handling noise, 97
handset taps, 202
hardware
    beercasts and, 179
    digitizing, 50
    improving setup, 320–324
    for interviews, 195, 198
    selecting microphones, 75–87
    setting up home studio, 61–75
    sound mixers, 87–94
Harmony Central web site, 87
Harry Fox Agency, 154, 356

headphones
  alternate commentary and, 150
  field recording and, 368
  host role and, 58
  monitoring with, 198
  music shows and, 156
  noise reduction, 96, 309
  public spaces and, 4
  recommendations, 324
  setting up home studio, 61
  sound cards and, 66
  splitters, 150
  talking naturally and, 118
  telephone hybrids and, 205
headsets
  hands-free, 62
  USB, 62, 75, 209
Henshall, Stuart, 214
Herrington, Jack, 148–152, 185–201,
      209–214
hertz (Hz), 305, 314
high pass effect, 112
high-pass filters, 308
Hill, Louis, 140
HiMD recorders, 366
hiss
  DATA recorders and, 365
  frequency filters and, 308
  headsets and, 62
  incorporating effects with, 334
  podcasts from car, 370
  removing, 314
  signal path noise, 97
  software filters and, 99
  studio setting and, 324
History Channel, 143
home studio
  building, 326–328
  compression and limiting, 304
  setting up, 61–75, 320–328
hosting
  bandwidth and, 237, 238, 239
  file services, 238
  free content service, 237
  making money with, 264
  MP3 files, 229
  web servers, 239, 240
hosts
  multiple, 127, 164
  role of, 57–59

HotRecorder application, 213
House of Representatives, 143
HTML
  displaying show notes in, 298
  Podcastamatic and, 225, 226
  soundseeing tours and, 377
  Tk support, 300
HTMLServerSide variable
      (Podcastamatic), 226
hum
  frequency filters and, 308
  headsets and, 62
  monitoring with headphones, 198
  recording interviews and, 195
  removing, 314
  signal path noise, 97
  software filters and, 99
  studio setting and, 324
Hurricane Electric service, 241
hydration, host role and, 58
hypercardioid microphones, 77

I

IB Audio, 358
Ibbot, Brian, 153–161, 255, 272
IBM, 342
iChat, 208
ID3 tags
  editing, 165
  formatting, 243–246
  LAME software and, 109
  licensing information, 360
  overview, 108
  Perl modules and, 31
  purpose, 49
  setting, 290, 291
  unlicensed materials, 354
Idiotarod, 183
IEEE-1394 standard (see FireWire)
IIS (Internet Information Services), 34,
      35–37
iLink (Sony), 379
Illegal Art, 351
iMic (USB adapter), 70
iMovie, 382
impedance, 368
importing, podcasts into iTunes, 22,
      22–25, 27
independent artists, 155, 156, 358

Independent Radio Drama
        Productions, 191
IndieHeaven, 357
influences (see mash-ups)
informal networks, 269, 270
informational interview, 194, 195
input devices, setting, 291, 292
Inside the Magic podcast, 141
Insomnia Radio podcast, 155
installing Perl modules, 31–37
instant messaging, 264
instrumentals, finding, 349, 350
integrated file management, 38, 42, 43
intellectual property rights, 138
IntelliPrompter, 389
Intercot, 141
Interface Builder, 294–297
Internet
    connection to, 41, 42
    hosting MP3 files on, 50, 228
    independent bands and, 358
    MP3zines, 182
    speech synthesis on, 342–344
    trackers, 241, 243
Internet Archive storage system, 143,
        233, 237, 238
Internet Explorer browser, 3, 341
Internet Information Services (IIS), 34,
        35–37
Internet Movie Database, 149, 151, 165
interpretive interview, 194, 195
interview scripts, 216–218
interviews
    arranging for, 130
    background ambience, 336
    consent to recording, 202
    content elements and, 124
    editing, 195, 197, 214–221
    field recording and, 367
    host role and, 57
    marketing and, 263
    MP3zines, 182, 183
    political podcasts, 145
    recording, 193–201, 206
    recording events and, 374
    recording on Skype, 209–214
    recording telephone, 202–208, 229
    sports podcasts, 168, 169
    stereo microphones, 367

for stories, 134–135
technology podcasts, 172
tips for, 53–55
two-enders and, 208
introduction
    audio editors, 279
    audio theatre, 191
    copyrighted material and, 355
    fade outs and, 216
    need for, 125
    podcasts and, 338
    scripting, 166
    in shows, 124
    soundseeing tours and, 377
    speech synthesizers and, 338–344
    technology podcasts, 176
investigative reporting, 128
IP addresses, 239, 241, 242
iPodcast Producer, 282
iPodder
    BitTorrent network and, 242
    discussion board, 267
    iTunes support, 7
    podcast directories, 11
    podcast maintenance, 12
    submissions and, 256
ipodder-dev mailing list, 267
ipodder.org Sports Directory, 169
iPodderSP program, 41
iPodderX
    demonstration, 8–10
    forcing genres, 13
    iTunes support, 8
    podcast directories, 11
    submissions and, 256
iPodderX Lite, 8
iPods
    Audio Hijack Pro support, 289
    downloading iTunes, 4
    field recording and, 364
    Flash playback device, 338
    Griffin iTalk, 337
    Griffin iTrip, 315
    microphones and, 378
    PodGuides and, 378
    recording events, 373
    soundseeing tours, 375
    synchronizing, 30
    updating automatically, 22, 24

iRiver (MP3 recorder)
    field recording and, 92, 364
    recording ambience, 337
    recording events, 373
    sample setups, 73
    soundseeing tours, 375
Isay, David, 61
ISDN, 208, 323
iSpeak It application, 30
ISPs
    bandwidth overage and, 237
    blog software and, 222, 227, 233
    cgi-bin directory and, 34
    hosting service and, 238–239
    podcasts and, 50, 249–252
    uploading scripts to, 16
    web seeding and, 242
IT Conversations (see Kaye, Doug)
iTunes
    AIF files, 333
    Audio Hijack Pro support, 289
    ID3 tags and, 165, 243, 244
    importing podcasts, 22–25, 27
    integrating recordings, 280
    locating song files, 157
    maintaining library, 12–13
    podcatcher support, 4–7, 8
    simulating rewind, 315
    synchronizing iPods to, 30

J

Jabra BT250 headset, 62
JazlerShow cart application, 283
Jewell, Mike, 161
JK Audio, 202, 204, 323
jokes, 186
journalism, 127–129, 132
JPEG/JPG images, 231, 316

K

K7 voice mail line, 168
k7.com service, 175
Kahn, Tony, 133–135, 161
Kaye, Doug
    optimizing compression, 109
    reverb, 310
    room equalization, 325
    TechNation podcast, 175
    telephone interviews, 203

Kempenaar, Adam, 165
Keyboard Maestro application, 294
Kjaerhus Audio Classic Series
        plug-ins, 288
Klass, Dan, 157
Knight, Jesse, 168
Krug, Kris, 180
KVR Audio web site, 287

L

LAME software
    Audacity and, 274
    converting text-based blogs, 29
    encoding with, 108, 110
    free version, 107
large-small-large technique, 144, 201
Las Vegas soundseeing tour, 378
lastBuildDate field (RSS), 225
lavalier microphones
    interviews and, 195
    pick-up patterns, 79, 80
    podcasts from car, 370
    recording events, 373
    soundseeing tours and, 375, 376
    surround sound and, 100
leading blank segments, 59, 216
legal considerations
    alternate commentary, 150
    audio theatre, 192
    copyrighted material, 350, 355–362
    grabbing audio, 351–355
    interviews and, 55
    libel and slander, 354
    mash-ups, 351
    podcasts from cars, 371
    recording calls, 202
Letterman, David, 124
libel, 354
Liberated Syndication, 50, 232
Libsyn (see Liberated Syndication)
licensing
    audio theatre, 190
    commercial status and, 266
    copyrighted material, 332, 356
    Creative Commons, 353, 354,
        359–362
    free content service and, 237
    GarageBand.com site and, 334
    grabbing audio legally, 351–355

licensing *(continued)*
music shows and, 154, 155
Ourmedia service and, 233
statutory, 357
"lifting the script off the page", 189
Limbaugh, Rush, 142
Lime podcast, 161
limiters, 304
linear narrative, 136, 187
link field (RSS), 225
links, 262, 377
$linkTAG variable, 227
Linux environment
Audacity application, 48
installing Perl modules, 32–34
mpgtx tools, 110
Perl language support, 31
podcatcher support, 7
remote control and, 106
SoX tool, 112
Lipscomb, Joe, 48
listening
detail in storytelling and, 136
developing skills, 51
editing transitions for, 220
field recording and, 368
MP3zines, 182
as rewarding experience, 126
for structure, 51
Logic Express, 279
Logitech keyboard/mouse, 106
--longhelp command-line argument
(lame), 110
lossy compression (see MP3 format)
Lost & Found Sound site, 335
loud signals, 300, 302, 304
low pass effect, 112
low-pass filters, 307, 313
Lucent Technologies, 344
LWP::Simple module, 16, 22, 31
LWP::UserAgent module, 31

M

Mac OS X environment
installing Perl modules, 32–34
mpgtx tools, 110
Perl language support, 31
Safari browser, 2
Salling Clicker program, 102

SoX tool, 112
telephone hybrids and, 206
Mac::Glue module, 25, 32
Macintosh environment
ANT client, 26
Audacity application, 48
audio editors, 274, 275
BitTorrent clients, 240
blogging service, 229
building sound cart, 294–298
cart applications, 283
downloading photos, 47
hands-free headsets, 62
helper applications, 284
importing podcasts into iTunes, 25
mash-ups, 346
NetNewsWire aggregator, 10
OdeoSyncr application, 233
Perl language support, 22
PlayStation Portable and, 46
podcasting applications, 283
podcatcher support, 7, 8–10
recording on Skype, 209–213
remote control and, 106
sound effects, 189
sound recording applications, 280
speech synthesis on, 30, 338–340
telephone hybrids and, 206
teleprompter software, 389, 390
USB standard, 67
videocasting, 382
Mackie sound mixers, 91, 321
Mac::Path::Util module, 25
MadTracker web site, 287
Mail::Box module, 35
mailing lists, 243, 257, 267
major chords, 158
Marantz
digital recorders, 365
portable recorders, 92, 369, 371
solid-state recorders, 100, 101, 150,
363, 375
Mark of the Unicorn (see MOTU)
marketing podcasts, 262–264
Marshall microphones, 85, 141
MAS (MOTU Audio System)
plug-ins, 288
mash-ups, 153, 345–351
master gain, 88, 89, 317
master use rights, 356, 357

M-Audio
  FireWire audio adapters, 72, 161
  microphone preamps, 93
  MobilePre USB device, 68
  PCI sound cards, 64
  studio microphones, 85
  USB interface, 141
  USB sound adapters, 68
MaxEmail service, 331
Mbox device (Digidesign), 70, 274, 321
McCoy, Quincy, 57
McLeish, Robert, 60, 194
McVicar, Gregg, 325
MDA VST Effects plug-ins, 288
MDF (medium density fiberboard), 387
mechanical license/rights, 154, 356, 357
media trainers, 117
memory management, 38, 44
memory sticks, 46
Merrick, Viki, 114–120
Microphone Flags, 55
microphone preamp
  defined, 66
  field recording and, 364
  listed, 92–94
  mixers and, 321
  MP3 recorders, 73
  noise and, 98
  recommendations, 66, 322
  sample setups, 73
microphones
  beercasts and, 179
  cabling and, 367
  compressors and, 304
  computer noise and, 56, 62
  environmental noise and, 96
  flags for, 55
  host role and, 58
  interviews and, 195, 197
  mixers and, 92
  monitor headphones and, 61
  noise gates and, 304
  off axis, 75
  podcasts from car, 369
  positioning, 75
  proximity effect, 58
  purchasing, 48
  recommendations, 285, 321
  recording ambience, 337

sample setups, 73
selecting, 75–87, 363
self-noise, 98
sound quality and, 367
soundseeing tour and, 375
speakerphones and, 207
speaking into, 114, 117
stereo sound and, 81, 88
talking naturally, 118–120
technology podcasts on, 173
telephone hybrids and, 204
tunable noise filtering, 308
two-enders and, 208
unidirectional, 62
USB, 63
windscreens, 97, 102
XLR standard, 66, 68, 321
(see also specific types of
    microphones)
Microsoft, 31, 288, 341
Middle Atlantic Products, 323
MIDI (Musical Instruments Digital
    Interface) standard, 66, 302,
    337
mini-disc recorders
  beercasts and, 179
  overview, 72, 365
  recording ambience, 337
  recording events, 373
  soundseeing tours, 375
mini-DV video cameras, 380
minor chords, 158
MixCast Live, 283
mix-down operation, 191, 316
mixers (see sound mixers)
MixMeister Technology, 283
mobile phones (see cell phones)
Modem Spy, 206
modems, 206, 331
Mogami, 322
monitoring systems, 324
mono sound, 67, 81–82, 316, 318
Morning Stories (WGBH-FM), 133,
    135, 161
Morris, Errol, 194
MOTU Audio System (MAS)
    plug-ins, 288
MOTU (Mark of the Unicorn), 64, 72,
    321

Movable Type
  automating podcasting to, 249–252
  category management, 234
  feeding MP3s to, 246–249
  first podcasts, 50
  overview, 230–231
  pinging and, 264
  RSS feeds and, 330
MovieWavs site, 334
Moyle, Bruce, 164
MP2 format, 113, 253
MP3 format
  beercasts and, 179
  Blogger service and, 228
  browser support, 2, 3, 4
  compression and, 49, 94
  constructing files, 107–114
  demand for, 174
  email feedback, 330
  feeding to Movable Type, 246–249
  finding files, 24
  hosting, 50, 229, 239
  ID3 tags, 31, 49
  microphone preamps and, 73
  music shows and, 155
  Odeo support, 233
  PDAs and, 38, 40, 41
  PlayStation Portable, 46
  Podcastamatic and, 225, 226
  podcasting applications and, 282
  podcasts and, 222
  speech synthesizers and, 27
  tagging files, 243–246, 360
  tools for, 110–113
  unlicensed material, 354
Mp3 Tag Tools, 244
MP3::Info module, 31, 225, 248
MP3zines, 181–185
MP4 format, 31
MP4::Info module, 31
MPEG-4 standard, 381
mpgcat utility, 112
mpgdemux utility, 112
mpginfo utility, 110, 111
mpgjoin utility, 110
mpgsplit utility, 112
mpgtx tools, 110–112
MSN Alerts service, 264
MT_DIR variable, 251
MT::Enclosure plug-in, 230, 249

MTEntries tag (RSS), 234
MTEntryEnclosures tag (RSS), 230
muddy, 80
multitrack editing, 316–319
music, building your own, 332–334
music loops (see sound loops)
music podcasts, 153–161
Music Womb web site, 287
Musical Instruments Digital Interface
        (MIDI) standard, 66, 302, 337
MusicPlayer, 235
MuVo MP3 player, 170
My Sports Radio Directory, 169
MySQL, 231
Mystery Science Theater, 148–152
mysties, 148

N

Nady portable mixers, 90
Narain, Greg, 177–181, 364
narrative arc, 136
narrowcasting, 124, 128
NAT (Network Address
        Translation), 241, 242
National Public Radio (NPR), 252–254
The Nationals Play-by-Play
        podcast, 167
Native Instruments Guitar Rig, 322
Net::FTP module, 32
Net::MovableType module, 246, 248
NetNewsWire aggregator, 10, 223
Net::SFTP module, 32, 248
Network Address Translation
        (NAT), 241, 242
networks
  building, 270
  commercial, 269
  informal, 269, 270
  joining, 270
  peer-to-peer, 7, 240–243
  podcast, 257–258, 268–271
Neumann
  condenser microphones, 76, 150
  field recording microphones, 85
  studio microphones, 86
Neutrik, 322
newPost handler (XML-RPC), 251
news editing, 215, 218–220
news podcasts, 127–132, 145

news sources
  anonymity, 131
  Google News, 143
  off-the-record information, 131
  overview, 129, 130
  political podcasts, 143, 147
  press releases, 130
nodes, 324, 325
noise
  ambient, 219
  audio theatre, 188
  beercasts and, 178
  computers and, 56, 62, 96, 323
  condenser microphones and, 76
  connections and, 367
  editing out, 215
  frequency filters and, 308
  headphones and, 62, 198
  headsets, 62
  high-pass filters and, 308
  lavalier microphones and, 376
  lavaliers and, 79
  measuring, 284
  mic distance and, 198
  microphones and, 58
  nervous habits and, 119
  recording interviews and, 195, 197
  recording problems and, 198
  reducing, 94–99, 309, 369
  software filters, 99
  Sound Forge application, 276
  soundseeing tours and, 376, 377
  training filters, 99
  wind, 102, 198, 313
  (see also signal path noise)
noise floor, 94, 325
noise gates, 304, 325
Nokia, 380
normalization, 215, 216, 224, 304
NPR (National Public Radio), 252–254
NTONYX Virtual Audio Cable 3
      system, 214
n-Track Studio, 277

O

Obi Show podcast, 140
observations, 137
Odeo, 50, 232, 233
OdeoSyncr application, 233

Odyssey, 324
off axis, 75, 77
off-the-record information, 131
Ogg Vorbis format
  defined, 113
  HotRecorder application and, 214
  Perl modules and, 31
  recommendations, 174
Ogg::Vorbis::Header module, 31
Old Wave Radio podcast, 157
omnidirectional microphones
  field recording and, 80, 367
  interviewing and, 198
  mounted lavaliers, 370
  pick-up patterns, 77
  recording events, 373
  soundseeing tours and, 375, 376
  speakerphones and, 207
OmniOutliner document, 55
Onebox service, 331
one-hour specials, 254
Open Directory Project, 259
Open Podcast, 257, 258
opinions, review shows, 168
OPML directories
  availability of, 259
  example, 260
  show notes and, 55
  submissions and, 255–257
OSXAudio web site, 287
OSXvnc, 106
OurMedia service, 50, 233
outline element (OPML), 260
Outline Processor Markup Language
      (see OPML directories)
output devices, setting, 291, 292
outtros
  audio editors, 279
  audio theatre, 191
  scripting, 166
  technology podcasts, 176
overtones, voice, 305
ownerEmail field (OPML), 261
ownerName field (OPML), 261
oXygen editor, 261
OziPhotoTool, 377

P

P2P (peer-to-peer) networks, 7,
    240–243
pace, 116, 117
Palermo, Tony, 185–192
Palm-powered PDAs, 44–45, 380
pan control, 88, 318, 337
parametric equalizers, 307, 325
parody, 185
parties, 101, 178
Patchett, Craig, 268–271, 355–362
PayPal service, 265, 266
PC Card adapters, 67
PCI sound cards, 63–67
PCM (pulse code modulated)
    format, 113, 366
PDAudio CF card, 366
Peak tool, 274, 275, 286
Peavey portable mixers, 90
peer-to-peer (P2P) networks, 7,
    240–243
Pehl, Mary Jo, 152
PenguinRadio, 256
performance, audio theatre, 188–191
Perl modules, 31–37
permission
    copyrighted material, 353
    downloading sounds, 335
    independent artists, 155, 358
    letter of introduction, 154
    virtual directories and, 36
personal revelation, 136
personal shows, 135–142
Pew Center for Civic Journalism, 132
phantom power
    condenser microphones and, 66, 68,
        80, 92, 322, 368
    defined, 76
    microphone preamps, 93
    mixers and, 91, 321
phase cancellation, 195
phaser effect, 112
phone (see telephone)
photos, downloading, 46, 47
Photoshop program, 316
PHP scripts, 224, 227, 231
phpBB bulletin board system, 330
pick-up patterns, 76–78
piece listing, 253

pinging, 264
pipe symbol (|), 251
Pipeline Comic Book Podcast, 166
pitch, 115, 305, 315
pitch shifting, 112, 312, 348
Plain Old Telephone Service
    (POTS), 323
Plantronics headset, 62
play through, 159
playlists, 157, 235
PlayStation Portable (PSP), 46–47
plosives
    defined, 74
    monitoring with headphones, 198
    off axis and, 75
    omnidirectional microphones
        and, 78
    stop, 115
    windscreens and, 165
Pluggo plug-ins, 288
plug-in power, 80
plug-ins
    adding effects, 310–312, 322
    Audacity and, 273
    developing, 288
    equalizer, 306
    extraction tools, 350
    functionality, 272
    headphones and, 156
    overview, 286–289
    standards for, 274, 288
    VST, 275, 286
plugs, trading, 262
Plugzilla web site, 287
Pocket PC PDAs
    podcatching with, 38–44
    portable videocasts, 381
    recording devices, 366
    video formats, 380
Pocket RSS program, 41
Pocket Tunes player, 45
Pod Razor web site, 4
Podcast Alley
    bulletin board, 267
    checking for tools, 159
    podcast directories, 11
    podcatcher list, 8
    sports directory, 170
    submissions and, 256
    voting, 264

Podcast Bunker, 126, 256
podcast networks, 257–258, 268–271
Podcast Promos, 262
podCast411, 256
Podcastamatic, 50, 222, 224, 225–227
PODCAST_DIR constant, 252
Podcasters mailing list, 267
podcasting applications, 282–283
Podcasting News, 256
Podcasting Tools, 257
podcast-review mailing list, 267
Podcastrevolution mailing list, 267
podcasts
    adopting formats for, 121–127
    audio theatre, 185–192
    beercasts, 177–181
    blogs and, 135, 222, 227–236, 258
    building networks, 268–271
    from car, 369–372
    categorizing feeds, 234
    converting text-based blogs, 27–31
    directories listed, 11, 256
    duration of, 122
    by email, 249–252
    at events, 372–374
    exporting show notes, 55
    importing into iTunes, 22, 22–25, 27
    introductions, 338–344
    Libsyn directory of, 232
    listening on PDAs, 37–45
    listening on Web, 1–13
    making money with, 264–266
    making the first, 48–51
    marketing, 262–264
    MP3zines, 181–185
    music, 153–161
    Mystery Science Theater, 148–152
    news, 127–132
    personal shows, 135–142
    political shows, 142–148
    professional-quality, 52–60
    protecting, 358–362
    recording, 159
    review, 162–166
    sample setups, 73
    speaking well for, 114–116
    sports, 167–171
    statutory licenses and, 357
    story shows, 133–135
    in surround sound, 100–102

syndication to radio, 252–254
technology, 172–176
without blogs, 222–227
PODCAST_URL constant, 252
podcatchers
    Blugg.com, 10
    building, 17–22
    demonstration, 8–10
    enclosure tags, 230
    integrated file management, 43
    iTune support, 7, 8
    iTunes and, 4–7
    naming files, 245
    Palm-powered PDAs, 44–45
    PlayStation Portable, 46–47
    Pocket PC PDA, 38–44
    RSS aggregators and, 223
    RSS feeds and, 11, 224
    testing podcasts, 229
PoddumFeeder podcatcher, 8
PodGuides, 378
Podscope service, 4
Polanco, James, 148–152, 320–328
political shows, 142–148
pop stoppers
    costs for, 75
    defined, 74
    microphone diaphragms, 78
    positioning mics, 58
    recording problems and, 198
POP3 email box, 252
Popplewell, Georgia, 160
port forwarding, 242
port triggering, 242
portable videocasts, 381
POTS (Plain Old Telephone
        Service), 323
power, 97, 116
Powers, Bill, 171
Poynter Institute, 132
ppm (Programmer's Package Manager)
        utility, 34, 35
practice, recommendations, 59
preamps (see microphone preamp)
preparation
    alternate commentary and, 149
    host role and, 57, 59
    interviewee and, 196, 200
    for interviews, 194–195
    review shows and, 163

Presentation Prompter, 389, 390
PreSonus, 72, 93
press releases, 130
Pro Prompter, 390
Pro Tools (Digidesign), 274, 288, 321
producer, role of, 52–55
production elements, 123, 125
Programmer's Package Manager (ppm)
          utility, 34, 35
promotion
    beercasts, 180
    connecting with
          community, 267–268
    get listed, 255–258
    honing, 200
    launching categories, 259–261
    making money, 264–266
    marketing podcasts, 262–264
    podcasting networks, 268–271
    podcasts, 160
promotional spots (promos)
    defined, 126
    diffing, 311
    trading, 262
prompters, making, 383–386
Propaganda, 283
proximity effect, 58, 313, 314, 373, 376
PRX (Public Radio Exchange)
          service, 252–254
pseudo pellas, 350
PSP (PlayStation Portable), 46–47
psychoacoustics, 312
public performance rights, 356
Public Radio Exchange (PRX)
          service, 252–254
publicists
    producer role and, 53, 54, 55
    technology podcasts, 176
publicity (see promotion)
PubSub service, 258, 268
pulse code modulated (PCM)
          format, 113, 366
punctuation, 116

Q

Q value, 307
Q-Dog, 164
Qmail, 251
QuakeMap, 377

quality sound
    alternate commentary, 150
    Audioblog and, 232
    brightening, 312
    building sweet sound, 305–309
    considerations for, 286–289
    constructing MP3 files, 107–114
    editing, 337
    engineer's role, 56
    feedback on, 170
    ISDN and, 208
    microphones and, 367
    mobile phones and, 102–107
    obtaining, 324–328
    podcasts from cars, 370
    reducing noise, 94–99
    setting up home studio, 61–75
    sound design and, 324
    sound mixers, 87–94
    studio setting and, 324
    surround sound, 100–102
    telephone hybrids and, 206
    (see also microphones)
questions
    concentration and, 201
    contemplative silence, 218
    editing ethics, 220
    interview, 195, 196, 197
Quick News (RSS reader), 44, 45
Quick Take podcast, 168
QuickTap handset tap, 202
QuickTime Player
    AIF files and, 333
    locating song files, 157
    MP3 support, 2, 4
    music podcasts and, 161
    Soundflower tool and, 159
    videocasting and, 382
QVGA resolution, 380

R

rack systems, 323, 324
Radio Clash podcast, 153
Radio College, 132
radio shows, 123, 146
radio, simulating, 315
radio theatre, 56, 185–192
Radio UserLand service, 50, 229, 260,
          270

RadioShack, 147, 150, 376
Randi Rhodes Show, 147
ratio parameter (compression), 303, 304
Rattray, Chris, 164
rawness, 172
RCA inputs, 65, 373
RDon, 164
reading technique, 119
README file, 286
Real Audio media application, 4
Really Simple Syndication (see RSS)
RealVNC, 106
recorded announcement files, 160
recording
    ambience, 199, 337
    applications for, 280–282
    audio production software, 272
    audio theatre, 188
    background ambience, 336–337
    beercasts, 179
    blank sound, 219
    editing, 49, 89, 120
    first podcast, 48, 49, 159
    hardware systems, 323
    integrating, 280
    interviews, 193–201, 206
    interviews on Skype, 209–214
    mini-disc/flash memory, 72
    with mobile phone, 102–107
    MP3, 73
    phantom power and, 80
    recommendations, 367–368
    recommended locations, 96, 97
    record levels for, 198
    reducing noise during, 94–99
    sessions, 290
    solid-state, 363, 365, 375
    sound effects, 199
    telephone interviews, 202–208, 229
    through modems, 206
    (see also field recording)
Recording Bin, 289, 292
recording booths, 325
Recording Industry Association of
        America (see RIAA)
recurring segments, 182
Reel Reviews, 2, 162
relaxation, 57, 58, 200
release parameter (compression), 303

research
    journalism and, 129
    movies, 149
    MP3zines, 181
    music shows, 157
retakes, 215, 216, 313
reverb
    audio theatre, 189, 191
    mixers and, 89, 91
    overview, 310
    recommendations, 313
    SoX tool, 112
reverse effect, 112
review podcasts, 162–166, 173
review segments, 137, 145
rewind, simulating, 315
Rhodes, Randi, 147
RIAA (Recording Industry Association
        of America)
    licensing and, 357
    mechanical rights, 154
    performer rights, 356
    permission from, 353
Rice, Bill, 146
Ricoh Pro digital camera, 377
riding the gain, 59, 88
RingCentral service, 331
Ritenour, Adam, 222
RMS adapters, 67
roar of the crowd, 101
The Rock and Roll Geek Show, 2
Rode
    field recording microphones, 85
    mini-connectors, 367
    stereo microphones, 81, 161
    studio microphones, 85
Rogue Amoeba, 210, 280
Rolls microphone preamps, 93
room considerations, 324–326
room simulator (see reverb)
round tables, 101
routers, 243
royalties, 154
RSS Ads service, 265
RSS feeds
    Audioblog support, 233
    bandwidth considerations and, 239
    "best of", 16
    Bloglines, 10, 16

RSS feeds *(continued)*
  building, 32
  cataloging, 4
  comment support, 330
  converting text-based, 27, 29
  first podcast and, 49, 50
  full-text, 265
  informal networks and, 269
  Liberated Syndication and, 232
  monitoring, 11
  multitasking with, 39
  parsing, 32
  podcasting applications and, 282
  podcasts and, 222
  rebroadcasting, 14–16
  renaming files, 239
  speech synthesis and, 342
  sports podcasts, 170
  tracking blog mentions, 268
  unlicensed material, 354
  validating, 224, 225, 227, 229
RSS files
  blogless alternatives, 224–227
  hand-coded, 165
  podcasts and, 4, 222
  tagging, 361
RSS readers
  aggregators as, 223
  enclosures and, 10, 11, 44
  podcatchers and, 8
RSS (Really Simple Syndication)
  Atom feed and, 228
  BitTorrent support, 243
  Drupal support, 231
  news sources and, 143
  overview, 222–224
  Pod Razor web site and, 4
  videoblogs and, 26
  videocasting and, 379
  WordPress support, 231
RTAS plug-ins, 288
RubyTube plug-in, 288
run-down, 125
running gags, 149
RuyaSonic web site, 191

S

Safari browser, 2, 33, 223
Salling Clicker program, 102–105
Samson C01U-USB microphone, 63

saucer eyes, 126
Saunders, Scott, 1
scripted shows
  audio theatre, 187, 188
  review podcasts, 163
  review shows, 166
Scripting News, 2
ScriptQ, 389
search engines, 258, 264
SEC Helper application, 105
Secure Digital flash cards, 380
security considerations, 138
segment producer, 52
segments
  artful editing, 216
  creating, 124–125
  defined, 124
  downloading, 241
  15-minute, 254
  mash-ups and, 346
  MP3zines, 181, 182
  noise gates between, 305
  political podcasts, 145
  prerecording, 140
  recurring, 182
  review, 137, 166
  soundseeing tours and, 377
  sports podcasts, 168
  stingers and, 332
  technology podcasts, 172
self-noise, 98
Sendmail, 251
Sennheiser
  dynamic microphones, 76
  field recording microphones, 84
  headphones, 62
  shotgun microphones, 80, 337, 367
  studio microphones, 86
series, half-hour, 254
SESAC, 154, 356
sessions, recording, 290
SFTP standard
  feeding MP3s, 248
  functionality, 32
  uploading files, 225, 227
Shadel, Tim, 176
shotgun microphones
  field recording, 80
  pick-up patterns, 77
  podcasts from car, 369
  recording ambience, 337

recording events, 373
soundseeing tours and, 376
show notes
    displaying in browsers, 298
    displaying in Windows, 300
    exporting, 55
    highlighting, 56
    interviews and, 53
    preparing, 55–56
    sports podcasts and, 171
    technology podcasts, 174
    timestamping, 292–294
show prep, 52, 55
show producer, 52
shows (see podcasts)
Shure
    A96f cable, 368
    cardioid microphones, 80
    dynamic microphones, 76, 80, 337, 367, 369
    field recording microphones, 83, 85
    mini-connectors, 367
    stereo microphones, 81
    studio microphones, 86, 150, 321
signal path noise
    defined, 94
    editing out, 215
    effects boxes and, 322
    eliminating, 97–99, 314
    measuring, 284
signals
    amplifying, 92
    amplitude of, 300, 301
    attenuating, 302
    boosting, 304
    clipped, 89, 301, 304
    delay effects and, 310
    diffing, 311
    gain enveloping, 301
    ground loops and, 314
    microphone preamps and, 322
    muffled voices and, 314
    noise gates and, 304
    tunable noise filters and, 309
silence
    as effect, 112
    contemplative, 218
    noise gates, 304
    podcasts from car, 372
    preserving, 216
    recommendations, 312

Six Apart, 230
sketches, 186
Skinner, Edith, 117
Skype service
    feedback via, 174, 175
    headsets and, 62
    MP3zines, 182
    recording calls, 207
    recording interviews, 209–214
    Soundflower and, 284
    technology podcasts on, 173
slander, 132, 354
Slashdot service, 237
Sledhead Radio podcast, 167
Smart Playlist feature (iTunes), 12, 13
SmartElectronix plug-ins, 288
smartphones, 40, 41
Smith, Greg, 37–45, 379–383
Society of Professional Journalists, 131
soft signals, 300
software
    filtering options, 99
    improving setup, 320–324
    teleprompter, 389, 390
solid-state recorders
    field recording and, 363
    overview, 365
    recommendations, 323
    recording ambience, 337
    recording events, 373
    sample setups, 73
    soundseeing tours, 375
Sonic Foundry, 166
Sonifex, 323
Sonique media application, 4
Sony
    ACID, 166, 191, 277, 332, 346–349
    field recording microphones, 82, 83
    headphones, 368
    iLink, 379
    mini-connectors, 367
    Minidiscs, 365
    PlayStation Portable, 46–47
    Sound Forge, 276, 277
    stereo microphones, 81, 165
Soulseek service, 350
sound bed, 355
Sound Byte cart application, 283
sound cards, PCI, 63–67
sound carts, building, 294–300
Sound Devices digital recorders, 365

sound effects (see effects)
Sound Forge (Sony), 276, 277
sound loops, 148, 277, 332–334
sound mixers
    audio production software, 272
    hardware considerations, 321
    old consoles, 302
    overview, 87–94
    power to, 80
    variety in, 50
Sound on Sound web site, 87
sound recording applications, 280–282
sound (see quality sound)
sound treatment, 325
Soundcraft portable mixers, 90
Sounddogs.com, 334, 358
SoundExchange, 356, 357
Soundflower tool
    Audacity and, 159
    overview, 284
    recording Skype, 209–213
    rerouting audio with, 272
Soundflowerbed tool, 284
soundseeing tours
    binaural podcasts and, 101
    creating, 374–378
    music podcasts, 161
    podcasts from car, 371, 372
    sports podcasts, 170
SoundSoap plug-in, 288
Soundstudio, 156
Soundtrack, 161
soundtracks, alternate, 148–152
source format (videocasting), 379, 380
Southern Sports Week podcast, 171
SoX tool, 110, 112
spam messages, 137
S/PDIF connectors, 66
speakerphones, 207
speakers, monitoring, 324
special effects (see effects)
specialty journalism, 128
specials, one-hour, 254
speech
    cadence of, 218, 313
    classes for, 117
    stress and, 57
    training your voice, 114–120

speech synthesizers
    converting text-based blogs, 27–31
    music shows, 161
    podcast introductions, 338–344
speed
    changing, 312, 315
    of teleprompter, 386
speed filters, 312
Split at Cursor function (ACID), 347,
        348
sponsorship information, 125
The Sports Pod, 167
sports podcasts, 167–171
Stand Alone Inc., 44
starting out
    first podcasts, 48–51
    professional-quality podcasts, 52–60
statutory licenses, 357
Steinberg web site, 287
stereo sound
    adapters, 67
    adapters for, 70
    microphones and, 367
    multitrack editing and, 316
    overview, 81–82
    pan control and, 88
    surround sound and, 101
stingers, 279, 332
stop-plosives, 115
story podcasts, 133–135
storytelling
    audio theatre and, 185, 186
    details in, 375
    experimenting with, 161
    interviewing for, 134–135
    Morning Stories, 133
    podcasts from car, 372
    principles of effective, 136
    recommendations, 126
    soundseeing tours and, 378
    story podcasts, 133–135
stress, host role and, 57
stretch effect, 112
structure, listening for, 51
studio microphones, 85, 86
Studio Projects, 80, 85, 93
studio setup, 188, 218
style, 51, 59
submissions, 255–257, 264

subscriptions, 4, 7, 10, 258
sudo command, 33
Supreme Court, 143
surround sound, 100–102
sweet sound, 305–309
Switchcraft, 322
synchronization
    alternate commentary and, 150
    blogs, 229
    iPods to iTunes, 30
    video and audio, 277
syndication to radio, 252–254

T

tagmp3 utility, 110, 112
talk shows, 122, 173, 177–181
Tapco portable mixers, 90
tape syncs, 207, 208
taper access, 373
Tascam
    audio adapters, 72
    recording systems, 323
    sound adapters, 68
    sound mixers, 321
TC Electronic PowerCore
    processor, 322
TDM (Time Division Multiplexing)
    plug-ins, 288
teasers, 125
TechNation radio show, 175
technical elements, 51
technology podcasts, 172–176
TechPodcasts, 258
teleconferencing systems, 206
telephone
    audio feedback via, 331
    recording interviews, 202–208, 229
    simulating, 314
telephone hybrids, 204–206, 323
teleprompters
    building, 387–390
    making, 383–386
Telos Systems, 323
templates, 230, 232, 234
text editors, 165, 338
TextEdit text editor, 165, 338
theatre of the mind, 136, 374, 377
TheForce.Net podcast, 166
theme songs, 156, 182

themes
    customizing feeds by, 16
    interviewee knowing, 200
    review shows, 163
    selecting for music show, 153
The Theory of Everything podcast, 253
This American Life, 185, 194
This and That with Jeff and Pat
    podcast, 140
three-and-a-half-minute drop-ins, 254
threshold parameter
    (compression), 303, 304
Time Division Multiplexing (TDM)
    plug-ins, 288
timeliness, 142
timestamping show notes, 292–294
timing, 149, 189, 347
Tip-Ring-Sleeve (TRS) connectors, 82
Title field
    MP3 files, 244
    Podcastamatic, 226
title field
    OPML, 261
    RSS, 225
$titleTAG variable, 227
Tk toolkit, 32, 299–300
Tomato Torrent, 240
"Top Ten List", 124
tops, adding, 332–335
.torrent file, 7, 240–243
Torrone, Phillip, 172–176
Total Recorder Pro, 189, 335, 341
Total Sound Recorder, 281
Towne, Jeff, 75–87, 363–368
Track field (MP3 files), 244
trackers, Internet, 241, 243
tracks
    ambient noise, 219
    mash-ups, 345–351
    multiple, 191, 316–319
    news editing and, 218
trade journalism, 128
trailing blank segments, 59, 216
transition elements, 124
Transom web site, 193
Triathlete's Garage podcast, 170
trivia questions, 168
TRS (Tip-Ring-Sleeve) connectors, 82
trust, 144
Tufnel, Nigel, 320

tunable noise filters, 308, 309, 314
tuning mash-ups, 348
Turtle Beach sound cards, 65
Two Rights podcast, 146
two-enders, 207, 208
two-person shows, 56, 144, 165
two-source rule, 131

U

"ums", 216, 282
undertones, voice, 305
Unicode, 108
Universal Audio processor, 322
Universal Serial Bus (see USB)
Unix environment, 248, 252
unlicensed materials, 354
up cuts, 220
urban legends, 186
USB (Universal Serial Bus) standard
    call recording and, 207
    DAW and, 321
    headsets, 62, 75, 209
    microphones, 63
    mini-discs and, 366
    sample setups, 73
    solid-state recorders and, 365
    support for, 67–70
    video cameras and, 380
Utilidors, 141

V

Vancouver Beercast Squad, 180
Varga, Adam, 181–185
variable bit rate (VBR) encoding, 107,
    113
Various and Sundry DVD podcast, 165
Vbox feature, 275, 286
VBR (variable bit rate) encoding, 107,
    113
video bit rate, 379
video compression codec, 379
video devices, 379, 380, 388
video frame rate, 379
Videobloggers mailing list, 267
videoblogs
    creating videocasts, 379–383
    teleprompters, 383–390
    tuning into, 26

videocasts, 39, 379–383
Viking Youth Power Hour podcast, 141
virtual directories, 35, 36
Virtual Directory Creation Wizard, 35
Virtual Network Computing
        (VNC), 106
Virtual Studio Technology (see VST
        standard)
visudo command, 33
VNC (Virtual Network
        Computing), 106
vocal skills
    audio theatre, 188
    first podcast and, 49
    hard consonants, 75
    monitoring, 61
    off axis, 75
    podcasting voice, 114–120
    recommendations, 59
voice mail service, 139, 175, 331
"voice of the people" interviews, 196
voice over effect, 280
Voice over IP, 203, 331
VoiceMix Studio, 342
voices
    amplitude of, 305
    chorus effect and, 310
    frequency of, 305
    of God, 315
    mash-ups of, 345–351
    muffled, 314
    obscuring, 313
    trapping, 315
volume
    adjustments to, 112
    ambience and, 337
    consistency in, 156
    editing, 215
    hand signal for, 189
    mic distance and, 198
    music shows, 157
    pitch and, 115
    power and, 116
    recommendations, 117
    recorders and, 368
Vonage service, 331
voting, 264
Vox Pop, 196
Voxengo plug-ins, 288

VST (Virtual Studio Technology)
  standard
    Audacity and, 274
    Audition and, 276
    DSP-Quattro and, 275
    extraction tools and, 350
    overview, 286
    plug-in sites, 287, 288
    Sound Forge and, 276
    tunable noise filters, 309

W

Walcott, Chris, 320–328
Walker, Benjamen, 253, 254
walla effect, 190
WAV format
    AIF files and, 333
    defined, 113
    HiMD recorders and, 366
    HotRecorder application and, 214
    podcasting applications and, 282
    PRX service and, 253
    solid-state recorders and, 73
    voice mail and, 175
    Win32::Sound module and, 299
Waves plug-in, 322, 350
WavSite, 335
WDW Magic, 141
web browsers (see browsers)
Web (see Internet)
web seeding, 241, 242
web servers
    hosting, 239, 240
    Perl support, 31–37
    resuming downloads, 42
    uploading videoblogs, 381
web sites, 184, 265
WebIntellects service, 239
weblogs (see blogs)
wet signal, 58, 310
WGBH-FM, 133, 135
WhisperRoom, 325
White House, 143
WiFi, 41, 42, 106
Win32::OLE module, 23, 300
Win32::Sound module, 299
WinAmp media application, 4
wind noise, 102, 198, 313
    (see also windscreens)

window glass, 387, 388
Windows environment
    ActiveState Perl and, 34–37, 225
    Audacity application, 48
    audio editors, 274, 277
    BitTorrent clients, 240
    blogging service, 229
    building sound cart, 299–300
    cart applications, 283
    COM interfaces, 22
    file formats, 174
    ID3 tags, 245
    importing podcasts into
        iTunes, 22–25
    mash-ups, 346
    mpgtx tools, 110
    OdeoSyncr application, 233
    Perl language support, 22, 31
    playing podcasts, 42
    PlayStation Portable and, 46
    podcasting applications, 282, 283
    podcatcher support, 7, 8
    recording on Skype, 213–214
    remote control and, 106
    sound effects, 189
    sound recording applications, 281
    SoX tool, 112
    speech synthesis on, 30, 31, 340–342
    telephone hybrids, 206
    teleprompter software, 389
Windows Media Audio (WMA)
        format, 114, 174
Windows Media Player, 3, 4, 42, 114
Windows Mobile devices (see PDAs)
Windows Movie Maker, 381
windscreens
    description, 97
    lavaliers and, 376
    plosives and, 165
    recommendations, 102
    recording problems and, 198
Winer, David, 2, 268
Winpodcast application, 283
WireTap software, 159
wiring, 322, 327
WMA (Windows Media Audio)
        format, 114, 174
word processors, 216

WordPress
   category feeds, 234
   category management, 234
   first podcasts, 50
   informal networks, 270
   overview, 231
   RSS feeds and, 330
work, talking about, 138
wow, 365
writer, role of, 55, 56

X

Xcode tool, 294, 295
XLR standard
   board access and, 373
   microphones and, 66, 68, 321
   signal path noise and, 98
   sound cards and, 65
   sound mixers and, 87
   telephone hybrids and, 204
XM Satellite radio, 173
XML, 32, 224
XML Shareable Playlist Format (XSPF)
      file, 235
XML::Atom module, 32
XML::DOM module, 32

XML::Parser module, 32
XML-RPC mechanism, 246, 251
XML::RSS module, 32
XML::RSS::Parser module, 32
XMLServerSide variable
      (Podcastamatic), 226
XML::Simple module, 32
XMLWebSide variable
      (Podcastamatic), 226
XML::XPath module, 32
XSPF (XML Shareable Playlist
      Format), 235

Y

Yahoo!
   directory of web pages, 259
   as mail provider, 331
   mailing lists, 267
   opml-dev group, 260
   Podcasters Group, 159
Yamaha portable mixers, 90
Year field (MP3 files), 244

Z

Zdot podcast, 176

Colophon

Our look is the result of reader comments, our own experimentation, and feedback from distribution channels. Distinctive covers complement our distinctive approach to technical topics, breathing personality and life into potentially dry subjects.

The tool on the cover of *Podcasting Hacks* is a bullhorn or megaphone. Useful at such events as sporting contests and protest rallies, the megaphone amplifies a single voice over the loud din of many voices. Its small size and simple handheld design make for a highly portable device. A high-end, 25-watt megaphone can be heard at distances up to 1,000 yards and typically includes such features as a built-in signal alarm and foghorn.

Adam Witwer was the production editor and Audrey Doyle was the copyeditor for *Podcasting Hacks*. Sada Preisch proofread the text. Matt Hutchinson, Marlowe Shaeffer, and Claire Cloutier provided quality control. Lucie Haskins wrote the index.

Ellie Volckhausen designed the cover of this book, based on a series design by Edie Freedman. The cover image was provided by Comstock Images. Karen Montgomery produced the cover layout with Adobe InDesign CS using Adobe's Helvetica Neue and ITC Garamond fonts.

David Futato designed the interior layout. This book was converted by Keith Fahlgren to FrameMaker 5.5.6 with a format conversion tool created by Erik Ray, Jason McIntosh, Neil Walls, and Mike Sierra that uses Perl and XML technologies. The text font is Linotype Birka; the heading font is Adobe Helvetica Neue Condensed; and the code font is LucasFont's TheSans Mono Condensed. The illustrations that appear in the book were produced by Robert Romano, Jessamyn Read, and Lesley Borash using Macromedia FreeHand MX and Adobe Photoshop CS. This colophon was written by Adam Witwer.